宁波市江北区行政服务中心

宁波市江北区行政服务中心（以下简称“中心”），是中共江北区委、区政府为全面贯彻“三个代表”重要思想，切实转变政府职能，改进机关作风，推进廉政勤政建设，方便投资者和人民群众，优化全区经济发展环境而成立的。

“中心”办事大厅由17个区管工作部门和5个市垂直管理部门组成，主要办事与我区经济和社会发展相关的行政审批、核准和服务事项，目前已达198项。区“96178廉政投诉中心”进驻“中心”，受理群众投诉事宜。

“中心”的运作方式是：一门受理，窗口运作，统一收费，承诺办结。

“中心”为江北区人民政府的派出机构，与2002年9月成立，内设行政办公室和业务（督查）科；主要负责中心的日常管理，制定中心的运作程序与规则，指导进驻中心各窗口依法规范运作和按职能要求开展工作。

江北区全程代理员例会

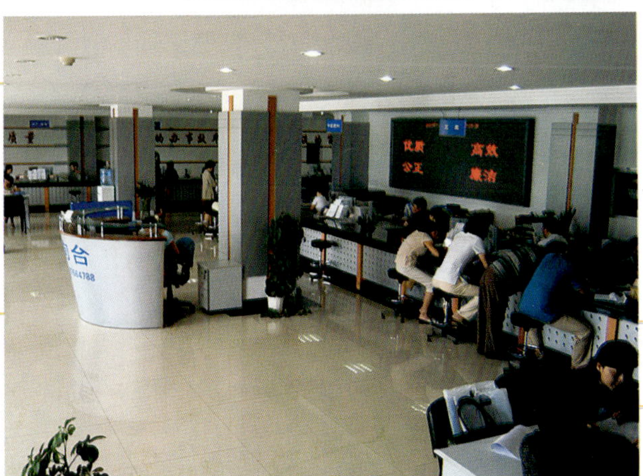

中心内景

中心地址：宁波市江北区白沙路1号

办证大厅咨询电话：87664788

监督电话：87385110

洪塘镇

洪塘是浙江省宁波市江北区的一个建制镇，宁波市综合实力廿强镇，位于宁波市区西北部，南临姚江，北靠马鞍山，全镇面积39.1平方公里,耕地面积2.3万亩,总人口2.4万。洪塘区位优势明显，江北大道横贯镇区，成为“上海2小时经济圈”交通大动脉——杭州湾大通道融入宁波中心城区的落脚点。全国重点文物保护单位保国寺座落镇内。

洪塘经济发展势头强劲，目前已建成洪塘工业A区、工业B区和洪塘工业城，形成刀片、扬声器、医疗器械、印刷包装、纺织以及工艺品等特色块状经济，2003年全镇工业总产值达13.55亿元。

座落于洪塘镇的宁波都市农业园区，规划面积7.88平方公里，是省级农业高科技示范园区，也是全市国内外农业名特优珍稀品种、高新技术的试验、推广基地，并成为2002年宁波市区十大新景点之一。

洪塘已形成完整的教育体系，拥有幼儿园、小学、中学、成人学校及两所民办学校（至诚学校、求知学校），全镇有全日制在校学生4000余名。青少年教育基地——宁波市绿色学校也座落镇内。

洪塘凭借独特的区位优势、明显的土地优势、开明的政策优势，政通人和业兴，开放势头强劲。

宁海县

西店镇

XIDIANZHEN

西店镇东濒象山港，北与奉化溪口相临，西达疗养胜地宁海南溪温泉。全镇区域面积102平方公里，下辖46个行政村（含11个居委会），常住人口4.3万人，暂住人口3.2万人。西店镇集全国重点镇、省小城镇综合改革试点镇、省中心镇、省文明镇、省教育强镇等荣誉于一身，是全国著名的“牡蛎之乡”和“中国蛋鸭之乡”。

近年来，西店镇大力实施“重工、强农、拓三产”战略，形成了以模具制造、学教用品、塑料制品、金属制品、家电制品等五大主导行业为主体的工业体系和蛋鸭、牡蛎、香鱼等10个区域化农业特色产业基地。2003年，全镇实现国内生产总值11.4亿元，完成工农业总产值44.6亿元，财政总收入1.3亿元。

西店镇将以加快经济建设为中心，以提高人民生活水平为根本出发点，进一步加强精神文明、民主法制和党的建设，努力把西店镇建设成为具备“经济中心、商贸重地、改革窗口、形象亮点”四大特征的现代化滨海经济强镇。

宁海县桥头胡街道

NING HAI XIAN

宁海县桥头胡街道东临象山港，南接宁海县科技园区，西依同三高速公路，北连宁海县临港开发区。区域面积59平方公里，下辖33个行政村，1个居委会，总人口2.3万，拥有工业企业388家，是规划中的宁波南部中等城市组团之一，设有县级汽车城、水产城。生态环境优越，景色怡人。

2004年，是撤镇建街道后的头一年，也是进一步理顺管理机制，集中精力抓经济、优服务、图发展，推动经济和社会发展迈上新台阶的关键一年。街道党工委和办事处坚持与时俱进，抢抓机遇，全面实施基础设施建设，在总体布局上实施四大举措：西扩、北连、东迁、中兴。街道配合有关部门投入100万元硬化学士路延伸段，投入250万元，完成桥洪头三角坛拆迁绿化工作，投入250万元完成老街拆建，投入260万元完成临海路的拆迁硬化工作，投入300万元完成店前王村等道路改造，促使城区形象日趋凸现。

桥头胡街道将以更宽的视野、更高的起点，整合发展优势、谋划发展方向、找准发展路子、增强经济实力，凸现城市形象和实现农业“双增”，优化服务质量，全力打造经济繁荣、环境优美、社会稳定、功能完善的现代化生态型商贸街道。

中国模具生产基地

中国文具生产基地

模具车间

宁海县 跃龙街道

跃龙街道是宁海县的政治、经济、文化中心，同三高速公路穿境而过，属宁波半小时交通圈；区域面积105平方公里，总人口13.5万人，是宁海人气最旺、经济最热、百姓最富的区域。

经济基础实力强大，形成了全方位、多层次的对外开放格局，经济总量位于全县乡镇、街道之首。2003年工业产值45.6亿，三产增加值5亿元。工业经济体系完善，特别是“四具一配”特色工业优势明显，是“中国模具生产基地”、“中国文具生产基地”的重要生产区域。商贸经济繁荣，是宁海县商贸中心、金融中心、三产服务中心、信息中心。农业经济形成了以粮食生产为主体，近郊蔬菜、瓜果生产和经济特产林、海涂养殖等为两翼的农业生产新格局，近郊农业示范区各具特色。

城市基础设施和服务功能完善，城区三产兴旺发达，社区服务丰富便捷。自然环境优美和谐，城市建设和发展融合了独特、宝贵的自然山水资源，已逐步形成山水相依的复合生态系统和人与自然和谐共存的生态绿洲城市。辖区内有柔石故居、王锡桐起义遗址、莲头山风景区、跃龙山风景区以及城区周边系列沿山生态休闲区，是工作之余休闲旅游的好去处。

充满生机与活力的跃龙街道正伸张双臂，竭诚欢迎各界人士前来投资发展，共创美好明天。

办公大楼

望府茶叶基地

潘天寿广场

宁海县

桃源街道

桃源街道位于宁海新城区中心，属宁波半小时交通圈，距宁波机场30分种车程，北仑港40分钟车程，杭州2小时车程。区域面积58平方公里，下辖50个行政村，总人口4.1万。2003年实现工农业总产值43亿元，三产增加值0.23亿元，农民人均纯收入7400元。

区位优势凸显，城市发展空间不断拓展。是规划中的市级公共中心，甬台温铁路站点设立在街道西端，高速公路、四自公路和兴宁北路组成交叉便捷的交通网络。国家交通主干线同三高速公路穿境而过，并设有互交式立交。

经济实力雄厚，生态建设步伐不断加快。拥有工业企业453家，其中规模以上企业29家，形成了模具制造、电子通讯等主导行业。辖区内设有省级经济开发区——科技工业园和新兴工业园区，规模效益企业不断向园区集聚，大量的人力资源也不断涌入。生态建设立足高起点、高标准，在中心区域建有6000亩的平原生态绿化林，成为城区生态“绿肺”。

人文资源丰富，城市品位不断提升。辖区内有国画大师潘天寿故居，占地面积280亩的柔石公园和占地100余亩的“5.19”开游节广场。

桃源街道正向“创一流街道，建现代城区”目标稳步迈进，一个具有现代文明气息、人和自然和谐统一发展的新兴街道正在逐步形成。

宁海县公路管理段

段长：张伟金

电话：65591559

地址：宁海县城关兴宁中路37号

宁海县公路管理段成立于1953年3月，属于全民事业单位。现有在职干部职工172人，其中党员64人。管养全县境内1100余公里公路、桥涵。行政上受县交通局领导，业务上受市公路管理局指导，行使政府赋予的公路建设、路政管理、养护的职责。由张伟金同志担任段长、党总支书记职务，段党内机构设有党总支（下设机关、路政、养护、公司、退休五个党支部）；行政机构设有办公室、路政管理大队（下设四自公路、宁南、桥头胡、力洋四个路政中队）、工程股、养护股、财务股、养护中心（下设宁海、梅林、深甽、力洋、亭头、长街、胡陈、桥头胡、强蛟九个养护站）。

鄞州区 塘溪

YINZHOUQU TANGXI ZHEN

塘溪，是一块神奇而秀丽的土地，镇域面积94.6平方公里，32个行政村，一个居委会，3万人口。境内群山环抱，山水秀美，有15000余亩良田，77000余亩山林，是浙江省黄金海岸线上的宁波市鄞东大嵩江发源地，是宁波鄞县的发祥地。

塘溪，凭借优越的自然资源和人才优势，迈入了新世纪，全镇工农业总产值达18亿元，村镇工业已迅速向外向型、知识型、科技型和个私企业发展。

塘溪，人杰地灵，名人辈出。著名生物学家童第周、书法大师沙孟海、一代书圣沙耆、昆虫学家周尧、舞蹈表演家杜红玲；建国后浙江省第一任省长沙文汉等都诞生在这块土地上。沙氏故居、浙江省第一教授村的童氏故居均已被列入文物保护单位和参观旅游景点。

人杰地灵 · 人杰地灵 · 人杰地灵 · 人杰地灵 · 人杰地灵 · 人杰地灵 · 人杰地灵

全镇人民热忱欢迎

国内外来宾光临

塘溪镇政府工业办公室

传真：88404258 88409715

邮编：315143

咨询电话：88409606

88409708

88404258

钟公庙街道

概况

钟公庙街道地处宁波市南郊，东邻下应街道，南接姜山镇，西隔奉化江与石碶街道相望，北连宁波市江东区，为鄞州新区府所在地。区域面积39平方公里，下辖29个行政村，14个社区居委会，总人口10万。地理位置优越，交通条件便捷，商贸服务齐全，公益设施完备，街道内大中学校、大型超市、高档酒店、医疗设施一应俱全。

随着鄞州新城区的开发建设，投资环境不断完善，优质高效的供电、供水、金融、邮电等服务，为全街道的发展提供了可靠保障。工业发展势头强劲，基本形成了以印刷包装、食品加工、服装辅料、建材化工为支柱的四大工业体系。2003年实现工业总产值65.8亿元，实现国内生产总值13.8亿元，完成财政总收入2.26亿元，农民人均纯收入8029元，被列为浙江省经济实力“百强镇”、宁波市“廿强镇”、和鄞州区“五强镇”之一。并多次被评为省教育强镇、市级卫生街道等。

步入新世纪的钟公庙街道，将再接再厉，全面提升“三个文明”建设水平，希望能与海内外贤能携手建设出更加文明富庶的钟公庙街道。

梁弄镇

余姚市

中共梁弄镇委员会书记：黄伟国

梁弄镇人民镇府镇长：徐康林

这是一片古老的土地，蜿蜒了千百年的长弄短街，哺育了一代又一代的名人学士；这是一片秀美的土地，满坡的翠竹摇曳着江南的灵秀，万顷碧波荡漾出迷人的流韵；这是一片英雄的土地，数以万计的热血儿女，曾会聚在这里，谱写了一曲抵御外侮、寻求真理的感人乐章。这片土地，就是浙江省历史文化名镇、浙江省中心镇余姚市梁弄镇。

梁弄现在已经是远近闻名的“中国灯具之乡”，近千个灯具经营部遍及全国各省市，500多家生产企业出产的庭园灯、投光灯、道路灯、高杆灯等十大系列800多个品种的灯具照亮了北京长安街，照亮了长江三峡工地，照亮了许多国家的首都。以四明湖环湖生态农业综合开发为主线的特色农业发展迅速，培育出省级名茶“瀑布仙茗”、“梁弄樱桃”，“田玉牌”笋丝干菜、果桑等名特优农副产品，形成了名茶、名果、花卉三大主导产业。得天独厚的自然景观和人文环境，静雅清丽的四明湖度假村，众多的革命遗址成为人们进行爱国主义教育和休闲观光的好地方。

湖光山色惹人爱，更有胜景看不厌。梁弄如镶嵌在四明山麓的一颗明珠，在二十一世纪的今天，正放射出越来越璀璨的光芒。

梁弄樱桃

旅游、观光、考察、合作

梁弄人民欢迎您来

电话：(0574) 62366608
传真：(0574) 62367059
邮编：315430
网址：www.ll.yy.gov.cn

桃源故里

横街镇

横街镇地处于宁波西乡、鄞县大道西端，距市区 10 公里，宁波飞机场 8 公里，108 路公交车直达镇区。下辖 28 个行政村，2 个居委会，在册人口 4.1 万，总面积 121.7 平方公里，列鄞州区前茅。

辖区内粮田肥沃、山林茂密、物产丰饶，气候宜人。名优茶、草席、竹笋、竹炭、花木等名闻遐迩。风光秀丽，环境幽静的休闲观光胜地 --- 溪下水库庄家溪生态旅游区正在规划之中。

几年来，镇党委政府坚持以“三个代表”重要思想为指导，按照全心全意谋发展、真情实意求引进、实事求是转作风、竭尽全力优环境的工作思路，以创经济强镇、农特重镇、环境美镇、服务优镇为目标，把发展作为第一要务，目前拥有华茂集团、东海集团、盛邦制衣等大型企业和林村水表、水家铝制品、芝岭气门嘴等块状经济，占地 2.5 平方公里的镇工业园区及上冯工业点已初具规模，企业群体的集聚和辐射功能充分体现。辖区内基础设施完善，投资环境较好，新村建设全面起步，农业产业化步伐不断加快，具有战略意义的溪下水库和山区规模移民工程已经启动，并已进入实质性的建设阶段，环境整治成效显著，居民的生活水平、居住条件和档次明显提高。

2003 年，全镇实现国内生产总值 14.4 亿元，工业产值 57 亿元，外贸出口交货值 15.5 亿元，镇财政总收入达到 1.1 亿元。如今，全镇上下社会稳定，经济繁荣，各业兴旺，人民安居乐业。

面对新形势，横街镇将在十六大精神推动下，进一步解放思想，实事求是，与时俱进，以“四镇”为目标，发扬“敢为、求实、争先”的鄞州精神，不断开创工作新局面。

强蛟——投资、开发的乐园

强蛟镇位于宁海东北部，地处象山港尾，与象山、奉化隔海相望。全镇陆地总面积58平方公里，海域面积34平方公里，辖21个行政村，总人口1.7万人。2003年全镇实现工农业总产值12.3亿元，完成财政收入3231.5万元，农民人均收入6160元。

工业经济发展迅猛，共有企业138家，销售500万元以上企业21家，一个以模具、塑料、机械、轻工、铸造为主的工业体系已初步构成。

海洋资源丰富，浅海滩涂面积4.26万亩，养殖总面积达1.1万亩，拥有网箱5300只，水产品口感鲜美，远销日本、韩国。

人文景观丰富，素有“海上千岛湖”之称的强蛟群岛像颗颗珍珠镶嵌在强蛟镇东部，横山岛上风景独特，环境幽静，“小普陀”之名闻名遐尔。

投资环境优越，境内临港开发区正在积极筹建，浙能国华宁海电厂辐射带动效应日益凸现。水陆空三路交通便捷，供水、供电、邮电、通讯等基础设施完备。

精神文明协调发展，获得市双拥模范镇、市六好乡镇党委、县社会治安综合治理先进集体、县优秀理论学习中心组、省十佳科技学校等光荣称号。

东吴镇

鄞州区东吴镇地处宁波市东郊，距甬城20公里，自东吴出发约20分钟可到达鄞州中心区。西南与东钱湖风景区相邻，北与北仑铁路、沿海大通道“同三线”相通，鄞州大道、宝瞻公路穿镇而过，地理位置优越，交通便捷。全镇区域面积80平方公里，辖12个行政村，1个居委会，常住人口1.7万余人。镇内有驰名中外的东南佛国天童寺，融自然景观于一体的天童国家级森林公园和三溪浦水库，山青水秀，风景宜人，是鄞州区第一个宁波市生态示范镇。2003年全镇共实现国内生产总值6.5亿元，工农业总产值23.8亿元，财政收入6884万元。

几年来，镇党委、政府始终坚持以富民强镇，率先基本实现现代化总揽全局，该镇经济建设和社会各项事业得到蓬勃发展，城镇面貌日新月异。工业经济已形成以机械电梯、冶金铸造、针织服装为支柱的产业体系，拥有欣达集团、日月集团等国家级高新技术企业二家，市百家重点企业二家，草原皇服饰为国家免检产品。位于鄞州大道两侧占地2.4平方公里的镇工业园区已初具规模，企业梯队群体的集聚和辐射功能充分体现。

在迈向现代化的征途中，东吴人民将充分利用相对的发展优势，锐意改革，致力创新，把东吴建设成“实力型经济、生态型环境、稳定型社会”的新东吴。竭诚希望各地客商、各界人士前来观光旅游、投资开发，经商洽贸，共同开创东吴新的辉煌。

地址：宁波市鄞州区东吴镇
电话：0574-88341592
邮编：315113

宁波金田铜业（集团）股份有限公司

宁波金田铜业（集团）股份有限公司位于千年古镇——慈城，是一家以铜加工为主的大型企业。沪杭甬铁路、61省道和在建的杭州湾大桥南岸连接线穿越于公司附近。现占地面积69万平方米，总资产10余亿元，职工3700多人，主要产品有标准阴极铜、铜及铜合金棒、板、带、线、管，漆包线、铜阀门、管接件、水表以及钕铁硼磁性材料等。其中铜系列产品为宁波市名牌产品，标准阴极铜为浙江省唯一的在上海期货交易所注册的产品，生产磁性材料的磁业公司为浙江省高新技术企业。

2003年铜产品总量达到19.5万吨，销量27亿元，利税1400多万元，比上年翻一番左右；外贸出口1659万美元，比上年增长330%。

公司遵循“天天求变，永不满足，勇于竞争，追求卓越”的企业精神，贯彻“做大做强”的发展战略，企业得到快速健康发展。先后获得中国优秀民营企业、全国乡镇企业100强、浙江省民营企业50强，以及省市文明单位和AAA重合同守信用单位等称号。

JINTIANTONGYE

昌祺 CHANG QI 宁波昌祺氟塑料制品有限公司

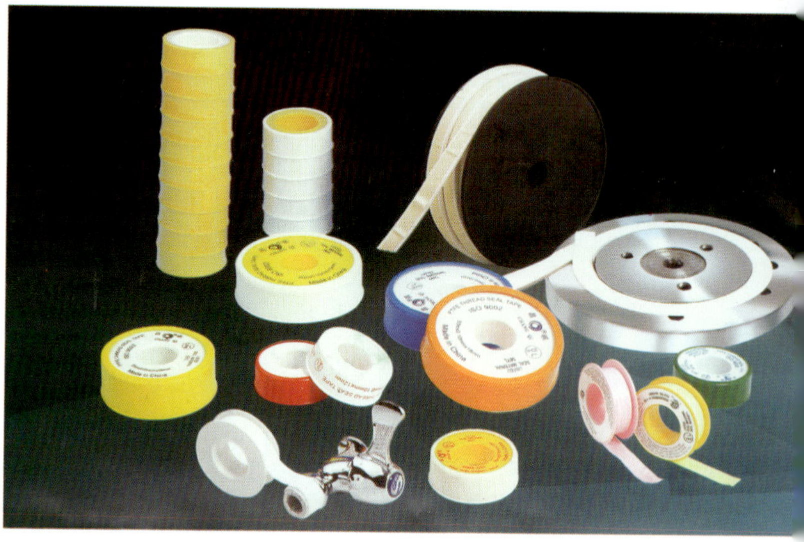

宁波昌祺氟塑料制品有限公司（中美合资）设立于1993年，地处宁波市近郊，距北仑深水港25公里，宁波机场18公里。

公司主要生产聚四氟乙烯（PTFE）压延膜、拉伸膜、弹性盘根及特种塑料桶和一般塑料制品，具有进出口经营权。

其中PTFE生料带产品月产量达到2000万卷。是目前中国最大生料带生产厂。95%以上销往国际市场，是中国唯一能大批量进入日本和美国市场的企业。由于生料带产品在国际市场的竞争中具有明显的综合优势，使企业在过去的10年中得以年平均35%的速度发展。

公司遵循市场为导，质量为先，人才为本的经营方针。建立了完整的质量管理体系，先后取得了ISO9001：2000认证、美国UL、加拿大CSA和日本JIS认证。是全球通过JIS认证的五家生料带厂之一，是中国唯一通过JIS认证的企业。

公司所采用的工艺技术、生产测试手段领先国内同行企业，压延膜的厚度、均匀度，拉伸膜的白度和厚度均匀性等技术指标能满足国际市场中最高领域的市场要求。

公司由于在生产管理条件和规模上的优势，形成了品质和成本上的优势。确保长期稳步、高速的发展。

国电浙江北仑第一发电有限公司

北仑发电厂是我国第一个利用世界银行贷款建设的火力发电厂,分二期建设。一期工程安装2台600MW亚临界燃煤机组，与1988年1月开工建设，至1994年建成投产。二期工程安装3台600MW亚临界燃煤机组，与1996年6月开工建设，至2000年全部建成。一期、二期总装机容量达到300万千瓦，是二十世纪中国最大的火力发电厂。

北仑发电厂总投资170多亿元，建设资金中利用世界银行贷款和由世界银行提供担保的联合融资贷款近10亿美元。主设备全部通过国际招标从国外引进，其中，1号锅炉由美国燃烧工程公司设计制造，1号汽轮发电机由日本东芝公司设计制造，2号锅炉由加拿大柏勃考克公司设计制造，2号汽轮发电机由法国阿尔斯通公司设计制造，二期工程3号机组的锅炉由日本石川岛播磨设计制造，汽轮发电机由日本东芝公司设计制造。北仑发电厂采用的设备比较先进，自动化程度比较高，它的建成投产是浙江电力工业向现代化迈进的里程碑。

北仑发电厂从建厂以来一直把培育北电特色的企业文化，作为企业思想政治工作的重要内容，有效地促进了电力生产经营。通过发展丰富“严谨、求实、高效、创一流”的北电企业精神，明确了“为社会提供永续动力”企业使命、树立了“以人为本，服务民生”的企业价值观，形成了“安全稳发促生产，科技环保图发展，创新管理铸辉煌”的企业经营理念，养成了“让业绩说话”的工作作风；“北电的光彩，你我的风采”成为每位员工的信条，“北仑发电、动力无限”更是企业的最强音。

地 址：宁波·北仑
电 话：0574-86892542
传 真：0574-86883246
邮 编：315800

宁波(骆驼)机电工业园区

位于宁波市中心城区西北，分别距市中心10公里，镇海港15公里，北仑港25公里，宁波栎社机场18公里，杭州湾大通道连接线入口8公里。园区规划面积10.5平方公里，近年来基础设施投入4.8亿元，开发面积6平方公里，水、电、路和通讯等基础设施已全面完成。以发展高附加值、无污染、科技含量高的电子、机械制造工业为主，着力建成高效、专业、生态、特色工业区。随着园区开发建设规模扩大，投资环境不断改善和服务水平不断提高，园区的知名度和影响力不断扩大，相继有170余家知名企业来园区落户，其中来自日本、新加坡、美、英、法、泰等国和港、台地区的投资者60余家。目前有75%的企业在建或已投产，正在洽谈的客商相继不断，投资热潮方兴未艾。

宁波金狮啤酒有限公司

NINGBO LION BREWERY CO.,LTD.

宁波金狮啤酒有限公司是中外合资兴建的现代化大型啤酒生产企业。2002年，英特布鲁入主公司后为宁波金狮啤酒带来了全新的生机。英特布鲁（Interbrew)，总部设立于比利时布鲁塞尔之上市公司，是全球第一大啤酒公司，也是世界上最悠久的啤酒公司之一。其经营战略为The World's Local Brewer（全球化的当地啤酒酿造商），在全球各主要啤酒市场建立强大坚实的地方化平台。目前，英特布鲁在世界各地拥有逾二百个品牌，雇有员工超过35,000名，公司业务遍及美洲、欧洲和亚太区21个国家。宁波金狮啤酒有限公司座落在山清水秀的宁波市西郊，占地面积近20万平方米，注册资金达2.4亿元人民币。目前的年产啤酒能力达35万吨，在宁波及周边地区拥有80%以上的市场份额，是浙江省啤酒主要生产企业之一，在全国同行业中享有较高的声誉。

酿造车间啤酒发酵集散控制系统

宁波金狮生产的啤酒以得天独厚的鄞江澄浪潭优质地下潜水和进口澳麦为基本原料，并与德国最大的啤酒生产企业—— DAB公司进行技术合作，使产品科技含量大大增加，产品质量不断提高。公司生科的“KK啤酒”、“K牌啤酒”等系列产品以泡沫洁白细腻、口感清洌爽口，具有典型的国际流行口味而备受广大消费者的厚爱。“K牌啤酒”作为宁波市名牌产品还分别荣获“浙江省著名商标”、“浙江省名牌产品”和“全国啤酒行业优质产品奖”等称号。2002年6月，公司主动把握啤酒消费市场动态，及时投入巨资，引进一条具有国际领先水平的纯生啤酒灌装生产线，成功地研制出“壹周纯生”啤酒，并在全国同行中首先提出并实施纯生啤酒“一周召回”承诺，产品一面市便迅捷占领市场。壹周纯生啤酒的成功上市意味着宁波地产啤酒品牌的生产设施、技术含量、工艺水平、管理措施及产品品质已与国际顶级品牌趋于同步。

德国产啤酒过滤系统

至今公司已在上海、杭州、绍兴等地建立了销售机构，市场占有率不断提高。通过资产重组、优化产品结构，引进英特布鲁先进的管理和销售模式，使企业实力再上新台阶，产品从区域名牌一跃成为全国名牌。

秀美的酿造车间全景

全自动成品包装车间

酿造车间一景

测试分析中心

ISO9001:2000.HACCP国际认证企业

宁波能大食品有限公司

宁波能大食品有限公司位于风景秀丽的象山港畔的象山县--国家确认的一级天然氧吧的现代化生态型滨海城市。水陆交通便捷，距宁波国际机场90公里，宁波北仑港100公里，象山港45公里，石浦港15公里。公司主要从事真空冷冻干燥（FD），速冻保鲜（IQF），热风干（AD）食品的开发、生产和销售，拥有自营进出口权。公司现有员工230人，研发人员22人，以及一批多年在食品行业中从事农产品的专业管理人才。2003年10月被宁波市人民政府确认为市农业龙头企业。

目前，公司已具备研发、生产各类果蔬、水产品、肉禽类等真空冷冻干燥、速冻，热风干燥的能力，且各项指标均符合出口食品卫生标准。公司完全遵循ISO9001：2000HACCP质量管理体系，从原料采购、生产、储运各方面进行CCP点的控制，使产品的品质得到了保证。目前产品不仅打开了国内市场，而且已远销欧美、德国、丹麦、日本等地。

公司以质量第一，诚信客户，求得自身发展的同时，坚持创高新科技，出名优产品，誉公司品牌，不断开拓冻干（FD）食品的新领域，以满足国内外市场消费者的需求。宁波能大食品有限公司全体员工竭诚欢迎海内外朋友光临指导，共创大业。

宁波市鄞州区

福泉山茶场茶叶系列产品

宁波市鄞州区福泉山茶场，位于风光秀丽的东钱湖旅游度假区。系浙东天台山余脉的支干，她南邻象山港，北接东钱湖，与太白山遥遥相望，方圆10.5平方公里，主峰为海拔596米，距宁波市区31公里，是一个以茶为主，兼营工业、林业、贸易一条龙综合经营的大型国有茶场。已拥有杉木林8000亩，茶园3600亩，其中有无性繁殖良种茶园1500亩，引种国内各高等院校及科研单位提供的无性繁殖36个。主要生产名茶“东海龙舌”、“云雾春”、“白茶”等系列产品,其名茶“东海龙舌”产品，在国内享有较高声誉。该茶场具有40余年办场历史，是一个典型的林特生产基地。

该场茶叶生长的自然生态环境十分优越，植被完整，远离城镇，自然形成了独特的无污染区域，营造了得天独厚的茶叶生态小气候。这种由天时、地利、人和所造成的独特氛围，为创造名茶“东海龙舌”等系列产品的优良品质奠定了扎实基础，其主导产品“东海龙舌”品质优良，市场信誉好，在国内外消费市场有口皆碑。

“东海龙舌”自创名牌以来，相继荣获各项殊荣：

1988至1990年荣获宁波市一类名茶三连冠，列入计划单列市名茶开发新产品和著名商标；

1991年获中国·杭州国际茶文化节名茶新秀奖；

1993年获中国优质农产品科技成果展览银奖；

1998年获浙江省优质农产品奖；

1999年获省13届一类名茶奖，同年6月在农业部茶叶质量监督检验测评中心的各项标准鉴定均达到国际先进水平；

1999年9月获中国国际农业博览会名牌产品证书；

2001年被宁波市人民政府授予宁波市名牌产品；

2002年获中国精品名茶博览会金奖；

2002年获浙江省无公害名特优茶，并在当年被浙江省授予无公害产品标志证书和无公害农产品基地，同年又被宁波市评为绿色农产品茶叶基地；

2003年获宁波市知名商标；

2004年获浙江省著名商标，同年又被中国农业科学院茶叶研究所认证为有机茶。

宁波市鄞州区福泉山茶场将一如既往，以“全心投入、正直诚实、以人为本、勇攀高峰、团对精神、顾客导向”作为企业理念，竭诚为广大消费者服务！

法定代表：郑金灿

地址：浙江省宁波市鄞州区东钱湖镇大寺

邮编：315134

电话：0574-88401777　88401445

传真：0574-88375066

余姚市城区

胜利瓦筒厂

厂长：施胜利

余姚市城区胜利瓦筒厂是专业生产Φ300-Φ1200Ⅱ级平口式及承插式钢筋混凝土管，本厂工艺先进，质量保证，讲究信誉，代办托运，热忱欢迎新老客户来我厂参观、洽谈、合作。

地址：余姚市西北街道康山村
电话：62665998
邮编：315400

慈城中心小学

慈城中心小学创办于1932年，原名“尚志小学”，由原效实中学高才生冯景曾先生一手创办。到1958年改名为“慈城中心小学”。

“以德育人，立人为本”是我们慈城中心小学的办学理念，也是我们追求教育境界和自我完善的目标；是我们为学生生命奠基，追求人生价值的目标；更是我们师生尊重生命、珍爱生命和体验生命意义的过程。

崇尚人文精神是我们的管理理念。我们在管理中强调以人为本，充分发挥人的主观能动性，使人尽其才，事得其人，人事相宜。我们还注重校园文化建设，优化校园自然环境，校园的每个角落留下了孩子们愉悦的足迹和清脆的笑声。

奠定学生幸福人生的基础是我们的教学理念。我们每一位教师在教学中呵护着学生的生命，关注学生生命的全部内容。我们冲破了以教材为中心，以课堂为中心，以教师为中心的樊篱，去超越教材、超越课堂、超越教师，让学生的学习焕发生命的活力，让学生的学习充满成长的气息。

我们学校在改革中奋进，在创新中发展，我们正满怀着信心向着更高的目标迈进。

余姚市第二中学

校长:吴傲琪

余姚二中是一所城区公办普通高中，占地达到102亩，由东南，西北两个校区组成（东南为余姚二中原址，西北为余姚中学原址）现有33个班级，学生1759人，教职工127名，其中有高级教师39人，中级教师40人，专任教师102人，学历均达到大学本科，具有研究生学历47人；教师平均年龄37岁，90%以上的教龄都在10年以上，教育教学经验丰富，师德高尚。

余姚二中是英才的摇篮，育人的殿堂。随着学校占地面积的扩大，作为一流的省A级普高，余姚二中目前正在积极向省级重点中学的目标迈进，她将成为有特色，高质量，并深受余姚人民放心的现代化窗口学校。

校址：
东南校区为余姚市东南街道东旱门路71号（花园新村东首）
西北校区为余姚市西北街道舜水北路3号（原余姚中学）
电话：0574-62722358 62663988
传真：0574-62722358
E-mail:x0002@yyedu.org

奉化市职业技术学校

转制三年初展风采

奉化市职业技术学校，有48年办学历史。1983年率先由普通完中转为职业高中。2000年8月，经市政府同意，由公办转为民办。转制三年多来，学校以发展为第一要务，构筑中高职教育相衔接的“立交桥”，开创职高、普高相沟通，中等教育与高等教育同步发展的新局面，在奉城东郊这块热土上初展风采。

汽车维修与驾驶专业

扩大了办学规模。在校生成倍增加，由转制时不到300人，增加到现在的近700人，今秋能超千名。

机械电子专业

提高了办学效益。毕业生一次性就业率达98%以上，近年报考高职院校上线率在92%左右。

拓宽了与高等院校联合办学路子。2000年9月建立了中国农业大学园艺学院奉化分院。教授上课，名校文凭，热门专业，灵活学制，受到省、市有关园艺园林规划设计单位的青睐。首届毕业生均已走上了工作岗位。

电脑财会专业

试办了综合高中班。一流的师资，一流的管理，取得了家长的信赖。参加省普通高中会考成绩优良。

改善了办学条件。转制后学校加大了投入，新建的400米标准田径运动场已投入使用，一幢五层综合教学楼即可竣工，师生休闲广场工程亦将启动。

发展前景灿烂。学校地处市区东郊，占地100余亩，有一个幽雅宜人的学习环境，交通便捷，发展空间大。宁波市教学评估组认为，这是一所充满活力、发展前景灿烂的学校！

综合高中

园艺园林设计专业

奉化市第二中学

FengHuaerzhong

刻苦 上进 和谐 文明

书记、校长：谢定生

学校简介

奉化市第二中学坐落于象山港畔，九峰山麓的莼湖镇西北角，依山傍海，环境幽美，系市属重点中学，省A级普通高中。学校创建于1952年7月，初称“奉化县第二初级中学”，曾先后易名为“奉化县初级中学”、“奉化县第一初级中学”。1958年增设高中部，定名为“奉化县第二中学”，1988年撤县建市遂改为“奉化市第二中学”。至今已有五十年的历史。目前学校有正式教职工103名，中高级教师37名，24个教学班，近1400名学生。

五十年的历史可分为四个阶段：1952年至1957年为艰苦创业阶段，虽然校舍设施陈旧简陋，但砥砺全校师生艰苦奋斗，勤俭办学，学校初具规模；1958年至1976年为巩固发展阶段，规模逐步扩大，群体活动初露头角，教学质量稳步提高；1977年至1992年为突飞猛进阶段，群体活动闻名于省内外，教学质量几度名列奉化市榜首；1993年至今为再度创业阶段，学校融资近1000万元，拆建了甬港联谊教学楼、杨大毅教学楼、学生宿舍楼、学生公寓楼、学生餐厅及教师宿舍楼等，装修了行政楼和高中教学楼，改造了运动场、彩砖天井，新增2000平方米绿化面积，配备了一套现代化的教学、办公设施，办学硬件日臻完善，校容校貌焕然一新。

经过50年的艰苦创业，学校已积淀了深厚的文化底蕴，创造了优良的人文环境，产生了一支“团结、民主、务实、创新”的领导班子和教学水平高、事业心强、充满朝气和活力的教职工队伍，形成了鲜明的办学特色：勤教苦学、群体活跃、“刻苦、上进、和谐、文明”的校风已深入人心。培养了1万余名初高中毕业生，涌现了一大批在国际国内享有盛誉的校友。如中国工程院院士沈昌祥，享受国务院特殊津贴的裘熙定、卓海通、刑照贤、裘古坊、胡才茂、张素娥等。

50年的不懈奋斗，几代人的心血和汗水，赢得了几多荣誉。学校曾被评为全国群体先进单位，多次被评为浙江省群体先进单位、浙江省体育卫生工作先进单位、浙江省业余训练先进单位、浙江省体育传统项目学校、宁波市示范性文明学校、宁波市先进团组织、奉化市文明单位、奉化市先进党组织、奉化市文明学校等。高考捷报频传，多次受上级教育行政部门嘉奖。

回顾历史，继承传统，展望未来，开拓进取，面对机遇与挑战，“二中人”以务实的作风，坚定的信心，矫健的步伐，执着追求，与时俱进，向着省重点中学的目标迈进。

学校荣誉

学校远景规划图

地址：浙江省奉化市莼湖镇

电话：0574-88743018

邮编：315506

网址：www.fhez.net

QIU ZHEN SHOOL

宁波求真学校

NINGBO QIUZHEN SHOOL

校长：周雪侦

简介 JIANJIE

宁波求真学校创办于2000年3月。校园占地56亩，建筑面积近20000平方米。建有多媒体室、计算机室、校园网络、理化生实验室、塑胶田径场、学生公寓等现代化教学、生活设施。学校现有教学班31个，在校学生1300多名，拥有一支爱岗敬业，素质优良的教师队伍。

学校建立了学前段、小学段、初中段十二年一贯制的办学体系和全寄宿的管理模式，形成了独树一帜的“成功教育”特色，突出了计算机、英语教育。办学四年，学校相继荣获市文明单位、市社会力量办学先进单位、优质特色教学民办学校等荣誉，成为中国青少年研究中心学习科学研究室实验学校。《体验成功快乐成长》课题被列为省教育科学规划课题。2002、2003两年“中考”，初中毕业生的全面质量均居奉化市前二位。奉化日报、中国教育报等新闻媒体都热情报道了学校跨越式发展的办学经验。

一个目标

“教全体学生学好，让每个家长满意”是学校已基本实现，并继续作为永恒追求、全面实施的办学目标。

二个一流

设施一流：学校不仅拥有占地面积3.5万平方米，建筑面积近2万平方米雅洁优美的校园，而且现代化教学设施和高档生活设施尽善尽美。

师资一流：60名专任教师平均年龄32岁，平均教龄12年，高学历、高职称占60%，县市级以上教坛新秀、教学能手、优秀班主任和骨干教师占60%。

三大优势

封闭管理，爱严相济，不轻视一个“育”。
班额适中，教学得法，不轻视一节“课”。
形式多样、价格实惠，不忽视学生一“方”。

四大亮点

学生成绩提高快。
学生品行优化快。
学生的全面素质好。
学生的学习方法好。

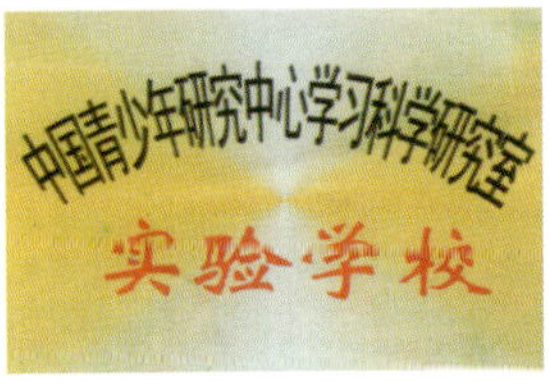

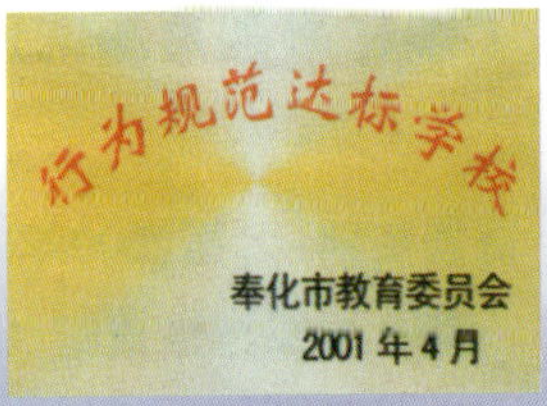

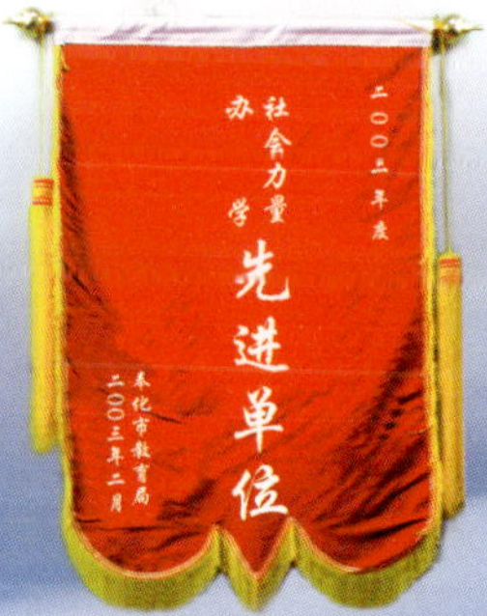

地址：宁波市奉化城区金钟路51号
电话：0574-88935237
0574-88935625-13

中国名茶
奉化曲毫
宋代雪竇寺住持廣聞禪師作《御書應夢名山記》景
年，宋仁宗趙禎夢游『八極之表』，後詔，『圖天下
山川以進』。自此，進山者，得天地之靈氣，取山中
之幽闌藍。御書應夢，謂，茶齊不同畝，曲毫幽而獨芳。
2000年荣获国际名茶金奖
2000年荣获浙江省名茶证书
2001年荣获宁波市农业名牌产品
2002年荣获中国精品名茶金奖
2003年荣获浙江省农博会金奖
2004年荣获中绿杯金奖
奉化曲毫茶叶
宁波市名牌产品
宁波绿色农产品基地
金奖
地址：宁波奉化南街2号
电话：0574-88982714
传真：0574-88966520
邮编：315500
电邮：fhfqy@eyou.com

宁波市统计局 • 编
NINGBO MUNICIPAL STATISTICS BUREAU

2004
宁波统计年鉴
NINGBO STATISTICAL YEARBOOK

中国统计出版社
China Statistics Press

（京）新登字 041 号

图书在版编目（CIP）数据

宁波统计年鉴 .2004/宁波市统计局编 .—北京：中国统计出版社，2004.6
ISBN 7－5037－4385－9

Ⅰ.宁… Ⅱ.宁… Ⅲ.统计资料－宁波市－2004－年鉴
Ⅳ.C832.553－54

中国版本图书馆 CIP 数据核字（2004）第 046941 号

宁波统计年鉴—2004

作　者/宁波市统计局
责任编辑/陈越月
E－mail/yearbook@stats.gov.cn
责任校对/徐卫民　朱晓瑜
封面设计/江西宜春资料印务有限公司
出版发行/中国统计出版社
通信地址/北京市西城区三里河月坛南街 75 号　中国统计出版社
邮　编/100826
电　话/（010）63262295
印　刷/江西宜春资料印务有限公司
经　销/新华书店
开　本/890×1240 毫米　1/16
字　数/95.8 万
印　张/28.25
印　数/10000 册
版　别/2004 年 6 月第 1 版
版　次/2004 年 6 月第 1 次印刷
书　号/ISBN 7－5037－4385－9/F·1848
定　价/258.00 元

编辑:宁波市统计局
出版:中国统计出版社

Edit by :Ningbo Municipal Statistics of Bureau
Published by: China Statisticcal Publishing House

编 者 说 明

《宁波统计年鉴－2004》以大量统计数据，全面、系统地反映了2003年宁波经济、科技、社会各方面的发展情况，是一本信息密集的资料性年刊和工具书。

年鉴内容包括：2003年宁波市国民经济和社会发展概况；综合；农业；工业、原材料、能源消费和电力；固定资产投资和建筑业；港口、交通运输、邮电业；批发零售贸易业、餐饮业；对外经济、旅游；科学技术；文化、教育、卫生、体育；财政、金融、保险；劳工工资、劳保福利、从业人员；物价指数、人民生活；城市建设、环境保护、民政、司法、企业景气及其他等十四个部分。

年鉴辑入的统计数据，以2003年为主，为方便读者使用，主要指标还列示了改革开放以来主要年份的统计数据，并对过去发表的统计数据重新予以核实，凡与本年鉴有出入的，均以本年鉴为准。在前几年出版的年鉴基础上，根据统计制度的变化，作了一些调整和改进，并与前几年版本在编辑体例、内容结构、指标体系、统计口径等方面保持了连贯性。

年鉴中凡带有续表的资料，如有注解均注在第一张表的下方。

本年鉴中的符号说明："…"表示数据不足本表最小单位数；"空格"表示该项统计数据不详或无该项统计数据；"#"表示其中数。

《宁波统计年鉴》出版以来，受到社会各界的关心、支持，不少读者对于年鉴的内容和编辑工作提出了许多宝贵的意见，对此，我们深表感谢。并欢迎读者一如既往地对年鉴的不足之处给予批评指正，以进一步提高编辑水平。

Complier's Note

Ningbo Statistical Yearbook 2004 is an annual publication which provides comprehensive and systematic data covering the economic, technological and social development in Ningbo Municipality in 2003.

This yearbook is comprised of 14 parts including :1. Brief Introduction of 2002 Ningbo National Economy and Social Development; 2. General Survey; 3. Agriculture; 4. Industry, Raw Materials, Energy Consumption and Electricity; 5. Investment in Fixed Assets and Construction; 6. Port, Transportation, Post and Telecommunication; 7. Wholesale and Retail, Domestic Trade and Catering; 8. Foreign Trade and Tourism; 9. Science and Technology; 10. Education , Culture, Health and Sports; 11. Finance, Banking and Insurance; 12. Wages, Welfare and Employment; 13. Price Index and People's Livelihood; 14. Civil Administration, Environmental Protection, Social Welfare, Legal System and Others; 15. Prosperity Index on Enterprises. The content of this yearbook are comprised of mainly the statistic of 2002 and statistical data of those key years after opening to the outside world. The data in this yearbook have been already checked. If ever the readers find inconsistency of data here as compared with those in previous year books, please refer to this yearbook as accurate and final. On the basis of past years' publication, this yearbook has made some due adjustment and improvement with the changes in statistical guidelines, however still keeping in conformity with the past years' yearbooks on editorial style, content makeup, indication selection and statistical approach.

The footnotes are placed at the first page, if the table is a continued one. Explanations on symbols used in this yearbook: "…"indicates that the data are not large enough to be rounded into the minimal unit; "space" indicates that the data is unknown or indicates the data not available; " # " indicates the component items.

Here we'd like to express our sincere thanks to the readers who have provided us so many invaluable suggestions on content selection and compilation of the yearbook. Our thanks also go to those friends in all circles of society who have shown their support and care to the publication of the yearbook. We welcome any suggestions and comments from readers at large so as to help us to further improve our work of compilation.

目　　录
CONTENTS

一、综　　合
CHAPTER 1 GENERAL SURVEY

二、农　　业
CHAPTER 2 AGRICULTURE

三、工　　业
CHAPTER 3 INDUSTRY

四、固定资产投资、建筑业
CHAPTER 4 INVESTMENT IN FIXED ASSETS AND CONSTRUCTION

五、港口、交通运输、邮电
CHAPTER 5 PORT, TRANSPORTATION, POSTAL AND TELECOMMUNICATION SERVICE

六、贸易、餐饮业
CHAPTER 6 DOMESTIC TRADE AND CATERING TRADE

七、对外经济、旅游
CHAPTER 7 FOREIGN TRADE AND TOURISM

八、科学技术
CHAPTER 8 SCIENCE AND TECHNOLOGY

九、文教、卫生、体育

CHAPTER 9 CULTURE, EDUCATION, PUBLIC HEALTH AND SPORTS

十、财政、金融、保险

CHAPTER 10 FINANCE, BANKING AND INSURANCE

十一、劳动工资、劳保福利、从业人员
CHAPTER 11 WAGES, WELFARE AND EMPLOYMENT

十二、物价及人民生活
CHAPTER 12 PRICES AND PEOPLE'S LIVELIHOOD

十三、市政、环保、民政福利、计划生育、政法
CHAPTER 13 CIVIL FACILITIES, ENVIRONMENT, SOCIAL WELFARE, JUDICATURE AND OTHERS

十四、企业景气指数
CHAPTER 14 PROSPERITY INDEX ON ENTERPRISES

2003年宁波市国民经济和社会发展统计公报

2003年是贯彻落实党的十六大精神,全面建设小康社会取得良好开局的第一年。全市人民在中共宁波市委、市人民政府的领导下,万众一心,开拓进取,坚持"五个统筹",有效化解各种矛盾,成功抵御了非典疫情和高温干旱、缺水少电等因素对社会经济的冲击,顺利完成了年初确定的各项任务,经济发展的活力和动力明显增强,人民生活持续改善,社会事业全面进步。

综　　合

国民经济运行快速、协调、健康。初步核算,全年实现GDP1769.9亿元,按可比价格计算,比上年增长15.3%,增长速度为近6年以来最高。人均GDP超过3400美元。第一产业增加值112.0亿元,比上年增长4.0%;第二产业增加值1007.0亿元,增长18.0%;第三产业增加值650.9亿元,增长13.3%。三次产业构成为6.3:56.9:36.8。第二产业对GDP的贡献率达65.9%,仍是拉动宁波经济的主要力量。

农村经济

农业生产和农村经济持续稳定发展。全年实现农林牧渔业增加值112.0亿元,比上年增长4.0%。农业结构继续调整,效益农业发展势头强劲,粮棉油面积继续调减,优质高效农产品面积增加,粮食与经济作物播种面积的比例从上年45:55调整到40:60。

积极实施科教兴农战略,加快实施种子种苗工程和农业科技示范园区建设。市级财政投入1000万元支持园区建设。11个园区共建设高标准农田2267公顷,大棚面积316公顷,发展了以温室、喷滴管等为主的现代农业设施。加速推进农业产业化,有23家农业龙头企业产值超亿元。

以市场为导向,大力发展绿色特色农产品。全市已有国家级绿色食品基地面积1350公顷,浙江省无公害农产品基地和市级绿色农产品基地面积10600公顷。已通过认定的国家级有机食品和绿色食品15个,省级绿色农产品29个。外向型农业发展加快,全年引进农业外资项目9个,项目总投资12955万美元,实际利用外资1584万美元。农产品出口3.92亿美元,增长19.4%。积极发展各类农村专业合作经济组织,全市有各类农村专业合作经济组织327个。

工业和建筑业

工业生产快速增长,经济运行质量稳步提高。全年工业增加值为910.1亿元,比上年增长18.0%,工业增加值占GDP的比重达51.4%。全市规模以上工业企业实现工业总产值2627.4亿元,工业销售产值2582.2亿元,分别比上年增长28.1%、29.4%,是近五年来增长最快的一年。工业产品产销率为98.28 %,比上年提高1.04个百分点。

各种所有制工业全面快速增长,其中,产值总量占全市规模以上工业五分之四的股份制企业和外商及港澳台投资企业分别比上年增长31.1 %和29.5 %,高于全市平均增幅3个和1.4个百分点。新产品产值增势较快,实现新产品产值348亿元,比上年增长43.6%。

工业规模效应进一步突现,优势骨干企业对工业经济拉动作用明显。工业总产值绝对额最大的前20家企业完成工业总产值822.8亿元,占规模以上工业总产值的三分之一,产值平均增长速度高于全市平均4.2个百分点。

重工业增长快于轻工业,增幅达31.6%,比轻工业高8个百分点。在38个工业大类中,有14个行业的增幅高于全市平均,其中,通信设备业、黑色金属工业、化学纤维制造业、交通运输设备制造业增长最快,增幅超过40%。作为我市支柱产业之一的石化工业,增幅为28.4%。

经济效益持续提高。全年实现工业利税总额318.47亿元,增长19.4%,其中利润189.18亿元,增长23.3%。11项经济效益指标考核得分为 230.52，比上年提高 9.87 分，居全省首位。

建筑业生产增长较快。全年建筑业实现增加值 96.9 亿元，比上年增长 18.1%。完成各类房屋建筑施工面积 6247.9 万平方米，比上年增加 2046.3 万平方米；竣工面积 2605.7 万平方米，增加 827.6 万平方米。建筑施工企业按总产值计算的全员劳动生产率为 12.77 万元/人，比上年提高 1.13 万元/人。

固定资产投资

固定资产投资增速加快。完成全社会固定资产投资 837.6 亿元，增长 39.3 %。投资增幅是 1995 年以来的最高水平。其中限额以上完成 740.9 亿元，比上年增长 43.7%。新开工项目增多、规模进一步扩大，全年限额以上投资新开工项目 1858 个，增长 15.8%，项目平均规模达 5528 万元，比上年扩大 1 倍。民间投资活跃，完成非国有投资 459.3 亿元，比上年增长 45.1%，比重占限额以上固定资产投资的 54.8%。

工业投资和房地产开发投资是推动全社会固定资产投资快速增长的主要力量，两项相加占全社会固定资产投资的比重达到 69.6%。其中，工业投资完成 398.9 亿元，比上年增长 64.1%。房地产供需两旺。全年完成房地产开发投资 184.3 亿元，占全社会投资的五分之一强，增幅比全社会投资高 7 个百分点。住宅仍是我市房地产开发投资的主要方向，占房地产开发投资比重达 74.3%。新开工房屋面积 1029.7 万平方米，增长 62.2%，其中住宅面积 831.1 万平方米，增长 66.1%；竣工面积 632.3 万平方米，增长 44.2%，其中住宅面积 526.6 万平方米，增长 54.4%。全年销售面积 537.6 万平方米，增长 39.9%，其中住宅销售面积 455.0 万平方米，增长 48.4%。

国内贸易与旅游

消费需求回升加快。全年实现社会消费品零售总额 521.5 亿元，比上年增长 12.7%，其中：限额以上批发零售贸易业增长 36.3%，高于全市平均 23.7 个百分点；餐饮业在非典疫情过后回升较快，全年餐饮业零售额为 67.2 亿元，增长 17.9%。居民消费升级倾向明显，住房、汽车、通信器材持续旺销。全市住宅销售额达 114.48 亿元，比上年增长 59.3%，其中个人住宅销售所占比重达 99.7%。汽车零售额达 21.2 亿元，增长 57.4%；家电及音像类、通讯器材类分别增长 53.6%和 115.9%。

旅游业成功抵御了非典疫情的冲击。2003 年全市接待入境旅游者 22.15 万人次，比上年增长 7.8%，旅游创汇 9976 万美元，增长 12.8%；接待国内旅游者 1720 万人次，增长 7.5%，国内旅游收入 155.83 亿元，增长 8.0%；旅游总收入达 164.06 亿元，增长 8.4%；全市旅游饭店平均客房出租率达 71.1%，继续保持全国 21 个重点旅游城市前列。

对外经济

对外贸易持续高位增长。全市自营进出口总额 188.1 亿美元，比上年增长 53.3%。其中：出口 120.7 亿美元，进口 67.4 亿美元，分别增长 47.9%和 63.9 %。三资企业、集体企业、私营企业出口占全市的 63.1%，其中私营企业出口 17.6 亿美元，增速高达 119.5%。

利用外资规模、质量同步突破。全年新批外商投资企业 1209 家，总投资 78.18 亿美元，合同利用外资 34.44 亿美元，实际利用外资 17.27 亿美元，分别比上年增长 18.9%、59.3%、58.6%和 56.6%。大项目居主导地位，“以外引外”成效显著。全市新批外资项目中，投资总额在 1000 万美元以上的大项目有 218 个，投资总额 56.97 亿美元，合同利用外资 22.89 亿美元，分别占项目总数的 18.0%、72.9%和 66.5%，分别增长 38.6%、41.3%和 7.0%。全球 500 强企业已有 27 家来甬投资。

对外经济合作稳步推进，出境劳务、投资取得新进展。全市对外承包劳务营业额 3.71 亿美元，增长 22.8%；外派劳务 1453 人，期末在外劳务 7025 人。企业境外投资的主动性不断增强，全年新批境外企业 74 家，项目总投资 2103 万美元，中方投资 1858 万美元。

财政、金融

财政增收较好。2003年全市完成财政总收入330亿元,增长25.9%,完成财政一般预算收入325亿元,同口径计算,比上年增长25.8%,其中:地方财政收入139.4亿元,增长32.4%;中央财政收入185.6亿元,增长21.2%。各主要税种继续保持快速增长,其中:完成增值税136亿元,增长21.2%(剔除免抵调增增值税因素,同口径增长22%);营业税完成41.3亿元,增长29.4%;企业所得税完成59.7亿元,增长28.7%;个人所得税完成24.4亿元,增长34.4%。财政支出结构调整,投向重点突出。全市财政总支出187.09亿元,比上年增长24.1%。其中农林水气支出10.5亿元,增长24%;医疗卫生支出7.55亿元,增长31.7%;坚持"科教兴市"战略和"文化大市"政策,保障教育投入,促进科技创新;大力推进社会保障体系建设,社保支出和医疗卫生支出分别比上年增长43.9%和31.7%。

金融对经济发展的支持力度加大。年末金融机构本外币存款余额达到2764.3亿元,比年初增加730.52亿元,比上年增长35.9%。其中城乡居民人民币储蓄存款余额为1059.63亿元,比年初增加197.27亿元。贷款规模进一步扩大。年末金融机构本外币贷款余额达到2223.02亿元,比年初增加668.63亿元,增长43.0%。金融机构资产质量进一步好转,全市银行业不良贷款已连续三年实现"双降",年末不良贷款率为4.95%,比年初下降3.8个百分点。信贷结构进一步优化,以国家重点工程项目、企业技术改造为主的中长期固定资产投资贷款209.9亿元,增长57.8%。个人消费信贷持续发展,年末贷款余额为231.92亿元,比年初增加89.9亿元,增量比上年多32.93亿元。

保险业持续稳健发展。全年保险金总额达9927.47亿元,总保险费收入38.36亿元,分别比上年增长80.2%和23.1%。其中:财产保险费收入13.35亿元,人寿险保费收入25.01亿元。全年总保险赔付金额达9.45亿元,比上年增长25.8%。

城市建设

城市化进程不断加快,基础设施建设力度进一步加大。新一轮城市总体规划修编工作基本完成,东部新城区、余慈组团、杭州湾新区等重点区域的规划不断深化。全年完成环境和公共设施投资90.4亿元,其中市区投资54.3亿元。市区重点建设南外环、北外环、宁姜路、大闸路、育才路、通途路等城市骨架道路桥梁工程。建设日湖公园、福明公园、南站广场、滨江大道及景观二期。全年新建、扩建城市道路长度120公里,其中市区40公里;新增公共绿地面积266公顷,其中市区136公顷。

交通、邮电

全年交通邮政及仓储业投资达49.87亿元,比上年增长15.9%。宁波杭州湾跨海大桥及南岸连接线、绕城高速西段相继开工。从郁浪浦到甬江口全线94公里300吨级航道的杭甬运河也已建成。全市新建公路134公里,改建公路264公里。农村公路投资1.27亿元,完成路基139公里,路面186公里。全市完成客运量2.5亿人次、货运量1.46亿吨,分别比上年增长4.9%和18%。车船运力快速增长,运力结构不断改善。全社会汽车拥有量超过21万辆,增长26%。其中载客汽车11.92万辆、78.84万客位;营运载客汽车9217辆,12.88万客位。快速客运集散网络初具规模,全年共开通高速和快速客运线路达73条。

港口建设有新突破。2003年新竣工5万吨级码头2个,集装箱码头4个。全年港口货物吞吐量达到1.85亿吨,名列大陆沿海港口第二位,比上年增长20.9%;集装箱吞吐量277.22万标准箱,增长49.2%,增幅已连续5年保持全国第一位。世界排名前20位的班轮公司均已落户宁波港。集装箱月航班突破460班,在欧洲、地中海、北美等主要贸易地区,达到了日均一班以上的密度,初步形成了覆盖全球的集装箱运输网络。

邮政、电信业务稳步增长。全年邮政和电信业务总量分别为4.72亿元和53.9亿元。全市电话普及率达68.76部/百人,其中城市电话普及率119.7部/百人,农村电话普及率49.99部/百人。

环境保护

环境保护工作力度加大,成效明显。建立并完善环保法律法规体系,制定并出台了《宁波市排污费征收管理实施办法》、《宁波市秸秆禁烧管理办法》。严格按国家产业政策,加强项目选址管理。全市共否决各类不符要求项目600余个,有效地控制了新污染源的产生。全市有35家单位被命名为环保模范单位。建成烟尘控制区19个,面积295.9平方公里;环境噪声达标区14个,面积1 35平方公里。宁海县已通过国家级生态示范区验收;余姚市泗门镇、慈溪市周巷镇通过了创建全国环境优美乡镇省级验收;全市有5个乡镇和12个行政村的生态示范区建设通过省(市)验收。宁波保税区、开发区等49家区域和企业通过IS014000认证。大气环境质量继续保持良好水平,Ⅰ、Ⅱ级环境质量优良天数336天,占全年总数92%。

科技、教育

全年共组织实施市级各类科技计划1431项,获得国家级项目115项,专利授权量3300件。新认定市级高新技术企业43家,新增国家级高新技术企业9家;国家级高新技术产业化基地5家。技术创新体系建设步伐加快,目前已建省级重点实验室4家、省级工程技术研究中心48家,并积极推进与中科院、兵科院、浙江大学、哈工大"两院两校"为重点的国内科技合作,全年共引进高新技术项目269项,引进、共建技术开发机构31个,引进各类人才2.85万人,其中博士、博士后72人,硕士762人,高级职称300多人。截至2003年底,全市人才资源总量已达38万人,其中专业技术人员30万人,高级职称1.3万人,中级职称8.7万人。

教育优先发展战略进一步加强。全市拥有各级各类全日制学校2701所(含技校),在校学生111万人。九年义务教育人口覆盖率达100%,义务教育的入学率、巩固率分别保持在100%和99.9%。高等教育进一步发展,高教南区基本建成,高教北区启动建设,普通高校在校学生人数为7.99万人,高等教育毛入学率达32%,全国高校统考报名录取率85.9%,继续保持全省领先地位。职业教育与成人教育有新发展,全市职业中专(含职高)招收学生2.67万名,成人中专普通班招收1323名,参加实用新知识、新技术培训的农村劳动力达35万人次,企业全员培训率38%。社会力量办学热情进一步激发,全市颁发社会力量办学许可证的学校(园)共有1642所,民办教育机构的资产从上年的23.7亿元增加到29.9亿元。"三残"儿童义务教育入学率超过96%。

文化、体育

组建了艺术剧院控股的股份制"大地艺术团"、宁波民乐团及与上海联和院线合资的宁波联和影视有限公司,成为国内第一家跨省合作组建的电影院线。成功承办了第七届宁波国际服装节开幕式和相关系列文化活动,全年又有10个镇通过省、市两级"东海明珠"验收,"东海明珠"乡镇覆盖率达83%。永丰库遗址考古成果荣获"2002年度全国十大考古新发现"。音乐厅、图书信息中心建成并正式启用,大剧院、美术馆完成主体工程。全市有线电视用户达127.5万户,广播电视人口综合覆盖率达99.98%。

成功承办了中国男子篮球联赛宁波主场赛、宁波国际城市围棋赛、全国艺术体操冠军赛、全国A类桥牌俱乐部锦标赛、第二届全国沿海城市长跑邀请赛等重大国际国内赛事10余项。各类群众体育活动蓬勃开展,四级全民健身工作网络日益完善,全市体育健身场所807家,"1154"全民健身工程继续实施,投资1亿元的市游泳健身中心主体工程建成,市老年体育活动中心也已结顶,并在社区和农村建成180条全民健身路径(园),全市健身路径总量达到580个。运动成绩不断提高,在第五届全国城市运动会上,全市共获金牌2枚、银牌6枚、铜牌6枚,总分163分,并获得体育道德风尚奖。

卫生事业

城乡居民医疗卫生条件进一步改善。年末医院、卫生院床位数达1.47万张,拥有专业卫生人员2.5万人。全市居民平均期望寿命达到75.8岁。以大病统筹为主、医疗救助为补充的新型农村合作医疗制度试点相继在镇海、余姚、慈溪、北仑、鄞州等地稳步开展，年末参加农村新型合作医疗的人数达159万多人。城市社区卫生服务网络体系不断健全，已建成省市级示范社区卫生服务中心13个、市级示范站10个，并设立了16个全科医学社区实践基地。疾病预防控制和卫生监督执法工作成效显著，有效地控制了非典疫情的发生和蔓延，全市无偿献血量占临床用血量的108%，传染病总发病率为210.31/10万，食品卫生抽检合格率为87.6%，食物中毒发生率为3.74/10万，均明显好于上年。2003年顺利通过国家卫生城市省级验收。

人口、人民生活和社会保障

人口继续保持低生育水平。年末全市总人口549.07万人，比上年末增加2.88万人，其中市区人口206.91万人，增加3.50万人。全市计划生育率达98.7%，已婚育龄妇女综合避孕率91.29%，流动人口计划生育管理率达92.3%。全市人口出生率7.42‰、死亡率6.28‰。

城乡居民收入稳步上升，生活质量进一步提高。全年市区城镇居民人均可支配收入14277元，比上年增长10.1%。市区城镇居民人均总支出14987元，比上年增长9.5%。其中，消费性支出10463元，增长11.3%，购房与建房支出达1844元，占总支出比重为12.3%。年末平均每百户市区城镇居民家庭拥有彩色电视机167台、影碟机59台、家用电脑50台、空调机117台、移动电话132部、健身器材8台(套)。

全市农村居民人均纯收入6221元，增长7.9%。平均每百户农村居民家庭拥有彩电129台，洗衣机50台，电冰箱73台，空调机21台，热水器37台，比上年分别增长10%、3.3%、4.8%、74.3%和8.3%。

全市年末私人汽车拥有量达到7.64万辆，比上年增长76.9%。

居住条件不断改善。市区城镇居民人均住房使用面积达到17.13平方米，住房成套率达98.25%。全市农村居民人均住房面积46.9平方米，比上年增加1.1平方米。

就业和再就业工作扎实推进。全年新增就业岗位13万个，开发社区就业岗位2.9万个，开发社区公益性岗位3553个，建立非正规就业组织418家。对3.1万名失业人员进行再就业培训，其中2.76万人获得各类合格证书，培训后就业率53%。至年底，全市有6.15万名失业人员实现再就业，城镇登记失业率4.02%，控制在预定目标内。

社会保险覆盖面进一步扩大。全市企业职工基本养老保险参保人数达118.79万人，实际缴费人数82.03万人，比上年净增10.77万人。有18.06万名离退休人员享受养老待遇，月人均养老金861元。有84.25万人参加医疗保险，参保人数比上年净增11.63万人。失业保险参保人数70.73万人，全年享受失业保险待遇62.3万人次，累计发放失业保险金和医疗补助金2.14亿元。年末生育保险参保人数33.62万人，工伤保险参保人数47.4万人，分别比上年增长33%和24%。年末被征地人员养老保障参保人数9.59万人，其中有3.81万名符合条件的参保人员享受了按月领取养老金待遇，共支付养老金3790万元。农村养老保险参保人数80万人，全年支付养老金2650万元。全市共有社会福利事业单位181个，床位1.14万张，收养0.92万人，享受低保的城乡居民达7.76万人。

注：公报中所列数据为初步统计数。

Statistics of National Economy and Social Development of Ningbo, 2003

The year, 2003, carried out and fulfilled the spirit of the 16th Party Congress in 2002, and opened a good phase of constructing well – off society in all – round way. Under the leading of CPC committee of Ningbo and municipal government, all Ningbo citizens of one mind insisted on "Five – Overall Planning", dissolved contradictions and resisted impacts on the national economy from the elements of SARS, high temperature, drought, water depletion and electric power shortage successfully, with the spirit of exploitation and enterprise. As a result, all the assignments, which were established and prearranged at the beginning of the year turned out to have generally been fulfilled and accomplished remarkably. Vigor and driving force of the economy development were strengthened evidently. Citizen's living standard was improved continuously and social undertaking was progressed in all – round way.

Comprehensive summary

National economy operated speedily, moderately and healthily. According to the preliminary statistics, in the year 2003, GDP amounted to 176.99 billion RMB, 15.3% increase that of the last year, computed by comparable price. The speed of increase is the highest in the recent 6 years. GDP per capita exceeded 3400 USD.

The contribution of primary industry to GDP increased 11.20 billion RMB compared with the last year, which is 4.0% increase that of 2002; the secondary industry contribution to GDP increased 100.70 billion RMB compared with the last year, which is 18.0% increase; the third industry contribution to GDP increased 65.09 billion RMB compared with the last year, which is 13.3% increase. Industrial structure was 6.3: 56.9: 36.8. The secondary industry still occupied the dominant position in the national economy of Ningbo, whose contribution rate of GDP reached 65.9%.

Agriculture

Agricultural production and economy sustained steady development. The realized value of agriculture, forestry, pasturage and fishery increased 11.20 billion RMB, 4.0% higher that of the last year. The force of plantation structure regulation was still seen on the full swing. The area of cotton, gain and edible oil continued to decrease, while the area of high grade and efficient agricultural products kept increasing. The ratio of the area of sown crops to it of industrial crops was adjusted from 45:55 to 40:60.

The strategy of developing agriculture with science and technology was implemented at full speed. The process of implementation of Seedling Project and construction of Technological Agricultural Demonstration Park was accelerated. The government has put an appropriation valued 10 million RMB from the financial budget to support the construction of the Park. The government mapped out 2267 hectares of farmland of high standard, 316 hectares greenhouse plants in eleven Technological Agricultural Demonstration Parks, and developed modern agricultural establishments mainly of greenhouse, drip pipe, etc. By speeding up the process of agriculture modernization, there are 23 leading agricultural corporations with production value of more than 100 million RMB.

Oriented by the market, green agricultural products are greatly developed. There exist 1350 hectares of state level green foods produce bases, 10600 hectares of province – level no environmental pollution agriculture produce bases and city – level green agriculture produce bases. 15 farm produce bases of state level organic foods and green foods and 29 produce bases of province – level green foods are authenticated. The speed of developing open agriculture was continuously given a boost. In the year 2003, 9 agriculture foreign investment projects were introduced in, with total investment 12.955 million USD and total utilization of investment valued 1.584 million USD. The total amount of agricultural products export reached 392 million USD, which increased 19.4% compared with the last year. There are 327 such rural cooperation organizations under the policy of actively developing various rural specialty cooperation economic organizations.

Industry and Construction Industry

Industrial production kept a rapid growth still, and the quality of economic performance kept increasing steadily. The industry increased value in 2003 was 91.01 billion RMB, up 18.0%, which accounted for 51.4% in GDP. City - level industries achieved total industry production value of 262.74 billion RMB and sales volume realized 258.22 billion RMB, increasing 28.1% and 29.4% respectively relative to 2002, which was the fastest in the recent five years. Production and sales were linked up in harmony with the ratio of 98.28%, 1.04% higher than the last year.

State - owned industries and non - state - owned industries developed in all - round way speedily. The production volume of stock enterprises and foreign or Hong Kong, Macao, Taiwan owned investment enterprises, which account for four fifth production volume of all city - level industries, increased 31.1% and 29.5% respectively, and 3 and 1.4 percentage points respectively higher than the average amount of increase in the Ningbo city. New products mounted up stupendously; the value of the output was as much as 34.8 billion RMB, up 43.6%.

The industry scale effects raised a step further. The effect of pushing the economy progress of preponderant pillar enterprises was pretty distinct. The top 20 enterprises with the highest industry production absolute value realized total industry production value of 82.28 billion RMB, accounting for one third of the total production value of all enterprises of the city. The average increase rate of production value was 4.2 percentage points higher than the city level.

The increase speed of heavy industries was higher than that of the light industries, with the amount of increase of 31.6%, 8 percentage points higher than the amount of increase of light industries. In the 38 broad headings of industry, 14 trades had the amount of increase higher than the average level of the city. Thereinto, the speed of increase of communication apparatus, ferrous metal industry, chemical fiber manufacture, and transport and communication facilities manufacture was the fastest, with more than 40% amount of increase. As the pillar trade, petrochemical industry had 28.4% amount of increase.

Economic benefit kept increasing continuously. The tax revenue generated by industrial enterprises was 31.847 billion RMB, up 19.4%, and total profit achieved by these enterprises was 18.918 billion RMB, 23.3% higher than the last year. The qualifying mark of the 11 economic benefit indexes was 230.52, which was the highest in the province, and 9.87 higher than the last year.

The construction industry progressed in good time. The increased value of the construction industry was 9.69 billion RMB, up 18.1%. The constructing area was 62,479,000sqm, added by 20,463,000sqm; the accomplished area was 26,057,000sqm, increased by 8,276,000sqm. The personnel work productivity of construction enterprises calculated by total output value was 127700 RMB per capita, with 11300 RMB per capita rise.

Investment of Fixed Assets

The prospect as for the investment of fixed assets emerged with full - scale development. Overall social fixed assets investment was 83.76 billion RMB, up 39.3%, which was the highest amount of increase from 1995. The realized amount exceeding the amount prescribed was 74.09 billion RMB, up 43.7%. New projects were increasing and the scale was expanding further.

New investments besides the amount prescribed were 1858, increasing 15.8%, with the average scale of 55.28 million RMB, which was twice as much as the last year.

The social aspiration of investment cheered with the ever more non - governmental investment of 45.93 billion RMB, a rise by 45.1%, which took up 54.8% of the prescribed fixed assets investment.

Industry investment and real estate investment were the main power of pushing the social fixed assets investment mounting up speedily, which took up 69.9% of the amount of investment of all fixed assets. And from the two parts, investment on industry were realized 39.89 billion RMB, up 64.1%

The supply and demand of real estate investment both flourished with thriving and prosperity. In the last year, the amount of investment on real estate were 18.43 billion RMB, which accounted for more than one fifth of all amount of social investment, and the amount of increase was 7 percentage points higher than all investment. Housing investment was the main aspect of real estate investment of the city, which took up 74.3% of all amount of real estate investment. The new operation area was 10,297,000sqm with the growth rate of 62.2%, from which residence area was accomplished 8,311,000sqm, up 66.1%. Accomplished area was 6,323,000sqm, raised by 44.2%, from which residence area was 5,266,000sqm, raised by 54.4%. The sales area of last year of commercial building was 5,376,000sqm, up 39,9%, from which sales area of residence was 4,550,000sqm, increased by 48.4%.

Domestic Trade and Tourism

The consumer market was on the increasing rise. The sales volume of retail trade was realized 52.15 billion RMB, up 12.7%. The sales volume of the quotas wholesale and retail trade increased 36.3%, which was 23.7 percentage points higher than the average level of the city. With the high speed of rebounding of the income of restaurants after the epidemic situation of SARS, the restaurants income was 6.72 billion RMB in the last year, raised by 17.9%.

The tendency of improving and upgrading citizen's consumption was evident, and the sales of residence, automobile and communication apparatus kept high sales volume. The sales volume of residence was 11.448 billion RMB, with a rise of 59.3%, from which 99.7% were private residence. The retail sales volume of automobile was 2.12 billion RMB, increased by 57.4%. The growth rate of domestic electric appliance, audio video and communication apparatus was 53.6%, 115.9% respectively.

The tourism resisted the impact of the epidemic situation of SARS successfully. In 2003, the number of foreign tourists amounted to 221,500 annually increased by 7.8% and earned foreign exchange of 99.76 million USD increased by 12.8%. The number of domestic tourists was 17,200,000 with a rise of 8.4%, with the domestic tourist income of 15.583 billion RMB, up 8.0%. Total tourist revenue reached 16.406 billion RMB with 8.4% rise and Ningbo, the average rent rate of whose tourism hotel reached 71.1% and maintained its position as one of the 21 key tourist cities.

Foreign Economy

Import and export of foreign trade retained substantial performance. The total quantity of imports and exports surmounted 18.81 billion USD, with a rise by 53.3%, of which the export being 12.07 billion USD and import 6.74 billion USD, up 47.9% and 63.9% respectively. The export proportion of foreign, joint venture, collective and private enterprises surpassed 63.1% of total export volume of the city, of which the export volume of private enterprises was 1.76 billion USD, with the growth rate of 119.5%.

The scale and quality of making use of foreign capital got breakthrough simultaneously. New ratified foreign invested projects and enterprises amounted to 1209, with the total foreign capital of 7.818 billion USD, among which the utilized foreign capital in contracts was 3.444 billion USD and the real utilization was 1.727 billion USD, with a rise of 18.9%, 59.3%, 58.6%, and 56.6% respectively. Large projects were in the dominant position with the remarkable effect of "attracting foreign capital with existing foreign capital". Of the new ratified foreign invested projects, large ones whose net investment increment surpassed 10 million UDS was 218, with the respective ratio of overall investment of 5.697 billion USD and investment in contracts of 2.289 billion USD being 18.0%, 72.9% and 66.5%, whose rate of increase was 38.6%, 41.3% and 7.0% compared with the last year. From Global 500, there were 27 foreign enterprises invested in Ningbo.

The cooperation of foreign economy goes on wheels, and service personnel sent abroad and investment abroad is making new progress. The turnover of constructed projects and service cooperation was 371 million USD, increased by 22.8%. The number of service personnel sent abroad was 1453, and those already abroad were 7025 at the end of quarter. With the increasing activity and passion of investing abroad, 74 new external enterprises were ratified, with total investment amount of 21.03 million USD and of which 18.58 million USD investment were from domestic enterprises.

Finance

Financial income increment remained high speed. The annual total financial income of the city in 2003 was 33.0 billion RMB, 25.9% more than the last year, and accomplished annual budget income 32.5 billion RMB, raised by 25.8% compared with the last year on the same calculation base. Regional financial income was 13.94 billion RMB up 32.4%, and central government financial income was accomplished 18.56 billion RMB, with a rise of 21.2%. The income of various items of taxation kept increasing fast. Value added tax was 13.6 billion RMB, up 21.2% (picking off the factor of exempt from offsetting adjusting increment value added tax, up 22% on the same calculation base). Sales tax, corporation income tax and individual income tax were 4.13, 5.97 and 2.44 billion RMB, raised by 29.4%, 28.7% and 34.4% respectively.

Financial expenditure fluxed into several key areas with the adjustment of the expenditure structure. The total financial expenditure was 18.709 billion RMB, 24.1% more than the last year. The expenditure on agriculture, forestry, water, gas, medical and health were 1.05 billion and 755milliom RMB, with the rise of 24% and 31.7% respectively. We insist the strategy and policy of "developing the city by relying on science and education" and "cultural city", ensure education expenditure, promote technology innovation, and push on the construction of social security system. The financial expenditure of social insurance and medical and health system were 43.9% and 31.7% higher than the last year respectively.

The support of finance to economy development was increased. By the end of the last year, RMB and other currency deposit balance of financial institution achieved 276.43 billion, 73.052 billion more than the year's commencement, 35.9% more than last year in amplitude. RMB deposit balance was 105.963 billion, 19.727 billion more than the year's commencement. Total amount of loan increased with preeminence. By the end of last year, loan balance of financial institution achieved 222.302 billion RMB, 66.863 billion more than the beginning of last year, 43.0% more in increment. The capital quality of financial institution was improving further. The bad debts of banking system achieved double reducing for the continuous three years. By the end of the year, the bad debts rate was 4.95%, 3.8 percentage points decreasing compared with the beginning of the year.

The credit and loan structure was optimized further. Medium term and long term credit loan on fixed assets investment mainly in national priority project item and technique reform reached 20.99 billion RMB, raised by 57.8%. Individual consumption credit kept developing. By the end of the year, loan balance was 23.192 billion RMB, 89.9 billion more than the beginning of the year, and 3.293 billion RMB more in increment compared with the last year.

Insurance went forward with a moderate development. The annual total coverage reached 992.747 billion RMB and total insurance premium achieved 3.836 billion RMB, raised by 80.2% and 23.1% respectively. Wealth insurance income was 1.335 billion RMB; age insurance income was 2.501 billion RMB. The payout compensation achieved 945 million RMB, up 25.8%.

City Planning

The process of city planning was mending, and the step of urban infrastructure establishment construction was fastened. New round modification of "overall project compendium of Ningbo City" was finished basically. Some key areas planning as the East New City Zone, Yuyao&Cixi Frame, Hangzhou Bay New District was deepening. Annual total investment on environment and public establishment reached 9.04 billion RMB, among which 5.43 billion RMB went to downtown. The city skeleton traffic and bridge projects, like Southern Exterior Circle Road,

North Exterior Circle Road, Ningjiang Road, Dazha Road, Yucai Road and Tongtu Road were constructed as key projects of city planning. Sun Lake Park, Fu Ming Park, South Station Square, Binjiang Avenue and landscape second stage project were being constructed. Newly constructed and extended roads in the city reached 120 km, among which 40 km was in the downtown. Newly increased public green areas were 266 hectare, among which 136 hectare were in the downtown.

Transportation and Post Telecommunication

The annual total investment on network – system construction of transportation, post telecommunication and warehousing was 4.987 billion RMB, with a rise of 15.9%. Ningbo Hangzhou Bay Sea Crossing Bridge, South Bank Connecting Line and Circuitous Highway West Sect began to construct subsequently. Hangyong Canal from Yulang Inlet to Yongjiang River Entrance with 94km in length and 300 – tonner channel were accomplished. The new constructed roads reached 134km and reconstructed roads 264km. The investment volume on country roads was 127 million RMB, among which subgrade 139km and road surface 186km. The overall volume of passenger transportation was 250 million, and freight service 146 million tons, augmented by 4.9% and 18% respectively. The transportation capacity of Ningbo was on the speedy rise, and of amendatory structure. The possession of automobiles was exceeding 210,000, 26% more than the last year, among which passenger service vehicles were 119,200 with 788,400 seats, and working passenger service vehicles were 9217 with 128,800 seats. The passenger traffic fast distribution net possessed primary scale. The highways and fast passenger traffic lines were opened 73.

The port transportation made its competitive breakthrough by exploring its advantage as a port-city. In 2003, two 50,000 – tonner docks and 4 container ports were newly completed. The cargo loading and unloading capacity reached 185 million tons and ranked the second position in all mainland coastal ports, up 20.9%. The container loading and unloading capacity was 2.7722 million standardizing cases, increased by 49.2%, and the amount of increase kept the first place for 5 continuous years. Shipping companies with containers which were the top 20 in the world have settled in Ningbo port. The container scheduled flight broke through 460 per month, even reached the consistency of one flight every day to the main trade areas like Europe, Mediterranean Sea and North America. The global container transportation net has been formed primarily.

Post and telecommunication business rose steadily with the yearly total being 472 million and 5.39 billion RMB respectively. The rate of telephone popularization was 68.76 per hundred people, of which 119.7 per hundred people and 49.99 per hundred people separately in urban and rural areas.

Environmental Protection

The environmental protection work was making further progress, and had distinct effects. Establishing and consummating the laws and regulations system, 《Charges for Disposing Pollutants Levy Management Implementation Measures of Ningbo City》, 《Straw Stalk Burning Prohibition Management Measures of Ningbo City》were established and enacted. According to national industrial policies strictly, the management of project address selection was strengthen. More than 600 various unqualified projects were voted down, so as to control the generation of new pollution sources efficiently. 35 enterprises and institutions were nominated environmental protection model. 19 smoke dust control areas with 295.9 km2, and 14 noise criterion areas with 135km2 were set up. Ninghai was listed as National Ecological Demonstration Area, and Simen town of Yuyao, Zhouxiang town of Cixi were listed as National Environmental and Ecological Villages and Towns in the province. 5 villages and towns and 12 executive villages were listed as Ecological Demonstration Area in the province (or the city). 49 districts and enterprises including Ningbo Tariff Protection Area and Development Area were granted ISO14000 certificate. Atmosphere quality remained upstanding level, and kept environmental quality I – II level for 336 days, which took up 92% in the whole year.

Technology, Education

In 2003, 1431 various technology plans of the city level were carried into execution, 115 national level projects were introduced to Ningbo and 3300 projects were granted patent. 43 city level high – tech companies were newly authenticated, 9 national key high – tech companies and 5 national high – tech industrialization bases were developed and carried out. The construction of technology innovation system was fastening. 4 province level key laboratories and 48 province level engineering and technology research centers had been established. The technology cooperation with CAS, Chinese Academy of Weapon Sciences, Zhejiang University and Haerbin Institute of Technology based on "Two Academies and Two Universities". We introduced 269 high – tech projects, 31 technology exploitation organization, 28500 various persons of talent, among which 72 doctors and post – doctorates, 762 post – graduates and more than 300 persons with senior professional title. By the end of 2003, the human resource reached 380 thousand persons, with 300 thousand professional technicians, 13 thousand persons with senior professional title and 87 thousand persons with semi – senior professional title.

The strategy of education priority was strengthened further. There were 2701 full time school in total in Ningbo (including technical secondary schools), with 1.11 million students in school. Fundamental education developed steadily, 9 – year compulsory education coverage reached 100%, the rate of enrollment and consolidation rate remained 100% and 99% respectively. High education speeded up. South Education District was completed basically, and north Education District began to construct. The number of students on campus of common colleges/universities achieved 79.9 thousand, and the rate of college/university enrollment achieved 32%. The passing rate of entrance examination to college/university achieved 85.9%, being in the lead position of the whole province. Vocational and adults education made new progress. Vocational technical secondary schools recruited 26700 students, and adult technical secondary school common classed recruited 1323 students. 350 thousand labour force took part in new knowledge and new technology training. The rate of training in companies reached 38%. The enthusiasm of the social strength to run a school was further stimulated. 1642 organizations of social strength were granted license to run a school. The capital of education institution run by the local people increased from 2.37 billion to 2.99 billion RMB. The enrollment rate of compulsory education for disabled children exceeded 96%.

Culture, Sports

We organized and established joint – stock "Mother Earth Art Group" controlled by Art Theater, Traditional Instruments Orchestra of Ningbo, and Ningbo Lianhe TV&Movie Co., Ltd cooperated with Shanghai Lianhe Theater Line which is the first trans – province cooperated Theater line. We held the opening pageant of the 7th Ningbo International Custom Festival and other relevant cultural activities successfully. 10 towns were titled as municipal and provincial following 8 towns titled in 2002. the coverage of towns titled as "Pearl of East Sea" reached 83%. The achievement of archaeological site of Yongfeng Storehouse was honoured "National Ten New Archaeological Discovery in 2002". The Concert Hall and the Books Information Center were completed and launched officially, and the main part projects of Great Theater and Gallery were finished. The customers of CATV reached 1.275 million, and the general coverage of radio and TV reached 99.98%.

Successfully we undertook more than ten significant international and national contests, such as Ningbo host competition of CBA, International City Go Competition, National eurythmics Championship Competition, National A class Bridge Club Championship Competition, and the Second Coastal City Long – distance Running Invitation Competition. Various people sports activities were developed vigorously, and the four levels people keeping – fit networks were consummated increasingly. There were 807 sports and keeping – fit sites, the "1154 Entire People Physical Training Network" of municipal government was carried into execution, the main body of Swimming & Keeping – fit Center with the investment of 100million RMB was completed, senior citizen sports activity center was almost finished, 180 Keeping – fit Route/Garden were completed in communities and rural areas, and the total amount of Keeping – fit Route reached 580. We achieved more and more in significant sports. In the 5th National City Game, we won 2 golden medals, 6 silver medals, 6 brass medals with total scores of 163, and won sports morality award.

Sanitation

The medical treatment and hygienic conditions for both urban and rural residents were further improved. By the end of last year, there were 14.7 thousand beds and 25 thousand professional hygienic service personnel in hospitals, public health clinics. The average expected length of life of all residents of Ningbo reached 75.8 ages old. The new - style rural cooperative medical service system giving priority to comprehensive arrangement for serious disease and supported by medical salvage was developed steadily in Zhenhai, Yuyao, Beilun and Yinzhou orderly. By the end of last year, number of people taking part in rural cooperative medical service reached 1.59 million.

Urban community hygienic service network was improved continuously. 13 demonstration community hygienic service centers of province and city level, 10 demonstration stations of city level, and 16 comprehensive medical community practice bases were set up. The work of disease precaution control and hygienic supervision and execution gained prominent effects. The occurrence and spreading SARS were efficiently controlled. The amount of gratis - donated blood occupied 108% of the total sum of clinical blood used. The total rate of infectious disease incidence was 210.31 per 100 thousand people, the percentage of pass of spot check of food hygiene was 87.6%, and the incidence rate of food intoxication was 3.74 per 100 thousand people, which were all evidently better than last year. In 2003, Ningbo was checked and accepted as national hygiene city of province level successfully.

Population, People's Life and Social Security

The birth level still remains low. By the end of the year, the total population was 5.4907 million, 28.8 thousand more than the last year, among which the urban population composed 2.0691 million, 35 thousand increasing. The family planning qualification rate came to 98.7%, the comprehensive contraception ratio of married women of child - bearing age achieved 91.29%, the birth control management ratio of transient population achieved 92.3%. The capita birth rate was 7.60‰, the death rate was 6.28‰.

The income of both urban and rural residents grew steadily and the living standard got improved. The annual urban per capita disposable personal income achieved 14277 RMB, raised by 10.1%. The annual urban per capita overall expenditure reached 14987 RMB, raised by 9.5%, among which residential consumption expenditure was 10463 RMB, up 11.3%. The expenditure of house purchasing and building achieved 1844 RMB, taking up 12.3% of the total. By the end of last year, every one hundred urban household occupied 167 color TV, 59 VCD, 50 personal computers, 117 air - conditioners, 132 mobile phones and 8 keep - fit equipments.

The annual rural per capita net income attained 6221 RMB, increased by 7.9%. Every one hundred rural household occupied 129 color TV, 50 washing machines, 73 refrigerators, 21 air - conditioners, 37 water heaters, increased by 10%, 3.3%, 4.8%, 74.3% and 8.3% respectively compared with the previous year.

By the end of last year, the amount of possession of private automobiles reached 76.4 thousand, with a rise of 76.9%.

Dwelling condition improved continuously. The resident area of urban per capita housing achieved 17.13m2, 98.25% formed a complete suite. While that of rural per capita housing achieved 46.9m2, 1.1m2 more than last year.

The work of employment and re - employment was pushed further. 130 thousand employment positions were increased newly. 29 thousand community employment positions, 3553 community welfare positions and 418 informal employment organizations were created and set up. 31 thousand unemployed men accepted the re - employment training, among which 27.6 thousand unemployed men gained qualifications and certifications for various occupations, and the employment rate after training reached 53%. By the end of last year, 61.5 thousand unemployed men were re - employed and found a job finally. The registered unemployment rate of urban residents was controlled under the prearranged index of 4.02%.

The coverage of social securities developed further. The number of endowment insurance enrollment of all employers reached 1.1879 million, among which the number of those who actually had paid fees achieved 820.3 thousand, 107.7 thousand more than last year. 180.6 thousand people who were dismissed or retired from the post were benefited from their pension of 816 RMB per capita monthly. The total number of medical insurance enrollment reached 842.5 thousand, 116.3 thousand more than last year. 707.3 thousand people enrolled in unemployment insurance, and the total number of people who were actually benefited from unemployment insurance was 623 thousand. The accumulative number of unemployment insurance and medical subsidies was 214 million RMB. By the end of last year, the number of the birth insurance for female employees enrollment reached 336.2 thousand, and the number enrolled in accident insurance in job reached 474 thousand, raised by 33% and 24% respectively. The number enrolled in endowment insurance of people from requisition areas reached 95.9 thousand, among which 38.1 thousand qualified people were benefited from the pension monthly. The total amount of the pension was 37.90 million RMB. The number of endowment insurance enrollment in rural areas reached 800 thousand, with total amount of pension of 26.50 million RMB. There were 181 social welfare enterprises, 11.4 thousand beds, 9200 people adopted. 77.6 thousand both urban and suburban residents were benefited from relief fund from the nation.

P.S: the above - mentioned figures were primary statistics.

1

综　合

CHAPTER 1 GENERAL SURVEY

综合
General Survey

宁波的经济发展
Economic Development of Ningbo

		2003	比上年增长(%) Increase Over Last Year
国内生产总值(亿元)	Gross Domestic Product(100 million yuan)	1786.85	15.6
第一产业	Primary Industry	112.23	3.6
第二产业	Secondary Industry	1001.21	16.9
第三产业	Tertiary Industry	673.41	14.9
规模以上工业总产值	Gross Output Value of Above Designated Sized Industry	2630.3	31.5
全社会固定资产投资	Investemnt in Total Fixed Assets	835.9	39.0
社会消费品零售总额	Total Retail Sales of Consumer Goods	521.5	12.6
财政总收入	Total Financial Revenue	330.0	25.9
港口货物吞吐量(万吨)	Ports Cargo Handling Capacity(10000 tons)	18543	20.4
#集装箱吞吐量(万标箱)	Container Handled at Ports(10000 TEU)	277.2	49.1
自营出口额(亿美元)	Directive Export(USD 100 million)	120.7	47.9
实际利用外资	Amount of Foreign Capital Actually Used	17.3	38.5

宁波的一天
One Day in Ningbo

国内生产总值	Gross Domestic Product	48955	万元	10000 yuan
工业增加值	Value - added of Industry	24457	万元	10000 yuan
农业增加值	Value - added of Agriculture	3075	万元	10000 yuan
全社会固定资产投资额	Total Investment of Fixed Assets	22901	万元	10000 yuan
社会消费品零售额	Retail Sales of Consumer Goods	14289	万元	10000 yuan
财政总收入	Total Financial Revenue	9042	万元	10000 yuan
地方财政收入	Local Financial Revenue	3957	万元	10000 yuan
港口货物吞吐量	Ports Cargo Handling Capacity	50.80	万吨	10000 tons
集装箱吞吐量	Container Handled at Ports	7595	标箱	TEU
自营出口额	Directive Export	3308	万美元	USD 10000
用电量	Electricity Consumption	5178	万千瓦时	10000 kwh

1－1　行政区划(2003 年末)
Administrative Division (End of 2003)

单位:个　　　　(unit)

地区	Region	镇 Town	乡 Township	街道办事处 Subdistrict Offices	居民委员会 Neighborhood Committee	村民委员会 Villages Committee
全市	**Whole Municipality**	**91**	**12**	**50**	**506**	**3823**
市区	**Urban Area**	**27**	**2**	**29**	**277**	**1129**
海曙区	Haishu District			8	63	16
江东区	Jiangdong District			7	68	6
江北区	Jiangbei District	4		4	48	110
北仑区	Beilun District	2	1	6	30	273
镇海区	Zhenhai District	2		4	22	65
鄞州区	Yinzhou District	19	1		46	659
县级市	**Cities at County Level**	**64**	**11**	**21**	**229**	**2684**
余姚市	Yuyao	14	2	6	52	259
慈溪市	Cixi	20		3	66	308
奉化市	Fenghua	6		5	30	580
象山县	Xiangshan	12	5	3	56	706
宁海县	Ninghai	12	4	4	25	831

1－2　部分年份国民经济主要指标

项目		Item	
人口		**Population**	
年末总人口	**（万人）**	**Year－end Population**	**（10000 persons）**
#非农业人口	（万人）	# Non－Agriculture Population	（10000 persons）
国内生产总值	**（亿元）**	**Gross Domestic Product**	**（100 million yuan）**
第一产业增加值	（亿元）	Added Value of Primary Industry	（100 million yuan）
第二产业增加值	（亿元）	Added Value of Secondary Industry	（100 million yuan）
第三产业增加值	（亿元）	Added Value of Tertiary Industry	（100 million yuan）
人均国内生产总值	**（元）**	**Per Capital GDP**	**（yuan）**
农业		**Agriculture**	
农村实有劳动力	（万人）	Rural Labor force	（10000 persons）
粮食产量	（万吨）	Yield of Grain Crops	（10000 tons）
工业		**Industry**	
全部工业增加值	（亿元）	Added Value of Industry	（100 million yuan）
运输、邮电和通信		**Transportation. Post and Telecommunications Services**	
港口货物吞吐量	（万吨）	Cargo Handled at Ports	（10000 tons）
集装箱吞吐量	（万标箱）	Container Handled at Ports	（10000 stand boxes）
旅客运输量	（万人）	Passenger Traffic	（10000 persons）
货物运输量	（万吨）	Freight Traffic	（10000 tons）
固定电话用户	（万户）	Number of Local Telephone Subscribers	（10000 subscribers）
电话普及率	（部/百人）	Number of Telephone Sets Owned per 100 persons	（set/100 persons）
全社会用电量	**（亿千瓦时）**	**Total Consumption of Electricity**	**（100 million kwh）**
#工业用电	（亿千瓦时）	Electricity Consumption for Industry Use	（100 million kwh）
生活用电	（亿千瓦时）	Electricity Consumption for Urban and Rural Residents	（100 million kwh）
全社会固定资产投资总额	**（亿元）**	**Total Investment in Fixed Assets**	**（100 million yuan）**
基本建设投资完成额	（亿元）	Capital Construction	（100 million yuan）
更新改造投资完成额	（亿元）	Technical Updates and Transformation	（100 million yuan）
房地产开发投资	（亿元）	Real Estate Development	（100 million yuan）

注：1.本表价值量指标按当年价格计算，发展速度按可比价格计算。2.城镇居民人均可支配收入、农村居民人均纯收入发展速度均已扣除价格变动因素。

Main Indicators of National Economy in Partial Year

1978	1990	1998	1999	2002	2003	指数(2002 为以下各年%) Index(2002 As Percentage of the Following Years)			平均年增长(%) Average Annual Growth Rate(%)	
						1978	1998	2002	1979 – 2003	1999 – 2003
457.70	**510.76**	**535.27**	**538.41**	**546.19**	**549.07**	**120.0**	**102.6**	**100.5**	**0.7**	**0.5**
63.42	102.98	130.48	137.12	162.43	168.81	266.2	129.4	103.9	4.0	5.3
20.17	**141.40**	**973.44**	**1041.74**	**1500.34**	**1786.85**	**3156.7**	**182.3**	**115.6**	**14.8**	**12.8**
6.52	29.35	88.84	93.16	107.15	112.23	334.2	126.1	103.6	4.9	4.7
9.69	80.31	542.98	581.88	828.88	1001.21	5659.4	189.4	116.9	17.5	13.6
3.96	31.74	341.62	366.70	564.31	673.41	3495.0	187.1	115.8	15.3	13.4
437	**2845**	**18219**	**19405**	**27541**	**32629**	**2485.7**	**178.2**	**115.0**	**13.7**	**12.3**
195.42	254.12	259.23	257.77	270.04	290.30	148.6	112.0	107.5	1.6	2.3
180.51	189.06	180.39	173.67	94.89	75.61	41.9	41.9	79.7	– 3.4	– 16.0
8.62	72.12	492.34	529.96	749.60	892.68	7069.8	188.2	115.7	18.6	13.5
214	2554	8707	9660	15398	18543	8665.0	213.0	120.9	19.5	16.3
	2.21	35.25	60.10	185.87	277.22		786.4	149.2		51.1
2966	7378	21736	22211	23752	24938	840.8	114.7	105.0	8.9	2.8
1385	4763	9952	10344	12429	13919	1005.0	139.9	112.0	9.7	6.9
1.07	6.19	83.74	104.13	203.58	242.00	22616.8	289.0	118.9	24.2	23.6
0.49	2.41	23.88	29.16	52.20	68.54	13987.8	287.0	131.3	21.9	23.5
7.09	**31.49**	**79.93**	**91.49**	**152.10**	**189.00**	**2665.7**	**236.5**	**124.3**	**14.0**	**18.8**
4.37	23.38	56.06	66.46	114.66	141.66	3241.6	252.7	123.6	14.9	20.4
0.43	4.30	13.15	13.68	18.72	23.86	5548.8	181.4	127.5	17.4	12.7
5.02	**39.28**	**309.81**	**318.93**	**601.27**	**835.90**	**16651.4**	**269.8**	**139.0**	**23.9**	**24.4**
2.91	14.29	130.12	109.53	212.03	310.94	10685.2	239.0	146.6	20.7	17.6
0.07	4.02	19.53	29.83	49.94	43.76	62514.3	224.1	87.6	34.6	34.4
	2.49	43.87	46.54	125.97	184.26		420.0	146.3		40.6

1. Figures in value terms are calculated at current prices, While the indices and growth rates are calculated at comparable prices. 2. The indices of Per capital Annual Disposable income of Urban households and Per-capital Annual net income of rural households are deducted the factor of changes in prices.

项目		Item	
财政金融		**Finance and Banking**	
财政总收入	(亿元)	Financial Revenue	(100 million yuan)
财政支出	(亿元)	Financial Expenditure	(100 million yuan)
年末金融机构存款余额	(亿元)	Balance of Deposits of Financial Institutions	(100 million yuan)
#城乡居民储蓄年末余额	(亿元)	Saving Deposits of Urban and Rural Residents	(100 million yuan)
年末金融机构贷款余额	(亿元)	Balance of Loans of Financial Institutions	(100 million yuan)
社会消费品零售总额	**(亿元)**	**Total Retail Sales of Consumer Goods**	**(100 million yuan)**
对外经济		**Foreign Trade**	
进出口总额	(亿美元)	Total Exports and Imports Value	(USD 100 million)
#出口总额	(亿美元)	Total Exports Value	(USD 100 million)
进口总额	(亿美元)	Total Imports Value	(USD 100 million)
合同利用外资	(亿美元)	Foreign Investment Contracted	(USD 100 million)
实际利用外资	(亿美元)	Foreign Investments Actually Use	(USD 100 million)
城乡居民收入		**Living Standard**	
市区城镇居民人均可支配收入	(元)	Per Capital Disposable Income of Urban Households	(yuan)
市区城镇居民人均消费性支出	(元)	Per Capital Annual Expenditure for Consumption of Urban Households	
农村居民人均纯收入	(元)	Per Capital Annual Net Incomeof	
教育		**Education**	
高等学校在校学生数	(万人)	Students Enrollment in Institutions of Higher Education	(10000 persons)
中等专业学校在校学生数	(万人)	Students Enrollment in Specializad Secondary Schools	(10000 persons)
中学在校学生数	(万人)	Students Enrollment in Secondary Schools	(10000 persons)
小学在小学生数	(万人)	Students Enrollment in Primary Schools	(10000 persons)
教师	(万人)	Teachers	(10000 persons)
卫生事业		**Health Care**	
卫生技术人员数	(万人)	Number of Medical Technical Personnel	(10000 persons)
#医生	(万人)	Doctor	(10000 persons)
卫生机构床位数	(张)	Number of Beds in Health Institutions	(bed)

continued

1978	1990	1998	1999	2002	2003	指数(2002为以下各年%) Index(2002 As Percentage of the Following Years)			平均年增长(%) Average Annual Growth Rate(%)	
						1978	1998	2002	1979 – 2003	1999 – 2003
4.97	15.89	92.36	108.58	262.18	330.03	6640.4	357.3	125.9	18.3	29.0
1.12	9.71	64.61	74.05	150.16	187.08	16703.6	289.6	124.6	22.7	23.7
4.84	63.80	855.28	1008.02	1906.24	2629.03	54318.8	307.4	137.9	28.6	25.2
1.52	46.12	459.63	529.64	862.39	1059.63	69712.5	230.5	122.9	29.9	18.2
6.50	80.41	670.08	773.48	1479.47	2102.78	32350.5	313.8	142.1	26.0	25.7
7.07	**54.98**	**313.36**	**345.76**	**462.86**	**521.53**	**7376.7**	**166.4**	**112.7**	**18.8**	**10.7**
	2.98	42.12	50.09	122.73	188.10		446.6	153.3		34.9
	2.80	29.64	34.77	81.63	120.74		407.4	147.9		32.4
	0.18	12.48	15.32	41.10	67.36		539.7	163.9		40.1
	0.56	5.12	6.57	32.00	34.44		672.7	159.0		46.4
	0.22	5.03	5.20	12.47	17.27		343.3	157.0		28.0
306	1963	9193	9492	12970	14277	4665.7	155.3	110.1	16.6	9.2
299	1628	7912	7493	9396	10463	3499.3	132.2	111.3	15.3	5.7
	1254	4697	4798	5764	6221		132.4	107.9		5.8
0.10	0.49	1.25	1.68	6.20	7.99	7990.0	639.2	128.9	19.2	44.9
0.29	0.90	2.55	2.73	1.92	1.87	644.8	73.3	97.4	7.7	-6.0
27.16	19.65	29.00	25.12	30.86	30.99	114.1	106.9	100.4	0.5	1.3
59.11	42.70	43.91	43.36	44.55	45.26	76.6	103.1	101.6	-1.1	0.6
3.55	3.34	4.40	4.81	5.27	5.61	158.0	127.5	106.5	1.8	5.0
0.93	1.58	1.86	1.89	2.01	2.15	231.2	115.6	107.0	3.4	2.9
0.36	0.75	0.91	0.93	0.99	1.06	294.4	116.5	107.1	4.4	3.1
5989	11449	13689	13795	14653	15279	255.1	111.6	104.3	3.8	2.2

1－3　各县(市)社会经济基本情况

(2003)

项目		Item	
人口、劳动力及土地面积		**Population, Employment and Land Areas**	
年末总人口	(万人)	Year－end Population	(10000 persons)
#非农业人口	(万人)	Non－Agriculture Population	(10000 persons)
年平均人口	(万人)	Annual Average Populations	(10000 persons)
暂住人口(一个月以上)	(万人)	Stay Populations(One month and Above)	(10000 persons)
年出生人口	(人)	Birth Population	(10000 persons)
年死亡人口	(人)	Death Population	(10000 persons)
年末总户数	(万户)	Total Households of Year－end	(10000 households)
年末国有等单位从业人员数	(万人)	Total Number of Employed Persons in State and Collective Units	(10000 persons)
第一产业	(万人)	Primary Industry	(10000 persons)
第二产业	(万人)	Secondary Industry	(10000 pers)ons
第三产业	(万人)	Tertiary Industry	(10000 person)s
私营和个体从业人员	(人)	Employed Persons Individuals and Private Enterprises	(person)
年末城镇登记失业人员数	(人)	Unemployed Persons in Urban Areas at Year－end	(person)
行政区域土地面积	(平方公里)	Land Area	(sq.km)
#建成区面积	(平方公里)	Land Area of Builds Up	(sq.km)
综合经济		**General Economy**	
国内生产总值(当年价格)	(亿元)	Gross Domestic Product(at Current Price)	(100 million yuan)
第一产业增加值	(亿元)	Value－added of Primary Industry	(100 million yuan)
第二产业增加值	(亿元)	Value－added of Secondary Industry	(100 million yuan)
#工业增加值	(亿元)	Value－added of Industry	(100 million yuan)
第三产业增加值	(亿元)	Value－added of Tertiary Industry	(100 million yuan)
人均国内生产总值	(元)	Per Capital GDP	(yuan)
国内生产总值增长率	(%)	Increase Rate Over 2001	(%)
财政、金融、保险		Finance, Banking and Insurance	
财政一般预算收入	(万元)	Total Financial Bdugetary Revenue	(10000 yuan)
#中央财政预算内收入	(万元)	Revenue of Central Government	(10000 yuan)
地方财政一般预算内收入	(万元)	Local Financial Revenue	(10000 yuan)

Major Indicators of National Economy by County

全市 Total	市区 Urban District	# 鄞州 Yinzhou	余姚 Yuyao	慈溪 Cixi	奉化 Fenghua	象山 Xiangshan	宁海 Ninghai
549.07	206.91	75.58	82.43	100.71	48.15	52.63	58.24
168.81	109.95	19.90	16.44	15.13	9.94	10.10	7.25
547.63	205.15	74.92	82.52	100.64	48.30	52.75	58.27
171.56	93.27	36.85	23.05	39.71	4.93	5.67	4.93
42445	14069	5478	5945	8497	3597	5060	5277
35173	11524	4970	6222	7079	3303	3853	3192
203.47	80.29	29.13	28.56	38.70	17.46	17.83	20.63
65.34	40.04	5.00	4.66	4.59	2.63	11.19	2.24
0.22	0.06	0.02	0.04	0.08	0.01	0.01	0.03
34.18	20.22	1.77	1.82	1.35	0.89	9.51	0.40
30.94	19.75	3.21	2.80	3.16	1.73	1.68	1.81
519353	270119	405223	71575	25154	37298	71084	44123
41029	30097	2200	1502	2645	2280	2874	1631
9365	2560	1527	1316	1154	1253	1172	1880
	109.51		35.12	30.00	11.64	13.51	21.56
1786.85	1025.03	232.31	213.36	245.57	95.15	107.54	100.20
112.23	27.88	14.24	19.67	18.19	10.57	21.73	14.18
1001.21	561.24	160.02	126.24	144.49	54.80	56.03	58.42
892.68	492.33	148.23	117.23	131.53	51.46	49.04	51.09
673.41	435.92	58.05	67.45	82.89	29.78	29.78	27.60
32629	49963	31006	25884	24400	19701	20389	17195
15.6	17.7	15.7	14.8	15.6	18.0	15.6	17.6
3250008	2287571	371960	262283	350058	112888	107128	130080
1855916	1327932	200587	142407	181863	68833	60450	74431
1394162	959709	154731	119876	168195	44055	46678	55649

1－3 续表 1

项目		Item	
各项税收	（万元）	Every Tax Revenue	(10000 yuan)
地方财政一般预算内支出	（万元）	Local Ordinary Budgetary Expenditure	(10000 yuan)
年末金融机构存款余额	（万元）	Balance of Deposits of Financial Institutions	(10000 yuan)
#城乡居民储蓄年末余额	（万元）	Saving Deposits of Urban and Rural Residents	(10000 yuan)
年末金融机构各项贷款余额	（万元）	Balance of Loans of Financial Institutions	(10000 yuan)
承保额	（万元）	Total Insurance	(10000 yuan)
保费收入	（万元）	Premium Income	(10000 yuan)
已决赔款	（万元）	Indemnity Expenditure	(10000 yuan)
农业		**Agriculture**	
农林牧渔业总产值		Gross Output Value of arming, Forestry, Animal Husbandry and Fishery	10000 yuan
年末实有耕地面积	（公顷）	Cultivated Area at Year－end	(ha)
蔬菜产量	（吨）	Output of Vegetable	(ton)
水果产量	（吨）	Output of Fruits	(ton)
肉类总产量	（吨）	Output of Meat	(ton)
奶类产量	（吨）	Output of Milk	(ton)
水产品产量	（吨）	Output of Aquatic Products	(ton)
工业		**Industry**	
国有及年销售收入500万元以上非国有工业企业主要经济指标		All State－owned and non－state－owned industrial enterprises with annual sales income of over 5 million yuan	
工业企业数	（个）	Number of Industrial Enterprises	(unit)
工业总产值（当年价）	（万元）	Gross Output Value of Indutry (at current price)	(10000 yuan)
从业人员年平均人数	（万人）	Annual Average Employees	(10000 persons)
产品销售收入	（万元）	Sales Revenue of Products	(10000 yuan)
本年应交增值税	（万元）	Value－added Taxes Payable in This Year	(10000 yuan)
利润总额	（万元）	Total Profits	(10000 yuan)
交通运输、邮电通信、能源电力		**Transport, Post & Telecommunications, Energy and Electricity**	
铁路客运量	（万人）	Railway Passenger Traffic	(10000 persons)
铁路货运量	（万吨）	Railway Freight Traffic	(10000 tons)
民用汽车拥有量	（辆）	Number of Civil Motor Vehicles	(unit)

continued 1

全市 Total	市区 Urban District	# 鄞州 Yinzhou	余姚 Yuyao	慈溪 Cixi	奉化 Fenghua	象山 Xiangshan	宁海 Ninghai
3230843	2267826	352872	257334	346006	117897	110912	130868
1802545	1220526	193859	157319	196946	68004	76440	83310
26290346	18459097	3787098	2338793	3220476	938461	665833	667686
10596339	6393243	1758782	1220682	1743076	531780	366996	340562
21027772	14767050	2582251	1705415	2501054	724468	605727	724058
99274700	73969600	10533000	6184800	9331800	4119900	2968300	2700300
383646	243628	34240	33736	51616	19846	17738	17082
94512	55265	11380	10156	14011	5471	4570	5040
1737503	417487	208970	277571	265719	166106	405938	204682
211054	64416	33610	38999	43477	21425	19996	22742
2750438	795694	514204	830568	637484	80897	212506	193289
1140565	320436	206371	149442	271460	82148	136841	180238
155431	65823	31407	30207	15107	9415	20676	14203
22125	20981	12112	100	338	605	15	86
903301	63798	21802	21951	53622	79259	564199	115860
4672	2119	989	715	838	249	358	393
26302862	15944163	4605100	2672195	3348667	1786863	1293618	1257356
91.96	45.99	20.52	10.49	17.48	4.96	5.23	7.81
26048962	15867906	4580963	2646140	3367129	1745592	1275751	1146444
854470	586390	145681	70781	83279	33067	41152	39801
1892997	1286454	427253	186077	174593	73179	93688	79006
438.30	336.20		102.10				
1157.72	1133.02		16.50	8.20			
210852	121116	29840	29397	31429	10204	9971	8735

项目		Item	
#私人汽车拥有量	（辆）	Number of Private Car	(unit)
公路客运量	（万人）	Highways Passenger Traffic	(10000 persons)
公路货运量	（万吨）	Highways Freight Traffic	(10000 tons)
境内公路里程	（公里）	Length of Highways	(km)
水运客运量	（万人）	Waterways Passenger Traffic	(10000 persons)
水运货运量	（万吨）	Waterways Freight Traffic	(10000 tons)
年末邮电局(所)数	（处）	Number of Post Offices at Year－end	(unit)
邮政业务总量	（万元）	Business Value of Post	(10000 yuan)
电信业务总量	（万元）	Business Value of Telecommunications	(10000 yuan)
本地电话用户数	（万户）	Number of Subscribers of Local Telephone	(10000 subscribers)
#农村电话用户	（万户）	Rural Telephone Subscribers	(10000 subscribers)
年末移动电话用户数	（户）	Number of Mobile Telephone Subscribers at Year－end	(subscriber)
国际互联网用户数	（户）	User of International Computer Network	(user)
全年用电量	（万千瓦时）	Electricity Consumption	(10000 kwh)
贸易、外经		**Domestic Trade, Foreign Trade and Tourism**	
社会消费品零售额	（万元）	Total Retail Sales of Consumer Goods	(10000 yuan)
当年合同外资金额	（万美元）	Foreign Investment Contracted in This Year	(USD 10000)
当年实际使用外资金额	（万美元）	Amount of Foreign Capital Actually Used	(USD 10000)
进口额	（万美元）	Total Import	(USD 10000)
出口额	（万美元）	Total Export	(USD 10000)
固定资产投资		Investemnt in Fixed Assets	
全社会固定资产投资	**（万元）**	**Total Investment in Fixed Assets**	**(10000 yuan)**
基本建设投资完成额	（万元）	Capital Construction	(10000 yuan)
更新改造投资完成额	（万元）	Innovation	(10000 yuan)
其他投资完成额	（万元）	Others	(10000 yuan)
房地产开发投资完成额	（万元）	Real Estate Development	(10000 yuan)
全年新增固定资产	（万元）	Newly Increase Fixed Assets in This Year	(10000 yuan)
文教、卫生、科技		**Culture, Education, Public Health, Science**	

continued 2

全市 Total	市区 Urban District	# 鄞州 Yinzhou	余姚 Yuyao	慈溪 Cixi	奉化 Fenghua	象山 Xiangshan	宁海 Ninghai
76377	40880	10187	12873	14005	2955	2903	2761
24320	13860	2785	2410	2740	2020	1600	1690
9070	5197	1205	1015	1230	580	470	578
5520.0	1573.8	963.5	895.7	571.7	728.1	586.1	1164.6
114.9	28.2	4.9				69.5	17.2
3568.3	2728.9	187.9	3.0	9.9	54.8	642.8	128.9
379	144		44	63	44	43	41
39508	21132		4606	8028	1896	1901	1945
539000	326286.0		60335	67677	26175	28590	29937
242.0	107.1	31.2	34.7	41.5	18.4	16.6	23.7
107.2	39.6	26.5	16.1	24.0	8.8	8.9	9.8
3793124	2253495		408955	429877	188442	266500	245855
835674	444334		181939	91830	36900	34370	46301
1890027	1048965	268934	247985	370373	83538	53774	85391
5215347	2087957	556194	812864	1069647	337377	506590	400912
344382	227643	57280	55048	37069	5078	8572	10972
172727	116787	28060	25081	21159	3805	2217	3678
673564	514898	63312	28256	31988	89531	4610	4281
1207370	816968	184818	114938	160912	33011	48045	33496
8358947	**5212113**	**1312031**	**875076**	**1230993**	**264633**	**370602**	**405530**
3109421	2362311	285450	148886	305952	41094	107057	144121
437638	402127	20751	17282	15976		2253	
147186	75905	17247	9960	31903	9357	9942	10119
1842589	1187784	325375	136843	318732	59368	68504	71358
3292041	2493220	271334	210192	309459	63562	87396	128212

1－3 续表 3

项目		Item	
学校数(含高校、中专、中学、小学)	(所)	Number of Schools(Higher Education,Specialized Secondary Schools,Regular Secondary Schools,Primary Schools)	(unit)
专任教师数	(人	Full－time Teachers	(person)
在校学生数	(人)	Students Enrollments	(persons)
各类专业技术人员数	(万人)	Number of Specialized Technical Personnel	(10000 person)
公共图书馆图书藏量	(千册、件)	Collection of Public Libraries	(1000 copies)
医院、卫生院数	(个)	Number of Health Institutions	(unit)
卫生机构床位数	(张)	Number of Beds in Health Institutions	(bed)
卫生技术人员数	(人)	Number of Medical Technical Personnel	(person)
#医生数	(人)	Doctors	(person)
人民生活		**People's Livelihood**	
农村居民人均纯收入	(元)	Per Capital Annual Net Income of Rural Residents	(yuan)
城镇居民人均可支配收入	(元)	Per Capital Annual Disposable Income of Urban Residents	(yuan)
城镇居民人均消费支出	(元)	Per Capital Annual Expenditure for Consumption of Urban Residents	(yuan)
年末离休、退休、退职人员数	(万人)	Number of Retire Veterans,Retire and Resigned Persons in This Year	(10000 persons)
基本养老保险参保职工	(人)	Number of Staff and Workers Engaged Basic Endowment Insurance	(person)
基本医疗保险参保人数	(人)	Number of Personnel Engaged Basic Medical Insurance	(person)
失业保险参保人数	(人)	Number of Personnel Engaged Unemployment Insurance	(person)
居民最低生活保障线以下人数	(人)	Number Personnel Below Minimum Standard of Living	(person)
社会治安		**Social Security**	
交通事故件数	(件)	Number of Traffic Accidents	(case)
交通事故死亡人数	(人)	Death of Traffic Accidents	(person)
刑事案件立案数	(件)	Number of Criminal Cases Registered	(case)
犯罪人数	(人)	Number of People of the Crime	(person)
市政公用事业		**Civil Facilities,Environment Protection**	
年末实有铺装道路面积	(万平方米)	Area of Paved Roads(Year－end)	(10000 sq.m)
排水管道总长度	(公里)	Length of Drainage Pipelines	(km)
供水综合生产能力(包括自备水源)	(万吨/日)	General Productive Capacity of Tap Water Supply	(10000 tons/day)
全年供水总量	(万吨)	Total Volume of Tap Water Supply in This Year	(10000 tons)

continued 3

全市 Total	市区 Urban District	# 鄞州 Yinzhou	余姚 Yuyao	慈溪 Cixi	奉化 Fenghua	象山 Xiangshan	宁海 Ninghai
1166	419	162	214	204	105	100	124
44091	20957	5223	5439	7149	3145	3548	3853
926556	432535	123532	127956	157686	66688	63524	78167
39.68	28.3	3.67	3.38	2.12	1.71	1.83	2.34
1549.74	846.81	130.53	181.72	174.22	110.81	144.44	91.74
290	125	50	26	27	33	32	47
14871	8062	1254	1544	1637	1723	980	925
21473	11712	2434	2251	2599	1639	1441	1831
10630	6114	1126	1077	1260	784	635	760
6221	6665	6291	6777	5592	5382	5446	
13852	14277	12018	15096	12642	13294	12561	
9984	10463	8844	10007	10232	8543	8242	
18.06	12.21	1.77	2.00	1.44	0.82	0.76	0.83
1007332	623309	135491	120626	121590	52023	40504	49280
842524	591717	73216	77646	68825	36603	31034	36699
707303	441790	60772	70288	72534	40175	48616	33900
18563	14860	990	1361	738	556	550	498
4046	1966	482	418	498	432	261	471
947	376	141	194	186	66	45	80
66016	30740	8821	7192	13801	4400	5216	4667
8063	3513	1149	964	1721	516	753	596
	1409.2		471.7	395.1	103.2	222.5	237.5
	2141		221	299	102.5	184	287
	140.1		28.0	16.5	8.0	9.0	7.4
	34288		5671	4259	1925	2430	1766

1－3 续表 4

项目		Item	
#居民家庭用水量	(万吨)	for Residents	(10000 tons)
用水人口	(万人)	Population with Access Tap Water	(10000 persons)
液化石油气供气总量	(吨)	Total Volume of Liquefied Petroleum Gas	(ton)
#家庭用量	(吨)	for Residents	(ton)
用液化气人口	(人)	Population with Access Liquefied Petroleum Gas	(person)
年末实有公共汽(电)车营运车辆数	(辆)	Number of Public Transportations Vehicles Per 10000 Persons	(unit)
全年公共汽(电)车客运总量	(万人次)	Number of Passengers Carried with Public Transportations Vehicles	(10000 person－times)
年末实有出租汽车数	(辆)	Operating Taxes at Year－end	(unit)
园林绿地面积	(公顷)	Total Area of Parks, Gardens and Green Areas	(hectare)
#公共绿地面积	(公顷)	Public Green Areas	(hectare)
建成区绿化覆盖面积	(公顷)	Coverage Area of Afforestation in Developed Area	(hectare)
环境保护		**Environment Protect**	
环境污染治理投资额	(万元)	Investment in Environmental Protection	(10000 yuan)
三废综合利用产品产值	(万元)	Gross Output Value of Utilized Waste Water, Waste Gas and Waste Solid	(10000 yuan)
工业废水排放量	(万吨)	Valume of Industrial Waste Water Discharged	(10000 tons)
工业废水排放达标量	(万吨)	Volume of Industrial Waste Water Up to the Discharged Standard	(10000 tons)
工业二氧化硫去除量	(吨)	Valume of Sulphur Dioxide Removed from Industrial Waste Gas	(ton)
工业二氧化硫排放量	(吨)	Volume of Industrial Sulphur Dioxide Emission	(ton)
工业烟尘去除量	(吨)	Volume of Wipe off Industrial Soot	(ton)
工业烟尘排放量	(吨)	Volume of Industrial Soot Emission	(ton)
工业固体废物综合利用率	(%)	Rate of Industrial Solid Waste Treated and Utilized	(%)
生活污水处理率	(%)	Rate of Disposal Living Waste Water	(%)
生活垃圾无害化处理率	(%)	Innocuous Disposal Rate of Living Garbage	(%)
补充指标		**Append Indicator**	
全社会从业人员	(万人)	Total Employment Personnel	(10000 persons)
第一产业	(万人)	Primary Industry	(10000 persons)
第二产业	(万人)	Secondary Industry	(10000 pers)ons
第三产业	(万人)	Tertiary Industry	(10000 person)s

continued 4

全市 Total	市区 Urban District	#鄞州 Yinzhou	余姚 Yuyao	慈溪 Cixi	奉化 Fenghua	象山 Xiangshan	宁海 Ninghai
	10929		2024	2162	735	781	723
	108.84		30.52	24.93	10.79	9.80	8.67
	480106		17856	17325	4500	4600	5000
	99032		15980	16645	4000	4300	3700
	1088400		295200	245800	107900	96000	86700
	2044		277	136	444	166	162
	26922		2645	1920	1869	1265	2207
	2900		270	355	112	75	278
	3651.7		895.0	610.9	319.0	228.0	585.0
	1149.2		197.7	201.7	51.2	95.9	107.0
	4000.1		1134.0	801.0	409.0	255.0	733.0
28426	15870	850	6375	3618	1167	905	492
113394	76056	27915	6935	29232	817	354	
11751	7917	2026	1499	829	310	666	500
11345	7687	1975	1428	823	304	607	497
192235	182305		1712	5955	1087	941	233
190071	177881	2561	3670	4613	1116	1773	1017
2074969	2033477	5017	6721	15524	9787	4881	4578
22607	18812	726	1579	1128	205	588	296
77.47	74.50	94.08	100.00	81.28	99.39	96.52	96.49
39.45	42.05		36.82	26.43	25.97	35.71	
90.52	83.46	100.00	93.00	93.64	91.11	95.45	100.00
386.20	147.10	56.53	55.66	80.00	33.40	36.94	33.10
88.10	16.07	12.61	11.97	16.40	12.00	19.46	12.20
198.40	92.82	34.66	23.25	44.70	12.80	10.73	14.10
99.70	38.21	9.26	20.44	18.90	8.60	6.75	6.80

1－4 总产出、国内生产总值及增加值率

Total Output Gross Domestic Product and Rate of Value－Added

单位:亿元 (2003) (100 million Yuan)

项目	Item	2003	2002	发展速度(%) Increase Rate Over 2002(%)
总产出	**Total Output**	**6289.17**	**5039.11**	**119.0**
第一产业	Primary Industry	173.75	165.98	103.5
第二产业	Secondary Industry	4923.95	3882.22	119.9
工业	Industry	4449.01	3546.83	118.9
建筑业	Construction	474.95	335.39	131.5
第三产业	Tertiary Industry	1191.46	990.91	118.2
交通运输仓储邮政业	Transportation, Storage, Postal and Telecommunication	254.43	203.93	125.5
批发零售、餐饮业	Wholesale and Retail Trade and Catering Services	347.00	309.36	122.5
国内生产总值	Gross Domestic Product	1786.85	1500.34	115.6
第一产业	Primary Industry	112.23	107.15	103.6
第二产业	Secondary Industry	1001.21	828.88	116.9
工业	Industry	892.68	749.60	115.7
建筑业	Construction	108.53	79.28	129.0
第三产业	Tertiary Industry	673.41	564.31	115.8
交通运输仓储邮电业	Transportation, Storage, Postal and Telecommunication	114.43	100.23	114.9
批发零售、餐饮业	Wholesale and Retail Trade and Catering Services	192.95	170.54	115.6
增加值率(%)	**Rate of Value－Added(%)**			
第一产业	Primary Industry	64.6	64.6	
第二产业	Secondary Industry	20.3	21.4	
工业	Industry	20.1	21.1	
建筑业	Construction	22.9	23.6	
第三产业	Tertiary Industry	56.5	56.9	
交通运输仓储邮电业	Transportation, Storage, Postal and Telecommunication	45.0	65.0	
批发零售贸易餐饮业	Wholesale and Retail Trade and Catering Services	55.6	55.1	
人均国内生产总值(元)	**Per Capital GDP(yuan)**	**32629**	**27541**	**115.0**

1－5　按支出法计算的国内生产总值

Gross Domestic Product Calculated with Expenditure Approach

单位:万元　　　　(2003)　　　　(10000 yuan)

项目	Item	按当年价计算 at Current Price 2003	按当年价计算 at Current Price 2002	发展速度(%) Increase Rate Over 2002(%)
支出法国内生产总值	**Gross Domestic Product Calculated with Expenditure Approach**	**18197003**	**15016250**	**118.4**
最终消费	Final Consumption	6620983	5778974	113.1
居民消费	Resident Consumption	4551993	4149848	108.8
农村居民	Rural Resident	2299669	2168814	104.7
城镇居民	Urban Resident	2252324	1981034	113.5
政府消费	Government Consumption	2068990	1629126	123.6
资本形成总额	Total Capital Formation	9710202	7550746	125.2
固定资本形成总额	Fixed Capital Formation	8181900	6279279	126.9
库存增加	Stock Increased	1528303	1271467	116.7
货物和服务净流出	Net Export	1865817	1686530	106.6
流出	Export	16553321	7833180	205.8
流入	Import	14687504	6146650	233.4
统计误差	Statistical Error	－328462	－12815	

1—6 按行业划分的资本形成总额

Gross Capital Formation by Sector

单位:万元 (2003) (10000 yuan)

项目	Item	2003	2002
资本形成总额	**Gross Capital Formation by Sector**	**9710203**	**7550746**
固定资本形成总额	The Fixed Capital Forms Total Value	8181900	6279279
第一产业	Primary Industry	111789	129290
农林牧鱼业	Farming, Forestry, Animal Husbandry and Fishery	111789	129290
第二产业	Secondary Industry	3800287	2550142
采掘业	Mining and Quarrying	4177	9835
制造业	Manufacturing Industry	3426433	2391939
电力、煤气及水生产供应业	Electric Power, Gas and Water Production and Supply	359143	136339
建筑业	Construction	10534	12029
第三产业	Tertiary Industry	4269824	3599847
交通运输邮电通讯业	Transportation , Storage, Post and Telecommunications	498726	495010
批发和零售贸易、餐饮业	Wholesale, Retail Trade and Catering Services	77078	208126
金融保险业	Banking and Insurance	12407	16048
房地产业	Real Estate	2190028	1167774
其他行业	Others	1491585	1712889
库存增加	The Stock Increasing	1528303	1271467
第一产业	Primary Industry	5112	13042
农林牧鱼业	Farming, Forestry, Animal Husbandry and Fishery	5112	13042
第二产业	Secondary Industry	1080559	724758
工业	Industry	877664	666658
建筑业	Construction	202895	58100
第三产业	Tertiary Industry	442632	533667
交通运输邮电通讯业	Transportation, Storage, Post and Telecommunications	3762	10904
批发和零售贸易、餐饮业	Wholesale, Retail Trade and Catering Services	218415	352958
其他行业	Others	220455	169805

1－7 最终消费

Final Consumption

单位：万元 (2003) (10000 yuan)

项目	Item	2003	2002
最终消费	**Final Consumption**	**6620983**	**5778974**
居民消费	Resident Consumption	4551993	4149848
农村居民	Rural Resident	2299669	2168814
自给性消费	Self－sufficiency Consumption	135610	124198
商品性消费	Goods Consumption	1405378	1127877
文化生活服务消费	Culture and Live Service	578348	718030
住房及水电消费	Residence	180333	198709
#住房消费	House	138695	158732
城镇居民	Urban Resident	2252324	1981034
商品性消费	Goods Consumption	1185431	1124433
文化生活服务消费	Culture and Live Service	922747	756102
住房及水电消费	Residence	144146	100499
#住房消费	House	85938	57107
政府消费	Government Consumption	2068990	1629126

1－8 居民总消费水平

Resident Consumption Level

(2003)

项目		Item		2003	2002	2002年为2001年(%) Increase Rate Over 2002(%)
当年价居民消费水平	**(元/人)**	**Resident Consumption Level at Current Price**	**(yuan/person)**	**8312**	**7618**	**109.1**
农村居民	(元/人)	Rural Resident	(yuan/person)	6020	5588	107.7
城镇居民	(元/人)	Urban Resident	(yuan/person)	13599	12646	107.5
可比价居民消费水平	**(元/人)**	**Resident Consumption Level at Comparable Price**	**(yuan/person)**	**8222**	**7594**	**108.3**
农村居民	(元/人)	Rural Resident	(yuan/person)	5960	5605	106.3
城镇居民	(元/人)	Urban Resident	(yuan/person)	13438	12521	107.3
居民年平均人口	**(人)**	**Annual Population**	**(person)**	**5476317**	**5447687**	**100.5**
农村居民	(人)	Rural Resident	(person)	3820108	3881210	98.4
城镇居民	(人)	Urban Resident	(person)	1656209	1566477	105.7

1—9 主要年份国内生产总值

Gross Domestic Product in Main Years

单位:亿元 (100 million yuan)

年份 Year	国内生产总值 Gross Domestic Product	第一产业 Primary Industry	第二产业 Secondary Industry	#工业 Industry	第三产业 Tertiary Industry	人均国内生产总值(元) Per Capita GDP (yuan)
1978	20.17	6.52	9.69	8.62	3.96	437
1979	24.15	7.99	11.43	10.11	4.73	522
1980	29.53	8.69	15.54	14.21	5.30	634
1981	31.99	7.85	18.11	16.82	6.03	680
1982	36.88	11.20	18.79	17.26	6.89	776
1983	41.68	10.91	22.63	21.22	8.14	864
1984	53.17	14.93	28.23	26.02	10.01	1096
1985	71.05	16.85	40.40	36.96	13.80	1455
1986	80.22	18.61	44.47	40.59	17.14	1626
1987	95.99	22.11	53.99	48.76	19.89	1928
1988	118.62	27.11	66.43	60.28	25.08	2356
1989	137.25	31.13	77.69	71.02	28.43	2702
1990	141.40	29.35	80.31	72.12	31.74	2845
1991	186.93	32.70	97.93	88.22	56.30	3648
1992	232.94	34.08	128.20	115.70	70.66	4516
1993	328.05	44.25	186.18	163.78	97.62	6104
1994	463.51	63.73	263.25	229.74	136.53	8889
1995	637.63	81.60	371.81	328.46	184.22	12156
1996	795.86	92.96	450.44	398.14	252.46	15069
1997	897.43	85.39	511.25	462.98	300.79	16879
1998	973.44	88.84	542.98	492.34	341.62	18219
1999	1041.74	93.16	581.88	529.96	366.70	19405
2000	1175.75	95.77	658.84	600.41	421.14	21786
2001	1312.68	100.34	718.91	651.87	493.43	24213
2002	1500.34	107.15	828.88	749.60	564.31	27541
2003	1786.85	112.23	1001.21	892.68	673.41	32629

1－10　主要年份国内生产总值指数

Indices of Gross Domestic Product in Main Years

单位：%　　　　(1978＝100)　　　　(%)

年份 Year	国内生产总值 Gross Domestic Product	第一产业 Primary Industry	第二产业 Secondary Industry	#工业 Industry	第三产业 Tertiary Industry	人均国内生产总值 Per Capita GDP
1978	100.0	100.0	100.0	100.0	100.0	100.0
1979	113.4	106.4	116.4	114.1	119.2	113.6
1980	133.5	108.8	156.0	158.3	125.0	132.7
1981	145.9	103.1	181.6	190.5	139.2	143.6
1982	165.9	134.7	191.5	198.2	161.6	161.1
1983	195.2	143.1	239.0	240.4	185.8	187.5
1984	230.4	162.8	285.7	300.5	221.3	219.9
1985	295.1	163.6	403.9	422.8	278.2	279.8
1986	321.7	171.5	436.2	454.0	325.2	302.4
1987	367.0	177.3	515.6	538.5	361.3	341.4
1988	407.8	170.2	599.2	641.9	385.9	374.9
1989	426.1	163.6	651.9	688.1	368.1	388.0
1990	450.4	171.1	678.0	713.5	418.2	407.0
1991	562.5	188.7	801.3	884.8	635.6	479.9
1992	663.2	184.0	1011.3	1144.9	734.8	566.8
1993	801.2	203.0	1278.3	1573.1	847.9	664.9
1994	970.2	217.2	1567.2	1909.8	1056.5	803.1
1995	1169.1	247.6	1943.3	2373.8	1226.6	960.5
1996	1370.2	269.1	2302.8	2808.3	1446.2	1118.0
1997	1558.0	252.2	2680.5	3353.1	1666.0	1261.1
1998	1730.9	265.0	2988.7	3755.4	1867.6	1394.8
1999	1921.3	286.5	3308.5	4176.0	2104.8	1541.3
2000	2151.9	296.0	3725.4	4706.4	2388.9	1916.2
2001	2412.3	310.8	4209.7	5313.6	2685.1	1916.2
2002	2730.7	322.6	4841.2	6110.5	3018.1	2161.5
2003	3156.7	334.2	5659.4	7069.8	3495.0	2485.7

1－11　主要年份国内生产总值构成

Strucure of Gross Domestic Productoin in Main Years

单位:%　　(%)

年份 Year	国内生产总值 Gross Domestic Product	第一产业 Primary Industry	第二产业 Secondary Industry		第三产业 Tertiary Industry
				# 工业 Industry	
1978	100	32.30	48.00	42.78	19.70
1979	100	33.10	47.30	41.86	19.60
1980	100	29.40	52.60	48.11	18.00
1981	100	24.50	56.60	52.58	18.90
1982	100	30.40	50.90	46.81	18.70
1983	100	26.20	54.30	50.91	19.50
1984	100	28.10	53.10	48.94	18.80
1985	100	23.70	56.90	52.02	19.40
1986	100	23.20	55.40	50.60	21.40
1987	100	23.00	56.20	50.80	20.80
1988	100	22.90	56.00	50.82	21.10
1989	100	22.70	56.60	51.75	20.70
1990	100	20.30	55.20	49.77	24.50
1991	100	17.50	52.40	47.20	30.10
1992	100	14.60	55.00	49.67	30.40
1993	100	13.50	56.80	49.93	29.70
1994	100	13.70	56.80	49.56	29.50
1995	100	12.80	58.30	51.51	28.90
1996	100	11.70	56.60	50.03	31.70
1997	100	9.50	57.00	51.59	33.50
1998	100	9.10	55.80	50.58	35.10
1999	100	8.90	55.90	50.87	35.20
2000	100	8.20	56.00	51.07	35.80
2001	100	7.60	54.80	49.66	37.60
2002	100	7.14	55.25	49.96	37.61
2003	100	6.28	56.03	49.96	37.69

1－12　部分年份国民经济主要比例关系

Major Proportions of National Economy in Partial Years

单位:%　　　　(%)

项目	Item	1990	1995	1998	2002	2003
国内生产总值中三次产业比例	**Ratio of GDP by Type of Industry**					
第一产业	Primary Industry	20.3	12.8	9.1	7.0	6.3
第二产业	Secondary Industry	55.2	58.3	55.8	55.2	56.0
第三产业	Tertiary Industry	24.5	28.9	35.1	37.8	36.7
农林牧渔业产值比重	**Structure of Agricultural Gross Output Value**					
农业	Frming	66.2	54.2	52.7	45.1	44.6
林业	Forestry	3.2	3.4	3.0	3.0	2.9
牧业	Animal Husbandry	20.4	16.7	15.1	14.9	15.0
渔业	Fishery	10.2	25.7	29.2	37.0	36.3
农林牧渔服务业	Services					1.2
规模以上工业增加值比例	**Ratio of Added Value of Industry Above Designated**					
轻工业	Light Industry			44.9	45.2	43.8
重工业	Heavy Industry			55.1	54.8	56.2
全社会固定资产投资额比例	**Fixed Assets Investment Ratio**					
第一产业	Primary Industry	2.7	0.8	2.9	0.9	0.4
第二产业	Secondary Industry	44.5	34.8	49.6	40.6	47.8
第三产业	Tertiary Industry	52.8	64.4	47.5	58.5	51.8
自营进出口额比例	**Directive Import and Export Ratio**					
出口	Exports	93.7	58.9	70.4	66.5	64.2
进口	Imports	6.3	41.1	29.6	33.5	35.8
农业人口与非农业人口比例	**Ratio of Population by Agriculture and Non－argiculture**					
农业人口	Agriculture	79.8	78.1	75.6	70.3	69.3
非农业人口	Non－Agriculture	20.2	21.9	24.4	29.7	30.7

1-13 平均每天主要社会经济活动

Indicators on Average Daily Social and Economic Activities in Partial Years

项目		Item		1978	1990	1998	2002	2003
平均每天创造财富		**Daily Production**						
国内生产总值	(万元)	Gross Domestic Product	(10000 yuan)	553	3874	26670	41104	48955
#工业增加值	(万元)	Added - value of Industry	(10000 yuan)	236	1977	13489	20537	24457
一般预算财政收入	(万元)	Financial Budgetary Revenue	(10000 yuan)	136	435	2401	7060	8904
每天其他经济活动		**Other Daily Economic Activities**						
全社会固定资产投资额	(万元)	Total Invesment in Fixed Assets	(10000 yuan)	138	1076	8488	16473	22901
社会消费品零售总额	(万元)	Total Retail Sales of Consumer Goods	(10000 yuan)	194	1506	8585	12681	14289
港口货物吞吐量	(万吨)	Cargo Handled	(10000 tons)	0.59	7.00	23.85	42.19	50.80
集装箱吞吐量	(标箱)	Container Handled	(boxes)			966	5090	7595
用电量	(万千瓦时)	Electricity Consumption	(10000 kwh)	194	863	2190	4167	5178
客运量	(万人)	Passenger Traffic	(10000 persons)	8.1	20.2	59.6	65.3	68.3
货运量	(万吨)	Freight Traffic	(10000 tons)	3.8	13.1	28.3	33.8	38.1
进出口总额	(万美元)	Total Imports and Exports	(USD 10000)		82	1154	3363	5153
#出口	(万美元)	Exports	(USD 10000)		77	812	2236	3308
人口变动和婚姻		**Population Changes and Marriages**						
出生	(人)	Births	(person)	206	185	129	113	116
死亡	(人)	Deaths	(person)	72	84	90	88	96
结婚	(对)	(Marriages)	(couple)		137	122	129	115
离婚	(对)	Divorces	(couple)		7	10	12	15

注:本表价值量指标按当年价格计算。
Note:The data in value terms in the table are calculated at current prices.

1－14 部分年份国民经济主要指标人均水平

Major Per Capita Indicators of National Economy in Partial Years

单位:元 (yuan)

项目	Item	1990	1995	1998	2002	2003
国内生产总值	Gross Domestic Products	2845	12156	18219	27541	32629
农业总产值	Gross Agritural Output Value	796	2356	2547	2990	3164
工业增加值	Added－value of Industry Value	1416	6238	9215	13760	16301
全社会固定资产投资额	Total Investment in Fixed Assets	769	5021	5788	11008	15224
社会消费品零售总额	Total Retail Sales of Consumer Goods	1076	4311	5854	8474	9499
自营进出口额(美元)	Directive Exports and Imports(USD)	58	732	787	2247	3426
一般预算财政收入	Financial Budgetary Revenue	311	1009	1637	4731	5919
#地方财政收入	Financial Revenue of Local Government		470	780	2048	2539
财政支出	Financial Expenditure	190	672	1207	2749	3407
人民生活	People's Livelihood					
市区居民可支配收入	Disposable Income of Urban Residents	1963	7275	9193	12970	14277
市区居民消费性支出	Living Expenditures of Urban Residents	1628	5566	7912	9396	10463
农民纯收入	Net Income of Rural Residents	1254	3484	4697	5764	6221
城乡居民储蓄存款余额	Balance of Saving Deposits of Urban and Rural Households	903	3980	8587	15789	19299
人均生活用电量(千瓦时)	Residential Electricity Consumption (kwh)	85	193	246	344	435
人均绿地面积(平方米)	Per Capita Urban Public Green Area (sq.m)			5.27	8.15	10.56
每万人拥有高校在校学生数(人)	Students Enrollment of Higher Education Per 10000 Persons (person)	9.6	18.6	23.4	113.7	145.5
每万人拥有医生数(人)	Number of Doctors Per 10000 Persons (person)	14.7	16.5	17.0	18.1	19.4
每万人拥有电话机数(部)	Number of Telephone Sets Per 10000 Persons (set)	241	1243	2388	5520	6854

1－15 主要年份总户数和总人口

Households and Population in Main Years

单位:万户,万人 (10000 households,10000persons)

年份 Year	总户数 Total Households	总人口 Total Population	按性别分 By Sex		按农业和非农业分 By Agriculture & Non－agriculture	
			男性 Male	女性 Female	农业人口 Agriculture	非农业人口 Non－agriculture
1978	123.30	457.70	234.18	223.52	394.28	63.42
1979	124.48	462.07	235.78	226.29	394.31	67.76
1980	128.57	465.99	237.98	228.01	393.13	72.86
1981	136.86	471.76	240.95	230.81	394.39	70.37
1982	140.56	478.33	244.20	234.13	396.40	81.93
1983	143.27	481.46	245.79	235.67	397.68	83.78
1984	147.57	484.18	247.26	236.92	398.64	85.54
1985	153.57	487.74	249.24	238.50	394.50	93.24
1986	158.53	491.89	251.56	240.33	394.69	97.20
1987	164.78	498.15	254.80	243.35	399.48	98.67
1988	170.92	503.06	257.19	245.89	402.81	100.25
1989	175.12	507.64	259.75	247.89	406.08	101.56
1990	176.06	510.76	260.99	249.77	407.78	102.98
1991	179.22	514.16	262.68	251.48	409.61	104.55
1992	180.89	516.72	264.09	252.63	409.90	106.82
1993	182.80	519.85	265.72	254.26	410.17	109.81
1994	184.38	526.85	267.24	255.61	410.17	112.68
1995	186.26	526.20	268.72	257.48	410.94	115.29
1996	186.82	530.08	270.30	259.78	410.57	119.51
1997	188.83	533.31	271.89	261.42	409.81	123.50
1998	190.39	535.27	272.40	262.87	404.79	130.48
1999	192.52	538.41	273.65	264.76	401.29	137.12
2000	193.99	540.94	274.50	266.44	398.91	142.03
2001	196.10	543.34	275.50	267.84	392.48	150.86
2002	198.94	546.19	276.60	269.60	383.76	162.43
2003	203.47	549.07	277.64	271.44	380.26	168.81

1－16 主要年份人口自然变动情况
Population Natural Changes in Main Years

单位:人,‰ (persons,‰)

年份 Year	出生 Birth		死亡 Death		自然增长率 Natural Growth Rate
	人数 Birth Population	出生率 Birth Rate	人数 Death Population	死亡率 Death Rate	
1978	75180	15.06	26150	5.74	9.32
1979	71642	15.58	27393	5.96	9.62
1980	57417	12.37	27989	6.03	6.34
1981	78132	16.66	28557	6.09	10.57
1982	84905	17.87	28258	5.95	11.92
1983	69668	14.52	30875	6.43	8.09
1984	51040	10.57	28114	5.82	4.75
1985	53366	10.98	29483	6.07	4.91
1986	62535	12.77	28738	5.87	6.90
1987	83541	16.88	30239	6.11	10.77
1988	69248	13.83	30171	6.03	7.80
1989	71283	14.11	30364	6.01	8.10
1990	67464	13.25	30670	6.02	7.23
1991	60140	11.74	29329	5.75	6.01
1992	50700	10.22	30573	5.93	4.29
1993	55242	10.66	29169	5.63	5.03
1994	54990	10.55	30050	5.76	4.78
1995	59600	11.36	32689	6.23	5.13
1996	58282	11.04	30652	5.80	5.24
1997	55231	10.39	31417	5.91	4.48
1998	47116	8.82	32902	6.16	2.66
1999	51544	9.57	31237	5.80	3.77
2000	50168	9.30	33438	6.20	3.10
2001	39867	7.35	30632	5.65	1.70
2002	41404	7.60	32361	5.94	1.66
2003	42445	7.80	35173	6.40	1.30

1－17　各县(市)、区人口、户口情况

项目		Item		全市 Total	市区 Urban District	海曙 Haishu	江东 Jiangdong
总户数	**(户)**	**Total Households**	**(household)**	**2034740**	**803049**	**106975**	**90556**
总人口	**(人)**	**Total Population**	**(person)**	**5490725**	**2069098**	**292613**	**235463**
男性	(人)	Male	(person)	2776358	1035512	146534	118146
女性	(人)	Female	(person)	2714367	1033586	146079	117317
非农业人口	(人)	Non－agriculture Population	(person)	1688112	1099526	278431	230395
未落常住户口的	(人)	Non－registered Residence	(person)	16225	1354	16	6
平均人口	**(人)**	**Average Population**	**(person)**	**5476317**	**2051591**	**288700**	**231455**
出生人数	**(人)**	**Birth Population**	**(person)**	**42445**	**14069**	**1863**	**1812**
男性	(人)	Male	(person)	21610	7205	979	928
女性	(人)	Female	(person)	20835	6864	890	884
出生率	(‰)	Birth Rate	(‰)	7.8	6.9	6.5	7.8
死亡人数	**(人)**	**Death Population**	**(person)**	**35173**	**11524**	**1011**	**876**
男性	(人)	Male	(person)	19579	6258	573	474
女性	(人)	Female	(person)	15594	5266	483	402
死亡率	(‰)	Death Rate	(‰)	6.4	5.6	3.5	3.8
本年自然增加人数	(人)	Natural Growth Population	(person)	7272	2545	852	936
人口自然增长率	(‰)	Natural Growth Rate	(‰)	1.3	1.2	2.9	4.0
迁入人数	**(人)**	**Number of the Persons Moved in**	**(person)**	**105057**	**56476**	**12612**	**6011**
#省内迁入	(人)	From Zhejiang Province	(person)	76140	38960	8763	3139
省外迁入	(人)	From Other Province	(person)	28917	17516	3849	2872
迁出人数	**(人)**	**Number of the Persons Moved Out**	**(person)**	**80102**	**23878**	**6417**	**3114**
#迁往省能	(人)	To Zhejiang Province	(person)	65019	17058	4088	1524
迁往省外	(人)	To Other Province	(person)	15083	6820	2329	1590

Population and Households by County and District

江北 Jiangbei	北仑 Beilun	镇海 Zhenhai	鄞州 Yinzhou	余姚 Yuyao	慈溪 Cixi	奉化 Fenghua	象山 Xiangshan	宁海 Ninghai
87923	**139219**	**87058**	**291318**	**285567**	**386967**	**174559**	**178295**	**206303**
230900	**337641**	**216691**	**755790**	**824295**	**1007079**	**481529**	**526335**	**582389**
117174	169000	110435	374223	415521	503376	245840	271749	304360
113726	168641	106256	381567	408774	503703	235689	254586	278029
143109	132453	116110	199028	164388	151342	99398	100986	72472
78	327	41	886	3873	4388	837	4143	1630
230884	**334967**	**216336**	**749248**	**825133**	**1006440**	**482987**	**527457**	**582707**
1469	**2428**	**1019**	**5478**	**5945**	**8497**	**3597**	**5060**	**5277**
727	1215	554	2808	2994	4177	1846	2518	2870
742	1213	465	2670	2951	4320	1751	2542	2407
6.4	7.3	4.7	7.3	7.2	8.4	7.5	9.6	9.1
1219	**2190**	**1258**	**4970**	**6222**	**7079**	**3303**	**3853**	**3192**
1183	705	663	2660	3472	3901	1803	2294	1851
1007	469	595	2310	2750	3178	1500	1559	1341
5.3	6.5	5.8	6.6	7.5	7.0	6.8	7.3	5.5
250	238	-239	508	-277	1418	294	1207	2085
1.1	0.7	-1.1	0.7	-0.3	1.4	0.6	2.2	3.6
8736	**7438**	**2268**	**19411**	**16740**	**11785**	**6214**	**6672**	**7170**
6223	3655	1077	16103	13149	7304	4808	5907	6012
2513	3783	1191	3308	3591	4481	1406	765	1158
4570	**2477**	**1194**	**6106**	**17516**	**11948**	**9179**	**7750**	**9831**
3938	1645	674	5189	15420	8870	8001	6777	8893
632	832	520	917	2096	3078	1178	973	938

1－18　15个副省级市主要经济指标

(2003)

项目		Item	
工业总产值(规模以上、现价)	(亿元)	Gross Output Value of Industry Above Designated Size (current price)	(100 million yuan)
工业产品产销率	(%)	Sales Rate of Industrial Products	(%)
全社会固定资产投资额	(亿元)	Investment in Fixed Assets	(100 million yuan)
社会消费品零售总额	(亿元)	Retail Sales of Consumer Goods	(100 million yuan)
外贸进出口总额	(亿美元)	Total Value of Foreign Import and Export(Customs)	(USD 100 million)
#出口总额	(亿美元)	Export	(USD 100 million)
实际利用外资金额	(亿美元)	Actually Utilization of Foreign Capital	(USD 100 million)
地方财政一般预算收入	(亿元)	Financial Ordinary Budgetary Revenue of Local Government	(100 million yuan)
地方财政一般预算支出	(亿元)	Financial Ordinary Budgetary Expenditure of Local Government	(100 million yuan)
金融机构存款余额	(亿元)	Deposit of Financial Institution	(100 million yuan)
#城乡储蓄存款余额	(亿元)	Saving Deposits of Rural and Urban Residents	(100 million yuan)
金融机构贷款余额	(亿元)	Loans of Financial Institution	(100 million yuan)
市区城镇居民人均可支配收入	(元)	Per Capital Annual Disposable Income of Urban Residents	(yuan)
市区城镇居民人均消费性支出	(元)	Per Capital Annual Expenditure for Consumption of Urban Residents	(yuan)
国内生产总值	(亿元)	Gross Domestic Product	(100 million yuan)
第一产业	(亿元)	Primary Industry	(100 million yuan)
第二产业	(亿元)	Secondary Industry	(100 million yuan)
#工业增加值	(亿元)	Value Added of Industry	(100 million yuan)
第三产业	(亿元)	Tertiary Industry	(100 million yuan)

注:本册所列数据为初步统计数。

Main Economic Indicators of 15 Cites at Vice ProvincialLevel

宁波 Ningbo	杭州 Hangzhou	大连 Dalian	青岛 Qingdao	武汉 Wuhan	深圳 Shenzhen	厦门 Xiamen
2630.29	3202.52	1542.40	2559.30	1334.90	5073.77	1318.21
98.28	97.83	98.37	98.01	98.45	98.00	98.90
835.90	1006.74	506.90	739.40	645.06	946.49	244.61
521.53	587.52	568.45	512.20	853.99	801.77	230.34
188.09	182.37	173.00	206.60	31.36	1173.99	187.11
120.74	109.54	95.30	123.90	14.18	629.62	105.54
17.27	10.09	22.11	28.10	14.16	36.23	4.22
139.41	150.39	110.53	120.14	80.44	290.46	70.15
180.26	163.59	147.39	147.17		349.36	86.97
2764.30	4439.53	2263.30	1892.09	3032.07	6079.48	1001.17
1059.63	1466.42	1130.20	908.47	1285.53	2199.45	397.16
2223.02	3686.90	1879.30	1678.39	2525.13	4525.05	721.87
14277	12898	9101	10075	8524.52	25935.84	12915
10463	9950	7760	8056	7251	19960	9459
1786.85	2099.77	1632.60	1780.30	1662.40	2860.51	760.12
112.23	126.59	145.60	147.05	94.20	18.16	19.85
1001.21	1089.32	782.10	937.10	741.80	1685.37	443.61
892.68	948.68	697.10	825.50	598.80	1500.13	
673.41	883.86	704.90	695.70	826.40	1156.98	296.66

Note: This listed data on table are counted for preliminary statistics.

1－18 续表

项目		Item	
工业总产值(规模以上、现价)	(亿元)	Gross Output Value of Industry Above Designated Size (current price)	(100 million yuan)
工业产品产销率	(%)	Sales Rate of Industrial Products	(%)
全社会固定资产投资额	(亿元)	Investment in Fixed Assets	(100 million yuan)
社会消费品零售总额	(亿元)	Retail Sales of Consumer Goods	(100 million yuan)
外贸进出口总额	(亿美元)	Total Value of Foreign Import and Export(Customs)	(USD 100 million)
#出口总额	(亿美元)	Export	(USD 100 million)
实际利用外资金额	(亿美元)	Actually Utilization of Foreign Capital	(USD 100 million)
地方财政一般预算收入	(亿元)	Financial Ordinary Budgetary Revenue of Local Government	(100 million yuan)
地方财政一般预算支出	(亿元)	Financial Ordinary Budgetary Expenditure of Local Government	(100 million yuan)
金融机构存款余额	(亿元)	Deposit of Financial Institution	(100 million yuan)
#城乡储蓄存款余额	(亿元)	Saving Deposits of Rural and Urban Residents	(100 million yuan)
金融机构贷款余额	(亿元)	Loans of Financial Institution	(100 million yuan)
市区城镇居民人均可支配收入	(元)	Per Capital Annual Disposable Income of Urban Residents	(yuan)
市区城镇居民人均消费性支出	(元)	Per Capital Annual Expenditure for Consumption of Urban Residents	(yuan)
国内生产总值	(亿元)	Gross Domestic Product	(100 million yuan)
第一产业	(亿元)	Primary Industry	(100 million yuan)
第二产业	(亿元)	Secondary Industry	(100 million yuan)
#工业增加值	(亿元)	Value Added of Industry	(100 million yuan)
第三产业	(亿元)	Tertiary Industry	(100 million yuan)

continued

沈阳 Shenyang	长春 Changchuan	哈尔滨 Harbin	南京 Nanjing	济南 Jinan	广州 Guangzhou	成都 Chengdu	西安 Xi'an
1063.58	1510.20	707.80	2509.38	1318.82	4017.83	970.10	779.56
96.50	97.80	97.30	98.41	97.84	97.67	98.20	97.63
582.61	389.60	435.96	954.04	504.88	1157.77	862.97	478.98
721.54	438.30	624.17	600.24	533.20	1494.27	771.50	440.05
42.60	52.20	19.05	147.12	20.20	349.44	25.17	23.09
20.04	15.50	9.09	76.65	8.40	168.89	13.55	14.03
22.42	1.70	2.26	22.10	1.18	25.81	4.24	2.56
81.03	45.97	76.36	136.48	76.11	274.75	89.60	64.80
134.07	85.80	121.56	155.24	88.58	370.15	136.10	76.62
2691.74	1615.20	2015.22	3821.37	2449.48	8676.72	3241.00	2665.87
1422.96	831.40	1153.70	1253.85	758.35	3727.33	1494.00	1210.56
2172.18	1629.60	1919.48	3546.40	2475.08	6127.27	2588.00	1954.18
7961	7905	7892.76	10195.56	11013	15002.59	9641	7748
6690	6725	6230	7725	8395	11571	7058	6805
1602.01	1338.00	1414.80	1576.20	1367.80	3466.63	1870.80	940.35
87.44	155.90	216.40	65.10	105.00	104.14	153.20	49.21
759.17	630.30	524.50	804.40	599.60	1504.89	859.10	446.95
682.22		421.30	659.40	494.60	1336.48	670.40	347.10
755.40	551.80	673.90	706.70	663.20	1857.60	858.50	444.19

1－19　长江三角洲15城市主要经济指标对比

（2003）

项目		项目	
总人口	（万人）	Total Population at Year－end	（10000 persons）
国内生产总值	（亿元	Gross Domestic Product	（100 million yuan）
第一产业	（亿元）	Primary Industry	（100 million yuan）
第二产业	（亿元）	Secondary Industry	（100 million yuan）
#工业增加值	（亿元）	Value－Added of Industry	（100 million yuan）
第三产业	（亿元）	Tertiary Industry	（100 million yuan）
人均 GDP	（元）	Per Capital GDP	（yuan）
规模以上工业总产值	（亿元）	Gross Output Value of Industry Above Designated Size	（100 million yuan）
利税总额	（亿元）	Total Profits and Taxes of Industry Above Designated Size	（100 million yuan）
#利润总额	（亿元）	Total Profits	（100 million yuan）
工业用电量	（亿千瓦时）	Electricity Consumption for Industry	（100 million kwh）
全社会固定资产投资	（亿元）	Investment in Fixed Assets	（100 million yuan）
#房地产投资	（亿元）	Real EstateDevelopment	（100 million yuan）
社会消费品零售额	（亿元）	Retail Sales of Consumer Goods	（100 million yuan）
自营进出口总额	（亿美元）	Total Value of Foreign Import and Export（Customs）	（100 million USD）
#出口	（亿美元）	Export	（100 million USD）
合同利用外资	（亿美元）	Contract Utilization of Foreign Capital	（100 million USD）
实际利用外资	（亿美元）	Actually Utilization of Foreign Capital	（100 million USD）
财政一般预算收入	（亿元）	Total Financail Revenue	（100 million yuan）
地方预算内财政收入	（亿元）	Financial Revenue of Local Government	（100 million yuan）
地方预算内财政支出	（亿元）	Financial Expenditure of Local Government	（100 million yuan）
金融机构存款余额	（亿元）	Deposit of Financial Institution	（100 million yuan）
#城乡储蓄	（亿元）	Saving Deposits of Rural and Urban Residents	（100 million yuan）
金融机构贷款余额	（亿元）	Loans of Financial Institution	（100 million yuan）
市区城镇居民人均可支配收入	（元）	Per Capital Annual Disposable Income of Urban Residents	（yuan）
市区城镇居民人均消费性支出	（元）	Per Capital Annual Expenditure for Consumption of Urban Residents	（yuan）
居民消费价格指数	（%）	Residents Consumer Price Indices	（%）
农村居民人均纯收入	（元）	Per Capital Annual Net Income of Rural Residents	（yuan）

注：本册所列数据为初步统计数。

Main Ecnomy Indicators of The Cities Lies in Yangtze River Delta

宁波 Ningbo	杭州 Hangzhou	嘉兴 Jiaxing	湖州 Huzhou	绍兴 Shaoxing	舟山 Zhoushan	上海 Shanghai
549.1	642.8	333.0	256.8	433.8	97.1	1341.8
1786.9	2099.8	855.6	490.8	1089.3	172.3	6250.8
112.2	126.6	66.1	55.4	82.5	33.0	93.0
1001.2	1089.3	507.5	261.8	644.9	71.1	3130.7
892.7	948.7	441.4	229.1	572.3	55.6	2865.9
673.4	883.9	282.1	173.6	362.0	68.1	3027.1
32629	32819	25720	19102	25115	17679	45827
2630.3	3202.5	1113.5	588.6	1895.4	153.0	10342.8
322.0	347.8	112.6	64.5	187.6	11.4	1329.7
189.3	192.9	70.6	37.7	117.2	5.6	805.7
141.7	172.1	83.4	49.7	112.8	8.1	746.0
835.9	1006.7	525.5	268.0	535.0	98.0	2452.1
184.3	258.9	72.4	41.5	74.5	18.2	901.2
521.5	587.5	279.4	182.3	292.0	75.1	2220.6
188.1	182.4	57.1	12.2	59.6	6.2	1124.0
120.7	109.5	36.2	10.1	45.3	5.4	484.8
34.4	20.0	21.0	14.5	15.0	0.5	110.6
17.3	10.1	8.0	5.4	7.4	0.2	58.5
325.0	329.7	92.7	51.2	107.3	19.0	2828.9
139.4	150.4	41.2	25.3	50.5	11.4	899.3
187.1	163.6	47.2	30.5	57.1	23.1	1102.6
2629.0	4439.5	1027.9	486.4	1280.2	259.4	17318.4
1059.6	1466.4	541.5	260.6	664.9	127.9	6054.6
2102.8	3686.9	757.8	365.5	986.8	190.1	13168.1
14277	12898	12251	12607	13535	12745	14867
10463	9950	8727	8431	9305	9771	11040
101.2	99.5	100.7	100.0	100.0	101.3	100.1
6221	5740	6127	5536	6143	5018	6658

Note: This listed data on table are counted for preliminary statistics.

1－19 续表

项目		项目	
总人口	（万人）	Total Population at Year－end	（10000 persons）
国内生产总值	（亿元）	Gross Domestic Product	（100 million yuan）
第一产业	（亿元）	Primary Industry	（100 million yuan）
第二产业	（亿元）	Secondary Industry	（100 million yuan）
#工业增加值	（亿元）	Value－Added of Industry	（100 million yuan）
第三产业	（亿元）	Tertiary Industry	（100 million yuan）
人均 GDP	（元）	Per Capital GDP	（yuan）
规模以上工业总产值	（亿元）	Gross Output Value of Industry Above Designated Size	（100 million yuan）
利税总额	（亿元）	Total Profits and Taxes of Industry Above Designated Size	（100 million yuan）
#利润总额	（亿元）	Total Profits	（100 million yuan）
工业用电量	（亿千瓦时）	Electricity Consumption for Industry	（100 million kwh）
全社会固定资产投资	（亿元）	Investment in Fixed Assets	（100 million yuan）
#房地产投资	（亿元）	Real EstateDevelopment	（100 million yuan）
社会消费品零售额	（亿元）	Retail Sales of Consumer Goods	（100 million yuan）
自营进出口总额	（亿美元）	Total Value of Foreign Import and Export（Customs）	（100 million USD）
#出口	（亿美元）	Export	（100 million USD）
合同利用外资	（亿美元）	Contract Utilization of Foreign Capital	（100 million USD）
实际利用外资	（亿美元）	Actually Utilization of Foreign Capital	（100 million USD）
财政一般预算收入	（亿元）	Total Financail Revenue	（100 million yuan）
地方预算内财政收入	（亿元）	Financial Revenue of Local Government	（100 million yuan）
地方预算内财政支出	（亿元）	Financial Expenditure of Local Government	（100 million yuan）
金融机构存款余额	（亿元）	Deposit of Financial Institution	（100 million yuan）
#城乡储蓄	（亿元）	Saving Deposits of Rural and Urban Residents	（100 million yuan）
金融机构贷款余额	（亿元）	Loans of Financial Institution	（100 million yuan）
市区城镇居民人均可支配收入	（元）	Per Capital Annual Disposable Income of Urban Residents	（yuan）
市区城镇居民人均消费性支出	（元）	Per Capital Annual Expenditure for Consumption of Urban Residents	（yuan）
居民消费价格指数	（%）	Residents Consumer Price Indices	（%）
农村居民人均纯收入	（元）	Per Capital Annual Net Income of Rural Residents	（yuan）

continued

南京 Nanjing	苏州 Suzhou	无锡 Wuxi	南通 Nantong	常州 Changzhou	镇江 Zhenjiang	扬州 Yangzhou	泰州 Taizhou
572.2	591.0	442.5	777.6	346.2	453.6	267.2	503.7
1576.2	2802.0	1901.2	1006.7	900.2	647.2	643.6	580.0
65.1	78.5	54.0	141.0	47.3	71.4	32.6	73.0
804.4	1768.1	1093.0	515.8	519.1	330.6	366.9	299.7
659.4	1583.0	992.7	452.4	468.9	226.5	311.9	251.0
706.7	955.5	754.2	349.9	333.8	245.2	244.0	207.3
27283	47701	42962	12923	26110	14300	24089	11512
2509.4	4976.5	3284.7	1126.9	1527.3	837.2	855.4	736.7
249.3	332.7	259.5	88.9	112.3	65.0	62.1	67.2
112.5	214.5	161.3	54.9	65.6	29.5	26.9	33.5
129.7	304.1	200.1	71.2	91.5	46.9	56.6	47.4
954.0	1408.9	893.3	448.4	446.6	247.0	237.3	230.7
183.8	562.2	131.8	48.3	52.8	43.8	32.3	31.2
600.2	526.1	487.1	331.3	280.7	198.0	168.2	173.8
147.1	656.6	143.8	51.6	52.5	20.3	26.1	8.8
76.7	326.3	73.3	32.8	35.3	11.1	12.2	6.3
40.1	125.0	50.1	23.1	20.5	9.5	17.9	4.8
22.1	68.1	27.0	7.3	8.6	4.8	8.1	3.0
335.0	409.9	265.6	117.0	136.1	72.9	73.9	66.3
191.8	220.3	149.7	70.1	78.5	30.0	41.8	36.6
210.4	231.6		81.9	83.8	38.7	47.0	50.0
3821.4	3149.8	2156.9	1333.0	1170.6	721.0	580.9	596.3
1253.9	1470.5	997.8	882.1	622.9	449.1	338.2	395.0
3546.4	2359.3	1435.8	726.9	799.1	433.9	425.1	348.7
10196	12361	11647	9598	11307	8705	9451	8517
7725	9272	8360	6808	8944	5910	6969	5743
101.4	100.8	101.0	101.6	100.7	101.6	101.8	101.3
4923	6681	6329	4393	5550	4220	4733	4079

1－20 气象情况

Meteorological Date

(2003)

时间 Time	平均气温 (0.1℃) Average Temperature (0.1℃)	降水量 (0.1毫米) Precipitation (0.1 millimeters)	日照时数 (0.1小时) Sunshine Hours (0.1 hours)	相对湿度 (%) Relative Humidity (%)
全年 Annual	17.9	861.1	72.0	140.7
1月 Jan.	4.8	40.0	78.0	90.9
2月 Feb.	8.2	96.1	75.0	127.4
3月 Mar.	10.7	123.5	77.0	122.4
4月 Apr.	16.7	79.1	76.0	129.4
5月 May	20.8	104.0	76.0	151.7
6月 June	24.9	107.6	69.0	281.2
7月 July	31.5	37.6	75.0	205.9
8月 Aug.	29.9	106.9	75.0	216.4
9月 Sept.	26.6	53.3	70.0	201.5
10月 Oct.	19.2	22.0	76.0	124.2
11月 Nov.	14.4	58.8	68.0	160.7
12月 Dec.	7.4	32.2	74.0	1052.4

注:1.最高气温为38.3度,出现在8月24日。
2.最低气温为－2.0度,出现在1月9日。
3.无霜期为242天。
The highest temperature 38.3℃,24/08.
The lowest temperature －3.53℃,9/01.
Annual Non－frost days is 242.

主要指标解释

【国内生产总值(GDP)】 指一个国家(或地区)所有常住单位在一定时期内生产活动的最终成果。国内生产总值有三种表现形态,即价值形态、收入形态和产品形态。从价值形态看,它是所有常住单位在一定时期内生产的全部货物和服务价值超过同期中间投入的全部非固定资产货物和服务价值的差额,即所有常住单位的增加值之和;从收入形态看,它是所有常住单位在一定时期内创造并分配给常住单位和非常住单位的初次收入分配之和;从产品形态看,它是所有常住单位在一定时期内最终使用的货物和服务价值与货物和服务净出口价值之和。在实际核算中,国内生产总值有三种计算方法,即生产法、收入法和支出法。三种方法分别从不同的方面反映国内生产总值及其构成。

【三次产业】 根据社会生产活动历史发展的顺序对产业结构的划分,产品直接取自自然界的部门为第一产业;对初级产品进行再加工的部门称为第二产业;为生产和消费提供服务的部门称为第三产业。它是世界上通用的产业结构分类,但各国的划分不尽一致。我国的三次产业划分为:

第一产业:农业(包括种植业、林业、牧业、副业、渔业)。

第二产业:工业(包括采掘业、制造业、自来水、电力、蒸汽、热水、煤气)和建筑业。

第三产业:除第一、第二产业以外的其他各业。

【劳动者报酬】 指劳动者因从事生产活动所获得的全部报酬。包括劳动者获得的各种形式的工资、奖金和津贴,既包括货币形式的,也包括实物形式的;还包括劳动者所享受的公费医疗和医药卫生费、上下班交通补贴和单位支付的社会保险费等。

【生产税净额】 指生产税减生产补贴后的余额。生产税指政府对生产单位生产、销售和从事经营活动以及因从事生产活动使用某些生产要素(如固定资产、土地、劳动力)所征收的各种税、附加费和规费。生产补贴与生产税相反,指政府对生产单位的单方面收入转移,因此视为负生产税,包括政策亏损补贴、粮食系统价格补贴、外贸企业出口退税收入等。

【固定资产折旧】 指一定时期内为弥补固定资产损耗按照核定的固定资产折旧率提取的固定资产折旧,或按国民经济核算统一规定的折旧率虚拟计算的固定资产折旧。它反映了固定资产在当期生产中的转移价值。各类企业和企业化管理的事业单位的固定资产折旧是指实际计提并计入成本费中的折旧费;不计提折旧的政府机关、非企业化管理的事业单位和居民住房的固定资产折旧是按照统一规定的折旧率和固定资产原值计算的虚拟折旧。原则上,固定资产折旧应按固定资产的重置价值计算,但是目前我国尚不具备对全社会固定资产进行重估价的基础,所以暂时只能采用上述办法。

【营业盈余】 指常住单位创造的增加值扣除劳动者报酬、生产税净额和固定资产折旧后的余额。它相当于企业的营业利润加上生产补贴,但要扣除从利润中开支的工资和福利等。

【出生率(又称粗出生率)】 指在一定时期内(通常为一年)平均每千人所出生的人数的比率,一般用千分率表示。计算公式为:

出生率 = 年出生人数/年平均人数 × 1000‰

式中:出生人数指活产婴儿,即胎儿脱离母体时(不管怀孕月数),有过呼吸或其他生命现象。年平均人数指年初、年底人口数的平均数,也可用年中人口数代替。

【死亡率(又称粗死亡率)】 指在一定时期内(通常为一年)一定地区的死亡人数与同期平均人数(或期中人数)之比,一般用千分率表示。计算公式为:

死亡率 = 年死亡人数/年平均人数 × 1000‰

【人口自然增长率】 指在一定时期内(通常为一年)人口自然增加数(出生人数减死亡人数)与该时期内平均人数(或期中人数)之比,一般用千分率表示。计算公式为:

人口自然增长率 = (本年出生人数 - 本年死亡人数)/年平均人数 × 1000‰ = 人口出生率 - 人口死亡率

Explanatory Notes on Main Statistical Indicators

【Gross Domestic Product (GDP)】 refers to the final products of all resident units in a country (or a region) during a certain period of time. Gross domestic product is expressed in three different forms, i.e. value, income, and products respectively. The form of value refers to the total value of all products and services produced by all resident units during a certain period of time , minus total value of intimidate input of materials and services of the nature of non – fixed assets or the summation of the value – added of all resident units; the form of income includes all the income created by all resident units and distributed primarily to all resident and non – resident units; the form of products refers to the value of all final goods and services for final use by all resident units plus the value of net exports of goods and services during a given period of time. In the practice of national accounting, gross domestic product is calculated with three approaches, i.e. production approach, income approach, and expenditure approach, which reflect gross domestic product and its composition from different aspects.

【Three Industries Industry】 structure has been classified according to the historical sequence of development. Primary industry refers to extraction of natural resources; secondary industry involves processing of primary products; and tertiary industry provides services of various kinds for production and consumption. The above classification is universal although it various to some extent from country to country. Industry in China comprises; Primary Industry: agriculture (including farming, forestry, animal husbandry, sideline production and fishery). Secondary Industry: industry (including mining and quarrying, manufacturing, water supply, electricity generation and supply, steam, hot water, gas) and construction. Tertiary Industry: all other industries not included in primary or secondary industries.

【Labourers' Remuneration】 refers to the whole payment of various forms earned by the labourers from the productive activities they are engaged in. It includes wages, bonuses and allowances the labourers earned in monetary form and in kind. It also includes the free medical services provided to the labourers and the medicine expenses, traffic subsidies and social insurance fee paid by the labourers' working units for them.

【Net Taxes on Production】 refers to the residual of the taxes on production minus the subsidies on production. The taxes on production refers to the various taxes, extra charges and fees levied on the production units on their production, sale and business activities as well as on some factors of production, such as fixed assets, land and labour force, used in the production activities they are engaged in. In contrast to the taxes on production, the subsidies on production refer to the unilateral transfer of part of the government's revenue to the production units and is therefore regarded as negative taxes on production. They include subsidies on the loss due to implementation of government policies, price subsidies to the grain institutions, foreign trade corporations receipts from drawback, etc.

【Depreciation of Fixed Assets】 refers to the depreciation of fixed assets of a given period, drawn in accordance with the stipulated depreciation rate for the purpose of compensating the wear loss of the fixed assets or the depreciation of fixed assets calculated in a fictitious way in accordance with the stipulated unified depreciation rate in the national economic accounting system. It reflects the value of transfer of the fixed assets in the production of the current period. The depreciation of fixed assets in various enterprises and institutions managed as enterprises refers to the depreciation expenses actually drawn and calculated as part of the cost. In government agencies and institutions not managed as enterprises which do not draw the depreciation expenses, as well as for the houses of residents, the depreciation of fixed assets is the imputed depreciation, which is calculated in accordance with the stipulated unified depreciation rate. In principle, the depreciation of fixed assets should be calculated on the basis of the re – purchased value of the fixed assets. However, there is no actual condition to re – evaluate all the fixed assets in China. Therefore, the above – mentioned methods are temporarily adopted at present.

【Operating Surplus】 refers to the balance of the value added created by the resident units deducting the labourers' remuneration, net taxes on production and the depreciation of fixed assets. It is equivalent to the business profit of the enterprises plus subsidies on production, but the wages and welfare expenses paid from the profits should be deducted.

【Birth Rate or (Crude Birth Rate)】 refers to the ratio of the number of births to the average population (or mid – period population) during a certain period of time (usually a year) which is often expressed in ‰. Birth rate in the chapter refers to annual birth rate. The following formula is used:

Birth Rate = Number of Births/Average Number of Population × 1000‰

Number of births refers to live births i.e. the births when babies had showed any vital phenomena regardless of the length of pregnancy.

Annual Average Number of Population is the average of the number of population at the beginning of the year and that at the end of the year. Sometimes it is substituted for with the mid year population.

【Death Rate (or Crude Death Rate)】 refers to the ratio of the number of deaths to the average population (or mid – period population) during a certain period of time (usually a year) which is often expressed in ‰. Death rate in the chapter refers to annual death rate. The following formula is used:

Death Rate = Number of Deaths/Annual Average Number of Population × 1000‰

【Natural Growth Rate of Population】 refers to the ratio of natural increase in population (number of births minus number of deaths) in a certain period of time (unsually ayear) to the average population (or mid – period population) of the same period which is often expressed in ‰. The following formulas are applied:

Natural Growth of Population = (Number of Births – Number of Deaths)/Average Number of Population × 1000‰

Natural Growth Rate of Population = Birth Rate – Death Rate

2

农　业

CHAPTER 2 AGRICULTURE

农业
Agriculture

主要统计指标
Major Statistics Indicators

2003年农村劳动力	Rural Laborers in This Year	290.3	万人	10000 persons
比上年增长	Increase Over Last Year	7.5	%	
2003年耕地面积	Cultivated Area at Year - end	210954	公顷	hectares
比上年增长	Increase Over Last Year	-0.5	%	
2003年农业总产值	Gross Output Value of Agriculture	173.75	亿元	100 million yuan
比上年增长	Increase Over Last Year	4.3	%	
2003年粮食总产量	Total Yield of Grain Grops	755466	吨	ton
比上年增长	Increase Over Last Year	-20.4	%	
2003年油料总产量	Yield of Oil - bearing Crops	42053	吨	ton
比上年增长	Increase Over Last Year	-11.6	%	
2003年肉类产量	Output of Meat	155431	吨	ton
比上年增长	Increase Over Last Year	2.8	%	
2003花卉苗木播种面积	Sown Area of Flowers and Plants Nursery Stock	27731	公顷	hectares
比上年增长	Increase Over Last Year	66.3	%	
2003年水产品总产量	Total Aquatic Products	903301	吨	ton
比上年增长	Increase Over Last Year	1.8	%	

2-1 部分年份农村基本情况

Basic Statistics on Rural Areas in Partial Years

项目	Item	1995	1998	2002	2003
农村基层组织	**Rural Grass Roots Units**				
乡镇政府(个)	Number of Township and Town Governments (unit)	149	149	115	102
#镇政府	Number of Town Governments	118	122	100	89
乡政府	Number of Township Governments	31	27	15	13
农村街道办事处	Number of Subdistrict Offices			16	32
农村居民委员会	Number of Neighborhoood Committees			67	165
村民委员会	Number of Villages Committees	5077	4982	3831	3812
村民小组(万个)	Number of Villages Groups (10000 units)	3.86	3.82	3.44	3.39
农村住户数、人口	**Number of Rural Households and Population**				
农村住户数(万户)	Rural Households (10000 households)	140.78	140.75	153.73	168.06
#农业生产户数	Agricultural Produeing			121.49	115.69
农村居委会住户数	Neighborhoood Committees			3.99	13.87
外来住户数	Household from Other Places			14.93	25.23
农村人口(万人)	Rural Population (10000 persons)	413.05	408.84	426.29	466.71
#农村居委会住户人口数	Neighborhoood Committees			10.91	32.45
外来人口数	Population form Other Places			41.95	71.34
农村社会基础设施	**Social Basic Facilities in Rural Areas**				
自来水受益村数(个)	Number of Villages with Tap Water (unit)	3577	4258	3635	3606
通汽车村数	Number of Villages with Bus Services	4449	4668	3838	3754
通邮村数	Number of Villages with Post and Telecommunication Services			3895	3809
通电话村数	Number of Villages with Telephone Communication	4611	4891	3888	3802
通电村数	Number of Villages with Electricity		4982	3898	3811

2-2 各县(市)、区农村基本情况

(2003)

项目	Item	全市 Total	市区 Urban District
农村基层组织	**Rural Grass Roots Units**		
乡镇政府(个)	Number of Township and Town Governments(unit)	102	33
#镇政府	Number of Town Governments	89	30
乡政府	Number of Township Governments	13	3
农村街道办事处	Number of Subdistrict Offices	32	11
农村居民委员会	Number of Neighborhoood Committees	165	96
村民委员会	Number of Villages Committees	3812	1102
村民小组(万个)	Number of Villages Groups(10000 units)	3.39	0.85
农村住户数、人口	**Number of Rural Households and Population**		
农村住户数(万户)	Rural Households (10000 households)	168.06	60.90
#农业生产户数	Agricultural Produeing	115.69	35.88
农村居委会住户数	Neighborhoood Committees	13.87	9.33
外来住户数	Moving to Ningbo	25.23	12.71
农村人口(万人)	Rural Population (10000 persons)	466.71	153.39
#农村居委会住户人口数	Neighborhoood Committees	32.45	20.56
外来人口数	Population from Other Places	71.34	34.92
农村社会基础设施	**Social Basic Facilities in Rural Areas**		
自来水受益村数(个)	Number of Villages with Tap Water (unti)	3606	1073
通汽车村数	Number of Villages with Bus Services	3754	1091
通邮村数	Number of Villages with Post and Telecommunication Services	3809	1102
通电话村数	Number of Villages with Telephone Communication	3802	1099
通电村数	Number of Villages with Electricity	3811	1102

Basic Statistics on Rural Areas by Region

海曙 Haishu	江东 Jiangdong	江北 Jiangbei	北仑 Beilun	镇海 Zhenhai	鄞州 Yinzhou	余姚 Yuyao	慈溪 Cixi	奉化 Fenghua	象山 Xiangshan	宁海 Ninghai
		4	9	2	18	15	17	6	15	16
		4	7	2	17	14	17	6	10	12
			2		1	1			5	4
2	1			4	4	6	3	5	3	4
10	15			25	43	4	29		36	
16	3	110	259	40	653	269	317	580	712	832
0.01		0.10	0.17	0.11	0.44	0.43	0.75	0.47	0.43	0.46
3.45	1.89	4.69	9.66	7.61	32.57	23.15	40.18	13.60	13.90	16.33
0.04	0.13	3.84	6.70	3.82	20.96	16.5	28.84	11.99	10.30	12.18
1.71	0.76		0.41	1.23	4.73	0.29	2.57		1.69	
1.70	0.99	0.85	0.85	2.62	5.55	1.09	9.33	0.59	0.29	1.23
8.39	4.27	11.19	25.84	19.24	81.70	68.46	114.23	38.14	41.90	50.59
3.08	1.58			3.04	11.61	0.80	7.32		3.77	
4.04	2.38	2.41	2.43	7.99	15.21	3.31	27.11	1.78	0.81	3.41
16	3	110	246	40	641	262	310	539	677	745
16	3	110	259	40	646	269	316	574	679	825
16	3	110	259	40	653	269	316	580	712	830
16	3	110	259	40	653	269	316	580	712	826
16	3	110	259	40	653	269	316	580	712	832

2-3　各县(市)、区农村劳动力资源情况

单位:万人　　　　(2003)

项目	Item	全市 Total	市区 Urban District
农村劳动力资源总数	**Total Rural Labor Force**	**302.95**	**92.18**
劳动年龄内的人口数	Number of Population in Working Age	287.77	88.45
#劳动年龄内上学的学生数	Students Enrollmet	10.39	2.64
劳动年龄内丧失劳动能力的人口数	Lose Labour Capacity	3.76	1.11
不足或超过劳动年龄而参加劳动的人口数	Number of Population Insufficient or Exceeding Work Age	18.94	4.84
农村实有劳动力合计	**Rural Laborers**	**290.30**	**89.05**
#外出劳动力	Laborers Going Outside	33.81	11.57
#出省的劳动力	Going to Other Province	8.08	1.05
按性别分	Grouped by Sex		
男劳动力	Male	154.84	46.85
女劳动力	Female	135.46	42.20
按部门分	Grouped by Sector		
农、林、牧、渔业	Farming, Forestry, Animal Husbandry & Fishery	87.04	21.03
农业	Farming	72.11	18.37
林业	Forestry	4.10	0.96
牧业	Animal Husbandry	3.84	0.90
渔业	Fishery	6.99	0.80
工业	Industry	118.43	37.87
建筑业	Construction	16.65	2.77
交通运输、仓储业及邮电通讯业	Transportation, Storage, Post &Telecommunications	10.68	3.42
批发和零售业	Wholesale, Retail Sale & Catering Trades	15.11	4.32
餐饮业	Catering Trades	5.94	1.89
其它非农行业	Other Non-agricultural Trades	36.45	17.75
#外出临时工、合同工	Contract or Temporary Workers Going Outside	13.71	8.34
附报:外来劳动力	**Labor from Other Places**	**59.50**	**23.89**

Rural Labor Force by Region

(10000 persons)

海曙 Haishu	江东 Jiangdong	江北 Jiangbei	北仑 Beilun	镇海 Zhenhai	鄞州 Yinzhou	余姚 Yuyao	慈溪 Cixi	奉化 Fenghua	象山 Xiangshan	宁海 Ninghai
6.50	**2.32**	**7.64**	**15.82**	**13.04**	**45.34**	**47.38**	**75.55**	**25.61**	**29.11**	**33.12**
6.29	2.26	7.16	14.98	12.74	43.60	44.96	70.97	24.57	27.65	31.17
0.13	0.05	0.19	0.57	0.21	1.44	2.23	3.30	0.56	0.90	0.76
0.02		0.07	0.21	0.09	0.71	0.62	0.77	0.42	0.39	0.45
0.23	0.06	0.55	1.05	0.39	2.45	3.04	5.35	1.46	1.85	2.40
6.37	**2.26**	**7.37**	**15.15**	**12.58**	**43.81**	**42.97**	**73.08**	**24.90**	**28.02**	**32.28**
2.51	0.13	0.68	2.48	0.89	4.75	3.68	2.51	3.73	5.25	7.07
0.04	0.01	0.03	0.53	0.07	0.36	0.56	1.13	0.44	1.73	3.17
3.43	1.16	3.89	7.98	6.48	23.13	22.85	38.65	13.17	16.13	17.19
2.94	1.10	3.48	7.17	6.10	20.68	20.12	34.43	11.73	11.89	15.09
0.18	0.30	1.47	4.61	1.81	12.53	11.77	16.30	11.30	14.49	12.15
0.13	0.29	1.18	4.13	1.55	11.00	9.69	14.84	9.35	11.12	8.74
		0.13	0.05	0.06	0.72	1.10	0.30	0.92	0.26	0.56
0.05	0.01	0.12	0.14	0.16	0.41	0.61	0.38	0.42	0.48	1.05
		0.04	0.29	0.04	0.40	0.37	0.78	0.61	2.63	1.80
2.44	0.92	2.98	5.38	5.57	19.88	19.22	38.95	8.00	3.88	10.51
0.27	0.07	0.21	0.69	0.34	1.11	3.17	3.25	0.96	3.64	2.86
0.18	0.19	0.25	0.66	0.39	1.67	1.67	2.91	0.80	0.82	1.06
0.22	0.17	0.32	1.11	0.31	2.12	1.84	4.89	1.27	0.81	1.98
0.17	0.08	0.12	0.33	0.30	0.82	0.99	1.30	0.50	0.49	0.77
2.91	0.53	2.02	2.37	3.86	5.68	4.31	5.48	2.07	3.89	2.95
2.46	0.14	1.34	1.13	0.74	2.40	1.53	1.10	1.03	0.60	1.11
3.16	**1.30**	**1.82**	**1.68**	**5.70**	**9.93**	**7.89**	**23.46**	**1.24**	**0.53**	**2.49**

2-4　主要年份农村劳动力构成

Structure of Rural Labor Force in Main Years

单位:万人　　　　　(10000 persons)

年份 Year	乡村实有劳动力 Rural Labor force	第一产业 Primary Industry		第二产业 Secondary Industry		第三产业 Tertiary Industry	
		人数 Number	比重(%) Proportion	人数 Number	比重(%) Proportion	人数 Number	比重(%) Proportion
1978	195.42						
1979	196.47						
1980	197.16						
1981	197.91						
1982	201.95						
1983	211.75						
1984	225.96						
1985	234.79	131.71	56.10	80.37	34.23	22.71	9.67
1986	240.88	130.51	54.18	85.73	35.59	24.64	10.23
1987	246.55	131.22	53.22	90.79	36.82	24.54	9.96
1988	250.35	132.86	53.07	90.64	36.21	26.85	10.72
1989	252.37	138.57	54.91	85.19	33.76	28.61	11.33
1990	254.12	142.33	56.01	81.83	32.20	29.96	11.79
1991	256.36	141.80	55.31	83.49	32.57	31.07	12.12
1992	260.65	141.29	54.21	82.79	31.76	36.57	14.03
1993	261.89	132.39	50.55	87.99	33.60	41.51	15.85
1994	263.13	126.79	48.19	89.13	33.87	47.21	17.94
1995	260.40	116.99	44.93	91.08	34.98	52.33	20.09
1996	260.37	115.02	44.18	93.06	35.74	52.29	20.08
1997	259.99	110.34	42.44	93.18	35.84	56.47	21.72
1998	259.23	109.77	42.35	91.96	35.47	57.50	22.18
1999	257.77	105.86	41.07	93.36	36.22	58.55	22.71
2000	257.44	99.83	38.78	97.90	38.03	59.71	23.19
2001	266.14	95.70	35.96	107.68	40.46	62.76	23.58
2002	270.04	92.29	34.17	114.46	42.39	63.29	23.44
2003	290.30	87.04	29.98	135.08	46.53	68.18	23.49

2-5 主要年份农林牧渔总产值

Gross Output Value of Farming, Forestry, Animal Husbandry and Fishery in Main Years

单位:亿元 (100 million yuan)

年份 Year	农林牧渔业总产值 Gross Output Value	农业产值 Farming	林业产值 Forestry	牧业产值 Animal Husbandry	渔业产值 Fishery	农林牧渔业服务业
1978	8.83					
1979	10.93					
1980	11.70					
1981	11.07					
1982	14.79					
1983	14.81					
1984	19.68					
1985	21.89	15.40	0.83	3.53	2.13	
1986	24.31	16.85	0.93	4.26	2.27	
1987	28.99	19.47	1.13	5.71	2.68	
1988	36.23	23.41	1.28	7.53	4.01	
1989	40.98	27.37	1.52	8.31	3.78	
1990	40.68	26.94	1.30	8.30	4.14	
1991	45.86	29.35	1.74	8.42	6.35	
1992	51.47	31.51	1.57	9.59	8.80	
1993	69.89	40.29	2.40	11.75	15.45	
1994	96.40	51.60	3.00	17.26	24.54	
1995	123.95	67.22	4.18	20.71	31.84	
1996	138.65	75.77	3.92	22.85	36.11	
1997	129.44	67.19	4.22	21.65	36.38	
1998	136.36	71.92	4.09	20.53	39.82	
1999	142.82	73.04	4.34	20.16	45.28	
2000	148.37	71.57	4.59	20.45	51.76	
2001	156.43	74.31	5.14	22.21	54.77	
2002	163.31	73.65	4.92	24.25	60.49	
2003	173.75	77.42	5.03	26.03	63.10	2.17

注:本表按现行价格计算。
Note: Data in this table are calculated at current prices.

2－6　分地区农林业牧渔业总产值

单位：万元　　　　　　　　　　　　　　　　　　(2003)

项目	Item	全市 Total	市区 Urban District	海曙 Haishu
合计	**Gross Output Value**	**1737503**	**417487**	**4509**
农业产值	**Farming**	**774236**	**238322**	**1474**
#副产品产值	By－products	5482	1106	2
粮食作物	Grain	108084	28684	79
谷物	Cereal	84790	26412	79
豆类	Beans	17428	1685	
薯类	Tubers	5866	587	
油料	Oil－bearing Crops	10036	1485	
棉花	Cotton	9811	169	
甘蔗	Sugarcane	10289	1358	9
药材类	Crude Drugs	19299	17280	
蔬菜、瓜类	Vegetables & Melon Crops	263173	76927	645
食用菌	Edible Mushroom	1331	730	
花卉园艺	Flower & Horticulture	124183	49141	517
茶、桑、果	Tea,Mulberry & Fruits	200326	45711	37
其他	Others	24673	16474	187
采集野生作物	Wild Plant Collected	3031	363	
林业产值	**Forestry**	**50297**	**11752**	
人造林木生长	Artificial Forestry	7375	1352	
林产品	Forest Products	33414	7637	
村及村以下竹木采伐	Lumbering	9508	2763	
牧业产值	**Animal Husbandry**	**260277**	**99139**	**3031**
牲畜	Livestock Raising	93197	39707	1997
家禽饲养	Poultry Raising	55757	16816	45
活的畜禽产品	Livestock Products	81565	35590	960
捕猎野兽野禽	Hunting Wild Beast and Wild Fowl	683	3	
其他动物饲养	Other Animals Raising	29075	7023	29
渔业产值	**Fishery**	**630985**	**60010**	**4**
海水产品	Seawater	543347	43537	
淡水产品	Freshwater	87638	16473	4

注：本表按当年价格计算。

Gross Output Value of arming,Forestry,Animal Husbandry and Fishery by Region

(10000 yuan)

	江东 Jiangdong	江北 Jiangbei	北仑 Beilun	镇海 Zhenhai	鄞州 Yinzhou	余姚 Yuyao	慈溪 Cixi	奉化 Fenghua	象山 Xiangshan	宁海 Ninghai
	4809	**51669**	**95484**	**52046**	**208970**	**277571**	**265719**	**166106**	**405938**	**204682**
	2111	**25704**	**48004**	**27089**	**133940**	**182843**	**163785**	**64588**	**66155**	**58543**
		159	114	191	640	1055	1594	548	516	663
	18	4602	1979	4116	17890	24864	20398	10721	9520	13897
	18	4599	1141	3480	17095	20540	8872	10185	7536	11245
			706	608	371	3096	9587	298	962	1800
		3	132	28	424	1228	1939	238	1022	852
		62	294	107	1022	1676	4818	132	850	1075
			68	12	89	3588	4492		88	1474
		61	40	94	1154	1832	1999	82	4785	233
					17280	783	1100	13	100	23
	2052	9069	7339	11544	46278	83887	61836	8494	17532	14497
		88	593	49		123		273	146	59
	16	3736	26452	6342	12078	26380	22144	20711	5016	791
	17	4277	11239	4324	25817	38300	46914	18846	24342	26213
	8	3798		149	12332	1013	84	3932	3139	31
		11		352		397		1384	637	250
		2165	**1835**	**493**	**7259**	**12868**	**1141**	**13810**	**3601**	**7125**
		437	297	154	464	1558	40	1426	1677	1322
		1476	558	131	5472	9444	240	11126	1092	3875
		252	980	208	1323	1866	861	1258	832	1928
	2698	**15435**	**18499**	**19458**	**40018**	**45870**	**32504**	**23345**	**26687**	**32732**
	1656	8185	40	6331	21498	17641	8149	7284	10921	9495
	19	3241	2570	4821	6120	16205	6203	3629	5796	7108
	673	3785	11999	6865	11308	4828	6953	11206	9161	13827
		3				300		42		338
	350	221	3890	1441	1092	6896	11199	1184	809	1964
		7365	**24932**	**4706**	**23003**	**33990**	**61089**	**61907**	**308607**	**105382**
		5816	22587	3780	11354	5903	38398	55759	297668	102082
		1549	2345	926	11649	28087	22691	6148	10939	3300

Note: Data in this table are calculated at current prices.

2-7 部分年份农林业牧渔业分项产值

Gross Output Value of arming, Forestry, Animal Husbandry and Fishery by Branch in Partial Years

单位:万元 (10000 yuan)

项目	Item	1995	1998	2001	2002	2003
合计	**Gross Output Value**	**1239545**	**1363579**	**1564251**	**1633107**	**1737503**
农业产值	**Farming**	**672219**	**719193**	**743073**	**736488**	**774236**
#副产品产值	By - products	10666	11424	6900	6136	5482
粮食作物	Grain	261366	267697	148283	123600	108084
谷物	Cereal	241111	239576	124870	102801	84790
豆类	Beans	9450	14961	17932	15649	17428
薯类	Tubers	10805	13160	5481	5150	5866
油料	Oil - bearing Crops	20274	15179	12994	11249	10036
棉花	Cotton	38915	35106	11600	8836	9811
甘蔗	Sugarcane	5173	5586	9329	10802	10289
药材类	Crude Drugs	4553	2031	5922	11161	19299
蔬菜、瓜类	Vegetables & Melon Crops	148747	177533	257666	271235	263173
食用菌	Edible Mushroom		786	413	950	1331
花卉园艺	Flower & Horticulture			64704	94376	124183
茶、桑、果	Tea, Mulberry & Fruits	72870	85330	143179	166031	200326
其他	Others	35487	50612	14759	36133	24673
采集野生作物	Wild Plant Collected	7026	4246	2587	2115	3031
林业产值	**Forestry**	**41805**	**40863**	**51411**	**49218**	**50297**
人造林木生长	Artificial Forestry	4843	6590	10607	8686	7375
林产品	Forest Products	14761	15421	25318	27874	33414
村及村以下竹木采伐	Lumbering	22201	18852	15486	12658	9508
牧业产值	**Animal Husbandry**	**207055**	**205323**	**222069**	**242528**	**260277**
牲畜	Livestock Raising	110135	102316	97479	100449	93197
家禽饲养	Poultry Raising	22970	25533	40498	48810	55757
活的畜禽产品	Livestock Products	61200	57357	58187	63484	81565
捕猎野兽野禽	Hunting Wild Beast and Wild Fowl	131	904	948	485	683
其他动物饲养	Other Animals Raising	12619	19213	24957	29300	29075
渔业产值	**Fishery**	**318466**	**398200**	**547698**	**604873**	**630985**
海水产品	Seawater	282386	349113	484027	526498	543347
淡水产品	Freshwater	36080	49087	63671	78375	87638

注:本表按当年价格计算。
Note: Data in this table are calculated at current prices.

2－8 分地区农林牧渔业商品产值

Output Value of Farming,Forestry,Animal Husbandry and Fisery Commodities by Region

单位:万元　　　　(2003)　　　　(10000 yuan)

地区	Region	总计 Total	农业 Farming	林业 Forestry	牧业 Animal Husbandry	渔业 Fishery
全市	**Whole Municipality**	**1428795**	**567902**	**34622**	**224136**	**602135**
市区	Urban Area	337394	183269	8770	88443	56912
余姚	Yuyao	221036	136966	10508	41032	5621
慈溪	Cixi	208842	120210	927	28571	37056
奉化	Fenghua	131660	45979	8299	16897	54645
象山	Xiangshan	364339	47091	1559	22275	283293
宁海	Ninghai	165524	34387	4559	26918	96978

2－9 分地区农林牧渔业商品产值率

Commodity Rate Output Value of Farming,Forestry,Animal Husbandry and Fisery by Region

单位:%　　　　(2003)　　　　(%)

地区	Region	总计 Total	农业 Farming	林业 Forestry	牧业 Animal Husbandry	渔业 Fishery
全市	**Whole Municipality**	**83.7**	**73.4**	**80.7**	**86.1**	**95.4**
市区	Urban Area	82.8	77.0	84.3	89.2	94.8
余姚	Yuyao	80.7	74.9	92.9	89.5	95.7
慈溪	Cixi	80.8	73.4	84.2	87.9	96.8
奉化	Fenghua	81.2	71.3	67.0	72.4	97.7
象山	Xiangshan	90.3	71.2	81.0	83.5	95.1
宁海	Ninghai	81.8	58.8	78.6	82.2	94.6

2－10 农林牧渔业增加值

Value Added of Farming, Forestry, Animal Husbandry and Fishery

单位:万元 (2003) (10000 yuan)

项目	Item	总产值 Gross Output Value	中间消耗 Depreciation	增加值 Value－added	增加值率(%) Value－adding Rate
总计	**Total**	**1737503**	**615231**	**1122272**	**64.59**
农业	Farming	774236	170800	603436	77.94
林业	Forestry	50297	14819	35478	70.54
牧业	Animal Husbandry	260277	150967	109310	42.00
渔业	Fishery	630985	270057	360928	57.20
服务业	Services	21708	8588	13120	60.44

2－11 分地区农林牧渔业增加值

Value Added of Farming, Forestry, Animal Husbandry and Fishery by Region

单位:万元 (2003) (10000 yuan)

地区	Region	增加值 Value－added	农业 Farming	固定资产折旧 Depreciation of Fixed Assets	劳动者报酬 Compensation of Labourers	中间消耗 Intermediate Consumption
全市	**Whole Municipality**	**1122272**	**603436**	**47201**	**881317**	**615231**
市区	Urban Area	280935	181422	16655	234543	136552
余姚	Yuyao	196715	150466	2650	139667	80856
慈溪	Cixi	181897	125777	4276	139963	83822
奉化	Fenghua	103681	51538	5201	76409	62425
象山	Xiangshan	217329	50781	14569	156720	188609
宁海	Ninghai	141715	43452	3850	134015	62967

2-12 主要年份农作物播种面积及产量

Sown Areas and Yield of Major Farm Crops in Main Years

单位：面积：千公顷　　Sown: 1000 hectares
产量：万吨　　Yield: 10000 tons

年份 Year	农作物播种面积 Sown Area	粮食 Grain Crops		棉花 Cotton		油料 Oil-bearing Crops		蔬菜 Vegetables Crops	
		面积 Area	产量 Yield	面积 Area	产量 Yield	面积 Area	产量 Yield	面积 Area	产量 Yield
1978	638.43	422.61	180.51						
1979	638.61	420.13	196.36						
1980	625.37	413.95	171.60						
1981	622.19	396.91	153.88						
1982	626.41	402.19	191.11						
1983	624.95	410.17	166.30	51.88	4.79	40.21	5.97		
1984	616.76	410.39	213.70	51.36	6.98	32.96	5.99		
1985	612.90	380.39	188.52	48.13	3.91	44.45	7.99	34.57	143.97
1986	596.50	361.81	188.65	41.39	3.66	48.70	8.41	36.09	158.75
1987	595.54	372.05	185.23	34.27	2.95	45.09	7.77	42.89	166.61
1988	580.01	369.58	189.98	34.65	1.80	46.70	8.47	41.01	161.74
1989	579.97	360.69	183.84	31.30	2.07	49.44	7.55	47.79	151.00
1990	591.03	368.77	189.06	34.55	3.34	52.51	9.50	48.79	135.64
1991	587.53	372.02	205.63	33.84	3.84	52.08	9.19	44.58	135.36
1992	572.68	357.66	181.62	33.03	2.59	49.15	8.62	46.82	126.89
1993	522.02	317.08	175.44	27.37	2.36	32.28	6.13	52.73	152.20
1994	504.73	308.04	172.51	26.93	2.07	30.17	4.84	56.37	162.65
1995	512.08	316.57	172.76	27.59	2.48	40.29	7.34	50.04	144.62
1996	519.48	318.99	190.30	27.14	2.73	40.37	8.00	54.20	164.26
1997	502.21	316.44	173.73	24.19	1.53	35.27	6.81	51.86	158.10
1998	510.73	317.76	180.39	25.81	2.69	34.21	5.05	58.01	174.67
1999	504.82	308.98	173.67	14.75	1.59	36.16	7.37	69.73	207.62
2000	445.90	246.79	132.51	9.69	1.05	32.58	6.59	82.16	243.70
2001	406.64	200.16	112.17	10.20	1.18	27.28	5.59	99.25	299.22
2002	386.85	172.34	94.89	6.85	0.80	24.51	4.76	104.71	291.67
2003	348.64	136.73	75.61	6.55	0.76	19.98	4.21	98.86	275.04

2-13 各县(市)、区农作物播种面积和产量

单位:公顷,吨 (2003)

项目	Item	全市 Total	市区 Urban District	海曙 Haishu
农作物播种面积总计	**Sown Area of Farm Crops**	**348635**	**110378**	**582**
粮食作物播种面积	**Sown Area of Grain Crops**	**136733**	**37103**	**100**
总产量	Total Yield of Grain Grops	756137	244347	628
谷物面积	Sown Area of Cereal	101104	34109	100
总产量	Yield of Cereal	645039	231381	628
稻谷面积	Sown Area of Rice	91370	33296	100
总产量	Yield of Rice	608135	227496	628
#早稻面积	Sown Area of Early Rice	15834	6908	33
总产量	Yield of Early Rice	93813	40434	175
晚稻及单季稻	Sown Area of Late Rice & Single Season Rice	75536	26388	67
总产量	Yield Late Rice & Single Season Rice	514322	187062	453
小麦面积	Sown Area of Wheat	2140	28	
总产量	Yield of Wheat	5898	104	
大麦面积	Sown Area of Barley	1369	232	
总产量	Yield of Barley	4083	788	
豆类面积	Sown Area of Beans	31479	2491	
总产量	Yield of Beans	79594	7767	
蕃薯面积	Sown Area of Yam	4150	503	
总产量	Yield of Yam	31504	5199	
油料播种面积	**Sown Area of Oil-bearing Crops**	**19979**	**2726**	
总产量	Yield of Oil-bearing Crops	42053	7001	
油菜籽	Sown Area of Rapeseeds	14879	2066	
总产量	Yield of Rapeseeds	25809	3816	
花生	Sown Area of Peanuts	4347	656	
总产量	Yield of Peanuts	14928	3177	
芝麻	Sown Area of Sesame	753	4	

Total Sown Area and Yield of Major Farm Crops by Region

(hectare, ton)

江东 Jiangdong	江北 Jiangbei	北仑 Beilun	镇海 Zhenhai	鄞州 Yinzhou	余姚 Yuyao	慈溪 Cixi	奉化 Fenghua	象山 Xiangshan	宁海 Ninghai
1001	**15549**	**14605**	**13123**	**65518**	**64498**	**86761**	**24902**	**30240**	**31856**
19	**6599**	**2474**	**4967**	**22944**	**26558**	**31051**	**12120**	**13275**	**16626**
128	43122	11790	33291	155388	162434	125016	73731	66719	83890
19	6597	1225	4271	21897	22578	12176	11136	9432	11673
128	43104	7875	29850	149796	146269	69012	71084	55505	71788
19	6534	1116	4143	21384	20879	6914	10936	8984	10361
128	42923	7414	29050	147353	138751	49414	70348	54114	68012
	2006	117	978	3774	5815	687	1252	1172	
	11620	632	5834	22173	35977	4229	6474	6699	
19	4528	999	3165	17610	15064	6227	9684	7812	10361
128	31303	6782	23216	125180	102774	45185	63874	47415	68012
		1		27	72	1326	1	25	688
		2		102	224	3947	3	76	1544
	63	2	6	161	209	758	3	103	64
	181	7	19	581	702	2068	10	365	150
		1135	657	699	3270	18106	793	2602	4217
		2886	2602	2279	11407	46562	1495	4568	7795
	2	114	39	348	710	769	191	1241	736
	18	1029	839	3313	4758	9442	1152	6646	4307
	199	**603**	**216**	**1708**	**2928**	**9891**	**265**	**1290**	**2879**
	302	1191	454	5054	6401	20244	535	3192	4680
	199	537	189	1141	2275	7328	100	760	2350
	302	930	353	2231	4095	13061	142	1291	3404
		63	26	567	563	1973	159	496	500
		255	99	2823	2145	6101	384	1874	1247
		3	1		90	590	6	34	29

项目	Item	全市 total	市区 Urban District	海曙 Haishu
总产量	Yield of Sesame	1316	8	
棉花(皮棉)播种面积	**Sown Area of Cotton**	**6549**	**149**	
总产量	Yield of Cotton	7567	156	
甘蔗播种面积	**Sown Area of Sugarcane**	**1747**	**267**	**1**
总产量	Yield of Sugarcane	113482	15406	94
药材类播种面积	**Sown Area of Medicinal Material**	**2035**	**523**	
总产量	Yield of Medicinal Material	2291	1297	
蔬菜类播种面积	**Sown Area of Vegetables**	**98856**	**27084**	**256**
总产量	Yield of Vegetables	2750438	795694	4677
食用菌产量	**Edible Mushroom**	**2045**	**1598**	
果用瓜播种面积	**Sown Area of Melon as Fruits**	**20961**	**6832**	**19**
总产量	Yield of Melon as Fruits	642901	219311	449
西瓜播种面积	Sown Area of Watermelon	17451	6079	17
总产量	Yield of Watermelon	566915	198342	407
草莓面积	Sown Area of Strawberry	1240	211	
总产量	Yield of Strawberry	20637	5110	
花卉园艺	**Flowers and Horticulture**			
花卉苗木播种面积	Sown Area of Flowers and Plants Nursery Stock	27731	13290	46
花卉面积	Sown Area of Flowers	13896	8631	29
苗木面积	Sown Area of Plants Nursery Stock	13414	4427	17
盆栽类园艺(万盆)	Potted Horticulture	515	164	1
其他农作物播种面积	**Sown Area of Other Farm Crops**	**34044**	**22404**	**160**
绿肥面积	Sown Area of Green Manure	8077	4635	23
席草面积	Sown Area of Rush	13645	11235	50
总产量	Yield of Rush	111674	92140	743

continued (hectare, ton)

江东 Jiangdong	江北 Jiangbei	北仑 Beilun	镇海 Zhenhai	鄞州 Yinzhou	余姚 Yuyao	慈溪 Cixi	奉化 Fenghua	象山 Xiangshan	宁海 Ninghai
		6	2		161	1082	9	27	29
		78	**13**	**58**	**2029**	**3342**		**71**	**958**
		66	11	79	2314	3941		95	1061
	12	**7**	**24**	**223**	**361**	**344**	**29**	**665**	**81**
	943	395	1149	12825	22895	23525	1056	47854	2746
				523	**147**	**1269**	**4**	**79**	**13**
				1297	603	266	7	89	29
950	**2942**	**2912**	**3852**	**16172**	**23894**	**25911**	**4221**	**9975**	**7771**
25179	83223	61155	107256	514204	830568	637484	80897	212506	193289
	78	**1440**	**80**		**130**	**5**		**237**	**75**
9	**753**	**683**	**953**	**4415**	**1698**	**7084**	**1056**	**2079**	**2212**
243	14584	17962	23129	162644	68046	176979	25961	37365	115239
9	715	624	644	4070	1365	5374	758	1718	2157
243	13813	16501	17908	149470	58482	144274	20718	30831	114268
	6	5	113	87	30	589	236	157	17
	100	125	2528	2357	445	8163	4204	2420	295
5	1153	7309	1298	3479	3908	4458	3752	1637	686
3	356	6180	373	1690	1766	1227	1258	938	76
2	690	1112	914	1692	2115	3195	2382	685	610
	90	15	20	38	256	20	33	21	21
18	**3891**	**539**	**1800**	**15996**	**2975**	**3411**	**3455**	**1169**	**630**
	646	41	999	2926	1191	102	1297	268	584
	1441		40	9704	512	56	1842		
	10013			81384	6150	616	12768		

2－14　各县(市)、区耕地面积情况

单位:公顷　　　　　　　　　　　　　　　　　(2003)

项目	Item	全市 Total	市区 Urban District	海曙 Haishu
上年年末数	**Cultivated Area at last－Year**	**211965.0**	**65213.0**	**333.3**
本年内增加数	**Increased Area in the Year**	**4120.5**	**2096.0**	
围垦海涂	Reclaim Land from Tideland	280.3	280.3	
开荒	Bring Barren under Cultivation	1029.6	605.9	
土地整理	Recultivation	2318.8	915.2	
其他	Others	491.8	294.6	
本年内减少数	**Decreased Area in the Year**	**5031.8**	**2893.2**	**59.9**
国家基建占地	State Capital Construction	2351.5	2137.2	44.1
县以上兴修水利	Build Water Conservancy Projects	77.8	34.0	
铁路	Railway			
公路	Highway	122.6	54.0	2.0
其他	Others	2151.1	2049.2	42.1
乡村基建占地	Village Capital Construction	2424.2	735.0	15.8
乡村兴修水利	Build Water Conservancy Projects in the Rural Area	6.0	2.0	
农户建房	Building Room of Peasant Households	102.7	66.7	1.5
农村道路	Rural Road	42.6	2.0	
乡镇企业	Township Enterprise	1982.2	527.8	5.8
其他	Others	290.7	136.5	8.5
退耕还林面积	Conceding the Land to Forestry	225.3		
改桑、茶、果园面积	Construction for Mulberry, Tea and Fruit Areas			
挖鱼塘占地	Construction for Digging Fish Groad			
其他占地	Others	30.8	21.0	
本年年末数	**Cultivated Area at Year－end**	**211053.7**	**64415.8**	**273.4**
水田	Paddy Fields	145243.4	53125.8	264.0
旱地	Dry Fields	65810.3	11290.0	9.4

Change of Cultivated Area by Region

(hectares)

江东 Jiangdong	江北 Jiangbei	北仑 Beilun	镇海 Zhenhai	鄞州 Yinzhou	余姚 Yuyao	慈溪 Cixi	奉化 Fenghua	象山 Xiangshan	宁海 Ninghai
238.9	**7726.0**	**13503.0**	**8925.8**	**33976.0**	**38998.7**	**43614.7**	**21398.2**	**19928.0**	**22812.4**
	27.9	**881.8**	**430.3**	**756.0**	**704.7**	**712.5**	**300.5**	**143.0**	**163.8**
			280.3						
	8.2	426.7		171.0	300.2		75.5		48.0
	13.1	455.1	150.0	297.0	404.5	641.2	101.9	143.0	113.0
	6.6			288.0		71.3	123.1		2.8
33.6	**330.4**	**989.1**	**358.2**	**1122.0**	**704.7**	**850.7**	**273.6**	**75.0**	**234.6**
23.8	209.2	989.1	330.0	541.0	36.0	31.0	59.2	75.0	13.1
				34.0	36.0		7.8		
	2.4		8.6	41.0		25.9	39.6		3.1
23.8	206.8	989.1	321.4	466.0		5.1	11.8	75.0	10.0
9.8	121.2		28.2	560.0	668.7	795.3	203.7		21.5
				2.0		4.0			
	0.1		0.1	65.0	4.6	29.6	0.8		1.0
				2.0		40.1			0.5
5.2	93.7		11.1	412	664.1	567.5	202.9		19.9
4.6	27.4		17.0	79.0		154.1			0.1
						14.6	10.7		200.0
				21.0		9.8			
205.3	**7423.5**	**13395.7**	**8997.9**	**33610.0**	**38998.7**	**43476.5**	**21425.1**	**19996.0**	**22741.6**
118.4	6838.7	9206.7	6076.0	30380.0	30788.0	10076.8	19309.0	16354.0	15589.8
86.9	584.8	4189.0	2921.9	3230.0	8210.7	33399.7	2116.1	3642.0	7151.8

2-15 农业机械年末拥有量

(2003)

项目		Item		全市 Total
农业机械总动力	**(千瓦)**	**Total Power of AgriculturalMachinery**	**(kw)**	**2024864**
耕作机械		**Cultivation Machinery**		
耕作机械动力合计	(台)	Mechanical Power of Cultivation	(unit)	25893
	(千瓦)		(kw)	247890
大中型拖拉机	(台)	Large and Medium Sized Tractors	(unti)	1192
	(千瓦)		(kw)	27589
农用小型拖拉机	(台)	Mini - tractors for Agriculture	(unit)	22301
	(千瓦)		(kw)	199400
收获机械		**Harvest Machinery**		
收获机械动力合计	(台)	Mechanical Power of Harvesting	(unit)	121679
	(千瓦)		(kw)	271534
联合收割机	(台)	Combine Harvesters	(unit)	3540
	(千瓦)		(kw)	55421
谷物烘干机	(台)	Cereal Dryer	(unit)	86
植保机械		**Plant Protection Machinery**		
植保机械动力合计	(台)	Mechanical Power of Plant Protection	(unit)	27511
	(千瓦)		(kw)	35449
机动喷雾(粉)器	(架)	Motorized Sprayer	(unit)	26759
	(千瓦)		(kw)	34060
排灌机械		**Drainage &Irrigation Machinery**		
排灌机械动力	(台)	Mechanical Power of Drainage and Irrigation	(unit)	40931
	(千瓦)		(kw)	245870
农用水泵	(台)	Water Pump for Agricultural Use	(unit)	37514
农副产品加工机械		**Processing Machinery of Agricultural Products**		
农副产品加工机械动力合计	(台)	Mechanical Power of Farm Sideline Products Manufacturing	(unit)	19383
	(千瓦)		(kw)	157433
运输机械		**Transport Machinery**		
运输机械动力	(台)	Mechanical Power of Transportation	(unit)	38013
	(千瓦)		(kw)	725986
农用运输车	(辆)	Vehicles for Agricultural Use	(unit)	12689
	(千瓦)		(kw)	274124
运输型拖拉机	(辆)	Transport Tractors	(unit)	19359
	(千瓦)		(kw)	285112
其他农用机械		**Other Mechanical**		
其他农业机械动力合计	(台)	Other Mechanical Power	(unit)	41172
	(千瓦)		(kw)	340702

Possession of Agricultural Machinery by Region (End of Year)

市区 Urban District	海曙 Haishu	江东 Jiangdong	江北 Jiangbei	北仑 Beilun	镇海 Zhenhai	鄞州 Yinzhou	余姚 Yuyao	慈溪 Cixi	奉化 Fenghua	象山 Xiangshan	宁海 Ninghai
585567	**1372**	**3734**	**50502**	**162472**	**52933**	**314554**	**412353**	**393420**	**206203**	**218830**	**208491**
8624	39	21	977	920	1226	5441	5837	3964	3603	2685	1180
82468	327	212	10809	8479	11509	51132	53766	39515	32477	29036	10628
460		3	252	38	88	79	215	209	65	212	31
8344		53	4482	758	1592	1459	5302	6056	1273	5910	704
6419	5	18	475	826	856	4239	5445	3724	3424	2208	1081
59608	21	159	4184	7264	7545	39435	47165	33279	30270	20685	9393
44251	126	52	3771	8400	6599	25303	38603	13815	10012	11866	3132
91086	351	112	11305	14663	13703	50952	83935	34512	22431	30364	9206
1589	10	2	382	152	196	847	885	260	430	265	111
24064	150	37	5416	2245	2780	13436	14227	4920	5933	5361	916
49			6		16	27	24	4	3	3	3
610			27	40	284	259	11221	13437	44	184	2015
890			48	63	462	317	12436	18399	109	409	3206
610			27	40	284	259	11221	13423	44	65	1396
890			48	63	462	317	12436	18317	109	163	2145
15536	50	33	1994	2871	1424	9164	6301	8600	3042	5031	2421
73279	432	201	12907	13201	8887	37651	60873	39045	16213	36373	20087
14841	42	33	1247	2929	1423	9167	6547	7265	2794	4029	2038
6555	18	17	450	1710	414	3946	3814	2059	1955	3114	1886
47758	201	140	4333	12956	3866	26262	30070	15418	18407	28445	17335
7657		41	294	2249	492	4581	8154	8686	4566	4173	4777
219159		3069	8286	61539	9835	100440	126493	144847	92815	76330	102332
2594			3	948	319	1324	3121	3052	1994	411	1517
58575			76	18479	7031	32989	52703	62050	36108	9564	55124
3635			223	1097	159	2156	3893	4526	1249	2945	3111
70295			3251	33698	1433	31913	54980	49862	11402	51836	46737
21077	204		187	667	238	19781	3441	7540	6418	1110	1586
106917	61		2814	51571	4671	47800	44780	101684	23751	17873	45697

2-16 各县(市)、区灌溉和水利情况

(2003)

项目		Item		全市 Total	市区 Urban District
水库年末累	(座)	Total Number of Reservoirs	(set)	401	96
总库容量	(万立方米)	Capacity	(10000 cu.m)	154574	39342
#大型水库	(座)	Large-sized Reservoirs	(set)	5	1
总库容	(万立方米)	Capacity	(10000 cu.m)	67379	11981
中型水库	(座)	Medium-sized Reservoirs	(set)	21	6
总库容	(万立方米)	Capacity	(10000 cu.m)	53204	18310
小型水库	(座)	Small-sized Reservoirs	(set)	375	89
总库容	(万立方米)	Capacity	(10000 cu.m)	33991	9051
灌溉面积总计	(千公顷)	Total Irrigated Area	(1000 hectares)	190.97	65.30
有效灌溉面积	(千公顷)	Effective Irrigated Area	(1000 hectares)	176.81	60.89
有效实灌面积	(千公顷)	Effective Fact Irrigated Area	(1000 hectares)	176.64	60.89
旱涝保收面积	(千公顷)	Famland Area of Stable Yields Despite Drought or Excessive Rain	(1000 hectares)	125.86	39.22
机电排灌面积	(千公顷)	Mechanical and Electrical Irrigated Area	(1000 hectares)	162.15	59.59
水土流失治理面积	(千公顷)	Area of Soil Erosion under Control	(1000 hectares)	131.19	27.63
水闸座数	(座)	Sluice	(set)	802	194
堤防长度	(公里)	Total Length of Dikes	(km)	1683.98	361.49
机电井眼数	(眼)	Motor-electric-pumped Well	(unit)	312	31
机电排灌站、装机容量		Mechanical and Electrical Irrigated Station, Installed Capacity		177.35	59.56
固定机电排灌站处数	(处)	Regular Mechanical and Electrical Irrigated Station	(unit)	10607	2266
装机容量	(千千瓦)	Installed Capacity	(1000 kw)	118.24	23.56
水利工程年供水量	(亿立方米)	Annually Water Supply of Water Conservancy	(100 million cu.m)	17.10	6.20
农业供水	(亿立方米)	Water Supply for Agriculture	(100 million cu.m)	7.39	2.68
工业供水	(亿立方米)	Water Supply for Industry	(100 million cu.m)	4.59	1.76
城镇生活用水	(亿立方米)	Water Supply for Urban life	(100 million cu.m)	5.13	1.78

Irrigation and Water Conservancy Facilities of Farmland by Region

海曙 Haishu	江东 Jiangdong	江北 Jiangbei	北仑 Beilun	镇海 Zhenhai	鄞州 Yinzhou	余姚 Yuyao	慈溪 Cixi	奉化 Fenghua	象山 Xiangshan	宁海 Ninghai
		5	30	5	56	50	23	89	80	63
		2179	4026	3768	29369	24069	14339	31282	12065	33477
					1	1		2		1
					11981	12354		26204		16840
			1	1	4	2	4		5	4
			1610	2300	14400	5947	8450		7411	13086
		5	29	4	51	47	19	87	75	58
		2179	2416	1468	2988	5768	5889	5078	4654	3551
0.27	0.33	6.77	16.10	8.95	32.88	38.08	32.43	19.59	19.30	16.27
0.27	0.33	6.37	14.56	7.86	31.50	36.73	32.35	19.06	15.88	11.90
0.27	0.33	6.37	14.56	7.86	31.50	36.73	32.43	19.06	15.88	11.65
0.27	0.29	3.53	10.13	2.60	22.40	27.86	27.19	16.28	8.81	6.50
0.27	0.33	6.27	14.56	7.86	30.30	33.77	31.58	11.98	16.11	9.12
			8.45	0.40	18.78	49.91	3.00	43.64	3.87	3.14
		23	20	53	98	77	26	41	398	66
12.00	10.00	33.33	140.00	33.16	133.00	479.09	82.28	78.00	187.00	496.12
			25	6			5			276
0.41	0.68	5.96	5.70	11.61	35.20	56.73	14.33	11.01	21.95	13.77
44	15	578	730	204	695	4077	870	1184	936	1274
0.37	0.13	5.40	4.79	6.03	6.84	48.90	11.37	8.66	13.56	12.19
0.04	0.11	0.41	1.30	0.73	3.61	3.34	0.91	2.81	1.97	1.88
0.04	0.08	0.38	0.42	0.64	1.12	1.84	0.17	0.93	0.84	0.96
	0.03	0.01	0.10	0.05	1.57	0.95	0.32	0.59	0.44	0.54
	0.01	0.02	0.79	0.04	0.92	0.55	0.43	1.29	0.69	0.39

2－17　各县(市)、区林业生产情况

(2003)

项目	Item	全市 total	江北 Jiangbei
营林情况(公顷)	**Afforestation(hectare)**		
造林面积合计	Total Afforestation Area	1773	181
按方式分	By Way of Afforestation		
当年人工造林面积	Area of Afforest artificially in This Year	1773	181
按用途分	By Use of Afforestation		
经济林	Economic Forest	455	
防护林	Shelter Forest	1183	181
迹地更新面积	Area of Forest Updating	633	
封山育林面积	Area of Afforestation in Enclosed Mountain	60865	1840
零星(四旁)植树(万株)	Planting Trees Piecemeal(10000 trees)	124	10
育苗面积(公顷)	Area of Growing Seedings (hectare)	1949	53
幼林抚育实际面积	Area of Tending Seedings	7579	
幼林抚育作业面积	Area of Seedings Cultivated	13999	610
成林抚育面积	Area of Grown Forest Cultivated	31049	
低产林改造面积	Area of Transform Low Yield Forest	774	
抚育改造出材量(立方米)	Output of Transform and Foster (Cubic Meter)	11359	
主要林产品产量(吨)	**Output of Major Forest Products(ton)**		
笋罐头	Bamboo Can	12470	
板栗	Chestnut	938	
竹笋干	Dried Bamboo Shoots	18350	334
竹壳	Shell of Bamboo	943	2
白果	Gingko	278	
毛料	Bamboo	2172	300
人造板	Artificial Plank	6600	

Basic Statistics on Forestry by Region

北仑 Beilun	镇海 Zhenhai	鄞州 Yinzhou	余姚 Yuyao	慈溪 Cixi	奉化 Fenghua	象山 Xiangshan	宁海 Ninghai
47	400	98	113	117	106	205	412
47	400	98	113	117	106	205	412
14		29	46		74	125	167
33	400	55	67	117	32	5	199
		56	85		97	322	73
3333	1095	15000	12000	667	4867	1333	20730
8		15	25	35	14	5	12
666	500	92	73	474	30	20	14
540	150		3354	667	1317	451	880
400			6625	700	2634	960	1630
780	150	2000	6226	1000	2393	2500	6000
	181	526			67		
8300			1531				1528
1515					10955		
8			331	40	210	15	334
360	115	2100	6239	360	6090	300	2450
	5		833		3		100
4		250	8		16		
	5		1695		35		137
							6600

2－18 各县(市)、区茶叶和水果生产情况

(2003)

项目	Item	全市 Total	市区 Urban District	海曙 Haishu
茶叶生产	**Tea**			
茶园总面积(公顷)	**Tea Field Area(hectare)**	**12696**	**3693**	
本年新增	New－added in This Year	280	81	
本年采摘	Pluck in This Year	11431	3079	
茶叶总产量(吨)	**Output of Tea (ton)**	**19154**	**7770**	
春茶	Spring Tea	10927	4118	
夏茶	Summer Tea	5370	2043	
秋茶	Autumn Tea	2857	1609	
水果生产	**Fruits**			
果园面积合计(公顷)	**Area of Orchards(hectare)**	**42374**	**6507**	
柑桔园	Citrus	13117	2413	
梨园	Pears	5001	993	
桃园	Peaches	4346	366	
杨梅园	Red Bayberry	13141	1316	
枇杷园	Loquat	1471	40	
葡萄园	Grapes	1390	368	
其他果园	Others	3571	889	
水果总产量(吨)	**Output of Fruits (ton)**	**1140565**	**320436**	**449**
柑桔	Citrus	218260	60087	
柑	Mandarin Orange	72699	6663	
桔	Mandarin	123312	43458	
橙	Orange	12321	100	
柚	Shaddock	119	100	
梨	Pears	82182	15802	
桃子	Peaches	41336	3869	
杨梅	Red Bayberry	75395	6692	
枇杷	Loquat	7152	547	
葡萄	Grapes	41284	8083	
果用瓜	Melon Used as Fruits	642901	219311	449
其他	Others	28597	3923	

Basic Statistics on Tea and Fruits Production by Region

江东 Jiangdong	江北 Jiangbei	北仑 Beilun	镇海 Zhenhai	鄞州 Yinzhou	余姚 Yuyao	慈溪 Cixi	奉化 Fenghua	象山 Xiangshan	宁海 Ninghai
	205	**1194**	**78**	**2216**	**4173**	**270**	**1016**	**1140**	**2404**
	6	38	4	33	35	29	37	36	62
	108	824	74	2073	4070	241	875	994	2172
	332	**2214**	**104**	**5120**	**5500**	**289**	**1945**	**1431**	**2219**
	176	1523	66	2353	3429	225	895	840	1420
	113	425	24	1481	1678	41	712	392	504
	43	266	14	1286	393	23	338	199	295
	838	**1552**	**684**	**3433**	**7026**	**5675**	**5204**	**11302**	**6660**
	125	985	306	1000	156	649	1288	5902	2709
	363	118	84	428	1597	1577	64	217	553
	30	107	28	201	413	353	2364	458	392
	203	230	153	730	3630	2294	509	3438	1954
	1	6	28	5	13	6	11	747	654
	24	55	57	232	421	384	92	67	58
	85	22	23	759	700	391	858	444	289
243	**23206**	**54131**	**36036**	**206371**	**149442**	**271460**	**82148**	**136841**	**180238**
	2545	26047	8934	22561	3226	11216	19634	70082	54015
		3757		2906	1119	1828	39	58968	4082
	2545	21997	5934	12982	2080	9356	19595		48823
		263		737	20			11113	188
		30		70	7			1	11
	4755	3131	1194	6722	32463	30183	604	1829	1301
	192	1475	256	1946	5865	5506	23985	1131	980
	398	3223	591	2480	20000	28268	3948	10008	6479
	5	66	454	22	85	57	79	5518	866
	486	1253	929	5415	17930	12438	379	1792	662
243	14584	17962	23429	162644	68046	176979	25961	37365	115239
	157	136	203	3427	1102	6559	7464	8952	597

2－19 各县(市)、区畜牧业生产情况

(2003)

项目	Item	全市 Total	市区 Urban District
生猪(万只)	**Hogs (10000 heads)**		
年末存栏头数(含未断奶小猪)	Being Raised at Year－end	76.47	34.68
#能繁殖的母猪	Reproducable	4.97	3.03
年内肥猪出栏头数	Slaughtered Fattened Hogs	149.08	70.23
全年饲养量	Number of Hogs Raised	225.55	104.91
牛(头)	**Cattles & Buffaloes (head)**		
年末存栏头数	Being Raised at Year－end	22146	6992
#良种及改良种乳牛	Milch Cows of Fine Breed and Improved Varieties	5681	5098
年内出栏头数	Slaughtered Cattles & Buffaloes of the Year	5057	1440
羊(万只)	**Sheep & Goat(10000 heads)**		
年末存栏只数	Being Raised at Year－end	10.14	1.34
年内出栏只数	Slaughtered Sheep & Goat of the Year	11.09	1.40
家禽(万只)	**Poultry(10000 heads)**		
年末存栏只数	Being Raised at Year－end	1903.7	567.39
年内出栏只数	Slaughtered Poultry of the Year	3422.14	1066.13
兔(万只)	**Rabbits(10000 heads)**		
年末存栏只数	Being Raised at Year－end	64.89	25.97
年内出栏只数	Slaughtered Rabbits	74.43	25.78
养蜂年末箱数(箱)	**Number of Beehives(box)**	**162315**	**8305**
家禽产品产量(吨)	**Output of Livestock Production (ton)**		
肉类产量	Output of Meat	155431	65823
猪肉	Pork	98956	48250
牛肉	Beef	717	208
羊肉	Mutton	1675	260
兔肉	Rabbits Meat	1347	590
禽肉	Poultry Meat	52293	16492
其他	Others	443	23
禽蛋产量	Poultry Eggs	136758	54287
蜂蜜产量	Honey	11962	448
蜂皇浆产量(公斤)	Royal Jelly(kg)	314369	10538
牛奶产量(吨)	Milk (ton)	22125	20981
兔毛产量	Rabbit Wool	516	359

Basic Statistics on Animal Husbandry By Region

海曙 Haishu	江东 Jiangdong	江北 Jiangbei	北仑 Beilun	镇海 Zhenhai	鄞州 Yinzhou	余姚 Yuyao	慈溪 Cixi	奉化 Fenghua	象山 Xiangshan	宁海 Ninghai
1.36	1.68	5.58	3.00	3.91	19.15	14.5	6.05	5.00	9.24	7.00
0.08	0.22	0.53		0.26	1.94	0.75	0.49		0.70	
3.40	3.09	11.03	8.00	7.98	36.73	29.01	13.51	8.00	19.33	9.00
4.76	4.77	16.61	11.00	11.89	55.88	43.51	19.56	13.00	28.57	16.00
1738	18	678	398	687	3473	1700	716	2732	2048	7958
1731	7	450	131	354	2425	58	120	219	88	98
159	20	236	267	209	549	800	173	901	112	1631
		0.06		0.26	1.02	2.80	0.90	1.00	2.10	2.00
		0.07		0.33	1.00	2.50	1.00	1.00	3.19	2.00
1.23	7.69	123.20	44.00	154.23	237.04	366.00	246.86	211.00	213.45	299.00
3.34	1.34	236.77	102.00	314.56	408.12	915.00	390.32	205.00	372.69	473.00
	0.12	1.34	3.00	12.63	8.88	8.00	21.34	3.00	4.58	2.00
0.67	0.16	1.32	7.00	11.09	5.54	6.00	28.80	6.00	4.85	3.00
		570	**1048**	**1670**	**5017**	**21000**	**90736**	**3805**	**10373**	**28096**
2611	2220	10605	7638	11342	31407	30207	15107	9415	20676	14203
2514	2175	6784	5954	5861	24962	15254	7425	5630	14658	7739
21	6	33	31	35	82	100	27	134	16	232
		13	71	26	150	350	150	248	422	245
14	5	30	148	310	83	98	432	128	41	58
62	34	3745	1434	5095	6122	14075	7021	3273	5539	5893
				15	8	330	52	2		36
193	1247	6090	18415	10570	17772	10000	10706	20154	19333	22278
		13	66	34	335	1500	7154	635	539	1686
		1526	4	5516	3492	35000	204097	3598	17011	44125
5580	9	2830	161	289	12112	100	338	605	15	86
		1	206	87	65	50	85	2	5	15

2－20 各县(市)、区水产品产量及养殖面积

单位:吨　　(2003)

项目	Item	全市 Total	市区 海曙 Haishu	江东 Jiangdong	江北 Jiangbei
水产品总产量	**Total Aquatic Products**	**903301**			**12799**
海水产品产量	**Seawater Aquatic Products**	**828816**			**11018**
按生产性质分	By Production Character				
海洋捕捞	Catching in Ocean	560991			11018
鱼类	Fish	406169			4800
虾蟹类	Shrimps.Prawns and Crabs	101934			
贝类	Shell－Fish	5914			
其他类	Others	1617			
海水养殖	Seawater Aquiculture	267825			
鱼类	Fish	18294			
虾蟹类	Shrimps.Prawns and Crabs	35989			
贝类	Shell－Fish	208604			
其他类	Others	188			
淡水产品产量	**Freshwater Aquatic Products**	**74485**			**1781**
按生产性质分	By Production Character				
淡水捕捞	Catching in Freshwater	5821			155
淡水养殖	Freshwater Aquiculture	68664			1626
按类别分	By Category				
鱼类	Fish	55126			1613
虾蟹类	Shrimps.Prawns and Crabs	14762			78
贝类	Shell－Fish	2801			
其他类	Others	1771			90
海水养殖面积(公顷)	**Seawater Aquiculture Area(ha)**	**44268.5**			
淡水养殖面积(公顷)	**Freshwater Aquiculture Area(ha)**	**21806**			**551**

Output and Area of Artificially Cultured of Aquatic Production by Region

(ton)

Urban Districts			余姚 Yuyao	慈溪 Cixi	奉化 Fenghua	象山 Xiangshan	宁海 Ninghai
北仑 Beilun	镇海 Zhenhai	鄞州 Yinzhou					
23948	**5249**	**21802**	**21951**	**53622**	**79259**	**564199**	**115860**
21524	**4455**	**10247**	**3700**	**29827**	**76199**	**554384**	**112880**
17263	3942	5010	3100	5521	42674	454100	14120
2595	3530	4230	1605	2232	38335	339678	5935
1506	247	665	335	987	911	92642	4600
15		30	624	1965	100	560	2620
25			384	337		300	
4261	513	5237	600	24306	33525	100284	98760
302	156	72	160	3132	5759	7733	980
1311	197	2334	304	5158	1908	12486	12190
2633	160	2693	136	15828	24851	76525	85540
				188			
2424	**794**	**11555**	**18251**	**23795**	**3060**	**9815**	**2980**
732	152	1183	1520	1283	546		250
1692	642	10372	16731	22512	2514	9815	2730
1482	742	8116	13740	20699	2013	5108	1608
340	27	3022	2210	2399	752	4585	1349
520	25	150	1362	421	265	35	23
82		267	939	276	30	87	
1592	**576**	**1121**	**186**	**8721**	**3154**	**13317**	**15575**
1239	**266**	**4222**	**3644**	**4962**	**1587**	**3017**	**2306**

2－21 各县(市)、区农村能源和农业物资消耗情况

单位:吨 (2003)

项目	Item	全市 Total	市区 Urban District	海曙 Haishu
农村用电量(万千瓦小时)	**Electricity Consumed for Rural(10000 kwh)**	**766120**	**271926**	**7540**
农用化肥施用量	**Agricultural Consumption of Chemical Fertilizers**			
按实物量计算	Calculated by Fact Use	397159	173074	837
氮肥	Nitrogenous Fertilizer	216266	93107	421
磷肥	Phosphate Fertilizer	92131	44626	217
钾肥	Potash Fertilizer	31257	15451	84
复合肥	Compound Fertilizer	57505	19890	115
按标准量计算	Calculated by Standard	575198	225257	1268
氮肥	Nitrogenous Fertilizer	317740	114791	737
磷肥	Phosphate Fertilizer	117725	52074	217
钾肥	Potash Fertilizer	37221	18613	84
复合肥	Compound Fertilizer	102512	39779	230
按折纯法计算	Calculated by Pure Consumption	120131	46867	267
氮肥	Nitrogenous Fertilizer	66723	24103	155
磷肥	Phosphate Fertilizer	21187	9372	40
钾肥	Potash Fertilizer	9309	4657	21
复合肥	Compound Fertilizer	22912	8735	51
农用塑料薄膜使用量	**Plastic Film Use for Agriculture**	**5859**	**2311**	**11**
# 地膜使用量	Use of Plastic Film	2944	1170	10
地膜覆盖面积(公顷)	Overcast Area of Plastic Film (hectate)	27456	9150	39
农用柴油	**Consumption of Diesel Oil**	**259138**	**17501**	**14**
农药使用量	**Consumption of Pesticide**	**6952**	**2462**	**2**

Consumption of Energy and Agriculture Materials in Rural Areas by Region

(ton)

江东 Jiangdong	江北 Jiangbei	北仑 Beilun	镇海 Zhenhai	鄞州 Yinzhou	余姚 Yuyao	慈溪 Cixi	奉化 Fenghua	象山 Xiangshan	宁海 Ninghai
6411	**30400**	**22567**	**36200**	**168808**	**140708**	**226622**	**52003**	**23524**	**51337**
1120	25054	8264	21600	116199	38442	79484	52865	33428	19866
574	14630	3524	14820	59138	24225	36254	28845	21178	12657
265	5552	2615	4833	31144	8730	18453	11405	6446	2471
142	2203	250	826	11946	1418	9157	3347	1234	650
139	2669	1875	1121	13971	4069	15620	9268	4570	4088
1541	32550	16528	43200	130170	45418	114506	89015	66856	34146
856	17372	7048	29640	59138	27132	58006	55727	42356	19728
265	5552	5230	9666	31144	8730	27683	11405	12891	4942
142	4289	500	1652	11946	1418	10073	3347	2470	1300
278	5337	3750	2242	27942	8138	18744	18536	9139	8176
323	6893	3358	8870	27156	6414	24182	18669	13842	7157
178	3648	1480	6224	12418	5698	12182	11702	8895	4143
48	999	941	1740	5604	1571	4983	2052	2319	890
37	1073	125	413	2988	355	2518	837	617	325
60	1173	812	493	6146	1790	4499	4078	2011	1799
17	**161**	**98**	**237**	**1787**	**320**	**2151**	**364**	**506**	**207**
7	85	54	117	897	65	1230	169	189	121
89	1270	120	1396	6236	760	12870	1644	1362	1670
8	**1024**	**7901**	**2922**	**5632**	**7500**	**3774**	**28423**	**191552**	**10388**
8	**226**	**156**	**827**	**1243**	**1400**	**949**	**452**	**1224**	**465**

主要指标解释

【农林牧渔业总产值】 指以货币表现的农、林、牧、渔业全部产品的总量。它反映一定时期内农业生产总规模和总成果。

农林牧渔业的统计范围是：

⑴ 农业 包括种植业和其他农业。

⑵ 林业 包括林木的栽培(不包括茶园、桑园和果园的栽培、管理和收获等活动)、林产品的采集和村及村以下合作经济和农户的竹木采伐。

⑶ 牧业 包括除渔业养殖以外的一切动物饲养和放牧以及野生动物的捕猎和饲养。

⑷ 渔业 包括水生动物和海藻类植物的养殖和捕捞。

农林牧渔业总产值的计算方法通常是按农林牧渔产品及其副产品的产量分别乘以各自单位产品价格求得，少数生产周期长，当年没有产品或产品产量不易统计，则采用间接方法匡算其产值，然后将四业产品产值相加即为农林牧渔业总产值。

1957年以前的农业总产值包括了厩肥和农名自给性手工业(如农民自制衣服、鞋、袜，自己从事粮食加工等)。1958年以后的农业总产值，林业中增加了村以及村以下的竹木采伐产值；牧业取消了厩肥产值；副业中取消了农民自给性手工业产值，增加了村以及村以下的工业产值；渔业中增加了海洋捕捞产品产值。1980年及以后的农业总产值，在副业中增加了农民家庭兼营工业商品部分的产值。从1984年起村以及村以下半工业产值划归工业。从1993年起，取消副业，将野生动物的捕猎划入牧业，野生植物采集和农民家庭兼营商品性供规划归农业。

【粮食产量】 指全社会的产量。包括国有经济经营的、集体统一经营的和农民家庭经营的粮食产量，还包括工矿企业办的农场和其他生产单位的产量。粮食除包括稻、小麦、玉米、高粱、谷子及其他杂粮外，还包括薯类和豆类。其产量计算方法，豆类按去豆荚后的干豆计算；薯类(包括甘薯和马铃薯，不包括芋头和木薯) 1963年以前按每4公斤鲜薯折1公斤粮食计算，从1964年开始及以后改为按5公斤鲜薯折1公斤粮食计算。城市郊区作为蔬菜的薯类(如:马铃薯等)按鲜品计算，并且不做为粮食统计。其他粮食一律按脱粒后的原粮计算。

【油料产量】 指全部油料作物的生产量。包括花生、油菜籽、芝麻、向日葵籽、胡麻籽(亚麻籽)和其他油料。不包括大豆，也不包括木本油料和野生油料。花生以带壳干花生计算。

【水产品产量】 指人工养殖的水产品和天然生长的水产品的捕捞量。包括海水的鱼类、虾蟹类、贝类和藻类以及内陆水域的鱼类、虾蟹类和贝类，不包括淡水生植物。

【猪、牛、羊肉产量】 指当年出栏并已屠宰后除去头蹄下水后带骨肉(即胴体重)的重量。

【耕地面积】 指年初可以用来种植农作物、经常进行耕锄的田地，除包括熟地、当年新开荒地、连续撂荒未满三年的耕地和当年的休闲地(轮歇地)外，还包括以种植农作物为主并附带种植桑树、茶树、果树和其他林木的土地，以及沿海、沿湖地区已围垦利用的“海涂”、“湖田”等面积。但不包括属于专业性的桑园、茶园、果园、果木苗圃、林地、芦苇地、天然或人工草地面积。

【农作物播种面积】 指实际播种或移植有农作物的面积。凡是实际种植有农作物的面积，不论种植在耕地上还是种植在非耕地上，均包括在农作物播种面积中，同时还包括因遭灾而重新改种和补种的农作物面积。

【农用化肥施用量】 指本年内实际用于农业生产的化肥数量。包括氮肥、磷肥、钾肥和复合肥。化肥施用量要求按折纯量计算数量。折纯法化肥施用量是把氮肥、磷肥和钾肥分别按含氮、含五氧化二磷、含氧化钾的百分之一百成份折算后的数量。复合肥按其所含主要成分折算。

【农业机械总动力】 指主要用于农、林、牧、渔业的各种动力机械的动力总和。包括耕作机械、排灌机械、收获机械、农产品加工机械、运输机械、植物保护机械、牧业机械、林业机械、渔业机械和其他农业机械内燃机按引擎马力折成瓦(特)计算，电动机按功率折成瓦(特)计算。不包括专门用于乡、镇、村、组办工业、基本建设、非农业运输、科学试验和教学等非农业生产方面用的动力机械与作业机械。

Explanatory Notes on Main Statistical Indicators

[Gross Output Value of Farming, Forestry, Animal Husbandry and Fishery] refers to the total volume of products of farming, forestry, animal husbandry and fishery in value terms, which reflects the total scale and total result of agricultural production during a given period of time.

The statistical coverage of farming, forestry, animal husbandry and fishery is as follows:

(1) Farming includes cultivation of farm crops and other agricultural activities.

(2) Forestry refers to planting trees of various kinds (excluding tea plantations, mulberry fields and orchards), gathering of the forest products, and cutting and felling of bamboo and trees by villages and other cooperative organizations under villages.

(3) Animal Husbandry refers to raising and grazing of all animals except fishery and aquaculture, and hunting and raising of wild animals.

(4) Fishery refers to cultivation and catching of fish and other aquatic animals and cultivation and collection of seaweed and other aquatic plants.

Gross output value of farming, forestry, animal husbandry and fishery is obtained by first multiplying the output of each product by its price, resulting in the output of each single item. For a small number of products, animal output of which is not available or difficult to get due to the long production/growing process involved, the output value is estimated through an indirect approach. The sum of output value of all products of farming, forestry, animal husbandry and fishery is then equal to their gross output value.

Prior to 1957, China's gross agricultural output value included barnyard manure and handicraft products for self-consumption (clothes, shoes, stockings, and initial grain processing undertaken by peasants). Since 1958, cutting and felling of bamboo and trees by villages and other cooperative organizations under villages have been included in forestry.; value of barnyard manure has been excluded from animal husbandry; self-consumed handicrafts have been excluded from sideline occupations, while the output value of industries run by villages and cooperative organizations under village has been included in sideline occupations and the output value of fish catches by motor fishing boats has been added to fishery. Since 1980, the value of handicraft products made for sale by individual in the households has been added to sideline occupations. Since 1984, industries run by villages and cooperatives organizations under villagers have been included in the sector of industry. Since 1993, the subdivision of sideline occupations has been canceled, and the hunting of wild animals has been classified into animal husbandry, and the gathering of wild plants and the gathering of wild plants and commodity industry run by rural household have been included in farming.

[Grain Yield] refers to the yield in the whole country including grains produced by state farms, collective units, industrial enterprises and mines. Grain includes rice, wheat, corn, sorghum, millet and other miscellaneous grains as well as tubers and beans. Output of beans refers to dry beans without pods. The output of tubers (sweet potatoes and potatoes, not including taros and cassava) was converted into that of grain at the ratio 4:1, I.e. Four kilograms of fresh tubers was equivalent to one kilogram of grain up to 1963. Since 1964 the ratio for conversion has been 5:1. Tubers supplied as vegetables (such as potatoes) in cities and suburbs are calculated as fresh vegetables and their output is not included in the output of grain. Output of all other grains refers to husked grain.

[Yield of Oil-bearing Crops] refers to the total yield of oil bearing crops of various kinds, including peanuts, (dry, in shell) rapeseeds, sesame, sunflower seeds, flax seeds, and other oil bearing crops. Soybeans, oil bearing woody plants, and wild oil-bearing crops are not included.

[Output of Aquatic Products] refers to catches of both artificially cultured and naturally grown aquatic products, including fish, shrimps, crabs and shellfish in sea and inland water as well as seaweed. Freshwater plants are not included.

[Output of Pork, Beef, and Mutton] refers to the meat of slaughtered hogs, cattle, sheep and goats with head, feet, and offal taken away.

[Cultivated Area (Area under cultivation)] refers to farmland which is plowed constantly for growing crops, including cultivated land, newly cultivated land in the current year, farmland left without cultivation for less than three years and fallow land in the current year, rotation land, rotation land of grass and crops, farmland with some fruit trees, mulberry trees and other trees and cultivated seashore land, lake land, and etc. The land of mulberry fields, tea plantations, orchards, nurseries of young plants, forest land, reed land, natural and man made grassland and other land are not included in cultivated land.

[Sown Area of Crops] refers to area of land sown or transplanted with crops regardless of being in cultivated area or non cultivated area. Area of land re sown due to natural disasters is also included, every sown hectare is calculated.

[Consumption of Chemical Fertilizers in Agriculture] refers to the quantity ofchemical fertilizers applied in agriculture in the year, including nitrogenous fertilizer, phosphate fertilizer, potash fertilizer and compound fertilizer. The consumption of chemical fertilizers is required in calculation to convert the gross weight into weight containing 100% effective component(e.g. 100% nitrogen content in nitrogenous fertilizer, 100% phosphorous pentoxide contents in phosphate fertilizer, 100% potassium oxide contents in potash fertilizer). Compound fertilizer is converted with its major component.

【Total Power of Farm Machinery】 refers to total mechanical power of machinery used in farming, forestry, animal husbandry, and fishery, including ploughing, irrigation and drainage, harvesting, transport, plant protection, stock breeding, forestry and fishery. The power of internal combustion engines is required to convert horsepower into watts and the power of electric motors is required to be converted into watts. Machinery employed for non agricultural purposes, such as the machines used in township run and village run industry, construction, non agricultural transport, scientific experiments and teaching, is excluded.

3

工业

CHAPTER 3 INDUSTRY

工业
Industry

主要统计指标
Major Statistics Indicators

2003 年规模以上企业数	Number of Industrial Enterprises Above Designated Size at Year - end	4672	家	unit
比上年增长	Increase Over Last Year	15.1	%	
2003 年规模以上工业总产值	Output Value of Industrial Enterprises Above Designated Size	26302862	万元	10000 yuan
比上年增长	Increase Over Last Year	31.5	%	
2003 年规模以上销售产值	Gross Industrial Products Sales of Industrial Enterprises Above Designated Size	25819475	万元	10000 yuan
比上年增长	Increase Over Last Year	32.9	%	
2003 年规模以上工业增加值	Value - added of Industrial Enterprises Above Designated Size	6053036	万元	10000 yuan
比上年增长	Increase Over Last Year	21.2	%	
2003 年规模以上实现利税	Total Profits and Taxes of Industrial Enterprises Above Designated Size	3220119	万元	10000 yuan
比上年增长	Increase Over Last Year	20.6	%	
2003 年规模以上企业实现利润	Total Profits of Industrial Enterprises Above Designated Size	1892997	万元	10000 yuan
比上年增长	Increase Over Last Year	24.3	%	
2003 年规模以上企业应交增值税	Value - added Taxes Payable of Industrial Enterprises Above Designated Size	854470	万元	10000 yuan
比上年增长	Increase Over Last Year	16.2	%	

3－1 全部国有及规模以上非国有工业企业单位数

Number of All State－owned and Non－state－owned Above Designated Size Industrial Enterprises

单位:个 (unit)

项目	Item	1999	2000	2001	2002	2003
工业企业单位数	**Number of Industrial Enterprises**	**2498**	**2803**	**3530**	**4060**	**4672**
按轻重工业分	**By Light and Heavy Industry**					
轻工业	Light Industry	1393	1542	1963	2251	2332
重工业	Heavy Industry	1105	1261	1567	1809	2340
按注册登记类型分	**By Registered Type**					
国有企业	State－owned Enterprises	146	100	54	49	43
集体企业	Collective－owned Enterprises	679	534	392	326	321
股份合作企业	Share Cooperative Enterprises	197	192	205	208	207
联营企业	Joint－owned	39	31	21	22	18
有限责任公司	Limited Liability Corporations	196	279	333	394	410
股份有限公司	Share－holding Corporations Ltd.	49	48	59	39	45
私营企业	Private Enterprises	643	990	1641	2093	2558
港澳台商投资公司	HongKong, Macao and Taiwan Funded	336	374	491	528	577
外商投资企业公司	Enterprises with Foreign Investment	213	255	334	401	490
在总计中:亏损企业	Of the Total: Loss Making Enterprises	362	295	318	320	371
在总计中:国有及国有控股	Of the Total: State－owned and State－holding Industrial Enterprises	241	202	144	148	114
在总计中:农村工业	Of the Total: Rural Industry	1665	1959	2504	3106	3463
按规模分	**By Size**					
大型企业	Large－Sized Enterprises	39	37	34	34	23
中型企业	Medium－Sized Enterprises	132	122	116	108	431
小型企业	Small－Sized Enterprises	2327	2644	3380	3918	4218

3-2 全部国有及规模以上非国有工业总产值

Gross Output Value of All State - owned and Non - state - owned Above Designated Size Industrial Enterprises

单位:万元 (10000 yuan)

项目	Item	1999	2000	2001	2002	2003
工业总产值	**Gross Industrial Output Value**	**10622865**	**14276977**	**16296574**	**20001637**	**26302862**
按轻重工业分	**By Light and Heavy Industry**					
轻工业	Light Industry	5458196	6652872	7642018	9223869	11204370
重工业	Heavy Industry	5164669	7624106	8654556	10777768	15098492
按注册登记类型分	**By Registered Type**					
国有企业	State - owned Enterprises	984893	1006234	1140380	1054879	1109306
集体企业	Collective - owned Enterprises	1898213	1571442	812819	705632	792419
股份合作企业	Share Cooperative Enterprises	513022	553706	662568	753153	820427
联营企业	Joint - owned	102654	99068	102458	108468	94536
有限责任公司	Limited Liability Corporations	731650	1610528	1896513	2814076	3287356
股份有限公司	Share - holding Corporations Ltd.	2306925	3689187	3997282	4586340	6391697
私营企业	Private Enterprises	1354819	2151257	3431000	4812764	6951380
港澳台商投资公司	HongKong, Macao and Taiwan Funded	1688207	1976240	2279452	2684180	3563627
外商投资企业公司	Enterprises with Foreign Investment	1042483	1619315	1974102	2482145	3283537
在总计中:亏损企业	Of the Total: Loss Making Enterprises	830511	717072	821116	877542	1092170
在总计中:国有及国有控股	Of the Total: State - owned and State - holding Industrial Enterprises	2775602	4178373	4153121	4342883	6432799
在总计中:农村工业	Of the Total: Rural Industry	5565750	6938626	8080884	11079017	14437306
按规模分	**By Size**					
大型企业	Large - Sized Enterprises	3229141	4780418	4916882	5126917	6479703
中型企业	Medium - Sized Enterprises	1280053	1438606	1514859	1632245	8966656
小型企业	Small - Sized Enterprises	6113671	8057954	9864833	13242475	10856503

注:工业总产值按现行价格计算。
Note: Gross industrial output value are calculated at current prices.

3－3 全部国有及规模以上非国有工业销售产值

Gross Industrial Products Sales of All State－owned and Non－state－owned Above Designated Size Industrial Enterprises

单位:万元 (10000 yuan)

项目	Item	1999	2000	2001	2002	2003
工业销售产值	**Gross Industrial Products Sales**	**10206854**	**13855876**	**15833472**	**19426768**	**25819475**
按轻重工业分	**By Light and Heavy Industry**					
轻工业	Light Industry	5231085	6402747	7382386	8906048	10984903
重工业	Heavy Industry	4975769	7453130	8451086	10520720	14834572
按注册登记类型分	**By Registered Type**					
国有企业	State－owned Enterprises	967584	995093	1113987	1058232	1124243
集体企业	Collective－owned Enterprises	1793664	1520747	791174	681969	769027
股份合作企业	Share Cooperative Enterprises	485438	527574	631190	731948	813786
联营企业	Joint－owned	99160	98205	97079	103784	91611
有限责任公司	Limited Liability Corporations	705050	1554885	1831178	2742155	3223829
股份有限公司	Share－holding Corporations Ltd.	2257788	3630052	3924362	4472342	6402979
私营企业	Private Enterprises	1258733	2044001	3285751	4610489	6742296
港澳台商投资公司	HongKong,Macao and Taiwan Funded	1649126	1938125	2230734	2614419	3476878
外商投资企业公司	Enterprises with Foreign Investment	990310	1547195	1928018	2411432	3166541
在总计中:亏损企业	Of the Total:Loss Making Enterprises	796665	699600	799276	850086	1054567
在总计中:国有及国有控股	Of the Total:State－owned and State－holding Industrial Enterprises	2735179	4145523	4092981	4340010	6413210
在总计中:农村工业	Of the Total:Rural Industry	5231942	6617444	7764344	10621972	14069895
按规模分	**By Size**					
大型企业	Large－Sized Enterprises	3178634	4715759	4832148	5048998	6489160
中型企业	Medium－Sized Enterprises	1243539	1399898	1480815	1573588	8729543
小型企业	Small－Sized Enterprises	5784681	7740219	9520509	12804182	10600772

注:工业销售产值按现行价格计算。
Note:Gross industrial products sales are calculated at current prices.

3－4 全部国有及规模以上非国有工业企业增加值

Value－added of All State－owned and Non－state－owned Above Designated Size Industrial Enterprises

单位:万元 (10000 yuan)

项目	Item	1999	2000	2001	2002	2003
工业增加值	**Value－added of Industry**	**2604169**	**3257877**	**3984459**	**4994376**	**6053036**
按轻重工业分	**By Light and Heavy Industry**					
轻工业	Light Industry	1245032	1485792	1813461	2257304	2652018
重工业	Heavy Industry	1359137	1772085	2170998	2737072	3401018
按注册登记类型分	**By Registered Type**					
国有企业	State－owned Enterprises	403146	527528	620145	639939	724268
集体企业	Collective－owned Enterprises	388844	315676	169427	151073	171364
股份合作企业	Share Cooperative Enterprises	106455	108374	153506	163564	166547
联营企业	Joint－owned	19339	21136	25032	27566	26043
有限责任公司	Limited Liability Corporations	163880	386327	462942	840443	886295
股份有限公司	Share－holding Corporations Ltd.	592204	652856	802034	942014	1142517
私营企业	Private Enterprises	307417	462443	755758	1095244	1487130
港澳台商投资公司	HongKong,Macao and Taiwan Funded	412565	442317	545409	616555	830024
外商投资企业公司	Enterprises with Foreign Investment	210321	341220	450208	517980	617704
在总计中:亏损企业	Of the Total:Loss Making Enterprises	114075	86804	117702	96701	138103
在总计中:国有及国有控股	Of the Total:State－owned and State－holding Industrial Enterprises	840053	1067442	1205816	1428563	1636214
在总计中:农村工业	Of the Total:Rural Industry	1201654	1479194	1790606	2414801	2964682
按规模分	**By Size**					
大型企业	Large－Sized Enterprises	941514	1230194	1446575	1599140	1213837
中型企业	Medium－Sized Enterprises	316961	357103	362020	404744	2282822
小型企业	Small－Sized Enterprises	1345694	1670581	2175864	2990492	2556377

注:工业增加值按现行价格计算。
Note:Value added value of industry are calculated at current prices.

3-5 主要年份工业企业主要经济指标
Main Economic Indicators of Industrial Enterprises in Main Years

单位:亿元，万人 (100 million yuan, 10000 persons)

年份 Year	总产值(当年价) Gross Industrial Output Value (current prices)	固定资产原值 Original Value of Fixed Assets	固定资产净值 Net Value of Fixed Assets	销售收入 Sales Revenue	利税总额 Total Profitsand Taxes	利润总额 Total Profits	职工人数 Number of Staff and Workers
1978	15.79	7.07			4.29	2.59	
1979	18.11	8.25	6.28	18.71	4.73	2.86	
1980	23.73	9.59	7.35	24.89	6.17	3.93	
1981	29.67	11.38	8.76	30.05	6.94	4.26	
1982	29.99	13.53	10.49	32.36	7.99	4.86	
1983	35.23	15.84	12.17	38.98	9.07	5.57	
1984	50.93	21.09	16.67	54.57	11.30	6.53	
1985	68.63	32.55	26.43	76.16	14.62	7.65	65.48
1986	81.96	38.43	30.49	86.67	15.86	7.94	68.69
1987	102.16	52.61	41.79	110.96	18.54	9.92	71.29
1988	132.17	62.81	48.85	147.85	23.24	12.00	72.06
1989	159.41	74.80	56.60	162.81	23.64	11.47	69.05
1990	200.00	89.31	64.39	167.35	20.99	8.21	67.71
1991	261.62	107.17	79.45	218.15	25.27	11.79	72.02
1992	341.42	128.57	95.03	282.90	31.65	14.82	73.15
1993	491.07	192.06	147.38	430.65	45.15	22.68	73.94
1994	642.18	276.98	225.18	480.46	53.56	26.06	71.53
1995	837.80	357.05	281.28	664.70	62.61	29.46	66.08
1996	843.48	407.73	312.70	722.15	66.57	28.63	64.60
1997	842.62	496.05	374.92	747.51	78.60	33.32	55.88
1998	940.59	567.09	423.50	835.24	88.00	37.52	50.78
1999	1062.29	668.71	490.07	985.32	118.65	61.21	52.38
2000	1427.70	829.69	601.93	1350.52	163.26	88.11	58.42
2001	1629.66	926.49	648.50	1538.70	213.72	115.95	66.90
2002	2000.16	1058.90	727.01	1945.02	267.09	152.34	77.22
2003	2630.29	1251.24	854.79	2604.90	322.01	189.30	91.96

注:1.1997 年以前为乡及乡以上独立核算工业企业。
2.1998 年为国有及年销售收入 500 万元以上的非国有工业企业。

Note: Data in this table refer to all state - owned enterprises and non - - state - owned industrial enterprises with annual sales income of over 5million yuan, before to enterprises at townships and above level.

3-6 全市及各县(市)、区规模以上工业企业总产值

单位:万元 (2003)

项目	Item	全市 Toal	市区 Urban District	海曙 Haishu
工业总产值	**Gross Industrial Output Value**	**26302862**	**15944163**	**902610**
按轻重工业分	**Grouped by Light and Heavy Industry**			
轻工业	Light Industry	11204370	6028734	757538
重工业	Heavy Industry	15098492	9915430	145072
按注册登记类型分	**Grouped by Registered Type**			
国有企业	State - owned Enterprises	1109306	1029344	8092
集体企业	Collective - owned Enterpriese	792419	376192	29756
股份合作企业	Share Cooperative Enterprises	820427	259689	16390
联营企业	Joint Owned Enterprises	94536	27431	
有限责任公司	Limited Liability Corporations	3287356	2280057	194183
股份有限公司	Share - holding Corporations Ltd.	6391697	4673127	211531
私营企业	Private Enterprises	6951380	2618738	32805
港澳台商投资企业	HongKong, Macao and Taiwan Funded	3563627	2384014	377994
外商投资企业	Foreign Funded Enterprises	3283537	2295572	31859
在总计中:亏损企业	Of the Total: Loss Making Enterprises	1092170	831059	5226
在总计中:国有及国有控股	Of the Total: State - owned and State - holding Industrial Enterprises	6432799	5075425	172228
在总计中:农村工业	Of the Total: Rural Indusdry	14437306	5968738	160195
按规模分	**Grouped by Enterprises Size**			
大型企业	Large - Sized Industrial Enterprises	6479703	4523488	118567
中型企业	Medium - Sized Industrial Enterprises	8966656	5524535	632559
小型企业	Small - Sized Industrial Enterprises	10856503	5896140	151484
按工业行业分	**Grouped by Sector**			
非金属矿采选业	Nonmetal Minerals Mining and Dressing	4739	3031	
农副食品加工业	Agricultural Non - staple Food Processing	695376	421614	
食品制造业	Food Manufacturing	164279	60154	
饮料制造业	Beverage Manufacturing	116000	35891	3452
烟草制品业	Tobacco Processing	516122	516122	
纺织业	Textile Industry	1687187	989624	242661

注:本表按 2002 年修订的国民经济行业标准统计。
表 3-7,3-8,3-9,3-17,3-19 同。

Gross Output Value of Above Designated Size Industrial Enterprises by Region(at Current Price)

(10000 yuan)

江东 Jiangdong	江北 Jiangbei	北仑 Beilun	镇海 Zhenhai	鄞州 Yinzhou	余姚 Yuyao	慈溪 Cixi	奉化 Fenghua	象山 Xiangshan	宁海 Ninghai
1277950	**869232**	**3880225**	**4217247**	**4605100**	**2672195**	**3348667**	**1786863**	**1293618**	**1257356**
711637	178744	1166147	389071	2830457	1208858	2081951	447504	671342	765981
566313	690488	2714078	3828176	1774643	1463336	1266716	1339359	622276	491375
530843	8147	225706	31414	33803	12889	38049	7737	12464	8823
34151	6921	62248	116614	126040	112760	230198	20256	37196	15817
49759	47081	1946	15581	128933	182149	206756		108556	63277
	14757	2500	1795	8379	26247		1453	39405	
99259	118874	654628	373366	839747	367921	235030	119040	46901	238407
156171	276754	217435	2799654	1011583	167579	26901	1122617	401473	
158178	172179	525195	341586	1388796	939725	1982903	346775	345262	717977
132409	137037	1073663	158439	504472	526163	304713	90277	188870	69590
117180	87483	1116905	378798	563347	329656	322644	78709	113490	143466
122242	52357	431356	91364	104550	97549	9200	84246	30759	39357
575375	27664	679375	3371521	55306	79075	50881	1131827	23099	72492
315978	609448	614695	403157	3864803	1859595	3034269	1701886	1134368	738450
	268804	317226	2893491	925402	228130	187457	1190699	349929	
836104	221266	1626296	653637	1530708	904118	1496535	182788	352114	506566
441846	379163	1936703	670119	2148991	1539947	1664675	413376	591575	750790
	721			2311				1708	
17125	7157	336006	3554	57773	67423	71833	10417	102647	21442
10911	2192	6420	10656	29976	29213		40820	8668	25424
				32439	25448	1809	996	5917	45939
516122									
14859	37736	139909	124238	430223	213252	327273	23665	71255	62118

Note: Statistics in this table are classified as the national economic category that was modified in 2002.
The same for table 3 - 7, 3 - 8, 3 - 9, 3 - 17, 3 - 19.

项目	Item	全市 Toal	市区 Urban District	海曙 Haishu
纺织服装、鞋、帽制造业	Textile Clothing. Shoes. Cap Manufacturing	1941425	1215651	93576
皮革、毛皮、羽毛(绒)及其制品业	Leather. Furs. Down and Related Products	59562	39291	
木材加工及木、竹、藤、棕、草制品业	Timber Processing, Bamboo, Cane, Palm Fiber and Straw Products	55614	43035	2055
家具制造业	Furniture Manufacturing	88023	43860	
造纸及纸制品业	Papermaking and Paper Products	480211	379387	235441
印刷业和记录媒介的复制	Printing and Record Medium Reproduction	211618	180248	2538
文教体育用品制造业	Cultural, Educational and Sports Goods	720915	390643	2055
石油加工、炼焦及核燃料加工业	Petroleum Processing, Coking & Nuclear Fuel Processing	2878686	2878686	
化学原料及化学制品制造业	Raw Chemical Materials and Chemical Products	799358	683482	2596
医药制造业	Medical and Pharmaceutical Products	67682	35172	9007
化学纤维制造业	Chemical Fiber	325210	80199	
橡胶制品业	Rubber Products	108353	25696	
塑料制品业	Plastic Products	1043021	566510	25294
非金属矿物制品业	Nonmetal Mineral Products	376769	268858	
黑色金属冶炼及压延加工业	Smelting and Pressing of Ferrous Metals	661491	491806	19430
有色金属冶炼及压延加工业	Smelting and Pressing of Nonferrous Metals	857179	540711	29286
金属制品业	Metal Products	948227	466797	12220
通用设备制造业	General Equipment Manufacturing	2020112	1095666	27047
专用设备制造业	Special Purpose Equipment Manufacturing	765948	571709	7607
交通运输设备制造业	Transport Equipment Manufacturing	1471971	733094	2132
电气机械及器材制造业	Electric Equipment and Machinery Manufacturing	3337033	1158675	111360
通信设备、计算机及电子设备制造业	Communication Equipment, Computer and Other Electronic Equipment Manufacturing	1858627	506570	60898
仪器仪表及文化、办公用机械制造业	Instruments, Meters, Cultural and Office Machinery	452080	231211	4920
工艺品及其他制造业	Handicraft and Others Manufacturing	304193	142844	9034
电力、热力的生产和供应业	Electric Power and Hot Power Production and Supply	1178339	1068025	
燃气生产和供应业	Gas Production and Supply	57172	52011	
自来水的生产和供应业	Tap Water Production and Supply	50339	27882	

continued (10000 yuan)

江东 Jiangdong	江北 Jiangbei	北仑 Beilun	镇海 Zhenhai	鄞州 Yinzhou	余姚 Yuyao	慈溪 Cixi	奉化 Fenghua	象山 Xiangshan	宁海 Ninghai
63912	11928	240200	33464	772573	19244	55934	220278	401622	28696
	3141	14363	6408	15379	13476	4609	2186		
	2213	2546	418	35801	4053	337	5949	955	1285
	11647	5128	2242	24843	20671	10229		4671	8592
11084	3051	46813	17538	65459	24181	30512	7415	8193	30523
6487	5591	8338	1371	155924	13426	3970	2151		11823
8236	23791	148632	17345	190584	43323	145575	8271	530	132573
4480		132367	2735791	6049					
20324	15054	227484	346873	71151	41042	13901	22095	11312	27526
6770		10104	6117	3176	3074	8553	12925	1992	5966
			74795	5404	42718	190187	5327	3228	3551
5475	7959		6036	6227	7672	29856		1235	43894
40268	54461	72372	91904	282212	209520	188876	3822	18587	55706
18418	34857	74092	19067	122423	35453	33944	8723	6981	22810
6167	10334	374476	6754	74646	49904	74152	15966	1212	28451
48404	282213	6684	83391	90732	125497	145274	11383	506	33808
19189	63662	70778	73038	227910	242325	98414	28185	19000	93506
139032	104989	172510	165446	486641	253540	377378	81945	80817	130766
44774	50301	291371	50795	126861	39409	23443	6751	54909	69727
80889	57398	358353	40731	193592	158164	214019	42384	285376	38934
46071	50361	203360	68558	678506	719564	1031372	52639	164437	210346
87304	16983	163685	24484	153217	120000	59047	1128811	13430	30769
43464	6335	41255	18003	117234	99719	48786	6480		65884
1948	5159	7301	1073	118330	10640	122510	16251	950	10998
16239		725679	179413	23584	32781	26746	19440	17681	13666
			7749			5161			
				3918	7467	4968	1586	5800	2636

3－7　全市及各县(市)、区规模以上工业企业销售产值

单位:万元　　(2003)

项目	Item	全市 Toal	市区 Urban District	海曙 Haishu
工业销售产值	**Value of Industrial Products Sales**	**25819475**	**15746161**	**877128**
按轻重工业分	**Grouped by Light and Heavy Industry**			
轻工业	Light Industry	10984903	5937734	735881
重工业	Heavy Industry	14834572	9808427	141247
按注册登记类型分	**Grouped by Registered Type**			
国有企业	State－owned Enterprises	1124243	1046361	8448
集体企业	Collective－owned Enterpriese	769027	365473	29200
股份合作企业	Share Cooperative Enterprises	813786	253480	16094
联营企业	Joint Owned Enterprises	91611	26639	
有限责任公司	Limited Liability Corporations	3223829	2240970	191206
股份有限公司	Share－holding Corporations Ltd.	6402979	4723502	190989
私营企业	Private Enterprises	6742296	2551591	32004
港澳台商投资企业	HongKong, Macao and Taiwan Funded	3476878	2322020	377446
外商投资企业	Foreign Funded Enterprises	3166541	2216124	31742
在总计中:亏损企业	Of the Total: Loss Making Enterprises	1054567	800723	5723
在总计中:国有及国有控股	Of the Total: State－owned and State－holding Industrial Enterprises	6413210	5091262	157373
在总计中:农村工业	Of the Total: Rural Indusdry	14069895	5818331	152092
按规模分	**Grouped by Enterprises Size**			
大型企业	Large－Sized Industrial Enterprises	6489160	4560892	103454
中型企业	Medium－Sized Industrial Enterprises	8729543	5408339	624871
小型企业	Small－Sized Industrial Enterprises	10600772	5776929	148802
按工业行业分	**Grouped by Sector**			
非金属矿采选业	Nonmetal Minerals Mining and Dressing	4406	2882	
农副食品加工业	Agricultural Non－staple Food Processing	666109	401554	
食品制造业	Food Manufacturing	153713	57192	
饮料制造业	Beverage Manufacturing	113749	34929	3192
烟草制品业	Tobacco Processing	533100	533100	
纺织业	Textile Industry	1667866	972540	226539

Value of Industrial Products Sales of Above Designated Size Industrial Enterprises by Region

(10000 yuan)

江东 Jiangdong	江北 Jiangbei	北仑 Beilun	镇海 Zhenhai	鄞州 Yinzhou	余姚 Yuyao	慈溪 Cixi	奉化 Fenghua	象山 Xiangshan	宁海 Ninghai
1295812	**839650**	**3792671**	**4257531**	**4491572**	**2574683**	**3299633**	**1752941**	**1257410**	**1188647**
723486	175249	1150268	387776	2769959	1169411	2054682	446745	651253	725078
572326	664401	2642403	3869755	1721613	1405272	1244951	1306196	606157	463569
547894	7746	225708	31713	33514	12889	35969	7737	12464	8823
33052	6913	59262	113280	123304	108916	222648	20224	36522	15244
49469	47548	1946	15563	122861	178097	217906		103439	60864
	14007	2473	1832	8327	25411		1412	38149	
97013	113509	643254	374504	821485	355456	233103	121415	45069	227816
163663	271318	217447	2874779	1005306	166658	25213	1092606	395000	
155985	166178	520119	331855	1345450	892655	1945908	338726	334167	679249
131684	126598	1045720	154867	485705	511701	301878	89532	185600	66147
117052	85833	1076741	359138	545620	316086	315537	81289	107001	130504
119731	46694	410025	91480	103107	94500	8731	83451	29715	37447
592923	26017	634342	3431138	55512	76869	48327	1101925	23099	71728
311798	589931	601554	394632	3767863	1785229	2989906	1666508	1103849	706072
	263640	309581	2971791	912427	224989	198818	1159462	344999	
853375	207255	1582048	632521	1484305	854593	1460343	186359	341999	477910
442437	368755	1901042	653220	2094840	1495102	1640472	407120	570412	710737
	779			2104				1524	
17070	7131	318861	3514	54979	64421	69961	10223	97435	22515
10105	2772	6564	9399	28352	25490		39945	7312	23774
				31737	24971	1521	1132	5802	45394
533100									
14545	36635	146327	124189	424307	204645	338031	23477	70325	58848

单位:万元　　3-7续表

项目	Item	全市 Toal	市区 Urban District	海曙 Haishu
纺织服装、鞋、帽制造业	Textile Clothing, Shoes, Cap Manufacturing	1901591	1187843	87434
皮革、毛皮、羽毛(绒)及其制品业	Leather, Furs, Down and Related Products	59119	39517	
木材加工及木、竹、藤、棕、草制品业	Timber Processing, Bamboo, Cane Palm Fiber and Straw Products	53661	41606	1784
家具制造业	Furniture Manufacturing	83925	41802	
造纸及纸制品业	Papermaking and Paper Products	482185	381666	237311
印刷业和记录媒介的复制	Printing and Record Medium Reproduction	206447	175869	2526
文教体育用品制造业	Cultural. Educational and Sports Goods	704752	384320	2325
石油加工、炼焦及核燃料加工业	Petroleum Processing, Coking & Nuclear Fuel Processing	2952709	2952709	
化学原料及化学制品制造业	Raw Chemical Materials and Chemical Products	775348	663433	2596
医药制造业	Medical and Pharmaceutical Products	64606	32695	8732
化学纤维制造业	Chemical Fiber	324582	84173	
橡胶制品业	Rubber Products	101960	24686	
塑料制品业	Plastic Products	1015457	552244	25117
非金属矿物制品业	Nonmetal Mineral Products	363678	258559	
黑色金属冶炼及压延加工业	Smelting and Pressing of Ferrous Metals	610035	444549	19418
有色金属冶炼及压延加工业	Smelting and Pressing of Nonferrous Metals	842704	532957	29311
金属制品业	Metal Products	920685	452445	12103
通用设备制造业	General Equipment Manufacturing	1967079	1069134	25369
专用设备制造业	Special Purpose Equipment Manufacturing	742007	555836	7986
交通运输设备制造业	Transport Equipment Manufacturing	1450724	730892	2136
电气机械及器材制造业	Electric Equipment and Machinery Manufacturing	3240021	1130100	110850
通信设备、计算机及电子设备制造业	Communication Equipment, Computer and Other Electronic Equipment Manufacturing	1799442	494197	58658
仪器仪表及文化、办公用机械制造业	Instruments, Meters, Cultural and Office Machinery	441483	227188	5056
工艺品及其他制造业	Handicraft and Others Manufacturing	294531	137641	8686
电力、热力的生产和供应业	Electric Power and Hot Power Production and Supply	1175896	1068025	
燃气生产和供应业	Gas Production and Supply	57118	52010	
自来水的生产和供应业	Tap Water Production and Supply	48790	27866	

continued (10000 yuan)

江东 Jiangdong	江北 Jiangbei	北仑 Beilun	镇海 Zhenhai	鄞州 Yinzhou	余姚 Yuyao	慈溪 Cixi	奉化 Fenghua	象山 Xiangshan	宁海 Ninghai
62117	12838	232206	33531	759716	18920	55914	222651	390728	25535
	3091	15354	6049	15023	12828	4462	2312		
	2282	2410	494	34637	3509	418	5987	858	1283
	11663	4212	1950	23977	19576	9941		4393	8213
11334	3037	46602	17540	65843	23596	30887	7273	8194	30569
6123	5506	9083	1564	151067	13187	3980	2104		11307
7852	22400	148868	17179	185697	42801	142280	8150	506	126695
4480		128137	2814091	6001					
19988	14885	233472	322718	69775	39903	13909	21044	11231	25828
6657		9638	4720	2948	3045	8318	12802	1882	5864
			78865	5308	41064	187151	5824	3060	3310
5277	7495		5858	6055	6945	28353		1210	40766
40335	51302	71900	87714	275877	202966	187472	3694	18073	51008
18121	29118	74166	18081	119073	34319	33793	8233	6897	21877
6231	10954	328214	6766	72967	48777	72696	16023	1152	26838
49009	276533	6529	81879	89697	123260	141360	11524	506	33097
18949	63063	70340	70520	217472	235881	96361	27870	17669	90459
139347	103592	168801	167588	464438	245292	369078	81426	77475	124674
43474	45713	286853	48890	122922	38141	23925	6391	52638	65076
82679	54173	361644	39791	190469	153395	208976	41102	282061	34298
44409	46937	199887	64649	662906	696899	1007054	51533	160840	193595
89975	16268	155224	24065	150007	105436	58471	1098835	13378	29125
46457	6262	34981	17694	116739	96347	47951	6462		63535
1941	5225	6721	1073	113994	9723	120947	15899	827	9494
16239		725679	179413	23584	32781	26349	19440	15635	13666
			7749			5108			
				3902	6566	4968	1586	5800	2004

3-8 全市及各县(市)、区规模以上工业企业增加值

单位:万元　　　　(2003)

项目	Item	全市 Toal	市区 Urban District	海曙 Haishu
工业增加值	**Value - added of Industry**	**6053036**	**3870797**	**182806**
按轻重工业分	**Grouped by Light and Heavy Industry**			
轻工业	Light Industry	2652018	1548320	152591
重工业	Heavy Industry	3401018	2322479	30215
按注册登记类型分	**Grouped by Registered Type**			
国有企业	State - owned Enterprises	724268	676854	1663
集体企业	Collective - owned Enterpriese	171364	78584	4901
股份合作企业	Share Cooperative Enterprises	166547	47388	3046
联营企业	Joint Owned Enterprises	26043	7587	
有限责任公司	Limited Liability Corporations	886295	636353	28511
股份有限公司	Share - holding Corporations Ltd.	1142517	902024	44162
私营企业	Private Enterprises	1487130	560208	6978
港澳台商投资企业	HongKong, Macao and Taiwan Funded	830024	562965	85264
外商投资企业	Foreign Funded Enterprises	617704	398831	8281
在总计中:亏损企业	Of the Total: Loss Making Enterprises	138103	91745	1056
在总计中:国有及国有控股	Of the Total: State - owned and State - holding Industrial Enterprises	1636214	1415436	36345
在总计中:农村工业	Of the Total: Rural Indusdry	2964682	1260193	30485
按规模分	**Grouped by Enterprises Size**			
大型企业	Large - Sized Industrial Enterprises	1213837	885631	27540
中型企业	Medium - Sized Industrial Enterprises	2282822	1512564	122859
小型企业	Small - Sized Industrial Enterprises	2556377	1472604	32406
按工业行业分	**Grouped by Sector**			
非金属矿采选业	Nonmetal Minerals Mining and Dressing	2360	931	
农副食品加工业	Agricultural Non - staple Food Processing	101507	55350	
食品制造业	Food Manufacturing	36650	14187	
饮料制造业	Beverage Manufacturing	39469	17612	982
烟草制品业	Tobacco Processing	386971	386971	
纺织业	Textile Industry	367578	191837	42579

Value – added of Above Designated Size Industrial Enterprises by Region

(10000 yuan)

江东 Jiangdong	江北 Jiangbei	北仑 Beilun	镇海 Zhenhai	鄞州 Yinzhou	余姚 Yuyao	慈溪 Cixi	奉化 Fenghua	象山 Xiangshan	宁海 Ninghai
538830	**155247**	**1009462**	**812764**	**1029903**	**579701**	**703998**	**329349**	**257384**	**311807**
425554	37472	250216	81602	591089	265093	418661	128619	113976	177349
113277	117775	759246	731162	438814	314608	285336	200730	143407	134458
389537	3370	120628	4016	15949	9227	18895	6577	6899	5816
6278	1857	12912	28332	24212	27188	44647	6505	10994	3446
7033	8285	379	4198	24448	32492	51752		20547	14368
	3853	1550	546	1638	9171		667	8618	
22357	25926	256754	100924	201882	80167	52396	41793	11644	63942
28132	23164	59179	519206	228181	28505	10225	135429	66334	
31848	38157	108524	60376	314326	190214	401613	87914	76427	170754
29724	30413	282832	34317	100414	129175	59961	27770	35069	15084
23921	20221	166704	60849	118852	72832	64095	22694	20854	38398
13569	8748	32717	11036	11217	14341	2109	16819	5160	7629
398667	9523	177259	629985	21752	23541	21915	142576	8614	24132
65366	93920	149708	80691	839933	382668	627914	294606	220094	179207
	21984	88835	559975	187298	54058	51715	162797	59636	
456288	50949	399603	105190	364271	209895	309549	56619	66861	127334
82543	82314	521024	147599	478334	315748	342734	109932	130887	184472
	67			864				1429	
2744	978	42431	738	8459	14099	17508	1183	10851	2516
3551	818	2225	1475	6119	7882		7281	1710	5590
				16630	5919	595	238	1226	13879
386971									
2437	7159	27987	27878	83796	54427	78386	6330	18321	18277

单位:万元

3-8 续表

项目	Item	全市 Toal	市区 Urban District	海曙 Haishu
纺织服装、鞋、帽制造业	Textile Clothing, Shoes, Cap Manufacturing	460245	300965	17529
皮革、毛皮、羽毛(绒)及其制品业	Leather, Furs, Down and Related Products	11791	7872	
木材加工及木、竹、藤、棕、草制品业	Timber Processing, Bamboo, Cane Palm Fiber and Straw Products	13507	10249	266
家具制造业	Furniture Manufacturing	16547	8513	
造纸及纸制品业	Papermaking and Paper Products	99153	80391	49345
印刷业和记录媒介的复制	Printing and Record Medium Reproduction	50490	43662	761
文教体育用品制造业	Cultural. Educational and Sports Goods	154755	84534	665
石油加工、炼焦及核燃料加工业	Petroleum Processing, Coking & Nuclear Fuel Processing	507012	507012	
化学原料及化学制品制造业	Raw Chemical Materials and Chemical Products	129840	105024	751
医药制造业	Medical and Pharmaceutical Products	13378	5685	2165
化学纤维制造业	Chemical Fiber	56934	15690	
橡胶制品业	Rubber Products	31010	6108	
塑料制品业	Plastic Products	214901	108378	4130
非金属矿物制品业	Nonmetal Mineral Products	83226	59649	
黑色金属冶炼及压延加工业	Smelting and Pressing of Ferrous Metals	80278	56511	3220
有色金属冶炼及压延加工业	Smelting and Pressing of Nonferrous Metals	92632	53785	3699
金属制品业	Metal Products	202030	93942	2178
通用设备制造业	General Equipment Manufacturing	518588	286853	6209
专用设备制造业	Special Purpose Equipment Manufacturing	208068	147966	1842
交通运输设备制造业	Transport Equipment Manufacturing	308050	167691	648
电气机械及器材制造业	Electric Equipment and Machinery Manufacturing	696848	236656	28949
通信设备、计算机及电子设备制造业	Communication Equipment, Computer and Other Electronic Equipment Manufacturing	306688	113133	14084
仪器仪表及文化、办公用机械制造业	Instruments, Meters, Cultural and Office Machinery	112629	53601	896
工艺品及其他制造业	Handicraft and Others Manufacturing	61307	27898	1911
电力、热力的生产和供应业	Electric Power and Hot Power Production and Supply	664709	607388	
燃气生产和供应业	Gas Production and Supply	-235	-806	
自来水的生产和供应业	Tap Water Production and Supply	24119	15552	

continued (10000 yuan)

江东 Jiangdong	江北 Jiangbei	北仑 Beilun	镇海 Zhenhai	鄞州 Yinzhou	余姚 Yuyao	慈溪 Cixi	奉化 Fenghua	象山 Xiangshan	宁海 Ninghai
12720	3473	77990	9025	180229	5181	10820	73752	63190	6337
	619	4084	1427	1742	2343	1037	539		
	923	708	76	8277	1133	112	1489	295	229
	1860	1108	714	4832	2964	1835		1282	1953
3049	741	9571	2767	14918	3671	6567	1398	1219	5907
1459	1503	1998	496	37445	2387	987	637		2817
1571	6769	36696	3389	35444	9928	24930	1621	78	33664
1433		125	504574	880					
5128	4590	37424	41055	16075	5086	2354	5085	2679	9612
-2107		2531	2264	833	481	2292	2467	896	1557
			14682	1009	10582	28681	1171	226	584
1309	1478		1271	2050	2680	6186		423	15613
5624	8244	20379	16819	53181	43326	43279	952	5785	13181
4378	8411	12209	4606	30046	7309	8409	1930	2241	3688
662	1211	40557	856	10006	4840	10814	2903	174	5036
3463	23370	1945	6581	14728	9601	21298	1857	179	5912
3224	12235	11668	14522	50116	55161	18280	9906	3976	20765
36440	26683	39668	46588	131266	57695	95499	25583	24177	28781
8284	12664	77777	13052	34347	9005	7219	2641	17894	23343
13413	13392	82544	7184	50513	37873	42485	10657	37321	12023
11443	10862	40290	18022	127000	148372	203368	14346	46795	47311
16623	4515	33225	5431	39256	25904	18306	137102	3862	8381
11249	1339	7391	3673	29053	32276	12152	2059		12541
558	1343	1387	88	22612	2442	24170	3637	254	2906
3206		395546	63497	16028	14922	13471	11386	9186	8356
			14			571			
				2151	2214	2391	1199	1718	1045

3－9 全市规模以上工业企业经济指标

单位:万元 (2003)

项目	Item	企业个数(个) Number of Enterprises (unit)	#亏损企业 Loss Making Enterprises	工业总产值(现价) Gross Industrial Output Value (Current Prices)
总计	**Total**	**4672**	**371**	**26302862**
按轻重工业分	**Grouped by Light and Heavy Industry**			
轻工业	Light Industry	2332	208	11204370
重工业	Heavy Industry	2340	163	15098492
按注册登记类型分	**Grouped by Registered Type**			
国有企业	State－owned Enterprises	43	9	1109306
集体企业	Collective－owned Enterpriese	321	22	792419
股份合作企业	Share Cooperative Enterprises	207	12	820427
联营企业	Joint Owned Enterprises	18	1	94536
有限责任公司	Limited Liability Corporations	410	39	3287356
股份有限公司	Share－holding Corporations Ltd.	45	5	6391697
私营企业	Private Enterprises	2558	145	6951380
港澳台商投资企业	HongKong,Macao & Taiwan Funded	577	72	3563627
外商投资企业	Foreign Funded Enterprises	490	66	3283537
在总计中:亏损企业	Of the Total:Loss Making Enterprises	371	371	1092170
在总计中:国有及国有控股	Of the Total:State－owned and State－holding Industrial Enterprises	114	24	6432799
在总计中:农村工业	Of the Total:Rural Indusdry	3463	203	14437306
按规模分	**Grouped by Size**			
大型企业	Large－Sized Industrial Enterprises	23		6479703
中型企业	Medium－Sized Industrial Enterprises	431	22	8966656
小型企业	Small－Sized Industrial Enterprises	4218	349	10856503
按工业行业分	**Grouped by Sector**			
非金属矿采选业	Nonmetal Minerals Mining and Dressing	6	1	4739
农副食品加工业	Agricultural Non－staple Food Processing	96	18	695376
食品制造业	Food Manufacturing	44	4	164279
饮料制造业	Beverage Manufacturing	23		116000
烟草制品业	Tobacco Processing	2		516122
纺织业	Textile Industry	371	24	1687187

Main Economic Indicators of Industrial Enterprises above Designated Size

(10000 yuan)

# 新产品产值 Value of New - products	工业销售产值 Value of Industrial Products Sales	# 出口交货值 Value of Export Products	工业增加值 Value Added of Industry	资产合计 Total Asset	流动资产小计 Circulating Funds	流动资产年平均余额 Average Balance of Circulating Funds	固定资产小计 Total Fixed Assets
3486873	**25819475**	**7778095**	**6053036**	**24460143**	**12841812**	**11564507**	**9332424**
804728	10984903	5051660	2652018	11035152	6164325	5604458	3672781
2682145	14834572	2726435	3401018	13424992	6677487	5960048	5659643
486	1124243	27087	724268	2050887	726458	698783	1220017
99074	769027	138779	171364	728286	491537	448858	185545
25781	813786	223743	166547	786499	491968	426492	207915
19437	91611	1253	26043	62698	41034	39641	18981
378629	3223829	711105	886295	3726271	1735339	1570977	1648806
1958410	6402979	880996	1142517	4829656	2256141	2064981	1940159
591335	6742296	2613322	1487130	5680081	3480000	3094290	1561099
258791	3476878	1748076	830024	3684459	2025445	1801357	1413971
154931	3166541	1432642	617704	2907489	1591230	1416945	1135298
62366	1054567	352876	138103	1546138	731265	699600	665944
1611188	6413210	505760	1636214	5421924	2049352	1879828	3015101
2498193	14069895	4934451	2964682	11818208	7307392	6429938	3229429
1927411	6489160	943002	1213837	4744579	2223036	1971444	1985615
1143421	8729543	3326176	2282822	9522312	5078830	4605398	3416031
416040	10600772	3508918	2556377	10193252	5539946	4987665	3930778
	4406		2360	8684	2796	2558	5812
13722	666109	150364	101507	590527	344206	310386	206542
190	153713	86835	36650	171512	88833	84494	70246
7917	113749	27179	39469	215121	109779	110950	62046
	533100	5387	386971	488563	297456	268123	171769
52927	1667866	829425	367578	1771059	1013688	876936	582641

单位:万元　　3-9 续表 1

项目	Item	企业个数(个) Number of Enterprises (unti)	# 亏损企业 Loss Making Enterprises	工业总产值(现价) Gross Industrial Output Value (Current Prices)
纺织服装、鞋、帽制造业	Textile Clothing, Shoes, Cap Manufacturing	453	52	1941425
皮革、毛皮、羽毛(绒)及其制品业	Leather, Furs, Down and Related Products	28	3	59562
木材加工及木、竹、藤、棕、草制品业	Timber Processing, Bamboo, Cane Palm Fiber and Straw Products	40	8	55614
家具制造业	Furniture Manufacturing	35	3	88023
造纸及纸制品业	Papermaking and Paper Products	69	7	480211
印刷业和记录媒介的复制	Printing and Record Medium Reproduction	55	8	211618
文教体育用品制造业	Cultural, Educational and Sports Goods	142	11	720915
石油加工、炼焦及核燃料加工业	Petroleum Processing. Coking & Nuclear Fuel Processing	7	2	2878686
化学原料及化学制品制造业	Raw Chemical Materials and Chemical Products	108	13	799358
医药制造业	Medical and Pharmaceutical Products	27	6	67682
化学纤维制造业	Chemical Fiber	43	1	325210
橡胶制品业	Rubber Products	38	1	108353
塑料制品业	Plastic Products	350	31	1043021
非金属矿物制品业	Nonmetal Mineral Products	83	6	376769
黑色金属冶炼及压延加工业	Smelting and Pressing of Ferrous Metals	75	7	661491
有色金属冶炼及压延加工业	Smelting and Pressing of Nonferrous Metals	86	5	857179
金属制品业	Metal Products	376	21	948227
通用设备制造业	General Equipment Manufacturing	633	45	2020112
专用设备制造业	Special Purpose Equipment Manufacturing	203	11	765948
交通运输设备制造业	Transport Equipment Manufacturing	304	17	1471971
电气机械及器材制造业	Electric Equipment and Machinery Manufacturing	542	31	3337033
通信设备、计算机及电子设备制造业	Communication Equipment, Computer and Other Electronic Equipment Manufacturing	177	16	1858627
仪器仪表及文化、办公用机械制造业	Instruments, Meters, Cultural and Office Machinery	109	7	452080
工艺品及其他制造业	Handicraft and Others Manufacturing	102	6	304193
电力、热力的生产和供应业	Electric Power and Hot Power Production and Supply	28	1	1178339
燃气生产和供应业	Gas Production and Supply	3	1	57172
自来水的生产和供应业	Tap Water Production and Supply	14	4	50339

continued 1 (10000 yuan)

# 新产品产值 Value of New－products	工业销售产值 Value of Industrial Products Sales	# 出口交货值 Value of Export Products	工业增加值 Value Added of Industry	资产合计 Total Asset	流动资产小计 Circulating Funds	流动资产年平均余额 Average Balance of Circulating Funds	固定资产小计 Total Fixed Assets
66310	1901591	1330094	460245	2008888	1114552	995950	638509
190	59119	33331	11791	34523	24785	23001	6863
12	53661	43518	13507	45701	27619	25453	15795
310	83925	64791	16547	83258	48201	41490	26227
55251	482185	19529	99153	786184	327859	336295	400451
42323	206447	43467	50490	230436	151344	137941	67115
54422	704752	418011	154755	551071	340391	297597	130694
456004	2952709	243141	507012	1520191	426729	386257	980151
35084	775348	69621	129840	628641	317118	290895	251087
12470	64606	22727	13378	134892	62450	63787	45994
10275	324582	15816	56934	376544	142012	137165	149929
16884	101960	22308	31010	106901	48482	44636	41487
31456	1015457	390036	214901	925997	558779	515743	288074
90667	363678	33536	83226	356053	184063	161261	148987
8966	610035	17620	80278	707650	323741	260973	348360
68384	842704	45594	92632	451437	277241	239588	121121
29717	920685	450907	202030	749208	487919	430764	186826
199370	1967079	844794	518588	2084363	1253834	1127609	603276
109206	742007	122289	208068	765995	501355	445001	214376
139319	1450724	313950	308050	1360156	820349	747163	353300
659937	3240021	1365831	696848	2738570	1727868	1556453	741248
1242193	1799442	304697	306688	1235786	817591	709864	302151
71384	441483	219945	112629	397508	258177	234642	105329
11983	294531	243354	61307	202868	130822	116845	58232
	1175896		664709	2376617	538596	512418	1797242
	57118		－235	44227	13555	7327	17311
	48790		24119	311015	59619	64945	193234

单位:万元　　3-9 续表2

项目	Item	固定资产原价 Original Value of Fixed Assets	# 生产经营用 Producting and Managing	累计折旧 Accumulative Total Depreciation	# 本年折旧 Depreciation in this year
总计	**Total**	**12512426**	**11814427**	**3964485**	**788237**
按轻重工业分	**Grouped by Light and Heavy Industry**				
轻工业	Light Industry	4621330	4257690	1307579	279532
重工业	Heavy Industry	7891096	7556736	2656905	508705
按注册登记类型分	**Grouped by Registered Type**				
国有企业	State - owned Enterprises	1824379	1796212	730659	116704
集体企业	Collective - owned Enterpriese	255867	238134	95817	15737
股份合作企业	Share Cooperative Enterprises	297023	263023	111436	19909
联营企业	Joint Owned Enterprises	24960	23917	8287	1413
有限责任公司	Limited Liability Corporations	2322963	2204775	788414	153087
股份有限公司	Share - holding Corporations Ltd.	2529110	2341366	784414	145801
私营企业	Private Enterprises	1882866	1740884	459863	127585
港澳台商投资企业	HongKong, Macao & Taiwan Funded	1947929	1853208	631865	122207
外商投资企业	Foreign Funded Enterprises	1426538	1352118	353574	85749
在总计中:亏损企业	Of the Total: Loss Making Enterprises	891354	852488	271864	49691
在总计中:国有及国有控股	Of the Total: State - owned and State - holding Industrial Enterprises	4423015	4232875	1667635	262807
在总计中:农村工业	Of the Total: Rural Indusdry	3883774	3554523	1008450	257219
按规模分	**Grouped by Size**				
大型企业	Large - Sized Industrial Enterprises	2708391	2480447	919550	156785
中型企业	Medium - Sized Industrial Enterprises	4641815	4390813	1542906	283124
小型企业	Small - Sized Industrial Enterprises	5162220	4943166	1502029	348328
按工业行业分	**Grouped by Sector**				
非金属矿采选业	Nonmetal Minerals Mining and Dressing	9619	9390	4443	341
农副食品加工业	Agricultural Non - staple Food Processing	268590	251612	72315	14646
食品制造业	Food Manufacturing	65600	60115	18015	3189
饮料制造业	Beverage Manufacturing	91059	88116	29759	5756
烟草制品业	Tobacco Processing	206574	205710	58289	13406
纺织业	Textile Industry	842920	753251	297711	51384

continued 2　　　　(10000 yuan)

固定资产净值年平均余额 Average Balance of Net Value of Fixed Assets	负债小计 Total Liabilities	流动负债小计 Circulting Liabilities	所有者权益 Creditors' Equity	实收资本 Total Capital Hold	国家资本金 State Capital	港澳台资本金 Invested Capital from Hongkong, Macao&Taiwan	外商资本金 Foreign Capital
8065316	**14062672**	**11451534**	**10397471**	**5163042**	**554908**	**850427**	**782128**
3136659	6437637	5668937	4597515	2247594	251669	357502	284750
4928657	7625035	5782597	5799957	2915448	303239	492925	497379
1037731	1106202	365907	944685	206893	147133		
158257	432624	399668	295662	106805	218	317	23178
179080	505104	443047	281394	106535	330	975	59
15779	30868	29424	31831	14143	4674		
1539083	2225735	1628333	1500536	775771	131479	9441	23504
1524445	2278187	1897516	2551469	802395	208378	86268	32763
1319699	3808478	3556286	1871603	926336	28	3558	14855
1284554	2152099	1770721	1532361	1159508	35085	746229	11739
1006124	1520770	1358027	1386719	1063958	27583	3640	675948
604218	991534	820869	554604	572540	98372	184282	172678
2497641	2600214	1639007	2821710	1079272	523346	88391	153164
2655401	7369401	6769420	4448808	1802839	13247	100556	138025
1557790	2352825	1958438	2391755	684281	192446	86329	13137
2917843	5142910	4387759	4379402	2328872	255466	364740	417323
3589683	6566938	5105338	3626315	2149889	106996	399358	351669
5291	1533	1524	7152	1925		91	
199935	378823	332435	211705	174355	8802	78001	39146
46350	109511	98539	62001	27851	361	3903	4827
60136	108065	103908	107056	80271	1102	172	28611
120938	54140	54140	434423	43696	43239		
519696	1079345	968513	691713	355896	42587	89013	39646

单位:万元　　3－9 续表 3

项目	Item	固定资产原价 Original Value of Fixed Assets	# 生产经营用 Producting and Managing	累计折旧 Accumulative Total Depreciation	# 本年折旧 Depreciation in this year
纺织服装、鞋、帽制造业	Textile Clothing, Shoes, Cap Manufacturing	729247	653206	167022	40723
皮革、毛皮、羽毛(绒)及其制品业	Leather, Furs, Down and Related Products	10537	9808	3962	481
木材加工及木、竹、藤、棕、草制品业	Timber Processing, Bamboo, Cane Palm Fiber and Straw Products	21890	20578	7166	1390
家具制造业	Furniture Manufacturing	30927	30314	6023	1920
造纸及纸制品业	Papermaking and Paper Products	553068	516635	184887	29770
印刷业和记录媒介的复制	Printing and Record Medium Reproduction	78941	72343	20239	4940
文教体育用品制造业	Cultural, Educational and Sports Goods	172256	159236	46599	11478
石油加工、炼焦及核燃料加工业	Petroleum Processing. Coking & Nuclear Fuel Processing	1436388	1389555	517722	78325
化学原料及化学制品制造业	Raw Chemical Materials and Chemical Products	349224	314431	105652	24266
医药制造业	Medical and Pharmaceutical Products	52005	49321	11736	2777
化学纤维制造业	Chemical Fiber	210035	198662	63074	10722
橡胶制品业	Rubber Products	53463	48934	16650	2917
塑料制品业	Plastic Products	373738	350138	111035	23316
非金属矿物制品业	Nonmetal Mineral Products	197384	187614	55352	12140
黑色金属冶炼及压延加工业	Smelting and Pressing of Ferrous Metals	379241	370403	64680	18438
有色金属冶炼及压延加工业	Smelting and Pressing of Nonferrous Metals	146529	131924	46056	9328
金属制品业	Metal Products	238537	220489	71445	14841
通用设备制造业	General Equipment Manufacturing	756318	703752	216879	50523
专用设备制造业	Special Purpose Equipment Manufacturing	260078	246527	73227	16275
交通运输设备制造业	Transport Equipment Manufacturing	436908	412163	112133	28440
电气机械及器材制造业	Electric Equipment and Machinery Manufacturing	877895	802406	214627	62114
通信设备、计算机及电子设备制造业	Communication Equipment, Computer and Other Electronic Equipment Manufacturing	357055	333281	77772	30210
仪器仪表及文化、办公用机械制造业	Instruments, Meters, Cultural and Office Machinery	127359	115455	30371	8725
工艺品及其他制造业	Handicraft and Others Manufacturing	72894	66612	16485	4251
电力、热力的生产和供应业	Electric Power and Hot Power Production and Supply	2871512	2820641	1176537	198177
燃气生产和供应业	Gas Production and Supply	18830	18516	6571	1069
自来水的生产和供应业	Tap Water Production and Supply	215808	203290	60049	11964

continued 3 (10000 yuan)

固定资产净值年平均余额 Average Balance of Net Value of Fixed Assets	负债小计 Total Liabilities	流动负债小计 Circulting Liabilities	所有者权益 Creditors' Equity	实收资本 Total Capital Hold			
					国家资本金 State Capital	港澳台资本金 Invested Capital from Hongkong, Macao&Taiwan	外商资本金 Foreign Capital
507336	1176086	994455	832802	366016	530	34699	42128
6610	20337	19708	14186	10684	235	5399	1441
14013	25813	24626	19888	13095	1138	2300	3584
22895	59986	52530	23272	18602	1400	1574	7152
374032	496610	292504	289574	232905	1292	40903	22206
55939	144306	137856	86130	29120	4183	5115	277
120242	289770	279137	261301	107153	2126	29321	13809
752260	560560	416860	959630	298005	180000	72664	37079
249408	352914	318623	275727	221320	31542	43073	110966
42132	80906	69290	53986	53185	8772	3734	3808
140486	255993	205192	120551	82441	48491	2546	409
34308	63122	52075	43779	22757	75	91	1986
245926	579268	533336	346729	205051	9701	51190	29048
134462	231697	206328	124356	76207		18757	6328
265000	301283	283355	406367	344521	2890	12695	104952
106115	312716	271106	138721	71250		2564	17586
162771	484864	465633	264344	150326	235	37686	25618
506012	1227938	1140368	856425	450367	10463	40560	86257
175423	451601	431851	314394	96231	695	12273	14826
314569	808034	708988	552122	255946	12377	36355	42699
610312	1669626	1560638	1068944	433083	7917	35326	33415
258895	718441	654239	517346	259806	9520	97531	43248
91905	220110	208792	177397	90755	702	30189	7869
48836	129624	117047	73244	38384	1273	6468	10020
1710154	1525518	329914	851099	464228	42349	56235	3189
15437	17844	7883	26383	2593	366		
147495	126288	110143	184726	85018	80545		

单位:万元　　3－9 续表 4

项目	Item	产品销售收入 Sales Revenue	产品销售成本 Cost of Sales	产品销售费用 Expenses of Sales
总计	**Total**	**26048962**	**21821106**	**738647**
按轻重工业分	**Grouped by Light and Heavy Industry**			
轻工业	Light Industry	10944119	8945522	447753
重工业	Heavy Industry	15104843	12875584	290894
按注册登记类型分	**Grouped by Registered Type**			
国有企业	State－owned Enterprises	1432007	962113	47839
集体企业	Collective－owned Enterpriese	764626	646256	16160
股份合作企业	Share Cooperative Enterprises	785025	675824	16167
联营企业	Joint Owned Enterprises	92434	69607	3468
有限责任公司	Limited Liability Corporations	3208738	2589988	110410
股份有限公司	Share－holding Corporations Ltd.	6423767	5470338	223856
私营企业	Private Enterprises	6659151	5705423	157498
港澳台商投资企业	HongKong,Macao & Taiwan Funded	3507476	2974282	87390
外商投资企业	Foreign Funded Enterprises	3167315	2719520	75840
在总计中:亏损企业	Of the Total:Loss Making Enterprises	1059530	982440	33424
在总计中:国有及国有控股	Of the Total:State－owned and State－holding Industrial Enterprises	6753919	5694315	114230
在总计中:农村工业	Of the Total:Rural Indusdry	13865870	11688907	487532
按规模分	**Grouped by Size**			
大型企业	Large－Sized Industrial Enterprises	6503180	5566210	223325
中型企业	Medium－Sized Industrial Enterprises	9090166	7356805	285094
小型企业	Small－Sized Industrial Enterprises	10455616	8898090	230228
按工业行业分	**Grouped by Sector**			
非金属矿采选业	Nonmetal Minerals Mining and Dressing	4411	3461	33
农副食品加工业	Agricultural Non－staple Food Processing	668292	608732	16458
食品制造业	Food Manufacturing	154476	132881	3952
饮料制造业	Beverage Manufacturing	113006	74914	13217
烟草制品业	Tobacco Processing	538585	167952	40565
纺织业	Textile Industry	1685022	1474137	26194

continued 4

(10000 yuan)

产品销售税金及附加 Sales Taxes and Extra Charges	管理费用 Management Expenses	税金 Tax	财产保险费 Property Insurance Expenses	劳动待业保险费 Job – waiting Insurance Expenses	财务费用 Financial Expenses	# 利息支出 Interest Expenditure	营业利润 Business Profits
472653	**1056889**	**28471**	**19962**	**18349**	**322904**	**251316**	**1726179**
291304	485037	13906	10283	8650	160584	120730	657505
181348	571852	14566	9679	9699	162321	130587	1068674
239725	51509	1114	1120	4730	10561	9671	124287
5253	35755	911	580	482	11743	10018	50847
5863	36492	869	508	1495	14464	9789	41882
880	5808	118	58	43	847	843	12065
25374	153919	4596	6248	3000	68635	53465	271547
130804	206503	3572	2645	3056	37181	32219	383444
56691	292434	9863	4763	2606	79485	66710	378560
4754	146678	3929	2364	1275	62498	38863	245369
3223	127616	3491	1675	1661	37416	29668	217867
4369	68503	2445	1223	1350	25523	20131	– 53671
361027	177956	4487	3097	7292	39676	34355	392300
86213	583857	15262	11377	6502	154122	128879	901062
127675	200160	3146	4484	2874	42619	34734	373615
282659	376819	10597	5993	9405	131747	103353	689344
62318	479909	14728	9485	6069	148538	113229	663220
120	371	7		3	55	54	571
2140	17033	792	398	115	9337	7988	24423
811	4776	217	97	128	2402	2185	9862
7846	10847	247	291	76	2455	2289	5658
236075	15814	453	490	1524	– 599	– 599	78378
6194	73732	1989	1275	2001	29743	19930	84997

单位:万元

3-9 续表 5

项目	Item	产品销售收入 Sales Revenue	产品销售成本 Cost of Sales	产品销售费用 Expenses of Sales
纺织服装、鞋、帽制造业	Textile Clothing, Shoes, Cap Manufacturing	1908652	1590208	92541
皮革、毛皮、羽毛(绒)及其制品业	Leather, Furs, Down and Related Products	59319	50397	2770
木材加工及木、竹、藤、棕、草制品业	Timber Processing, Bamboo, Cane Palm Fiber and Straw Products	53282	47027	809
家具制造业	Furniture Manufacturing	83161	69569	4242
造纸及纸制品业	Papermaking and Paper Products	473502	403531	11192
印刷业和记录媒介的复制	Printing and Record Medium Reproduction	206351	167525	3689
文教体育用品制造业	Cultural, Educational and Sports Goods	694974	572879	29560
石油加工、炼焦及核燃料加工业	Petroleum Processing, Coking & Nuclear Fuel Processing	3051171	2706637	12001
化学原料及化学制品制造业	Raw Chemical Materials and Chemical Products	771449	667381	17254
医药制造业	Medical and Pharmaceutical Products	64008	47105	7289
化学纤维制造业	Chemical Fiber	323930	289615	4823
橡胶制品业	Rubber Products	96741	74821	3196
塑料制品业	Plastic Products	1015310	857422	36885
非金属矿物制品业	Nonmetal Mineral Products	364907	303414	14785
黑色金属冶炼及压延加工业	Smelting and Pressing of Ferrous Metals	612350	557589	3454
有色金属冶炼及压延加工业	Smelting and Pressing of Nonferrous Metals	850300	796469	5519
金属制品业	Metal Products	920697	786447	23318
通用设备制造业	General Equipment Manufacturing	1943802	1591208	47142
专用设备制造业	Special Purpose Equipment Manufacturing	731606	558694	27114
交通运输设备制造业	Transport Equipment Manufacturing	1413781	1172478	32662
电气机械及器材制造业	Electric Equipment and Machinery Manufacturing	3199842	2604177	172379
通信设备、计算机及其他电子设备制造业	Communication Equipment, Computer and Other Electronic Equipment Manufacturing	1751064	1536547	56933
仪器仪表及文化、办公用机械制造业	Instruments, Meters, Cultural and Office Machinery	443398	359855	13940
工艺品及其他制造业	Handicraft and Others Manufacturing	294336	254908	8186
电力、热力的生产和供应业	Electric Power and Hot Power Production and Supply	1452992	1202258	31
燃气生产和供应业	Gas Production and Supply	57095	58849	374
自来水的生产和供应业	Tap Water Production and Supply	47152	32021	6143

continued 5 (10000 yuan)

产品销售税金及附加 Sales Taxes and Extra Charges	管理费用 Management Expenses	税金 Tax	财产保险费 Property Insurance Expenses	劳动待业保险费 Job – waiting Insurance Expenses	财务费用 Financial Expenses	# 利息支出 Interest Expenditure	营业利润 Business Profits
7713	87551	2409	3633	560	22360	20544	115757
217	2383	39	40	6	584	441	3084
438	1921	151	107	49	498	472	2729
377	4605	191	45	58	1836	1588	2810
1590	18153	855	409	373	28474	14184	11887
882	6208	280	123	75	2834	2598	25482
3726	35372	877	362	248	7225	6284	47263
116379	43896	1386	917	1075	10694	8785	167842
1453	31256	595	557	273	7178	5912	48029
357	7866	286	212	181	2365	2321	– 1160
1831	10732	225	228	648	5694	4630	11959
741	8089	257	94	113	2180	2064	8267
5147	47968	1241	714	746	12802	10245	56500
1940	15788	442	228	239	5890	5356	23595
1750	14360	1304	108	396	6357	5613	28828
2978	14748	556	235	271	10323	8881	21300
4913	43268	1231	565	686	10246	8846	54367
11640	112512	3027	1240	1239	22822	21320	164732
3099	41812	793	791	1106	7262	6197	95860
17399	74672	1438	781	795	16223	13906	105582
17038	158483	3571	1976	1438	33762	28271	223398
4357	75282	871	948	417	9657	7754	82005
2169	26305	947	216	413	4887	4203	37015
1148	12472	454	202	133	3059	1809	14704
9812	28524	984	2541	2331	40683	25017	176357
8	1039	11	28	7	39	35	– 2804
364	9052	348	115	630	3578	2194	– 3095

项目	Item	利润总额 Total Profits	# 应交所得税 Income Tax Payable
总计	**Total**	**1892997**	**453205**
按轻重工业分	**Grouped by Light and Heavy Industry**		
轻工业	Light Industry	728058	166736
重工业	Heavy Industry	1164939	286470
按注册登记类型分	**Grouped by Registered Type**		
国有企业	State－owned Enterprises	126021	45258
集体企业	Collective－owned Enterpriese	59670	15610
股份合作企业	Share Cooperative Enterprises	50315	13437
联营企业	Joint Owned Enterprises	12470	4577
有限责任公司	Limited Liability Corporations	342703	106927
股份有限公司	Share－holding Corporations Ltd.	434325	103129
私营企业	Private Enterprises	392280	105070
港澳台商投资企业	HongKong,Macao and Taiwan Funded	258763	29718
外商投资企业	Foreign Funded Enterprises	216137	29393
在总计中:亏损企业	Of the Total:Loss Making Enterprises	－60141	531
在总计中:国有及国有控股	Of the Total:State－owned and State－holding Industrial Enterprises	391096	117980
在总计中:农村工业	Of the Total:Rural Indusdry	1007777	230534
按规模分	**Grouped by Size**		
大型企业	Large－Sized Industrial Enterprises	422153	105151
中型企业	Medium－Sized Industrial Enterprises	721976	164221
小型企业	Small－Sized Industrial Enterprises	748868	183832
按工业行业分	**Grouped by Sector**		
非金属矿采选业	Nonmetal Minerals Mining and Dressing	610	50
农副食品加工业	Agricultural Non－staple Food Processing	22007	3284
食品制造业	Food Manufacturing	11339	2802
饮料制造业	Beverage Manufacturing	6922	1874
烟草制品业	Tobacco Processing	76258	25118
纺织业	Textile Industry	104037	21449

continued 6 (10000 yuan)

亏损企业亏损总额 Total Loss	利税总额 Total Profits and Taxes	本年应付工资总额 Total Wages Payable In This Year	本年应付福利费总额 Total Welfare Funds Payable In This Year	本年应交增值税 Value - added Taxes Payable in This Year	本年进项税额 Purchases Tax in This Year	本年销项税额 Sales Tax in This Year	全部职工年平均人数 Annual Average Employees (person)
60141	**3220119**	**1347570**	**148326**	**854470**	**3328923**	**3891364**	**919629**
34187	1376195	694102	74164	356833	1299988	1433997	519383
25954	1843924	653467	74162	497637	2028935	2457367	400246
5357	497990	48061	7453	132244	151260	358064	17438
1791	94672	45635	5939	29749	97333	123136	35022
1126	84350	48775	5906	28172	97245	120587	39273
1004	18204	4621	515	4854	10226	14530	2944
8488	520134	171274	20530	152057	364488	495952	108083
5894	725698	166425	23080	160570	930156	1039438	79484
6509	640163	464520	56255	191193	861893	970387	372309
12259	363810	227987	14749	100294	429166	416082	155001
17713	274564	169914	13877	55204	385916	351939	109769
60141	- 35780	68743	5873	19993	127848	125082	49724
11426	1003375	166824	23437	251252	928611	1230255	61295
11482	1484335	825214	90004	390345	1811760	2004845	621522
	728122	211415	25743	178294	936238	1039923	111086
14570	1305127	453941	49258	300492	1090706	1242966	296591
45571	1186870	682214	73325	375684	1301979	1608475	511952
52	1048	890	108	318	444	619	731
5503	33957	15451	1521	9810	75082	80649	11190
208	15822	9817	697	3672	19206	21092	10177
	22396	6664	330	7628	10753	17925	4079
	379006	7432	1430	66673	27821	92465	1831
4012	159677	109944	11700	49446	205724	230970	85540

单位:万元　　　　3-9 续表 7

项目	Item	利润总额 Total Profits	# 应交所得税 Income Tax Payable
纺织服装、鞋、帽制造业	Textile Clothing, Shoes, Cap Manufacturing	136857	22382
皮革、毛皮、羽毛(绒)及其制品业	Leather, Furs, Down and Related Products	3096	394
木材加工及木、竹、藤、棕、草制品业	Timber Processing, Bamboo, Cane Palm Fiber and Straw Products	3053	775
家具制造业	Furniture Manufacturing	3757	625
造纸及纸制品业	Papermaking and Paper Products	12831	3991
印刷业和记录媒介的复制	Printing and Record Medium Reproduction	28993	8207
文教体育用品制造业	Cultural. Educational and Sports Goods	48528	10536
石油加工、炼焦及核燃料加工业	Petroleum Processing, Coking & Nuclear Fuel Processing	155295	50437
化学原料及化学制品制造业	Raw Chemical Materials and Chemical Products	44499	7809
医药制造业	Medical and Pharmaceutical Products	-1013	651
化学纤维制造业	Chemical Fiber	12387	3610
橡胶制品业	Rubber Products	9118	2309
塑料制品业	Plastic Products	57843	12064
非金属矿物制品业	Nonmetal Mineral Products	27766	8443
黑色金属冶炼及压延加工业	Smelting and Pressing of Ferrous Metals	31228	4076
有色金属冶炼及压延加工业	Smelting and Pressing of Nonferrous Metals	36750	5768
金属制品业	Metal Products	58941	13588
通用设备制造业	General Equipment Manufacturing	183991	43472
专用设备制造业	Special Purpose Equipment Manufacturing	96911	15505
交通运输设备制造业	Transport Equipment Manufacturing	118451	24257
电气机械及器材制造业	Electric Equipment and Machinery Manufacturing	251578	60983
通信设备、计算机及电子设备制造业	Communication Equipment. Computer and Other Electronic Equipment Manufacturing	85444	17252
仪器仪表及文化、办公用机械制造业	Instruments, Meters, Cultural and Office Machinery	38745	10883
工艺品及其他制造业	Handicraft and Others Manufacturing	15854	2762
电力、热力的生产和供应业	Electric Power and Hot Power Production and Supply	213716	67427
燃气生产和供应业	Gas Production and Supply	-46	1
自来水的生产和供应业	Tap Water Production and Supply	-2746	421

continued 7

亏损企业亏损总额 Total Loss	利税总额 Total Profits and Taxes	本年应付工资总额 Total Wages Payable In This Year	本年应付福利费总额 Total Welfare Funds Payable In This Year	本年应交增值税 Value – added Taxes Payable in This Year	本年进项税额 Purchases Tax in This Year	本年销项税额 Sales Tax in This Year	全部职工年平均人数 Annual Average Employees (person)
2754	212799	185304	18313	68229	259273	250136	131274
106	5224	5014	457	1911	6333	7899	4057
364	6148	4470	456	2657	6290	8569	3663
178	5602	7188	557	1469	8515	7453	5838
2009	35132	16862	2612	20711	59295	78979	12162
580	36098	11187	935	6223	22865	28514	8442
819	64371	54276	5291	12118	75418	62764	42812
5818	338954	50201	7312	67281	443015	499703	9603
4822	66950	20357	2319	20997	101804	116301	10510
4605	2536	6526	750	3192	5631	7772	3899
286	22791	11162	1536	8573	45960	53702	7713
87	14413	9792	1153	4554	10317	14601	7975
2328	87371	64326	7044	24381	127788	142456	47574
1653	44335	16814	1768	14629	41291	54643	11818
604	42334	15931	1604	9356	103063	104253	9620
170	64652	18706	2120	24924	124093	148125	13355
1715	87269	66581	6763	23416	117600	122251	51105
5242	265355	161895	16937	69724	251107	276913	111820
1743	130033	48145	7524	30023	106897	128621	27902
1863	176238	73994	9084	40388	187680	209273	51380
1799	358305	173374	20072	89690	396211	422246	129835
2676	114492	65267	5183	24691	241588	251102	43954
1252	51927	33100	3290	11013	46214	44962	23912
2029	21547	25939	2103	4545	31072	27301	22534
359	353908	43121	6486	130380	162588	369723	10195
60	38	1022	133	76	7386	7462	455
4446	– 610	6816	741	1772	597	1922	2674

3-10 各县市区规模以上工业企业主要财务指标

单位:万元　　　　(2003)

项目	Item	全市 Toal	市区 Urban District	海曙 Haishu
企业单位数(个)	Number of Enterprises(unti)	4672	2119	93
#亏损企业	Deficits Enterprises	371	216	6
工业总产值(现价)	Gross Industrial Output Value(Current Prices)	26302862	15944163	902610
#国家、省级新产品产值	Value of New Products at State and Province Level	3486873	1419633	158157
工业销售产值(当年价)	Value of Industrial Products Sales(Current Prices)	25819475	15746161	877128
#出口交货值	Value of Export Products	7778095	3884191	343502
工业中间投入合计	Total of Input Among Industry	21104296	12659756	753012
工业增加值(当年价)	Value Added of Industry(Current Prices)	6053036	3870797	182806
资产合计	Total Asset	24460143	15431496	1131627
流动资产小计	Circulating Funds	12841812	7293819	514688
应收账款净额	Net Accounts Receivable	3369798	1824384	113070
产成品	Finished Products	1390788	788337	47706
流动资产年平均余额	Annual Average Balance of Circulating Funds	11564507	6686783	514234
长期投资	Long-Term Investment	1016918	703736	59427
固定资产小计	Total Fixed Assets	9332424	6807896	493696
固定资产原价	Original Value of Fixed Assets	12512426	9314997	689158
生产经营用	Producting and Managing	11814427	8880789	627945
累计折旧	Accumulative Total Depreciation	3964485	3050092	236215
本年折旧	Depreciation in this year	788237	571908	38320
固定资产净值年平均余额	Annual Average Balance of Net Value of Fixed Assets	8065316	5912425	464701
无形资产小计	Intangible Assets	716897	334447	22180
负债合计	Total Liabilities	14062672	8407094	700057
流动负债小计	Circulting Liabilities	11451534	6280486	480439
所有者权益合计	Total Creditors' Equity	10397471	7024402	431570
实收资本	Total Capital Hold	5163042	3531386	294544

Main Financial Indicators of Above Designated Size Industrial Enterprises by Region

(10000 yuan)

江东 Jiangdong	江北 Jiangbei	北仑 Beilun	镇海 Zhenhai	鄞州 Yinzhou	余姚 Yuyao	慈溪 Cixi	奉化 Fenghua	象山 Xiangshan	宁海 Ninghai
181	200	326	326	989	715	838	249	358	393
28	26	41	52	62	56	3	40	31	25
1277950	869232	3880225	4217247	4605100	2672195	3348667	1786863	1293618	1257356
116019	57680	105119	504377	478282	156903	466266	1140154	165226	138691
1295812	839650	3792671	4257531	4491572	2574683	3299633	1752941	1257410	1188647
313614	202944	871636	544201	1608287	1012175	1447143	336371	545954	552261
827013	742866	3020113	3521872	3720878	2163274	2727948	1490581	1077387	985350
538830	155247	1009462	812764	1029903	579701	703998	329349	257384	311807
1421602	648410	4455161	2661367	4273057	2451902	3266925	1017377	1080418	1212025
813404	401562	1970112	1053386	2435708	1496140	1940574	723180	665987	722112
177574	106165	516878	242926	664242	406406	559148	131461	229190	219209
71408	62331	164283	129697	311205	149968	140495	109710	96282	105996
750787	364481	1771115	980836	2206758	1299246	1732135	600496	583838	662009
92210	10771	90040	56877	343851	30516	147800	29840	57320	47706
461022	189649	2219217	1410218	1351952	758562	885397	236713	302637	341219
551247	271158	3303982	2136470	1577367	937456	1159096	304332	355979	440566
527293	253499	3258652	2004878	1430637	875926	1021775	282011	346257	407669
153810	93892	1165938	831589	379852	269248	336762	81297	100668	126418
34425	16665	215881	122649	93692	59441	85135	21752	22245	27756
371041	174301	2115685	1136532	1084002	641172	754352	203819	245310	308238
19603	30398	84839	55972	121061	101497	155789	19844	41610	63710
601301	420436	2420748	1205425	2359214	1499240	2096156	664229	651725	744228
512914	391822	1629582	1050998	2104171	1409606	1902557	600779	580442	677664
820301	227974	2034413	1455943	1913843	952662	1170769	353148	428693	467797
284602	123675	1480358	546066	756525	507829	600654	133439	149688	240046

单位:万元 3－10 续表

项目	Item	全市 Toal	市区 Urban District	海曙 Haishu
国家资本	State Capital	554908	450211	6122
港澳台资本	Invested Capital from Hongkong, Macao&Taiwan	850427	663999	53441
外商资本	Foreign Capital	782128	580831	3921
产品销售收入	Sales Revenue of Products	26048962	15867906	916915
产品销售成本	Cost of Sales	21821106	13136767	780682
产品销售费用	Expenses of Sales	738647	411276	25175
产品销售税金及附加	Sales Taxes and Extra Charges	472653	409151	1148
产品销售利润	Sales Profits	3016557	1910713	109909
管理费用	Management Expenses	1056889	599832	44548
税金	Tax	28471	16583	1271
财产保险费	Property Insurance Expenses	19962	9951	428
劳动、待业保险费	Job－waiting Insurance Expenses	18349	11298	650
财务费用	Financial Expenses	322904	200935	32252
#利息支出	Interest Expenditure	251316	156772	16885
营业利润	Business Profits	1726179	1169728	38999
利润总额	Total Profits	1892997	1286454	51370
应交所得税	Income Tax Payable	453205	318631	13241
亏损企业亏损总额	Total Loss	60141	50454	969
利税总额	Total Profits and Taxes	3220119	2281994	85727
本年应付工资总额	Total Wages Payable in This Year	1347570	746940	39808
本年应付福利费总额	Total Welfare Funds Payable in This Year	148326	84763	4792
本年应交增值税	Value－added Taxes Payable in This Year	854470	586390	33209
本年进项税额	Purchases Tax in This Year	3328923	2011582	115305
本年销项税额	Sales Tax in This Year	3891364	2477652	134716
全部职工年平均人数(人)	Annual Average Employees(person)	919629	459862	25217

continued (10000 yuan)

江东 Jiangdong	江北 Jiangbei	北仑 Beilun	镇海 Zhenhai	鄞州 Yinzhou	余姚 Yuyao	慈溪 Cixi	奉化 Fenghua	象山 Xiangshan	宁海 Ninghai
72216	9859	28230	267636	21977	56269	14203	10290	10162	13773
26606	34308	368451	101711	79482	108367	23359	22379	23575	8748
23281	13831	333792	82644	123363	80196	72562	14113	3353	31073
1306344	850287	3789236	4357017	4580963	2646140	3367129	1745592	1275751	1146444
819633	739803	3150893	3828859	3755615	2227589	2911223	1540337	1063405	941785
61697	18421	74571	37338	188413	85881	98992	65217	39399	37882
238215	2231	18314	121414	27769	15706	20853	7345	9949	9649
186800	89832	545458	369406	609166	316965	336061	132693	162998	157127
64786	46175	126690	99088	212482	126158	137227	63194	68795	61683
1409	1400	3735	2486	6131	4246	2859	804	1032	2947
932	498	3552	1673	2785	1847	2619	3974	499	1072
2812	886	1645	2193	2928	1860	3086	684	651	770
10034	7991	76958	25592	46974	30342	46215	9173	15850	20389
9483	7766	54456	23209	43844	21834	31558	7799	14161	19192
115818	37974	364616	253636	365346	165702	159313	71418	82544	77474
118917	48635	400544	243664	427253	186077	174593	73179	93688	79006
35984	8535	87369	70544	102959	35834	40194	17743	21651	19152
6260	3081	23913	6816	5471	4365	531	2352	871	1568
445025	79747	568208	482467	600703	272564	278725	113591	144789	128456
57446	51111	153914	142564	288891	146831	217333	73258	71502	91706
6759	4817	17401	17724	31011	14275	22081	8675	7561	10971
87893	28881	149351	117388	145681	70781	83279	33067	41152	39801
115177	107594	483327	603490	569608	333052	429264	275762	148210	131053
185915	128050	552048	696781	658231	358194	453768	274371	175949	151430
32717	36061	90780	66290	205198	104879	174818	49648	52349	78073

3－11 各县(市)、区国有控股工业企业主要财务指标

单位:万元 (2003)

项目	Item	全市 Toal	市区 Urban District	海曙 Haishu
企业单位数(个)	Number of Enterprises(unti)	114	80	11
#亏损企业	Deficits Enterprises	24	18	2
工业总产值(现价)	Gross Industrial Output Value(Current Prices)	6432799	5072806	172228
#国家、省级新产品产值	Value of New Products at State and Province Level	1611188	483142	15061
工业销售产值(当年价)	Value of Industrial Products Sales(Current Prices)	6413210	5088643	157373
#出口交货值	Value of Export Products	505760	458505	76042
工业中间投入合计	Total of Input Among Industry	5047837	3881764	138942
工业增加值(当年价)	Value Added of Industry(Current Prices)	1636214	1415225	36345
资产合计	Total Asset	5421924	4524692	229941
流动资产年平均余额	Annual Average Balance of Circulating Funds	1879828	1367241	85894
长期投资	Long－Term Investment	158643	129701	9230
固定资产原价	Original Value of Fixed Assets	4423015	4074297	143880
#累计折旧	Accumulative Total Depreciation	1667635	1552776	45214
固定资产净值年平均余额	Annual Average Balance of Net Value of Fixed Assets	2497641	2281295	103070
负债合计	Total Liabilities	2600214	2098667	117048
流动负债小计	Circulting Liabilities	1639007	1194190	101796
所有者权益合计	Total Creditors' Equity	2821710	2426025	112893
#实收资本	Total Capital Hold	1079272	963211	48892
产品销售收入	Sales Revenue of Products	6753919	5181462	175202
产品销售成本	Cost of Sales	5694315	4261715	152449
产品销售费用	Expenses of Sales	114230	71333	3286
产品销售税金及附加	Sales Taxes and Extra Charges	361027	358054	344
产品销售利润	Sales Profits	584346	490360	19123
管理费用	Management Expenses	177956	120481	11874
财务费用	Financial Expenses	39676	34233	3055
营业利润	Business Profits	392300	349172	5230
利润总额	Total Profits	391096	346735	14638
亏损企业亏损总额	Total Loss	11426	10625	715
本年应付工资总额	Total Wages Payable in This Year	166824	133425	8895
本年应付福利费总额	Total Welfare Funds Payable in This Year	23437	19706	916
本年应交增值税	Value－added Taxes Payable in This Year	251252	224182	3058
本年进项税额	Purchases Tax in This Year	928611	684560	17953
本年销项税额	Sales Tax in This Year	1230255	961933	19695
全部职工年平均人数(人)	Annual Average Employees(person)	61295	43046	7202

Main Financial Indicators of State Holding Shares Industrial Enterprises by Region

(10000 yuan)

江东 Jiangdong	江北 Jiangbei	北仑 Beilun	镇海 Zhenhai	鄞州 Yinzhou	余姚 Yuyao	慈溪 Cixi	奉化 Fenghua	象山 Xiangshan	宁海 Ninghai
12	7	15	20	12	11	6	4	7	6
3	1	2	6	3	3		1	2	
575375	27664	679375	3371521	55306	79075	50881	1131827	25718	72492
2381	2399		456004	7299	296	1189	1122617	486	3458
592923	26017	634342	3431138	55512	76869	48327	1101925	25718	71728
13100	60	71059	289145	9100	6184		28347	5521	7203
244789	19748	532621	2833074	38975	61691	33898	999449	18190	52845
398667	9523	177259	629985	21752	23541	21915	142576	8825	24132
568354	30210	831339	1914915	109953	188927	162673	407463	54042	84127
306135	17229	264731	538214	56647	93725	78699	272907	20546	46710
20302	705	5977	40075	2851	1344	1771	19221	1736	4870
250327	19260	938985	1871585	64699	109143	85267	62826	38710	52772
69784	8803	474212	742653	23332	45603	18761	14070	11024	25401
153934	9460	442225	967816	38665	64968	53963	42237	27931	27247
93811	14859	367194	760042	46062	82145	87618	262597	26475	42712
81353	14016	230388	626336	29999	60612	69935	253912	21318	39040
474543	15351	464145	1154874	63891	106782	75055	144866	27567	41415
66966	6981	372257	401817	20702	57565	14565	19966	10032	13933
601414	25915	629403	3515626	167242	170051	191737	1068351	43057	99261
224125	17681	533937	3117350	155322	153381	176400	972266	39250	91303
42184	372	3369	16039	428	723	601	40754	210	609
236223	180	2650	118140	466	501	385	1583	166	338
98882	7682	89447	264097	11026	15445	14352	53748	3431	7010
20840	5052	15288	55398	5993	9542	9239	32253	2400	4041
265	240	13137	16151	258	941	2064	991	493	954
78263	2780	64590	200004	4971	6161	3168	30522	991	2286
77404	2529	64373	187063	4664	6018	4480	31112	669	2082
213	184	3043	2396	129	649		48	104	
10987	2284	19245	74845	3984	5938	6008	12358	3041	6054
1841	326	2721	11148	494	664	858	957	422	830
68081	1607	30504	91537	5421	6157	4932	10199	1297	4485
36416	2938	87988	498373	23878	25045	27617	173546	5137	12706
101304	4065	109830	578005	27207	30822	32548	181873	5906	17173
3919	1070	6057	19301	1918	2873	3651	6208	1792	3725

3－12　各县(市)、区规模以上集体工业企业主要财务指标

单位:万元　　　　　　　　　　　　　　(2003)

项目	Item	全市 Toal	市区 Urban District	海曙 Haishu
企业单位数(个)	Number of Enterprises(unti)	321	155	12
＃亏损企业	Deficits Enterprises	22	16	
工业总产值(现价)	Gross Industrial Output Value(Current Prices)	792419	376192	29756
＃国家、省级新产品产值	Value of New Products at State and Province Level	99074	15927	1986
工业销售产值(当年价)	Value of Industrial Products Sales(Current Prices)	769027	365473	29200
＃出口交货值	Value of Export Products	138779	45991	3734
工业中间投入合计	Total of Input Among Industry	650804	311913	25768
工业增加值(当年价)	Value Added of Industry(Current Prices)	171364	78584	4901
资产合计	Total Asset	728286	333441	27261
流动资产年平均余额	Annual Average Balance of Circulating Funds	448858	222484	19389
长期投资	Long－Term Investment	15312	10332	309
固定资产原价	Original Value of Fixed Assets	255867	96084	6231
＃累计折旧	Accumulative Total Depreciation	95817	34110	2476
固定资产净值年平均余额	Annual Average Balance of Net Value of Fixed Assets	158257	57839	4022
负债合计	Total Liabilities	432624	189199	16773
流动负债小计	Circulting Liabilities	399668	177479	16698
所有者权益合计	Total Creditors' Equity	295662	144242	10489
＃实收资本	Total Capital Hold	106805	43617	3340
产品销售收入	Sales Revenue of Products	764626	358367	29170
产品销售成本	Cost of Sales	646256	303568	25885
产品销售费用	Expenses of Sales	16160	7058	347
产品销售税金及附加	Sales Taxes and Extra Charges	5253	2450	95
产品销售利润	Sales Profits	96958	45291	2844
管理费用	Management Expenses	35755	18943	1467
财务费用	Financial Expenses	11743	4338	540
营业利润	Business Profits	50847	22887	964
利润总额	Total Profits	59670	28633	1440
亏损企业亏损总额	Total Loss	1791	1673	
本年应付工资总额	Total Wages Payable in This Year	45635	22350	1069
本年应付福利费总额	Total Welfare Funds Payable in This Year	5939	3212	147
本年应交增值税	Value－added Taxes Payable in This Year	29749	14306	914
本年进项税额	Purchases Tax in This Year	97333	45389	4260
本年销项税额	Sales Tax in This Year	123136	58649	5150
全部职工年平均人数(人)	Annual Average Employees(person)	35022	16906	786

Main Financial Indicators of Collective – owned Aboved Designated Size Industrial Enterprises by Region

(10000 yuan)

江东 Jiangdong	江北 Jiangbei	北仑 Beilun	镇海 Zhenhai	鄞州 Yinzhou	余姚 Yuyao	慈溪 Cixi	奉化 Fenghua	象山 Xiangshan	宁海 Ninghai
6	8	18	59	51	67	55	14	19	11
	3		10	3	2		1	3	
34151	6921	62248	116614	126040	112760	230198	20256	37196	15817
1581		10698	647	1016	3450	79669		28	
33052	6913	59262	113280	123304	108916	222648	20224	36522	15244
3059	663	6119	10668	21737	24216	38734	6858	20958	2022
29024	5361	51038	93636	106702	89988	193034	14965	27867	13037
6278	1857	12912	28332	24212	27188	44647	6505	10994	3446
32739	8558	54735	128106	81752	83812	244633	22658	32332	11410
23418	4617	30310	91004	53565	52011	133466	13276	19520	8101
631		2684	5756	953	794	2421	1755	10	
10046	5431	14112	33098	27113	31486	96796	14128	13894	3479
2738	2015	4195	13136	9536	9705	37844	7414	5716	1028
7049	3010	8831	19389	15501	22855	60618	6485	8084	2376
21155	4565	34865	63937	47644	51856	157585	11481	15203	7300
20626	4524	28149	63887	43334	49609	141448	9804	14566	6762
11584	3993	19870	64169	34108	31956	87049	11177	17128	4110
7304	2643	4949	17066	8294	8133	45123	5142	3866	924
33459	6969	57042	112212	119033	109836	225184	20252	36103	14884
28997	5722	47233	92059	103242	91566	192779	16760	28997	12586
437	78	764	4015	1411	2386	5299	482	616	319
183	38	346	650	1131	990	1284	156	263	110
3843	1132	8699	15488	13249	14893	25823	2854	6227	1870
1571	683	2689	7348	5161	5478	7118	1208	1918	1090
270	120	757	1652	993	1222	5342	413	284	144
2031	389	5318	6746	7433	7974	13523	1505	4318	640
2383	495	6012	7071	11225	8502	14449	2119	5157	810
	157		943	573	24		66	28	
1748	822	3709	8542	6438	7780	9792	1943	2904	866
176	115	354	1661	759	1017	972	263	379	96
1151	296	1702	5353	4874	4416	7483	1213	1664	667
4530	1062	7380	13370	14721	12027	32096	1807	4396	1618
5654	1257	9046	18431	19028	16121	37220	2865	6030	2251
1033	597	2916	6084	5470	5583	7635	1622	2316	960

3-13 各县(市)、区规模以上大中型工业企业主要财务指标

单位:万元　　　　　　　　　　(2003)

项目	Item	全市 Toal	市区 Urban District	海曙 Haishu
企业单位数(个)	Number of Enterprises(unti)	454	224	16
#亏损企业	Deficits Enterprises	22	15	
工业总产值(现价)	Gross Industrial Output Value(Current Prices)	15446359	10048023	751126
#国家、省级新产品产值	Value of New Products at State and Province Level	3070832	1252899	149773
工业销售产值(当年价)	Value of Industrial Products Sales(Current Prices)	15218703	9969232	728326
#出口交货值	Value of Export Products	4269177	2338566	296360
工业中间投入合计	Total of Input Among Industry	12428486	8009129	628671
工业增加值(当年价)	Value Added of Industry(Current Prices)	3496659	2398194	150400
资产合计	Total Asset	14266891	9418077	991785
流动资产年平均余额	Annual Average Balance of Circulating Funds	6576842	4024931	417561
长期投资	Long-Term Investment	852060	610198	55299
固定资产原价	Original Value of Fixed Assets	7350206	5714216	639529
#累计折旧	Accumulative Total Depreciation	2462455	2004054	215388
固定资产净值年平均余额	Annual Average Balance of Net Value of Fixed Assets	4475633	3388555	433775
负债合计	Total Liabilities	7495734	4512440	611556
流动负债小计	Circulting Liabilities	6346196	3671228	397012
所有者权益合计	Total Creditors' Equity	6771157	4905636	380229
#实收资本	Total Capital Hold	3013153	2200467	266261
产品销售收入	Sales Revenue of Products	15593346	10195324	766427
产品销售成本	Cost of Sales	12923015	8339318	652479
产品销售费用	Expenses of Sales	508419	300310	21590
产品销售税金及附加	Sales Taxes and Extra Charges	410334	382361	586
产品销售利润	Sales Profits	1751578	1173333	91772
管理费用	Management Expenses	576980	342787	34038
财务费用	Financial Expenses	174366	113473	30340
营业利润	Business Profits	1062959	756891	32575
利润总额	Total Profits	1144130	807524	44127
亏损企业亏损总额	Total Loss	14570	13019	
本年应付工资总额	Total Wages Payable in This Year	665356	398299	28188
本年应付福利费总额	Total Welfare Funds Payable in This Year	75001	48224	3385
本年应交增值税	Value-added Taxes Payable in This Year	478786	359300	27945
本年进项税额	Purchases Tax in This Year	2026944	1325704	94642
本年销项税额	Sales Tax in This Year	2282889	1543755	109939
全部职工年平均人数(人)	Annual Average Employees(person)	407677	214408	17269

Main Financial Indicators of Large – scale and Medium – scale Above Designated Size Industrial Enterprises by Region

(10000 yuan)

江东 Jiangdong	江北 Jiangbei	北仑 Beilun	镇海 Zhenhai	鄞州 Yinzhou	余姚 Yuyao	慈溪 Cixi	奉化 Fenghua	象山 Xiangshan	宁海 Ninghai
19	20	57	22	89	58	91	19	22	40
3	3	6	1	1	3		2		2
836104	490069	1943522	3547128	2456110	1132248	1683992	1373487	702043	506566
93921	45681	91178	473541	398807	114733	348057	1128019	149029	78095
853375	470895	1891629	3604311	2396732	1079581	1659161	1345821	686998	477910
181064	68962	693056	329856	769270	481036	793435	157679	236794	261667
454394	433446	1522515	2976772	1982204	897855	1360334	1170733	596323	394112
456288	72933	488438	665165	551569	263953	361264	219417	126497	127334
966994	349748	2181294	2067606	2687162	1156135	1881851	665402	579022	566404
492309	189866	956359	631907	1312464	572009	960375	418315	313685	287527
76811	7085	64651	46622	321753	15951	117713	26049	46863	35286
383639	154951	1540280	1908348	958533	474763	667294	129313	153472	211148
106743	52352	627501	752772	209992	126402	193155	26474	48556	63814
248619	101508	858141	995948	670202	327768	429706	85511	100203	143890
304975	226389	1054918	855949	1400720	666329	1167137	450309	347466	352053
254245	204843	854048	715729	1192634	606281	1045375	409623	297398	316291
662020	123359	1126376	1211656	1286442	489807	714714	215093	231556	214351
192510	60692	755030	427319	454485	254073	333940	51423	57306	115944
859289	477312	1884538	3686080	2499279	1167073	1760072	1304030	692328	474519
430671	425841	1565787	3257629	1992099	966590	1509436	1156782	564997	385892
51763	9443	40618	21410	150128	48233	56038	55425	26953	21460
236833	1133	10941	118858	13961	5430	8025	4457	5284	4777
140022	40896	267191	288183	343090	146820	186573	87367	95095	62390
39286	20907	64991	62992	115243	56959	72058	40651	39618	24907
4498	4493	29034	18318	25647	12561	26610	4036	8275	9411
97233	17019	186817	214183	213299	79671	94286	53041	49357	29713
97896	26848	186038	201039	255522	90620	105106	54430	56687	29763
3830	1169	3346	644	86	772		299		480
29916	19387	95137	86760	135216	61143	102890	35825	28628	38571
3614	1620	11506	12147	15693	5532	10178	3901	2983	4183
74578	16310	67431	94809	77663	29560	37606	16663	20777	14880
61766	63361	268818	521908	314921	152897	217334	201140	78679	51190
127280	76868	269569	601650	358000	157975	226815	210061	91124	53159
13553	12096	54386	26356	89543	41429	81638	19572	18690	31940

3－14 各县(市)、区规模以上农村工业企业主要财务指标

单位:万元　　　　(2003)

项目	Item	全市 Toal	市区 Urban District	海曙 Haishu
企业单位数(个)	Number of Enterprises(unti)	3463	1328	35
#亏损企业	Deficits Enterprises	203	95	2
工业总产值(现价)	Gross Industrial Output Value(Current Prices)	14437306	5968738	160195
#国家、省级新产品产值	Value of New Products at State and Province Level	2498193	608388	3337
工业销售产值(当年价)	Value of Industrial Products Sales(Current Prices)	14069895	5818331	152092
#出口交货值	Value of Export Products	4934451	1880521	86879
工业中间投入合计	Total of Input Among Industry	11862968	4894377	133323
工业增加值(当年价)	Value Added of Industry(Current Prices)	2964682	1260193	30485
资产合计	Total Asset	11818208	5088292	121147
流动资产年平均余额	Annual Average Balance of Circulating Funds	6429938	2699851	77395
长期投资	Long－Term Investment	595619	338048	7644
固定资产原价	Original Value of Fixed Assets	3883774	1733076	25893
#累计折旧	Accumulative Total Depreciation	1008450	414834	6356
固定资产净值年平均余额	Annual Average Balance of Net Value of Fixed Assets	2655401	1207095	18168
负债合计	Total Liabilities	7369401	2988932	93960
流动负债小计	Circulting Liabilities	6769420	2719586	87088
所有者权益合计	Total Creditors' Equity	4448808	2099362	27187
#实收资本	Total Capital Hold	1802839	747810	12074
产品销售收入	Sales Revenue of Products	13865870	5799420	159288
产品销售成本	Cost of Sales	11688907	4794916	137505
产品销售费用	Expenses of Sales	487532	226942	6837
产品销售税金及附加	Sales Taxes and Extra Charges	86213	29637	301
产品销售利润	Sales Profits	1603218	747925	14645
管理费用	Management Expenses	583857	246915	6437
财务费用	Financial Expenses	154122	59417	1879
营业利润	Business Profits	901062	454894	6542
利润总额	Total Profits	1007777	524605	6963
亏损企业亏损总额	Total Loss	11482	6524	32
本年应付工资总额	Total Wages Payable in This Year	825214	355739	9729
本年应付福利费总额	Total Welfare Funds Payable in This Year	90004	40023	1286
本年应交增值税	Value－added Taxes Payable in This Year	390345	185836	3613
本年进项税额	Purchases Tax in This Year	1811760	755150	22783
本年销项税额	Sales Tax in This Year	2004845	872918	19611
全部职工年平均人数(人)	Annual Average Employees(person)	621522	256645	6865

Main Financial Indicators of Rural Above Designated Size Industrial Enterprises by Region

(10000 yuan)

江东 Jiangdong	江北 Jiangbei	北仑 Beilun	镇海 Zhenhai	鄞州 Yinzhou	余姚 Yuyao	慈溪 Cixi	奉化 Fenghua	象山 Xiangshan	宁海 Ninghai
83	127	122	142	818	579	772	226	320	238
9	18	4	22	40	35	2	32	27	12
315978	609448	614695	403157	3864803	1859595	3034269	1701886	1134368	738450
15159	36484	73577	38565	441266	82870	461698	1140154	113876	91207
311798	589931	601554	394632	3767863	1785229	2989906	1666508	1103849	706072
134239	122365	117800	146836	1272393	630039	1294334	299850	486122	343585
260754	536870	483957	334497	3144595	1523540	2478317	1436562	949384	580788
65366	93920	149708	80691	839933	382668	627914	294606	220094	179207
382390	363724	584028	333103	3303609	1410004	2828367	883886	900641	707018
185181	203814	318128	211987	1703163	814920	1502312	550949	482866	379040
51282	3815	22068	9206	244034	19687	127058	26619	50418	33789
102075	125679	194110	111139	1174129	486908	950860	201974	274562	236394
25228	32876	52960	36374	261024	132115	275397	52004	75357	58743
80119	92584	130609	73418	812158	329550	618953	136852	190110	172841
202778	243220	356004	198108	1894601	925325	1868194	598543	544389	444018
181994	225585	330639	190834	1703186	892002	1702855	553880	488840	412257
179612	120504	228024	134995	1409008	484679	960173	285343	356251	263000
104685	50922	64166	45577	470365	222274	506774	81828	120670	123483
316497	598785	600963	393637	3729769	1758622	2916327	1629723	1105565	656213
263824	534936	475153	338380	3044690	1480600	2510287	1445826	921697	535581
9210	10853	25350	8313	166373	51474	88855	62368	35733	22160
1287	1606	2266	1577	22592	13510	19943	7124	9186	6813
42177	51391	98194	45367	496114	213038	297242	114405	138949	91659
18432	21905	22433	20099	157585	74853	116216	55018	57588	33267
3134	5575	6330	4708	37786	20440	41789	7629	13096	11751
22084	24564	71021	21071	309606	119817	145357	62542	71221	47231
24270	34057	74214	22115	362979	132058	156239	65311	81274	48290
286	1107	72	2874	2155	1665	172	1801	740	580
20708	29714	35230	31530	228806	100852	194079	63544	59543	51457
2041	2842	5326	3020	25509	9945	20237	7495	6141	6163
10142	21341	18969	12031	119725	46612	71962	29281	35109	21545
38463	78199	97132	49724	468782	218212	370519	262518	130781	74580
43915	96813	108197	55362	548938	241952	391931	260000	153074	84970
13443	22842	22946	24934	165595	73823	157004	43522	44130	46398

3－15 各县(市)、区规模以上外商和港澳台投资工业企业主要财务指标

单位:万元 (2003)

项目	Item	全市 Toal	市区 Urban District	海曙 Haishu
企业单位数(个)	Number of Enterprises(unti)	1067	583	26
#亏损企业	Deficits Enterprises	138	81	3
工业总产值(现价)	Gross Industrial Output Value(Current Prices)	6847165	4679588	409854
#国家、省级新产品产值	Value of New Products at State and Province Level	413722	266997	124629
工业销售产值(当年价)	Value of Industrial Products Sales(Current Prices)	6643419	4538145	409188
#出口交货值	Value of Export Products	3180718	1747357	101385
工业中间投入合计	Total of Input Among Industry	5554935	3832600	335915
工业增加值(当年价)	Value Added of Industry(Current Prices)	1447727	961793	93545
资产合计	Total Asset	6591949	4645737	643356
流动资产年平均余额	Annual Average Balance of Circulating Funds	3218303	2161052	270452
长期投资	Long－Term Investment	102130	82796	38345
固定资产原价	Original Value of Fixed Assets	3374467	2661069	488077
#累计折旧	Accumulative Total Depreciation	985439	782762	177346
固定资产净值年平均余额	Annual Average Balance of Net Value of Fixed Assets	2290678	1817167	320939
负债合计	Total Liabilities	3672869	2477383	391383
流动负债小计	Circulting Liabilities	3128749	1992192	194207
所有者权益合计	Total Creditors' Equity	2919080	2168353	251973
#实收资本	Total Capital Hold	2223467	1724963	217510
产品销售收入	Sales Revenue of Products	6674791	4573828	407878
产品销售成本	Cost of Sales	5693801	3914180	335884
产品销售费用	Expenses of Sales	163230	101751	10613
产品销售税金及附加	Sales Taxes and Extra Charges	7977	3580	203
产品销售利润	Sales Profits	809783	554317	61179
管理费用	Management Expenses	274294	182395	18051
财务费用	Financial Expenses	99914	73586	25373
营业利润	Business Profits	463236	322550	20152
利润总额	Total Profits	474900	326271	19936
亏损企业亏损总额	Total Loss	29973	24827	387
本年应付工资总额	Total Wages Payable in This Year	397901	244737	16883
本年应付福利费总额	Total Welfare Funds Payable in This Year	28626	19713	1803
本年应交增值税	Value－added Taxes Payable in This Year	155498	114809	19607
本年进项税额	Purchases Tax in This Year	815082	550828	47718
本年销项税额	Sales Tax in This Year	768020	548735	65136
全部职工年平均人数(人)	Annual Average Employees(person)	264770	151612	8138

Main Financial Indicators of Foreign Funded and Enterprises Funded from Hongkong, Macao, Taiwan Above Designated Size Industrial Enterprises by Region

(10000 yuan)

江东 Jiangdong	江北 Jiangbei	北仑 Beilun	镇海 Zhenhai	鄞州 Yinzhou	余姚 Yuyao	慈溪 Cixi	奉化 Fenghua	象山 Xiangshan	宁海 Ninghai
49	45	143	82	238	195	133	46	64	46
8	7	28	14	21	31	2	13	6	5
249589	224520	2190568	537237	1067819	855819	627357	168985	302360	213056
41000	19019	23230	9362	49757	22398	69658	8232	19705	26732
248736	212430	2122462	514005	1031324	827787	617414	170821	292601	196651
123837	79249	690359	133891	618637	549411	422854	103230	229390	128476
201718	178780	1792226	453896	870066	667982	510542	122487	255607	165717
53645	50635	449537	95167	219266	202008	124056	50465	55923	53482
259593	229576	2331403	414460	767348	852503	498795	161822	205681	227411
130675	137491	1021109	189605	411720	451670	288262	70669	110234	136416
6631	4440	21962	1799	9621	6908	5834	964	978	4650
123741	103596	1390580	247483	307593	277689	181446	98648	79803	75812
38802	37546	371590	75708	81770	80471	53371	24600	20479	23756
81334	61229	968802	172674	212190	185783	115288	68790	52757	50893
142293	136648	1152890	219123	435047	537413	313070	84870	126827	133306
119814	129028	937558	206607	404977	519813	303515	69222	121664	122343
117300	92928	1178514	195337	332301	315090	185725	76952	78854	94106
76444	62607	1015896	145111	207395	217791	109065	62892	41889	66867
251663	216863	2136712	519493	1041220	831149	606402	174142	297896	191374
214910	178686	1848165	452547	883987	697403	524559	144452	260794	152413
6056	7717	42265	8343	26758	24554	18462	4035	6819	7609
235	48	1265	314	1515	1425	412	321	1711	528
30462	30413	245017	58288	128959	107768	62968	25335	28571	30824
12866	14288	78683	16113	42396	36687	25201	8320	10071	11620
2995	1982	28112	4919	10205	10123	7007	1914	3787	3497
15545	14993	153461	39681	78719	62789	31314	15082	15452	16049
16068	16284	148831	40544	84609	66127	34067	14495	17346	16594
821	1316	19586	1297	1421	3078	448	801	178	641
18839	17843	92359	22639	76174	54307	47372	15371	18946	17168
1366	800	8147	1223	6374	3107	1466	1719	1081	1540
5774	4895	51195	11825	21514	14171	7240	3967	9169	6142
25957	26571	271163	63797	115621	103841	71735	39784	30247	18647
22812	27667	250709	68861	113551	90042	55465	18076	36579	19123
10602	10817	54835	14490	52730	37196	38075	10758	13335	13794

3-16 工业主要产品产量

Output of Major Industrial Products

产品		Industrial Products		2000	2001	2002	2003
原盐	(万吨)	Salt	(10000 tons)	6.22	6.21	3.60	5.87
大米	(万吨)	Rice	(10000 tons)	1.42	6.82	3.98	4.26
小麦粉	(万吨)	Wheat Powded	(10000 tons)	6.00	4.00	3.70	3.41
配混合饲料	(万吨)	Blend Fodder	(10000 tons)	17.92	18.31	18.41	15.10
食用植物油	(万吨)	Edible Vegetable Oil	(10000 tons)	6.20	6.09	2.62	2.30
水产加工品	(万吨)	Processed Aquatic Products	(10000 tons)	4.05	5.99	6.86	9.25
罐头	(万吨)	Canned Food	(10000 tons)	10.07	10.78	11.51	14.28
味精	(万吨)	Monosodium Glutamate	(10000 tons)	1.23	1.41	1.93	2.18
饮料酒	(万吨)	Alcoholic Beverages	(10000 tons)	28.08	29.03	28.76	29.11
啤酒	(万吨)	Beer	(10000 tons)	26.04	27.21	26.12	26.90
黄酒	(万吨)	Millet Wine	(10000 tons)	1.82	1.62	2.43	1.94
软饮料	(万吨)	Soft Drink	(10000 tons)	5.44	6.82	6.40	7.43
瓶(罐)装饮用水	(万吨)	Bottled Drinking Water	(10000 tons)	4.73	6.08	5.67	7.19
精制茶	(万吨)	Refine Tea	(10000 tons)	1.18	1.28	1.83	2.28
卷烟	(万箱)	Cigarettes	(10000 cases)	37.52	40.92	42.75	44.61
纱	(万吨)	Yarm	(10000 tons)	8.00	9.11	11.54	10.77
布	(万米)	Cloth	(10000 m)	15111	17481	15343	18951
印染布	(万米)	Printing and Dyeing Cloth	(10000 m)	30508	38085	34121	43709
帘子布	(万吨)	Curtain Cloth	(10000 tons)	5.10	6.17	5.60	5.69
绒线(毛线)	(吨)	Knitting Wool	(ton)	3382	4468	4511	3672
呢绒	(万米)	Woolen Piece Goods	(10000 m)	766	1084	1337	1586
丝织品	(万米)	Silk Knitwear Goods	(10000 m)	3163	1963	616	868
服装	(万件)	Garment	(10000 units)	46056	53913	65570	81507

3－16 续表 1　continued 2

产品		Industrial Products		2000	2001	2002	2003
梭织服装	（万件）	Shuttle Woven Garment	（10000 units）	7365	7892	9351	11012
西服及西服套装	（万件）	Western－style Clothes	（10000 units）	905	964	1325	1477
衬衫	（万件）	Shirt	（10000 units）	3126	3761	3925	4772
针织服装	（万件）	Knitting Garment	（10000 units）	38625	45967	56136	70375
羽绒服装	（万件）	Eiderdown Garment	（10000 units）	66	53	83	120
机制纸	（万吨）	Machine Made Paper	（10000 tons）	2.48	4.18	7.28	5.24
机制纸板	（万吨）	Machine Made Paperboard	（10000 tons）	68.34	65.15	72.15	73.93
纸制品	（万吨）	Paper Products	（10000 tons）	12.28	17.46	20.64	26.24
玩具	（万元）	Toy	（10000 yuan）	74671	90881	73801	77178
原油加工量	（万吨）	Crude Oil Processed	（10000 tons）	1050.44	1072.19	1188.28	1360.97
汽油	（万吨）	Gasoline	（10000 tons）	168.16	164.44	184.82	230.72
煤油	（万吨）	Kerosene	（10000 tons）	105.93	85.02	100.4	110.31
柴油	（万吨）	Diesel Oil	（10000 tons）	370.07	425.00	473.66	531.53
石油沥青	（万吨）	Asphalt	（10000 tons）	40.96	32.82	44.32	57.25
液化石油气	（万吨）	Liquefied Petroleum，Gas	（10000 tons）	38.43	46.30	56.42	108.50
硫酸（折 100%）	（万吨）	Sulphuric Acid（100%）	（10000 tons）	9.61	11.00	11.60	8.84
盐酸（含量 31%以上）	（万吨）	Hydrochloric Acid（above 31% percent）	（10000 tons）	1.93	4.44	6.82	10.19
烧碱（折 100%）	（万吨）	Caustic Soda（100%）	（10000 tons）	6.70	9.15	10.70	10.72
合成氨	（万吨）	Synthetic Ammonia	（10000 tons）	32.83	35.89	36.25	33.44
农用化肥（折纯）	（万吨）	Chemical Fertilizers	（10000 tons）	26.69	28.29	28.96	26.12
氮肥（折含 N 100%）	（万吨）	Nitrogenous Fertilizer（100%）	（10000 tons）	25.53	27.26	28.03	25.69
尿素	（万吨）	Urea	（10000 tons）	24.36	26.26	26.77	25.69
磷肥（折合 P205 100%）	（万吨）	Phosphorus Fertilizer（100%）	（10000 tons）	1.16	1.03	0.93	0.42

3-16 续表 2　continued 2

产品		Industrial Products		2000	2001	2002	2003
化学农药	（吨）	Chemical Pesticide	(ton)	6228	5004	6255	4392
纯苯	（万吨）	Pure Benzene	(10000 tons)	4.79	4.24	5.10	5.55
甲醛	（万吨）	Formaldehyde	(10000 tons)	4.64	6.20	6.13	6.43
油漆	（万吨）	Paint	(10000 tons)	1.32	1.24	1.44	1.52
建筑涂料	（吨）	Building Dope	(ton)	2058	3015	1561	1868
染料	（吨）	Dye	(ton)	1784	1816	3028	2366
塑料树脂及共聚物	（万吨）	Plastic Resin and Copolyment	(10000 tons)	9.51	5.81	6.91	8.59
化学原料药	（吨）	Chemical Raw Medicine	(ton)	522.0	560.0	544.0	473.4
中成药	（吨）	Traditional Chinese Patent Medicine	(ton)	139	147	139	152
化学纤维	（万吨）	Chemical Fiber	(10000 tons)	19.50	22.11	24.34	27.32
塑料制品	（万吨）	Plastic Products	(10000 tons)	27.10	46.30	61.51	80.66
水泥	（万吨）	Cement	(10000 tons)	161.0	256.0	295.3	378.8
#散装水泥	（万吨）	Bulk Cement	(10000 tons)	126.0	204.0	247.9	325.4
砖（折标准砖）	（万块）	Bricks	(10000 pcs)	1786	2198	1214	1150
成品钢材	（万吨）	Rolled - steel Final Products	(10000 tons)	23.21	26.26	23.38	43.29
铜	（万吨）	Copper	(10000 tons)	3.80	3.89	3.42	3.08
铜加工材	（万吨）	Copper Material	(10000 tons)	16.50	18.32	25.66	37.72
铝材	（万吨）	Aluminium	(10000 tons)	4.03	4.59	4.81	5.97
钢丝绳	（吨）	Steel Cable	(ton)	12572	12769	8156	9918
日用精铝制品	（万吨）	Fine Aluminium Products Product for Daily Use	(10000 tons)	1.17	1.45	1.89	1.83
粉末冶金制品	（万吨）	Powder Metallurgy Products	(10000 tons)	1.01	1.30	1.38	1.78
塑料加工设备	（万吨）	Plastic Process Equipment	(10000 tons)	7.90	8.28	11.31	15.57
大中型拖拉机	（台）	Lager and Medium - sized Tractor	(unit)	2889	3998	5118	3392

3-16 续表 3　continued 3

产品		Industrial Products		2000	2001	2002	2003
医疗仪器设备	（万元）	Medical Instrument and Equipment	（10000 yuan）	5216	6303	8329	9136
汽车	（辆）	Motor Vechicle	（unit）	66	8887	17342	38888
轿车	（辆）	Car	（unit）			3317	15942
改装汽车	（辆）	Refit Automobile	（unit）	573	1230	1739	1837
摩托车	（万辆）	Motorcycles	（10000 units）	7.14	10.64	17.69	24.58
自行车	（万辆）	Bicycles	（10000 units）	35.87	38.34	49.52	64.26
民用钢质船舶	（综合吨）	Civil Steel Ship	（complex ton）	4000	13000	29250	83200
交流电动机	（万千瓦）	Alternating Current Motor	（10000 kw）	31.80	30.42	29.61	47.29
变压器	（万千伏安）	Transformer	（10000 kev）	77.34	98.44	128.18	298.51
通讯电缆	（万公里）	Telecommunications Cable	（10000 km）	14.45	61.74	68.91	7.65
电线	（万公里）	Electric Wire	（10000 km）	34.05	44.79	59.96	70.98
原电池(折一号电池)	(万只)	Primary Cells and Batterices	（10000 units）	62786	71817	92017	171943
家用洗衣机	（万台）	Household Washing Machine	（10000 units）	115.69	139.90	262.68	417.96
吸尘器	（万台）	Dust Catcher	（10000 units）	102.58	155.58	219.20	300.20
电风扇	（万台）	Electric Fan	（10000 units）	118.80	123.04	179.00	119.61
房间空气调节器	（万台）	Home Air Conditioner	（10000 units）	55.62	134.15	292.75	346.64
排油烟机	（万台）	Range Hoods	（10000 units）	188.76	161.16	119.21	95.48
移动电话机	（万部）	Mobile Phone	（10000 units）	93.48	279.21	734.24	1181.41
光学仪器	（万台）	Optical Instrument	（10000 units）	174.10	139.10	172.39	229.46
发电量	（亿千瓦小时）	Electricity	（100 million kwh）	205.06	284.77	285.69	329.54
供热量	（万百万千焦）	Heating Supply	（10000 million kjoule）	516.00	735.00	903.90	1109.79
自来水生产量	（万吨）	Tap Water Production	（10000 tons）	32188	35088	41149	47533

3－17　各县(市)、区规模以上工业企业综合能耗及产值能耗

(2003)

项目	Item	全市 Toal	市区 Urban District
综合能耗(吨标准煤)	**Final Energy Consumption(Ton of SCE)**	**8664195**	**6260814**
非金属矿采选业	Nonmetal Minerals Mining and Dressing	1119	811
农副食品加工业	Agricultural Non－staple Food Processing	139305	94833
食品制造业	Food Manufacturing	51597	21545
饮料制造业	Beverage Manufacturing	48539	21970
烟草制品业	Tobacco Processing	15855	15855
纺织业	Textile Industry	771500	337828
纺织服装、鞋、帽制造业	Textile Clothing.Shoes.Cap Manufacturing	241391	190838
皮革、毛皮、羽毛(绒)及其制品业	Leather.Furs.Feather and Related Products	4830	3208
木材加工及木、竹、藤、棕、草制品业	Timber Processing.Bamboo. Cane Palm Fiber and Straw Products	14840	12883
家具制造业	Furniture Manufacturing	6451	3170
造纸及纸制品业	Papermaking and Paper Products	417398	356075
印刷业和记录媒介的复制	Printing and Record Medium Reproduction	14555	9456
文教体育用品制造业	Cultural.Educational and Sports Goods	67300	25331
石油加工、炼焦及核燃料加工业	Petroleum Processing.Coking & Nuclear Fuel Processing	2420312	2420312
化学原料及化学制品制造业	Raw Chemical Materials and Chemical Products	366420	320850
医药制造业	Medical and Pharmaceutical Products	17821	5551
化学纤维制造业	Chemical Fiber	244531	104758
橡胶制品业	Rubber Products	50579	13672
塑料制品业	Plastic Products	216223	115320
非金属矿物制品业	Nonmetal Mineral Products	158008	109327
黑色金属冶炼及压延加工业	Smelting and Pressing of Ferrous Metals	244899	153600
有色金属冶炼及压延加工业	Smelting and Pressing of Nonferrous Metals	217982	123391
金属制品业	Metal Products	231108	141030
通用设备制造业	General Equipment Manufacturing	418591	276644
专用设备制造业	Special Purpose Equipment Manufacturing	61229	41490
交通运输设备制造业	Transport Equipment Manufacturing	140877	67400
电气机械及器材制造业	Electric Equipment and Machinery Manufacturing	393692	82294
通信设备、计算机及其他电子设备制造业	Communication Equipment.Computer and Other Electronic Equipment Manufacturing	79745	52012
仪器仪表及文化、办公用机械制造业	Instruments.Meters.Cultural and Office Machinery	44205	21204
工艺品及其他制造业	Handicraft and Others Manufacturing	30845	14620
电力、热力的生产和供应业	Electric Power and Hot Power Production and Supply	1499627	1078097
燃气生产和供应业	Gas Production and Supply	965	732
自来水的生产和供应业	Tap Water Production and Supply	31854	24603

Final Energy Consumption of Above Designated Size Industrial Enterprises by Counties and Districts

海曙 Haishu	江东 Jiangdong	江北 Jiangbei	北仑 Beilun	镇海 Zhenhai	鄞州 Yinzhou	余姚 Yuyao	慈溪 Cixi	奉化 Fenghua	象山 Xiangshan	宁海 Ninghai
471179	**211463**	**219295**	**553352**	**3029139**	**903084**	**750501**	**892889**	**173412**	**290519**	**296060**
		354			458				308	
	18892	2048	3802	1517	9420	6167	27247	1818	7784	1456
	5698	4852	294	1991	8333	15630		7858	1439	5125
1723					20247	2628	2027	63	844	21007
	15855									
114158	3531	11431	31652	37605	119232	92239	254569	2933	67939	15992
3546	3438	463	3013	1628	80987	1338	6175	17162	24589	1289
		647	71	596	1708	800	643	179		
772		1434		181	10468	719	131	713	190	204
		344		174	2518	1848	773		180	480
272858	1458	555	3124	16331	55422	14339	26032	4199	1266	15487
835	406	368	769	116	5977	1505	1234	815		1545
701	455	4094	8457	2670	5050	5169	20153	1651	4	14992
	2084		1838	2413100	526					
8916	44224	45109	10944	88229	13249	9710	2574	3928	13395	15963
2108	976		613	453	395	1896	6448	1780	961	1185
				103315	1444	46587	88422	1152	1682	1930
	1688	6506		2191	3287	1871	24493		447	10096
5051	8993	6241	7044	15540	66627	43906	44907	317	2099	9674
	4402	22588	3070	12892	40808	24339	10266	4212	3538	6326
6599	959	2617	83549	5127	54366	38876	25750	13772	456	12445
	8264	57884	10421	15463	31360	23732	52416	9947	167	8329
26976	4466	13256	13452	33763	47656	39316	18572	2093	3136	26961
10693	24744	13783	11968	39044	167149	33596	76191	12368	4184	15608
1755	2624	5638	15796	3970	8251	5237	2691	911	3790	7110
226	3748	9454	14450	4524	24413	18454	29588	6075	14822	4538
8405	2024	5779	11690	4647	47756	165842	108462	6530	6982	23582
4905	6093	1771	17073	936	17378	8181	9582	5381	1307	3282
221	2892	829	1391	1846	14026	9959	7192	714		5136
732	385	1247	548	7	11610	1333	11596	1762	407	1127
	43162		298323	221201	31113	132901	32501	64801	126766	64561
				83			233			
					1846	2486	2023	277	1836	629

3－17续

项目	Item	全市 Toal	市区 Urban District
产值能耗(吨标煤/万元)	**Energy Consumption of Output Gross Value (Ton of SCE/10000 yuan)**	**0.3303**	**0.3945**
非金属矿采选业	Nonmetal Minerals Mining and Dressing	0.2362	0.2676
农副食品加工业	Agricultural Non－staple Food Processing	0.2041	0.2318
食品制造业	Food Manufacturing	0.3141	0.3582
饮料制造业	Beverage Manufacturing	0.4184	0.6121
烟草制品业	Tobacco Processing	0.0307	0.0307
纺织业	Textile Industry	0.4591	0.3438
纺织服装、鞋、帽制造业	Textile Clothing. Shoes. Cap Manufacturing	0.1238	0.1559
皮革、毛皮、羽毛(绒)及其制品业	Leather. Furs. Feather and Related Products	0.0849	0.0877
木材加工及木、竹、藤、棕、草制品业	Timber Processing. Bamboo. Cane Palm Fiber and Straw Products	0.2690	0.3026
家具制造业	Furniture Manufacturing	0.0733	0.0723
造纸及纸制品业	Papermaking and Paper Products	0.8687	0.9379
印刷业和记录媒介的复制	Printing and Record Medium Reproduction	0.0669	0.0507
文教体育用品制造业	Cultural. Educational and Sports Goods	0.0953	0.0674
石油加工、炼焦及核燃料加工业	Petroleum Processing. Coking & Nuclear Fuel Processing	0.8411	0.8411
化学原料及化学制品制造业	Raw Chemical Materials and Chemical Products	0.4625	0.4746
医药制造业	Medical and Pharmaceutical Products	0.2627	0.1585
化学纤维制造业	Chemical Fiber	0.7519	1.3062
橡胶制品业	Rubber Products	0.4668	0.5320
塑料制品业	Plastic Products	0.2113	0.2109
非金属矿物制品业	Nonmetal Mineral Products	0.4194	0.4066
黑色金属冶炼及压延加工业	Smelting and Pressing of Ferrous Metals	0.3780	0.3212
有色金属冶炼及压延加工业	Smelting and Pressing of Nonferrous Metals	0.2633	0.2413
金属制品业	Metal Products	0.2337	0.2785
通用设备制造业	General Equipment Manufacturing	0.2089	0.2565
专用设备制造业	Special Purpose Equipment Manufacturing	0.0784	0.0708
交通运输设备制造业	Transport Equipment Manufacturing	0.0963	0.0930
电气机械及器材制造业	Electric Equipment and Machinery Manufacturing	0.1181	0.0714
通信设备、计算机及其他电子设备制造业	Communication Equipment. Computer and Other Electronic Equipment Manufacturing	0.0429	0.1030
仪器仪表及文化、办公用机械制造业	Instruments. Meters. Cultural and Office Machinery	0.0978	0.0917
工艺品及其他制造业	Handicraft and Others Manufacturing	0.1010	0.1015
电力、热力的生产和供应业	Electric Power and Hot Power Production and Supply	1.2737	1.0104
燃气生产和供应业	Gas Production and Supply	0.0169	0.0141
自来水的生产和供应业	Tap Water Production and Supply	0.6367	0.8824

continued

海曙 Haishu	江东 Jiangdong	江北 Jiangbei	北仑 Beilun	镇海 Zhenhai	鄞州 Yinzhou	余姚 Yuyao	慈溪 Cixi	奉化 Fenghua	象山 Xiangshan	宁海 Ninghai
0.5221	**0.1655**	**0.2549**	**0.2405**	**0.7221**	**0.1960**	**0.2804**	**0.2666**	**0.0971**	**0.2249**	**0.2351**
		0.4904			0.1982				0.1801	
	1.1032	0.2862	0.1222	0.4268	0.1631	0.0915	0.3793	0.1745	0.0760	0.0679
	0.5223	2.2140	0.0700	0.1869	0.2780	0.5350		0.1925	0.1660	0.2016
0.4991					0.6242	0.1033	1.1208	0.0632	0.1426	0.4573
	0.0307									
0.4704	0.2377	0.3029	0.4041	0.3027	0.2769	0.4301	0.7779	0.1240	0.9651	0.2574
0.0379	0.0538	0.0388	0.0666	0.0486	0.1048	0.0695	0.1104	0.0779	0.0612	0.0449
		0.2059	0.0157	0.0930	0.1056	0.0593	0.1395	0.0817		
0.3759		0.6479		0.4322	0.2924	0.1773	0.3876	0.1198	0.1993	0.1588
		0.0296		0.0775	0.1014	0.0894	0.0756		0.0386	0.0559
1.1589	0.1315	0.1820	0.2761	0.9312	0.8441	0.5930	0.8532	0.5663	0.1542	0.5074
0.3284	0.0625	0.0658	0.0689	0.0844	0.0382	0.1121	0.3107	0.3790		0.1307
0.3411	0.0552	0.2772	0.0824	0.1539	0.0265	0.1203	0.1384	0.1997	0.0084	0.1131
	0.4652		0.0164	0.8821	0.0870					
3.4344	2.1759	2.9966	0.7307	0.2544	0.1862	0.2366	0.1798	0.1778	1.1953	0.5799
0.2340	0.1442		0.3108	0.0741	0.1245	0.5584	0.7538	0.1377	0.4825	0.1987
				1.3813	0.2673	1.0906	0.4649	0.2162	0.5212	0.5433
	0.3084	0.8175		0.3631	0.5279	0.2439	0.8204		0.3615	0.2300
0.1997	0.2233	0.1146	0.2352	0.1984	0.2361	0.2091	0.2378	0.0831	0.1156	0.1737
	0.2390	0.6480	0.1967	0.6761	0.3333	0.6865	0.3024	0.4829	0.5090	0.2773
1.1314	0.1555	0.2533	0.2263	0.7591	0.7283	0.7790	0.3473	0.8626	0.3762	0.4374
	0.1707	0.2051	1.5590	0.1854	0.3456	0.1891	0.3608	0.8738	0.3302	0.2463
0.4896	0.2327	0.2082	0.2113	0.4623	0.2091	0.1617	0.1887	0.0743	0.1639	0.2883
0.3954	0.1780	0.1313	0.1730	0.2415	0.3430	0.1323	0.2018	0.1509	0.0518	0.1194
0.2337	0.0586	0.1121	0.0628	0.0766	0.0650	0.1329	0.1148	0.1349	0.0690	0.1019
0.1061	0.0463	0.1647	0.1791	0.1111	0.1258	0.1166	0.1383	0.1433	0.0520	0.1166
0.0755	0.0439	0.1147	0.0816	0.0731	0.0704	0.2302	0.1052	0.1247	0.0424	0.1111
0.0806	0.0698	0.1043	0.1535	0.0382	0.1134	0.0677	0.1623	0.0048	0.0951	0.1067
0.0448	0.0665	0.1308	0.0337	0.1025	0.1196	0.0999	0.1474	0.1102		0.0780
0.0811	0.1976	0.2418	0.1718	0.0067	0.0981	0.1253	0.0947	0.1084	0.4289	0.1025
	2.6580		0.4298	1.2384	1.3192	4.0542	1.2152	3.3335	7.1583	4.7243
				0.0107			0.0452			
					0.4711	0.3329	0.4072	0.1743	0.3344	0.2387

3－18　全市规模以上工业企业能源购、消、存情况

(2003)

项目		Item		年初库存 Stock (Year－head)	购进量 Purchases 实物量 Material Amount	购进量 Purchases 金额(万元) Value (10000 yuan)	消费量合计 Consumption
原煤	(吨)	Raw Coal	(ton)	424248	15324856	464599	15397431
煤制品	(吨)	Coal Products	(ton)	142	9164	363	9153
焦炭	(吨)	Coke	(ton)	3548	69526	3505	71529
原油	(吨)	Crude Oil	(ton)	312167	13809070	2790368	13619009
汽油	(吨)	Gasoline	(ton)	440	56866	17742	57230
煤油	(吨)	Kerosene	(ton)	297	19340	5892	19348
柴油	(吨)	Diesel Oil	(ton)	4038	168050	51316	173216
燃料油	(吨)	Fuel Oil	(ton)	26185	691110	141163	1263233
液化石油气	(吨)	Liquefied Petroleum Gas	(ton)	324	31995	8453	33810
炼厂干气	(吨)	Refinery Dry Gas	(ton)		75	10	394115
其他石油制品	(吨)	Other Petroleum Products	(ton)	62	20871	5734	666098
热力	(百万千焦)	Heat	(million kilo－joule)		7788817	34116	29400150
电力	(万千瓦时)	Electricity	(10000 kwh)		948364	577725	1186494
能源合计	(吨标准煤)	Total	(Ton of SCE)	815736	36297988	4102770	39725590

Purchases,Sales and Inventory of Energy of Above Designated Size Industrial Enterprises

工业生产消费 Consumptiop of Industrial Production	非工业生产消费 Consumptiop of Non – Industrial Production	年末库存 Stock (Year – end)	能源转出量 Energy Producing	能源投入 Energy Input	火力发电 Generation of Electric Power by Thermal Power	供热 Heat Supply	炼油投入 Input of Oil Refining
15365033	32397	329512		13870381	12681125	1189255	
8990	163	153					
71405	124	1596					
13618953	56	476467		13609740			13609740
40598	16632	352	2307276				
19288	60	296	1103104				
164560	8656	3984	5315375	8607	8607		
1263181	52	31212	704765	883276	733237	150039	
31866	1943	421	683407				
394115			394040				
666097	2	55	3705400	309264	150367	137826	21071
29242050	158100		32136995				
1159220	27274		3324986	21624			
39560542	165049	981172	30896347	31570114	10808470	1222014	19463946

3－19　主要能源按工业行业分组消费量

(2003)

项目	Item	能源合计 吨标准煤 Total Ton of SCE	原煤 (吨) Raw Coal (Ton)	焦炭 (吨) Coke (Ton)
按工业行业分	**Grouped by Sector**	**39725590**	**15397431**	**71529**
非金属矿采选业	Nonmetal Minerals Mining and Dressing	1144	57	
农副食品加工业	Agricultural Non－staple Food Processing	141015	23050	
食品制造业	Food Manufacturing	53799	38444	
饮料制造业	Beverage Manufacturing	49368	50697	
烟草制品业	Tobacco Processing	15856	654	
纺织业	Textile Industry	918429	593068	
纺织服装、鞋、帽制造业	Textile Clothing. Shoes. Cap Manufacturing	248248	93334	15
皮革、毛皮、羽毛(绒)及其制品业	Leather. Furs. Feather and Related Products	4958	2283	
木材加工及木、竹、藤、棕、草制品业	Timber Processing. Bamboo. Cane Palm Fiber and Straw Products	15058	1039	
家具制造业	Furniture Manufacturing	6851	169	
造纸及纸制品业	Papermaking and Paper Products	734533	502678	
印刷业和记录媒介的复制	Printing and Record Medium Reproduction	15587	1483	
文教体育用品制造业	Cultural. Educational and Sports Goods	69805	19446	51
石油加工、炼焦及核燃料加工业	Petroleum Processing. Coking & Nuclear Fuel Processing	22326683	51751	
化学原料及化学制品制造业	Raw Chemical Materials and Chemical Products	375231	105648	
医药制造业	Medical and Pharmaceutical Products	18076	13896	
化学纤维制造业	Chemical Fiber	327762	215934	6
橡胶制品业	Rubber Products	50936	27832	
塑料制品业	Plastic Products	222620	46244	96
非金属矿物制品业	Nonmetal Mineral Products	159484	75186	839
黑色金属冶炼及压延加工业	Smelting and Pressing of Ferrous Metals	246629	62793	658
有色金属冶炼及压延加工业	Smelting and Pressing of Nonferrous Metals	221680	52814	16369
金属制品业	Metal Products	235560	58442	3074
通用设备制造业	General Equipment Manufacturing	426372	86094	36208
专用设备制造业	Special Purpose Equipment Manufacturing	63259	6218	711
交通运输设备制造业	Transport Equipment Manufacturing	144739	14221	3042
电气机械及器材制造业	Electric Equipment and Machinery Manufacturing	404020	132695	8600
通信设备、计算机及其他电子设备制造业	Communication Equipment. Computer and Other Electronic Equipment Manufacturing	81620	1320	188
仪器仪表及文化办公用机械制造业	Instruments. Meters. Cultural and Office Machinery	46559	1512	1660
工艺品及其他制造业	Handicraft and Others Manufacturing	31667	5872	12
电力、热力的生产和供应业	Electric Power and Hot Power Production and Supply	12034949	13112556	
燃气生产和供应业	Gas Production and Supply	1173		
自来水的生产和供应业	Tap Water Production and Supply	31921		

Main Energy Consumption by Category Industrial Branch

原油 (吨) Crude Oil (Ton)	汽油 (吨) Gasoline (Ton)	柴油 (吨) (Ton)	柴油 (吨) Diesel Oil (Ton)	燃料油 (吨) Fuel Oil (Ton)	液化石油气 (吨) LPG (Ton)	其他油制品 (吨) Other Petroleum Products (Ton)	热力 (百万千焦) Heat (million kilo – joule)	电力 (万千瓦时) Electricity (10000 kwh)
13619009	**57230**	**19348**	**173216**	**1263233**	**33810**	**666098**	**29400150**	**1186494**
	4		3					313
	378	8	3048	3252	70		1590198	17300
1097	2786		1051	50	144		23370	5146
	132		412		89			3488
	28		224				181161	2527
	3877	34	12523	1205	325	3	3883696	93746
28	3604	83	7629	1471	52	24	1906825	27903
	142		300					766
	299	6633	348					1032
	231	8	836					1474
	786	5	4918	1725	33		3969808	65499
	831	418	545		5			3373
	2068	9	3126	267	94	1009		13336
13609740	384		7903	577437	1837	661350	11040681	99901
8000	2761	443	3353	2	1	624	1213200	67640
	170	2	474	500	4		24833	1611
	994	2	1784				2015082	28333
2	846	2	988			100	16398	7916
1	3225	317	7954	1195	521	1415	61261	47545
	1388	201	7470	2250	10923		35490	19191
5	381	94	7587	2028	13739		1234	46538
12	1026	457	10002	4363	1524	13	58662	40057
2	4645	1161	13642	9684	682	40	2574	41876
29	8740	8490	19390	525	249	1119	5992	78041
7	2581	228	4665	57	51	171		13375
4	3968	306	12634	80	588	146	1425	29998
83	5722	149	20868	146	2386	41	8084	72949
	1878	26	4002	52	235		15258	20225
	1107	124	2353	9	176	11		10855
	841	146	2016	6	83	29	2891	6490
	1234		10740	656931		3	3342028	308848
	72		318					172
	100		110					9032

3－20　规模以上工业企业主要经济效益指标

(2003)

项目		Item		全市 Total	市区 Urban District
产销率	(%)	Proportion of Products Sold	(%)	98.16	98.76
资产负债率	(%)	Assets Liability Ratio	(%)	57.49	54.48
成本费用利润率	(%)	Ratio of Profits to Industrial Cost	(%)	7.91	8.97
每百元资金实现利税	(元)	Pre－tax Profits Per 100 Yuan Funds	(yuan)	16.40	18.11
每百元固定资产原值实现利税	(元)	Pre－tax Profits Per 100 Yuan Original Value of Fixed Assets	(yuan)	25.74	24.50
每百元销售收入实现利税	(元)	Pre－tax Profits Per 100 Yuan Sales Revenue	(yuan)	12.36	14.38
流动资产周转次数	(次)	Number of Times of Turnover of Circulating Funds	(times)	2.25	2.37
全员劳动生产率	(元/人)	Overall Labor Productivity	(yuan/perso)n	65820	84173
工业增加值率	(%)	Ratio of Value Added of Industry	(%)	20.05	21.01
流动比率	(%)	Ratio of Circulating Funds to Current Liabilities	(%)	1.12	1.16
速动比率	(%)	Ratio of Quickassets to Current Liabilities	(%)	0.81	0.82
企业亏损面	(%)	Ratio of Number of Deficit Enterprises to Total Enterprises Number	(%)	7.94	10.19
盈亏率	(%)	Losing Rate	(%)	3.08	3.77
出口交货值占工业销售产值比重	(%)	Ratio of Exports Products Value to Industrial Sales Value	(%)	30.12	24.67
利润总额占利税比重	(%)	Ratio of Total Profits to Total Pre－tax	(%)	58.79	56.37
利润总额占增加值比重	(%)	Ratio of Total Profits to Value Added of Industry	(%)	53.20	58.95
存货周转次数	(次)	Number of Times of Turnover of Inventories	(times)	6.10	6.11
新产品产值率	(%)	Ratio of Value of New Type of Products to Total Products Value	(%)	13.26	8.90

Main Indicators on Ecnomic Benefit Industrial Enterprises Above Designated Size

海曙 Haishu	江东 Jiangdong	江北 Jiangbei	北仑 Beilun	镇海 Zhenhai	鄞州 Yinzhou	余姚 Yuyao	慈溪 Cixi	奉化 Fenghua	象山 Xiangshan	宁海 Ninghai
97.18	101.40	96.60	97.74	100.96	97.53	96.35	98.54	98.10	97.20	94.54
61.86	42.30	64.84	54.34	45.29	55.21	61.15	64.16	65.29	60.32	61.40
5.82	12.44	5.99	11.68	6.11	10.16	7.53	5.47	4.36	7.89	7.44
8.76	39.67	14.80	14.62	22.79	18.25	14.05	11.21	14.12	17.46	13.24
12.44	80.73	29.41	17.20	22.58	38.08	29.07	24.05	37.32	40.67	29.16
9.35	34.07	9.38	15.00	11.07	13.11	10.30	8.28	6.51	11.35	11.20
1.78	1.74	2.33	2.14	4.44	2.08	2.04	1.94	2.91	2.19	1.73
72493	164694	43051	111199	122607	50191	55273	40270	66337	49167	39938
17.62	36.81	15.57	22.78	16.54	19.57	19.13	18.51	15.98	17.51	22.13
1.07	1.59	1.02	1.21	1.00	1.16	1.06	1.02	1.20	1.15	1.07
0.81	0.97	0.66	0.86	0.66	0.85	0.79	0.81	0.72	0.86	0.79
6.45	15.47	13.00	12.58	15.95	6.27	7.83	0.36	16.06	8.66	6.36
1.85	5.00	5.96	5.63	2.72	1.26	2.29	0.30	3.11	0.92	1.95
39.16	24.20	24.17	22.98	12.78	35.81	39.31	43.86	19.19	43.42	46.46
59.92	26.72	60.99	70.49	50.50	71.13	68.27	62.64	64.42	64.71	61.50
46.90	82.59	51.37	56.29	59.36	58.33	47.02	39.59	34.49	56.25	41.20
6.14	2.60	5.21	5.61	10.66	5.86	5.77	7.29	5.26	6.42	5.02
17.52	9.08	6.64	2.71	11.96	10.39	5.87	13.92	63.81	12.77	11.03

3－21 全社会用电量

单位:万千瓦时 (2003)

项目	Item	全市 Total	为上年(%) The Preceding Year＝100(%)
总计	**Total**	**1890027**	**124.3**
全行业用电量	**Electricity Consumption for Non－Living Electricity**	**1651392**	**123.8**
农林牧渔水利业	Farming, Forestry, Animal Husbandry, Fishery and Water Conservancy	22305	85.4
#排灌	Irrigation and Drainage	7302	102.0
#农副业	Agricultural Sideline Production	2707	137.8
农业	Farming	12256	74.2
林业	Forestry	593	138.9
畜牧业	Animal Husbandary	1197	121.2
渔业	Fishery	954	83.1
水利业	Water Conservancy	3413	99.9
其他	Others	3892	107.2
工业	Industry	1416625	123.6
#乡村工业	Township and Village Industries	545632	126.3
轻工业	Light Industyr	574100	118.8
重工业	Heavy Industry	842525	127.0
地质普查和勘探业	Geological Prospecting	357	109.5
建筑业	Construction	21672	139.6
交通邮电通讯业	Transportation, Postal and Telecommunications Services	25326	115.5
交通运输	Transportation	16232	107.2
邮电通讯	Postal and Telecommunications	9094	133.8
商业饮食供销仓储业	Trade, Catering and Storage Services	74461	126.1
其他事业	Others	90646	141.5
公用事业等	Public Service	28712	131.6
卫生体育福利业	Health Care, Sports and Social Welfare	8869	127.5
文教广播电视	Education, Culture, Radio, Film and Television	12278	141.3
机关社会团体	Governments, Parties and Social Organizations	19920	157.2
城乡居民生活用电量	**Electricity Consumption for Urban and Rural Residents**	**238635**	**127.5**
乡村	Rural Residents	143019	126.7
城市	Urban Residents	95616	128.7

Total Electricity Consumption

(10000 kwh)

市区 Urban District	# 鄞州 Yinzhou	余姚 Yuyao	慈溪 Cixi	奉化 Fenghua	象山 Xiangshan	宁海 Ninghai
1048967	**268934**	**247985**	**370373**	**83538**	**53774**	**85390**
934701	**229028**	**221426**	**321353**	**66912**	**40142**	**66858**
12511	8080	3182	2896	483	1289	1944
3013	2159	1745	1178	273	924	169
208	208	791	518	32	95	1063
5466	3042	2536	2089	306	986	873
296	234	65	32	14	13	173
590	246	258	50	10	27	262
495	456	15	279	86	31	48
2551	2443	249	360	32	21	200
3113	1659	59	86	35	211	388
777794	204633	200972	297535	58697	30192	51435
179606	119880	118857	195125	6642	8687	36715
264121	98377	101694	141471	17802	21389	27623
513673	106256	99278	156064	40895	8803	23812
357	257					
13057	3578	1921	2095	943	906	2750
18814	1537	1305	1653	562	577	2415
13621	289	509	574	129	232	1167
5193	1248	796	1079	433	345	1248
46712	2707	6083	11235	2748	3660	4023
65426	8236	7963	5969	3479	3518	4291
21698	1392	2051	1830	1160	488	1485
5203	1028	1203	709	463	527	764
8348	2217	1441	931	553	482	523
13066	2395	1309	2285	541	1713	1006
114266	**39906**	**26559**	**49020**	**16626**	**13632**	**18532**
55773	36134	18668	40223	8709	7168	12478
58493	3772	7891	8797	7917	6464	6054

3－22 规模以下工业企业及个体工业单位主要经济指标(2003)

Main Economic Indicators of Industrial Enterprises Below Designated Sizeand Private and Individuals

单位:个,万元,人 (unit,10000 yuan,person)

项目	Item	企业单位数 Number of Enterprises(unit)	工业总产值 Gross Industrial Output Value	产品销售收入 Value of Industrial Products Sales	上缴税金 Tax Payment
规模以下全部工业	**Total**	**81088**	**14295841**	**6977227**	**668499**
小型企业	**Industrial Enterprises Below Designated Size**	**27891**	**7427117**	**6977227**	**415844**
#集体企业	Collective－owned Enterprises	3229	1531237	1440018	99381
股份合作公司	Share－holding Cooperative Enterprises	1127	273455	259786	15554
有限责任公司	Limited Liability Corporations	880	255989	244345	12883
股份有限公司	Share－holding Corporations Ltd.	33	8592	7302	602
私营企业	Private Enterprises	21141	4442346	4180155	222079
外商投资企业	Enterprises with Foreign Investment	651	116862	107149	6944
个体工业单位	**Individuals Enterprises**	**53197**	**6868724**		**252655**

续表

项目	Item	期末从业人员 Total Employees at Year－end	营业利润 Business Profits	应付工资 Wages Payable	折旧 Depreciation
规模以下全部工业	**Total**	**1257317**	**687416**	**513326**	**127242**
小型企业	**Industrial Enterprises Below Designated Size**	**778628**	**687416**	**513326**	**127242**
#集体企业	Collective－owned Enterprises	106606	235578	80717	21852
股份合作公司	Share－holding Cooperative Enterprises	43805	13583	29873	6353
有限责任公司	Limited Liability Corporations	29536	14226	20938	6391
股份有限公司	Share－holding Corporations Ltd.	606	386	404	169
私营企业	Private Enterprises	509128	273306	337169	67122
外商投资企业	Enterprises with Foreign Investment	11677	14719	6805	3065
个体工业单位	**Individuals Enterprises**	**478689**			

注:个体工业单位中,产品销售收入,营业利润,应付工资,折旧暂未列入统计范围。
Data in this table exclude value of industrial products sales, business profits, wages payable, depreciation of individuals enterprises.

3-23 2003年销售收入前20位

The First 20. Enterprises On Sales Income in 2002

序号 No.	企业名称 Name of Enterprises	注册类型 Registered Type
1	中国石化镇海炼油化工股份有限公司 Sinopec Zhenhai Refining & Chemical Co., Ltd.	股份有限公司 Share - holding Corporations Ltd.
2	宁波市波导股份有限公司 Ningbo Bird Co., Ltd.	股份有限公司 Share - holding Corporations Ltd.
3	宁波卷烟厂 Ningbo Cigarette Factory	国有企业 State - owned Enterprises
4	宁波三星集团股份有限公司 Ningbo Sanxing Group Co., Ltd.	股份有限公司 Share - holding Corporations Ltd.
5	浙江北仑发电有限公司 Zhejiang Beilun Power Co., Ltd.	其他有限责任公司 Other Limited Liability Corporations
6	宁波宝新不锈钢有限公司 Ningbo Baoxin Stainless Steel Co., Ltd.	中外合资经营 Chinese - forein Equity Joint Ventures Enterprises
7	宁波金田铜业(集团)股份有限公司 Ningbo Jintian Copper (Group) Co., Ltd.	股份有限公司 Share - holding Corporations Ltd.
8	宁波华翔集团股份有限公司 Ningbo Huaxiang Group Co., Ltd	股份有限公司 Share - holding Corporations Ltd.
9	宁波乐金甬兴化工有限公司 Ningbo Lejin Yongxing Chemical Industry Co., Ltd.	中外合资经营 Chinese - forein Equity Joint Ventures Enterprises
10	宁波中华纸业有限公司 Ningbo Zhonghua Paper Co., Ltd.	与港澳台商合资经营 Equity Joint Ventures with HongKong, Macao & Taiwan
11	浙江北仑第一发电有限责任公司 Zhejiang Beilun First Power Co., Ltd.	国有企业 State - owned Enterprises
12	金光食品(宁波)有限公司 Jinguang Food (Ningbo) Ltd.	外资企业 Enterprises with Foreign Investment
13	宁波海天股份有限公司 Ningbo Haitian Co., Ltd.	股份有限公司 Share - holding Corporations Ltd.
14	宁波申洲织造集团有限公司 Ningbo Shenzhou Weaving Group Co., Ltd.	与港澳台商合资经营 Equity Joint Ventures with HongKong, Macao & Taiwan
15	雅戈尔集团股份有限公司 Younger Group Co., Ltd.	股份有限公司 Share - holding Corporations Ltd.
16	慈溪市供电局 Cixi Power Supply Bureau	国有企业 State - owned Enterprises
17	浙江吉利汽车有限公司 Zhejiang Geely Automobile Co., Ltd.	私营有限责任公司 Private Limited Liability Corporations
18	浙江镇海发电有限责任公司 Zhejiang Zhenhai Power Co., Ltd.	其他有限责任公司 Other Limited Liability Corporations
19	华茂集团股份有限公司 Huamao Group Co., Ltd.	股份有限公司 Share - holding Corporations Ltd.
20	金轮集团股份有限公司 Jinlun Group Co., Ltd.	股份合作 Share - holding Cooperative Enterprises

主要指标解释

【工业总产值】 是以货币表现的工业企业在一定时期内生产的已出售或可供出售工业产品总量，它反映一定时间内工业生产的总规模和总水平。

工业总产值采用“工厂法”计算，即以工业企业作为一个整体，按企业工业生产活动的最终成果来计算工业总产值。

工业总产值的内容包括：生产的成品价值、对外加工费收入和自制半成品在产品期末初差额价值。

【工业销售产值】 是以货币表现的工业企业在一定时期内销售的本企业生产的工业产品量。它是反映一定时期内工业企业产品销售规模和总水平的重要指标。

【工业增加值】 是指工业行业在报告期内以货币表现的工业生产活动的最终成果。

【固定资产原价】 固定资产原值指企业在建造、购置、安装、改建、扩建、技术改造某项固定资产时所支出的全部货币总额。它一般包括买价、包装费、运杂费和安装费等。

【固定资产净值】 是指固定资产原价减去历年已提折旧额后的净额。

【流动资产】 流动资产是指可以在一年或者超过一年的一个营业周期内变现或者耗用的资产，包括现金及各种存款、短期投资、应收及预付货款、存货等。

【利税总额】 指企业利润总额、产品销售税金及附加和应交增值税之和。

【产品销售收入】 指企业销售产品的销售收入和提供劳务等主要经营业务取得的业务总额。

【产品销售成本】 指企业销售产品和提供劳务等主要经营业务的实际成本。

【产品销售税金及附加】 指企业销售产品和提供工业性劳务等主要经营业务应负担的城市维护建设税、消费税、资源税和教育费附加。

【产品销售利润】 指企业销售产品和提供工业性劳务等主要经营业务收入扣除其成本、费用、税金后的利润。

【资本金】 指企业在工商行政管理部门登记的注册资金合计。企业资本金按投资主体可分为国家资本金、法人资本金、个人资本金和外商资本金等。资本金合计包括企业各种投资主体注册的全部资本金。

【总资产】 指企业拥有或控制的全部资产。包括流动资产、长期投资、固定资产、无形及递延资产、其他长期资产、递延税项等，即为企业资产负债表的资产总计项。(1) 流动资产：指企业可以在一年内或者超过一年的一个生产周期内变现或耗用的资产合计。包括现金及各种存款、短期投资、应收及预付款项、存货等。(2) 固定资产：指企业固定资产净值、固定资产清理、在建工程、待处理固定资产损失所占用的资金合计。(3)：无形资产 指企业长期使用而没有实物形态的资产。包括专利权、非专利技术、商标权、著作权、土地使用权、商誉等。

【总负债】 指企业承担并需要偿还的全部债务。包括流动负债和长期负债、递延税项等，即为企业资产负债表的负债合计项。(1) 流动负债：指企业在一年内或者超过一年的一个营业周期内需要偿还的债务合计，其中包括短期借款、应付及预收款项、应付工资、应交税金和应交利润等。(2) 长期负债：指企业在一年以上或者超过一年的一个生产周期以上需要偿还的债务合计，其中包括长期借款、应付债务、长期应付款项等。

【所有者权益】 指企业投资人对企业净资产的所有权。企业净资产等于企业全部资产减去全部负债后的余额，其中包括投资者对企业的最初投入，以及资本公积金、盈余公积金和未分配利润，对股份制企业即为股东权益。

【能源消费总量】 指一定时期内全国物质生产部门、非物质生产部门和生活消费的各种能源的总和，是观察能源消费水平、构成和增长速度的总量指标。能源消费总量包括原煤和原油及其制品、天然气、电力，不包括低热值燃料、生物质能和太阳能等的利用。能源消费总量分为终端能源消费量、能源加工转换损失量和损失量三部分。

⑴终端能源消费量：指一定时期内全国生产和生活消费的各种能源在扣除了用于加工转换二次能源消费量和损失量以后的数量。

⑵能源加工转换损失量：指一定时期内全国投入加工转换的各种能源数量之和与产出各种能源产品之和的差额，是观察能源在加工转换过程中损失量变化的指标。

⑶能源损失量：指一定时期内能源在输送、分配、储存过程中发生的损失和由客观原因造成的各种损失量，不包括各种气体能源放空、放散量。

Explanatory Notes on Main Statistical Indicators

【Gross Industrial Output Value】 is the total volume of industrial products sold or available for sale in value terms which reflects the total achievements and overall scale of industrial production during a given period.

The gross industrial output value is calculated with "factory method". No double calculations are to be made within the same enterprise. However, double counting does occur among different enterprises.

It includes the value of the finished products, the value of industrial services rendered to other units and the changes in the value of the semi finished products and products in process between the beginning and closing of the period (only the enterprises with long production cycle are required to calculate the changes).

【Industrial Sales Output Value】 is the total volume of industrial products sold in value terms of an industrial enterprise, which reflects the total achievements and overall sales scale of industrial production during a given period.

【Value Added of Industry】 refers to the final results of industrial production of the industrial trade in money terms during the reference period.

【Original Value of Fixed Assets】 refers to the original value of all fixed assets owned by industrial enterprises, calculated at the cost paid at the time of purchase, installation, reconstruction, expansion, and technical innovation and transformation of the said assets, which includes expenses on purchase, package, transportation, and installation, etc.

【Net Value of Fixed Assets】 is obtained by deducting depreciation over years from the original value of fixed assets.

【Working Capital (Circulating Assets)】 refers to assets which can be cashed in or spent or consumed in an operating cycle of one year or over – one year, which includes cash, various deposits, short term investment, and receivable payments, and advance payments, stock, etc.

【Total Value of Profit and Tax(Pre tax Profits)】 refers to the sum of the total profits, products sales tax and surcharges and the value added tax payable of industrial enterprises. It is also called pretax profits.

【Sales Revenue of Industrial Products】 refers to the revenue from the sales of products by industrial enterprises and the revenue from services provided and etc.

【Sales Cost of Industrial Products】 refers to the actual cost of products of industrial enterprises and industrial services provided, etc.

【Tax and Extra Charges on Sales of Products】 refer to the tax on city maintenance and construction, consumption tax, resources tax and extra charges for education, which should be borne by the enterprises in selling products and providing industrial services.

【Sales Profit of Products】 refers to the profit gained by the enterprises by deducting cost, charges and taxes from the business income of the enterprises obtained in selling products and providing industrial services.

【Capital】 refers to the corporation's capital registered in the departments of administration for industry and commerce. According to the different nature of investors, corporations' capital can be divided into state capital, legal person's capital, personal capital, foreign capital, etc. Total capital includes total registered capital of all investors in the corporation.

【Total Assets】 refer to all assets which are owned or controlled by enterprises, including circulating assets, long – term investment, fixed assets, intangible assets and deferred assets, other long – term assets, and defertaxes, etc. The summation of above items is equal to total assets shown in the balance sheets of the enterprises. (1) Circulating assets (working capital) refer to assets which can be cashed in or spent or consumed in an operating cycle of one year or over one year, including cash, all kinds of deposits, short term investment, receivables, advance payment, stock, etc. (2) Fixed assets refer to the net value of fixed assets, clearance of fixed assets, project under construction, fixed assets losses in suspense. These are corporations' fund holdings. (3) Intangible assets refer to the assets without material form used by enterprises over a long time, such as patents, non – patent technologies, trade marks, copyright, land use right, business reputation, etc

【Total liabilities】 refer to the debts that enterprises are responsible for repayment, including liquid liabilities, long term liabilities and deferred taxes, etc. Total liabilities correspond to the summation item of liabilities shown in the balance sheets of the enterprises. (1) Liquid liabilities (also called quick liabilities or immediate liabilities) refer to enterprises total debt payable within an operating cycle of one year or over one year, including short term loans, payables and advance payments, wages payables, taxes payable and profit payable, etc. (2)Long – term liabilities refers to total debt payable within an operating cycle of one year or over one year, including long – term loans, payable liabilities, long – term payables, etc.

【Creditors' Equity】 refers to investors' ownership of net assets of the enterprise. It is equal to the total assets of the enterprise minus its total liabilities, including the primary input from investors, capital accumulation fund, surplus accumulation fund and undistributed profit. It is the stock holders' equity in stock companies.

【Total Domestic Energy Consumption】 refers to the total consumption of energy of various kinds by material production sectors, non material production sectors and households in the country in a given period of time. It is a comprehensive indicator to show the scale, composition and development of energy consumption.

The total energy consumption includes that of coal, crude oil and their products, natural gas and electricity, However, it excludes the consumption of fuel of low calorific value, bio – energy and solar energy. Total domestic energy consumption can be divided into three parts:

(1) Final Energy Consumption: It refers to the total energy consumption by material production sectors, non material production sectors and households in the country (region) in a given period of time, but excludes the consumption in conversion of the primary energy into the secondary energy and the loss in the process of energy conversion.

(2) Loss During the Process of Energy Conversion: It refers to the total input of various kinds of energy for conversion, minus the total output of various kinds of energy in the country in a given period of time. It is an indicator to show the loss that occurs during the process of energy conversion. (3) Loss: It refers to the total of the loss of energy during the course of energy transport, distribution and storage and the loss caused by any objective reason in a given period of time. The loss of various kinds of gas due to gas discharges and stocktaking is excluded.

4

固定资产投资、建筑业

CHAPTER 4 INVESTMENT IN FIXED ASSETS AND CONSTRUCTION

固定资产投资和建筑业
Investment Fixed Assets and Construction

主要统计指标
Major Statistics Indicators

2003 年全社会固定资产投资额	Total Value of Investment Fixed Assets	8358947	万元	10000 yuan
比上年增长	Increase Over Last Year	39.0	%	
2003 年基本建设投资额	Value of Investment in Capital Construction	3109421	万元	10000 yuan
比上年增长	Increase Over Last Year	46.7	%	
2003 年更新改造投资额	Value of Investment in Innovation	437638	万元	10000 yuan
比上年增长	Increase Over Last Year	-12.4	%	
2003 年房地产开发投资额	Value of Investment in Real Estate Development	1842589	万元	10000 yuan
比上年增长	Increase Over Last Year	46.3	%	
2003 年商品房销售面积	Floor Space of Commercial Building Sold	5485913	平方米	sq.m
比上年增长	Increase Over Last Year	37.8	%	
2003 年商品房实际销售额	Total Actually Sales of Commercial Buildings	1571945	万元	10000 yuan
比上年增长	Increase Over Last Year	51.1	%	
2003 年建筑业总产值	Gross Output Value of Construction	4746787	万元	10000 yuan
比上年增长	Increase Over Last Year	41.5	%	

4-1 主要年份全社会固定资产投资情况

Total Invesment in Fixed Assets in Main Years

单位:亿元 (100 million yuan)

年份 Year	全社会固定资产投资 Total	基本建设投资 Capital Construction	更新改造投资 Innovation	房地产开发投资 Real Estate Development	其他固定资产投资 Others	农村非农户投资 Non-peasant Households in Rural Area	城镇工矿区私人投资 Private Investment in Cites, Towns and Mining Areas	农户投资 Peasant Households in Rural Area
1978	5.02	2.91	0.07		0.04			
1979	5.79	3.15	0.30		0.07			
1980	6.50	3.48	0.54		0.26			
1981	6.39	2.40	0.79		0.34			
1982	8.57	3.01	1.50		0.49			
1983	7.69	2.49	1.31		0.68	1.44		1.77
1984	10.95	3.43	1.19		0.92	2.13		3.28
1985	18.08	5.22	1.82		2.17	3.73	0.42	4.72
1986	22.01	6.41	3.12		2.10	4.02	0.57	5.79
1987	29.46	6.65	4.03		3.13	6.63	0.83	8.19
1988	35.81	10.27	5.38		3.36	5.38	0.67	10.75
1989	32.79	12.06	3.29		2.75	5.06	0.61	9.02
1990	39.28	14.29	4.02	2.49	3.25	5.59	0.31	9.33
1991	51.42	16.03	4.85	3.00	4.81	11.22	0.44	11.07
1992	76.25	23.09	7.89	7.36	7.79	17.65	0.52	11.95
1993	129.27	27.84	12.31	25.44	13.46	35.65	1.13	13.44
1994	184.60	39.14	12.55	50.46	14.95	42.97	1.61	22.92
1995	264.19	63.03	19.52	71.59	14.18	58.74	4.33	32.80
1996	309.97	99.45	21.07	65.90	25.37	64.04	2.75	31.39
1997	300.57	120.86	16.98	51.92	16.91	61.96	3.34	28.60
1998	309.81	130.12	19.53	43.87	21.43	67.05	2.45	25.36
1999	318.93	109.53	29.83	46.54	28.62	77.51	2.18	24.72
2000	360.75	131.68	32.93	59.71	20.94	90.23	1.53	23.73
2001	470.28	181.45	42.38	87.08	14.06	122.11	2.98	20.22
2002	601.27	212.03	49.94	125.97	14.79	173.28	1.66	23.60
2003	835.90	310.94	43.76	184.26	14.72	258.74	1.01	22.47

4-2 各县(市)全社会固定资产投资完成情况

单位:万元 (2003)

项目	Item	全市 Total 本年 This Year	全市 Total 为上年(%) Preceding Year=100
全社会固定资产投资完成额	**Total**	**8358947**	**139.0**
基本建设完成额	Capital Construction	3109421	146.7
农、林、牧、渔	Farming, Forestry, Animal Husbandry and Fishery	5331	68.4
工业、建筑业	Industry and Construction	1344512	244.5
商业、运输邮电业	Business, Post and Telecommunications	354235	124.6
其他	Others	1405343	109.9
更新改造完成额	Innovation	437638	87.6
农、林、牧、渔	Farming, Forestry, Animal Husbandry and Fishery		
工业、建筑业	Industry and Construction	328464	99.2
商业、运输邮电业	Business, Post and Telecommunications	45229	32.3
其他	Others	63945	235.2
其他投资完成额	Others	147186	99.5
农、林、牧、渔	Farming, Forestry, Animal Husbandry and Fishery		
工业、建筑业	Industry and Construction	56827	70.4
商业、运输邮电业	Business, Post and Telecommunications	71826	118.0
其他	Others	18533	295.5
房地产开发投资完成额	Real Estate Development	1842589	146.3
#住宅	# Residential Buildings	1368423	138.7
农村非农户投资完成额	Investment in Fixed Assets of Non-peasant Households in Rural Area	2587357	149.3
城镇工矿区私人建房投资完成额	Private Buildings Constuction in Cites, Towns and Mining Areas	10084	60.7
农村农户固定资产投资额	Investment in Fixed Assets of Peasant Households in Rural Area	224672	95.2

Total Investment in Fixed Assets by Region

(10000yuan)

市区 Urban Disctict	#鄞州 Yinzhou	余姚 Yuyao	慈溪 Cixi	奉化 Fenghua	象山 Xiangshan	宁海 Ninghai
5212123	**1312031**	**875066**	**1230993**	**264633**	**370602**	**405530**
2362311	285450	148886	305952	41094	107057	144121
1509			3822			
1207007	57646	13323	54379	14281	13585	41937
251931	3199	28980	32123	987	14310	25904
901864	224605	106583	215628	25826	79162	76280
402127	20751	17282	15976		2253	
294913	20751	16332	14966		2253	
44219			1010			
62995		950				
75915	17247	9950	31903	9357	9942	10119
39760	3800		6673		5660	4734
26538	13447	8900	23340	7957	1706	3385
9607		1060	1890	1400	2576	2000
1187784	325375	136843	318732	59368	68504	71358
914055	286771	95441	184175	47931	61869	64952
1124104	622496	514066	491540	143848	159771	154028
			7090		2994	
59882	40712	48039	59800	10966	20081	25904

4－3 部分年份分产业全社会固定资产投资完成额

Total Fixed Assets Investment by Industry in Partial Years

单位:万元 (10000 yuan)

项目	Item	1990	1995	1998	2002	2003
总计	**Total**	**392836**	**2641914**	**3098083**	**6012703**	**8358947**
第一产业	Primary Industry	10503	20152	88988	51638	37216
第二产业	Secondary Industry	174839	918148	1538911	2442328	3991837
第三产业	Tertiary Industry	207494	1703614	1470184	3518737	4329894
基本建设	**Capital Construction**	**142955**	**630274**	**1301170**	**2120298**	**3109421**
第一产业	Primary Industry	5792	11104	76826	7799	5331
第二产业	Secondary Industry	82531	281408	802695	549886	1344512
第三产业	Tertiary Industry	54632	337762	421649	1562613	1759578
更新改造	**Innovation**	**40078**	**195129**	**195182**	**499380**	**437638**
第一产业	Primary Industry	546	550			
第二产业	Secondary Industry	28877	108036	116262	331019	328464
第三产业	Tertiary Industry	10655	86543	78920	167232	109174
其他	**Others**	**32538**	**141744**	**214317**	**147863**	**147186**
第一产业	Primary Industry	73	27	276		
第二产业	Secondary Industry	21221	59037	49674	80729	56827
第三产业	Tertiary Industry	11244	82680	164367	67134	90359
房地产开发	**Real Estate Development**	**24895**	**715949**	**438688**	**1259694**	**1842589**
#住宅建设	ResidentialBuildings	20743	346412	241561	986611	1368423
农村集体单位投资	**Rural Collective Owned Units**	**55885**	**587452**	**670525**	**1732848**	**2587357**
第一产业	Primary Industry	4092	8471	11886	42710	31885
第二产业	Secondary Industry	42210	469667	570280	1480694	2262034
第三产业	Tertiary Industry	9583	109314	88359	209444	293438
城镇工矿区私人建房	**Private Investment in Cites,Towns and Mining Areas**	**3136**	**43318**	**24594**	**16619**	**10084**
农村私人固定资产投资	**Private Investment in Rural Areas**	**93349**	**328048**	**253607**	**236001**	**224672**

4－4 部分年份城镇集体以上新增固定资产及房屋建筑面积

Newly Increase Fixed Assets and Floor Space of Buildings Above City and Town Over in Partial Years

单位:万元,万平方米 (10000 yuan,10000 sq.m)

年份	本年新增固定资产额 Newly Increase Fixed Assets	房屋施工面积 Floor Space of Buliding Under Construction	#住宅 Residential Buildings	房屋竣工面积 Floor Space of Buildings Completed	#住宅 Residential Buildings
1990	179769	308.76	137.73	180.48	77.30
1991	289108	362.09	175.07	182.28	88.11
1992	253780	518.29	254.60	209.38	91.38
1993	516881	906.08	501.36	383.28	224.91
1994	908056	1205.39	615.30	528.40	285.92
1995	1007217	1386.64	760.99	515.02	312.26
1996	1433274	1395.46	681.71	579.60	332.59
1997	1758309	1264.97	543.00	442.76	232.08
1998	1685871	1156.62	467.16	506.87	232.26
1999	1915400	1050.10	519.91	499.65	233.31
2000	2464806	1208.39	681.38	446.70	227.64
2001	2776661	1626.01	886.08	622.64	341.45
2002	2382537	2342.77	1132.48	745.33	365.88
2003	3292041	3401.43	1744.41	971.64	550.62

4－5　城镇集体以上固定资产投资完成情况

单位:万元　　(2003)

项目	Item	计划总投资 Total Investment Quota	累计完成投资 Accumulative Finish Total Investment	累计新增固定资产 Accumulative Newly In－creased Fixed Assets
总计	**Total**	**15032496**	**752689**	**3076581**
按登记类型	**By Registered Type**			
内资	Domestic－investment Enterprises	11402291	5446048	2573658
#国有	State－owned	6763673	3414165	1609044
港澳台投资	Hongkong,Macao and Taiwan Funded	1549128	516765	142061
外资	Foreign Funded Enterprises	2077077	1032916	360862
按隶属关系	**By Subordination**			
中央	Central	1729583	1196455	796177
地方	Local	13302913	5802274	2280404
按建筑性质	**By type of Construction**			
#新建	New Construction	8730352	3121671	1089643
扩建	Expansion	4485881	2690053	1490681
改建	Reconstruction	1211361	790996	287877
按国民经济行业分组	**By Sector**			
农、林、牧、渔业	Farming,Forestry,Animal Husbandry and Fishery	13950	10260	5372
制造业	Manufacturing Industry	5405139	2722090	1237539
电力、燃气及水的生产和供应业	Power.Gas and Hot Water Production and Supply	1924728	433848	150955
建筑业	Construction	7772	8192	6592
交通运输、仓储和邮政业	Transport,Storage and Post Industries	3023964	947056	575618
信息传输、计算机服务和软件业	Information Transmission,Computer Service and Software Industries	157314	139544	102859
批发和零售业	Wholesale and Retail Sale Trade	39911	32095	11806
住宿和餐饮业	Hotels and Catering Trade	80325	42578	18778
金融业	Banking	21175	13401	10937
房地产业	Real Estate Industry	119218	23810	12613
租赁和商务服务业	Leasing and Businessl Services	102791	94839	73773
科学研究、技术服务和地质勘查业	Scientific Research,Technology Services and Geological Prospecting	48656	10567	877
水利、环境和公共设施管理业	Water Conservancy,Environment and Public Facility Management	3048298	1775465	551355
教育	Education	473108	358168	171588
卫生、社会保障和社会福利业	Health Care,Social Security and Welfare Industry	190801	132142	39490
文化、体育和娱乐业	Culture,Sports and Entertainment	165471	96616	24282
公共管理和社会组织	Public Administration and Social Organizations	209425	157672	81721

注:城镇以上,不包括房地产开发情况。
本表按2002年修订的国民经济行业标准统计。表4－6同。

Investment in Fixed Assets of City and Town Collective Units & Above

(10000 yuan)

本年计划投资 PlanInvest－ment of This Year	本年完成投资 Investment Made This Year	建筑工程 Construc－tion	安装工程 Installa－tion	设备工器具购置 Purchase of Equipment and Instruments	按用途分 by Used 其他费用 Others	土地购置费 Purchase of Land	本年新增固定资产 Newly Increased Fixed Assets This Year	本年施工面积(平方米) Floor Space of Buildings Under Construction (sq.m)	本年房屋竣工面积(平方米) Floor Space of Buildings Competed (sq.m)
6873811	**3694245**	**1893389**	**231589**	**832059**	**737208**	**303062**	**2304036**	**13470369**	**3155122**
5298871	2663144	1391188	202996	466695	602265	211746	1916492	6728989	2461178
2863108	1737567	1084622	92304	192024	368617	104189	1373465	4185792	1767731
405388	295599	125307	5598	123881	40813	28395	130352	1077438	327117
1166552	732502	376094	22995	240083	93330	62171	257192	5663942	366827
467975	415732	56500	72752	264642	21838	1628	423937	289559	195429
6405836	3278513	1836889	158837	567417	715370	301434	1880099	13180810	2959693
4133076	1841063	1153412	87526	253682	346443	210517	887431	8690316	1906604
1894458	1154805	433712	89741	391023	240329	60816	982655	3270457	663313
573422	477114	199955	43743	109391	124025	13371	246147	235178	123871
5331	5331	4936	55	35	305	206	4487	17427	17427
1960018	1387816	516100	106601	552433	212682	136359	709442	7652523	1084108
793184	335951	155236	72285	74064	34366	3572	139623	592663	117404
6036	6036	1067	125	4844			4995	6264	
2131833	448221	314555	170	55607	77889	31126	431284	140345	90517
146178	103858	6823	1813	95222			102859		
27835	23069	15025	528	1742	5774	4651	10166	245966	81541
51735	34388	23878	806	2752	6952	4150	18327	146555	43950
13175	12401	3021	742	7625	1013		9781	37000	
36847	23810	21068	100		2642	1903	12613	865036	30525
16265	15528	10164			5364	3378	73773	268559	202305
27990	9901	7602		114	2185	983	705	102178	3000
1236886	932759	580691	5243	5542	341283	92342	496257	267076	
184718	159209	131145	5563	5574	16927	12386	156221	1629822	792050
69711	56965	35991	2343	12263	6368	3782	38606	447621	100651
69145	53518	21115	20890	591	10922	6441	23443	349418	164522
96474	85058	44713	14325	13484	12536	1783	71454	701916	427122

Note: Data in this table above urban collective－owned units, exclude Real Estate. Statistics in this table are classified as the national economic category that was modified in 2002. The same for table 4－6.

4－6 各县(市)城镇集体以上固定资产投资主要指标

单位:万元 (2003)

项目	Item	全市 Total	
		本年 This Year	为上年(%) Preceding Year＝100
计划总投资	**Total Investment of Plan**	**15020633**	**145.0**
实际需要投资	**Total Actual Need investment**	**14833291**	**152.7**
本年计划投资	**Total Investment of Plan This Year**	**6873811**	**202.1**
本年完成投资	**Finished Investment of This Year**	**3694245**	**133.5**
按经济注册类型分	**By Registration Status**		
#国有经济	State－Owned Units	1737567	100.7
集体经济	Collective－owned Units	22162	66.4
股份有限公司	Share－holding Corporation Units	425099	129.0
其他有限责任公司	Other Limited Liability Corporations	284645	208.4
外商投资经济	Foreign Investment	732502	219.3
港澳台投资经济	HongKong, Macao and Taiwan Funded	295599	231.7
其他经济	Others	196671	241.9
按隶属关系分	**By Administrative Relationship**		
#中央	Central Government	415732	93.7
省	Province	139805	557.3
省辖市	Municipalities Directly Under the Province Government	965664	117.0
县(市)、区	Counties and Districts	1643027	139.5
其他	Others	530017	179.5
按建设性质分	**By Type of Construction**		
#新建	New Construction	1841063	165.3
扩建	Expansion	1154805	119.0
改建	Reconstruction	477114	120.1
其他	Others	221263	77.2
按构成分	**By Use of Funds**		
#建筑工程	Construction	1893389	142.3
安装工程	Installation	231589	121.7
设备工器具购置	Purchase of Equipment and Instruments	832059	136.1
其他费用	Others	737208	116.1
按国民经济行业分	**By Sector**		
农、林、牧、渔业	Farming, Forestry, Animal Husbandry and Fishery	5331	

注:本表数据不包括房地产开发情况。

Main Indicators of Investment in Fixed Assets of City and Town CollectiveUnits & Above by Region

(10000 yuan)

市区 Urban District	# 鄞州 Yinzhou	余姚 Yuyao	慈溪 Cixi	奉化 Fenghua	象山 Xiangshan	宁海 Ninghai
11658111	**1296682**	**445125**	**1118827**	**147995**	**359485**	**1291090**
11493905	**1261667**	**440144**	**1117592**	**147895**	**364924**	**1268831**
5740835	**497264**	**238766**	**404998**	**63544**	**167527**	**258141**
2840343	**323448**	**176128**	**353831**	**50451**	**119252**	**154240**
1073171	179797	129615	271756	35495	80911	146619
3042		4260	1890		8236	4734
391531	20023	21036	1122		10523	887
231805	57842	15047	37443		350	
699245	16092		20014	6943	6300	
274421	13940	610	8404	2957	9207	
167128	35754	5560	13202	5056	3725	2000
414581	5680	611			540	
102426				310		37069
959370	54177	5923			371	
919621	217554	156869	300448	34830	116088	115171
444345	46037	12725	53383	15311	2253	2000
1455822	219762	75775	95370	31096	62446	120554
936730	51845	52462	116137	4000	34875	10601
264976	22604	36936	130270	10541	15072	19319
182815	29237	10955	12054	4814	6859	3766
1365737	218101	119283	196372	38655	81731	91611
195464	6760	7027	15284	993	4708	8113
754930	32933	12687	32721	6489	10760	14472
524212	65654	37131	109454	4314	22053	40044
1509			3822			

Note: Data in this table exclude Real Estate Trade.

项目	Item	全市 Total 本年 This Year	全市 Total 为上年(%) Preceding Year=100
制造业	Manufacturing Industry	1387816	
电力、燃气及水的生产和供应	Power. Gas and Hot Water Production and Supply	335951	
建筑业	Construction	6036	
交通运输、仓储和邮政业	Transport, Storage and Post Industries	448221	
信息传输、计算机服务和软件	Information Transmission, Computer Service and Software Industries	103858	
批发和零售业	Wholesale and Retail Sale Trade	23069	
住宿和餐饮业	Hotels and Catering Trade	34388	
金融业	Banking	12401	
房地产业	Real Estate Industry	23810	
租赁和商务服务业	Leasing and Businessl Services	15528	
科学研究、技术服务和地质勘查	Scientific Research, Technology Services and Geological Prospecting	9901	
水利、环境和公共设施管理业	Water Conservancy, Environment and Public Facility Management	932759	
居民服务和其他服务业	Resident Service and Other Service Industry	426	
教育	Education	159209	
卫生、社会保障和社会福利业	Health Care, Social Security and Welfare Industry	56965	
文化、体育和娱乐业	Culture, Sports and Entertainment	53518	
公共管理和社会组织	Public Administration and Social Organizations	85058	
新增固定资产	**Newly Increased Fixed Assets**	**2352704**	**131.5**
按资金来源分	**By Source of Funds**		
#国家预算内投资	State Budget	235895	105.2
国内贷款	Domestic Loans	883532	146.7
利用外资	Foreign Investment	425631	194.6
自筹资金	Fund Raising	2074698	134.8
房屋建筑面积(万平方米)	**Floor Space of Buildings (10000 sq.m)**		
施工面积	Floor Space of Buildings Under Construction	13746301	143.1
#住宅	Residential Buildings	1118340	278.3
竣工面积	Floor Space of Buildings Completed	3361085	111.5
#住宅	Residential Buildings	207846	102.7
本年竣工房屋价值(万元)	alue of Building Completed(10000 yuan)	414284	128.5
#住宅	Residential Buildings	18616	95.0

continued (10000 yuan)

市区 Urban District	# 鄞州 Yinzhou	余姚 Yuyao	慈溪 Cixi	奉化 Fenghua	象山 Xiangshan	宁海 Ninghai
1279869	74479	18681	57512	9900	17120	4734
255774	7718	10975	18506	4381	4378	41937
6036						
313577	13462	27861	55293	6872	16016	28602
97559		3248	3051			
9111	3184	10019	1180	2072		687
13018		1300	3000		15070	2000
9755	2226		70		2576	
20160	7200	2150				1500
8068	2703	6660	800			
9791					110	
559594	137940	79443	172929	14925	41509	64359
					426	
129148	46815	9392	9810	4108	4642	2109
35310	11967	2350	6387	5623	6775	520
40088	3645	1506	3253	363	4600	3708
45676	12109	5792	21269	2207	6030	4084
1817339	**143403**	**127587**	**195812**	**50029**	**61833**	**100104**
222453	30699	4664	1800	415	5963	600
722662	137405	51878	11408	600	31205	65779
396470	16008		12870	13183	3108	
1457160	177850	109205	320724	35645	65539	86425
10697004	1967304	454139	1715452	209821	473633	196252
925448	680831	94918	19200	16780	37761	24233
1812097	241656	305475	923179	146312	99481	74541
55954		89918	19200	16780	5761	20233
265328	27087	31312	80122	18912	9506	9104
5228		8810	773	1420	555	1830

4-7 全市房地产企业开发投资情况

单位:万元　　(2003)

项目	Item	总计 Total	按经济类型分 国有 State-owned	集体 Colloective-owned
计划总投资	**Total Investment of Plan**	**5148947**	**302885**	**179250**
本年计划投资	**Plan Investment of This Year**	**2328271**	**136408**	**96880**
本年完成投资	**Investment Made of This Year**	**1842589**	**117931**	**83477**
#商品房建设投资额	Investment of Commercial Houses	972184	87128	52621
土地开发投资额	Investment of Land Developed	41791	6003	2224
土地购置费	Purchase of Land	711899	16607	21565
按构成分	**By Composition**			
#建筑工程	Construction	973808	93042	53993
安装工程	Installation	40167	89	852
设备工器具购置	Purchase of Equipment and Instruments	4594	212	77
其他费用	Others	824020	24588	28555
按工程用途分	**By Purpose**			
#住宅	Residential Buildings	1368423	87864	71125
办公楼	Office Buildings	76782	8613	707
商业营业用房	Buildings for Commercial Business	200473	9044	9421
其他	Others	196911	12410	2224
本年新增固定资产	Newly Increased Fixed Assets This Year	939337	78508	47713
本年完成开发土地面积(平方米)	Land Space Developed This Year (sq.m)	3590221	391595	217714
待开发的土地面积	Land Space Needed Development	2154447	34432	110303
本年购置土地面积	Land Space Purchased This Year	7212975	888025	331397

Develop&Investment of Enterprises for Real Estate Development

(10000 yuan)

By Registration Status			按隶属关系分 By Administrative Relationship				
外商投资 Foreing Funds	港澳台投资 Invetsment Founds from Hongkong, Macao&Taiwan	其他经济 Others	中央 Central Government	地区 （省辖市） Municipality	县（县级市） Counties and Districts	乡（镇） Town and Township	其他 Others
92024	**304569**	**4270219**	**146029**	**1602434**	**1214352**	**523547**	**1662585**
46634	**128509**	**1919840**	**56384**	**634006**	**590925**	**265268**	**781688**
33917	**112448**	**1494816**	**44878**	**513767**	**456235**	**184247**	**643462**
27030	54587	750818	38063	256217	249835	134510	293559
290	1507	31767		5670	11106	6517	18498
5181	51304	617242	3389	216037	172788	34631	285054
26318	54242	746213	38063	249183	251476	134311	300775
1002	1852	36372		12704	9465	6716	11282
820	337	3148		1175	652	98	2669
5777	56017	709083	6815	250705	194642	43122	328736
21503	97523	1090408	32517	386563	319827	140996	488520
1867	1296	64299	7114	26775	14694	21403	6796
9249	5940	166819	4571	34574	78050	12904	70374
1298	7689	173290	676	65855	43664	8944	77772
11214	64751	737151	30318	309532	215148	90446	293893
74187	79844	2826881		642724	814359	474907	1658231
37008		1972704		578570	418202	260832	896843
63635	328220	5601698	423622	1494870	1280152	831307	3183024

4－8　全市房地产企业房屋施工及竣工情况

单位：平方米　　（2003）

项目	Item	总计 Total	按经济类型分 国有 State－owned	集体 Colloective－owned
施工房屋面积	**Floor Space of Buildings Under Consrtuction**	**20267994**	**1622225**	**1042969**
住宅	Residdential Buildings	16325769	1303663	882926
办公楼	Office Buildings	667034	89603	14648
商业营业用房	Buildings for Commercial Business	1901263	129568	87294
其他	Others	1373928	99391	58101
本年新开工房屋面积	**Floor Space of Buildings Newly Started This Year**	**10297277**	**924904**	**268928**
住宅	Residdential Buildings	8309874	788884	240814
办公楼	Office Buildings	288050	31698	1359
商业营业用房	Buildings for Commercial Business	915519	51759	17303
其他	Others	783834	52563	9452
竣工房屋面积	**Floor Space of Buildings Completed**	**6355274**	**585670**	**440307**
住宅	Residdential Buildings	5298341	464848	376672
办公楼	Office Buildings	121752	17438	419
商业营业用房	Buildings for Commercial Business	596251	47324	36211
其他	Others	338930	56060	27005
竣工房屋价值(万元)	**Value of Buildings Completed(10000 yuan)**	**869351**	**68802**	**42384**
住宅	Residdential Buildings	698663	50850	35882
办公楼	Office Buildings	24625	3202	59
商业营业用房	Buildings for Commercial Business	98132	7252	3956
其他	Others	47931	7498	2487
竣工住宅套数(套)	Completed Residencial House (flat)	44028	4157	3251
拆迁还建竣工房屋面积	Completed Housing Area on Old Sites	530060	24473	63857
统建代建竣工房屋面积	Completed Housing Area	426737	153050	7371
公益性建筑竣工面积	Area of the Completed Public Buildings	61972	9701	500

Buildings Construction and The Completed of Enterprises for Real Estate Development

(sq. m)

By Registration Status			按隶属关系分 By Administrative Relationship				
外商投资 Foreing Funds	港澳台投资 Invetsment Founds from Hongkong, Macao&Taiwan	其他经济 Others	中央 Central Government	地区 (省辖市) Municipality	县(县级市) Counties and Districts	乡(镇) Town and Township	其他 Others
383250	**1035036**	**16184514**	**711346**	**5377040**	**5009141**	**2643609**	**6526858**
259503	870182	13009495	594177	4220490	4141194	2340860	5029048
24696	12267	525820	60407	200267	152968	112468	140924
83503	88930	1511968	47952	328002	452629	126455	946225
15548	63657	1137231	8810	628281	262350	63826	410661
65602	**428755**	**8609088**	**361638**	**2438680**	**2425665**	**1615889**	**3455405**
38530	351202	6890444	328214	1789998	1973532	1471904	2746226
	5777	249216	18700	116197	62992	63153	27008
27072	22894	796491	14724	139425	233442	53881	474047
	48882	672937		393060	155699	26951	208124
120840	**373355**	**4835102**	**206883**	**1721469**	**1589307**	**767948**	**2069667**
112468	319461	4024892	181865	1416213	1318988	684143	1697132
		103895	10780	21659	53452	9914	25947
8372	51114	453230	9008	128110	162357	46821	249955
	2780	253085	5230	155487	54510	27070	96633
10951	**48652**	**698562**	**21011**	**282125**	**198850**	**87331**	**280034**
9246	40731	561954	16352	226322	160275	76337	219377
		21364	1928	5378	9488	1420	6411
1705	7087	78132	2071	25266	22667	6412	41716
	834	37112	660	25159	6420	3162	12530
938	3073	32609	1884	9694	11018	7451	13981
		441730		27328	112977	195947	193808
		266316	49983	302476	12394	8401	53483
240	120	51411	9623	30094	19767	246	2242

4-9 全市房地产企业房屋销售情况

单位:平方米 (2003)

项目	Item	总计 Total	按经济类型分 国有 State-owned	集体 Colloective-owned
商品房销售面积	**Floor Space of Building Sold**	**5485913**	**360822**	**350734**
住宅	Residdential Buildings	4633243	290432	304196
办公楼	Office Buildings	102463	24351	3485
商业营业用房	Buildings for Commercial Business	546968	32945	26516
其他	Others	203239	13094	16537
商品房预售面积	**Floor Space of Building Advance Sold**	**3474840**	**105900**	**172265**
住宅	Residdential Buildings	3065026	79701	154809
办公楼	Office Buildings	104395	17717	
商业营业用房	Buildings for Commercial Business	208560	7046	12772
其他	Others	96859	1436	4684
商品房空置面积	**Floor Space of Vacant Buildings**	**706004**	**91903**	**71085**
住宅	Residdential Buildings	375241	44020	49578
办公楼	Office Buildings	77016	25659	1237
商业营业用房	Buildings for Commercial Business	199838	19152	18946
其他	Others	53909	3072	1324
商品房出租面积	**Floor Space of Lease Buildings**	**140218**	**19933**	**30807**
住宅	Residdential Buildings	21292	682	
办公楼	Office Buildings	48858	12048	4600
商业营业用房	Buildings for Commercial Business	63418	7203	20107
其他	Others	6650		6100
商品房实际销售额(万元)	**Total Actually Sales of Commercial Buildings (10000 yuan)**	**1571945**	**98805**	**68830**
住宅	Residdential Buildings	1177246	66761	57340
办公楼	Office Buildings	37966	9011	1207
商业营业用房	Buildings for Commercial Business	305695	20300	8797
其他	Others	51038	2733	1486

Building Sale Situation of Enterprises for Real Estate Development

(sq. m)

By Registration Status			按隶属关系分 By Administrative Relationship				
外商投资 Foreing Funds	港澳台投资 Invetsment Founds from Hongkong, Macao&Taiwan	其他经济 Others	中央 Central Government	地区(省辖市) Municipality	县(县级市) Counties and Districts	乡(镇) Town and Township	其他 Others
102428	**383811**	**4288118**	**131130**	**1533930**	**1409099**	**534677**	**1877077**
93700	344652	3600263	94076	1294325	1210160	466022	1568660
	3279	71348	22821	26850	25696	10738	16358
8372	34571	444564	12653	140211	149519	41899	202686
356	1309	171943	1580	72544	23724	16018	89373
104675	**109960**	**2982040**	**81994**	**905133**	**673415**	**576132**	**1238166**
85925	103701	2640890	59107	862802	606753	515061	1021303
6000	3575	77103	17717	6521	13370	35429	31358
12750	2684	173308	5170	17712	34507	18660	132511
		90739		18098	18785	6982	52994
22166	**75242**	**445608**	**14817**	**74888**	**337274**	**93046**	**185979**
20522	47302	213819	2014	21226	163225	71331	117445
	2460	47660	11022	13586	50281		2127
1644	22908	137188	1781	19960	96927	17987	63183
	2572	46941		20116	26841	3728	3224
8408	**30835**	**50235**	**1330**	**67363**	**30859**	**1500**	**39166**
	18325	2285		265	682	1500	18845
		32210	606	16135	20284		11833
8408	12500	15200	724	44863	9343		8488
	10	540		6100	550		
29216	**114025**	**1261069**	**40262**	**543181**	**346744**	**149583**	**492175**
22672	85308	945165	22220	408237	263802	128097	354890
	653	27095	8693	11854	9194	3677	4548
6501	27507	242590	8569	98581	67338	14364	116843
43	557	46219	780	24509	6410	3445	15894

4-10 全市房地产企业经营情况

单位:万元 (2003)

项目	Item	总计 Total	按经济类型分 国有 State-owned	集体 Colloective-owned
本年资金来源合计	**Total Funds This Year**	**1956866**	**117496**	**85758**
上年末结余资金	Balance of Funds Last Year	64978	3664	888
本年资金来源小计	Subtotal Funds This Year	1891888	113832	84870
国内贷款	Domestic Loans	549966	37674	16082
利用外资	Foreign Investment	527		
自筹投资	Fund Raising	505385	17904	13489
其他资金来源	Others	836010	58254	55299
本年各项应付款合计	**Total Account Payable This Year**	**179847**	**56026**	**3550**
年末从业人员(人)	Employed Persons at Year-end(person)	6497	650	476
全年从业人员劳动报酬	Pay of All Empolyed Persons	18165	2664	900
实收资本合计	**Total Capital Hold**	**531888**	**29805**	**29266**
#国家资本	State Capital	27356		
年末资产负债情况	**Assets and Liabilities of Year-end**			
资产总计	Total Assets	5501231	428877	232067
固定资产累计折旧	Accumulative Total Depreciation of Fixed Assets	29818	2600	1193
负债总计	Total Liabilities	4584122	363352	179381
所有者权益合计	Creditors' Equity	917109	65525	52686
损益情况	**Expenditureznd Income**			
经营总收入	Total Income of Management	1601008	100508	78813
土地转让收入	Land Transferred	3062		
商品房销售收入	Commercial Buildings Sold	1520100	92368	75411
房屋出租收入	Buildings Leased	4811	766	482
其他收入	Others	73035	7374	2920
经营成本	Costs of Management	1171890	73634	55976
销售费用	Sales Funds	26065	916	509
经营税金及附加	Sales Taxes and Extra Charges	92913	5538	4365
管理费用	Manage Expenses	66349	8065	2874
财务费用	Finance Expenses	23186	2391	826
利润总额	Total Profits	260241	16005	19666

Main Economy Indicators of Real Estate Development

(10000 yuan)

By Registration Status			按隶属关系分 By Administrative Relationship				
外商投资 Foreing Funds	港澳台投资 Invetsment Founds from Hongkong, Macao&Taiwan	其他经济 Others	中央 Central Government	地区(省辖市) Municipality	县(县级市) Counties and Districts	乡(镇) Town and Township	其他 Others
32831	**124091**	**1596690**	**41423**	**531926**	**484844**	**193092**	**705581**
3300	1604	55522		13797	12048	2990	36143
29531	122487	1541168	41423	518129	472796	190102	669438
9420	25530	461260	7000	165068	130792	37365	209741
	527						527
6140	40260	427592	1406	128923	136035	51584	187437
13971	56170	652316	33017	224138	205969	101153	271733
2110	**4222**	**113939**	**55632**	**39387**	**35682**	**5225**	**43921**
147	410	4814	69	1546	1904	826	2152
447	1343	12811	470	6049	5137	1667	4842
22396	**55006**	**395415**	**3750**	**147955**	**114765**	**56679**	**208739**
	2024	25332		18529	4057		4770
120803	459351	4260133	87107	1816758	1232636	539221	1825509
386	4412	21227	583	9997	7056	2065	10117
92945	386261	3562183	73133	1545097	1030942	447072	1487878
27858	73090	697950	13974	271661	201694	92149	337631
33489	88182	1300016	35660	555008	377247	181926	451167
600	366	2096					3062
32538	84149	1235634	35614	550830	366986	178862	387808
351	811	2401	46	1940	1064	30	1731
	2856	59885		2238	9197	3034	58566
23817	54366	964097	23759	394395	286715	130751	336270
209	1923	22508	261	15571	4352	1515	4366
2156	5241	75613	2012	34248	21425	9720	25508
			1742	24858	17485	5288	
993	3989	14987	156	4644	7064	2268	9054
5429	21992	197149	7890	101527	55289	34098	61437

4－11 各县市农村非农户固定资产投资主要指标

单位:万元　　　　(2003)

项目	Item	全市 Total
本年完成投资	**Finished Investment of This Year**	**2587357**
按国民经济行业分	**By Sector**	
农、林、牧、渔业	Farming, Forestry, Animal Husbandry and Fishery	31885
采掘业	Mining and Quarrying	3412
制造业	Manufacturing Industry	2232579
电力、燃气及水的生产和供应业	Power. Gas and Hot Water Production and Supply	23192
建筑业	Construction	2851
交通运输、仓储和邮政业	Transport, Storage and Post Industries	50505
信息传输、计算机服务和软件业	Information Transmission, Computer Service and Software Industries	
批发和零售业	Wholesale and Retail Sale Trade	15519
住宿和餐饮业	Hotels and Catering Trade	4102
金融业	Banking	6
房地产业	Real Estate Industry	42352
租赁和商务服务业	Leasing and Businessl Services	3590
科学研究、技术服务和地质勘查业	Scientific Research, Technology Services and Geological Prospecting	220
水利、环境和公共设施管理业	Water Conservancy, Environment and Public Facility Management	109544
居民服务和其他服务业	Resident Service and Other Service Industry	5471
教育	Education	16815
卫生、社会保障和社会福利业	Health Care, Social Security and Welfare Industry	4747
文化、体育和娱乐业	Culture, Sports and Entertainment	5263
公共管理和社会组织	Public Administration and Social Organizations	35304

注:本表按 2002 年修订的国民经济行业标准统计。

Main Indicators of Investment in Fixed Assets of Non－peasant Households in Rural Area by Region

（10000 yuan）

市区 Urban Disctict	＃鄞州 Yinzhou	余姚 Yuyao	慈溪 Cixi	奉化 Fenghua	象山 Xiangshan	宁海 Ninghai
1124104	**622496**	**514066**	**491540**	**143848**	**159771**	**154028**
12158	7586	8274	2808	1619	4548	2478
1992	1840	1055			365	
927653	568597	428900	456531	134876	142822	141797
6437	3745	10671	1505	276	4093	210
2577	1235	274				
39273	500	2777	4150	2686	1361	258
11380	6241	2120	2010			9
3150		50	600		220	82
		6				
19912	3962	22115	325			
490			3100			
		220				
66082	24109	18341	15932	2610	4764	1815
1832	86		500	109	705	2325
6395	2415	7918	689		181	1632
1367	777	2307	314		157	602
1299	1090	1692	513	1204	40	515
22107	313	7346	2563	468	515	2305

Note：Statistics in this table are classified as the national economic category that was modified in 2002.

4-12 部分年份城镇集体以上固定资产投资主要指标

Main Indicators of Investment in Fixed Assets of City and Town Collective Units & Above in Partial Years

单位:万元 (10000 yuan)

项目	Item	1990	1995	1998	2002	2003
计划总投资	Total Investment of Plan	851483	7345261	9233556	10355586	15032496
累计完成投资	Accumulative Finished Investment	516537	2871454	5339505	5997523	6998729
本年计划投资	Total Investment Quota of This Year	258447	1916551	2385760	3400725	6873811
本年完成投资	Finished Investment of This Year	240466	1683096	2149357	2767541	3694245
按经济注册类型分	**By Registration Status**					
#国有经济	State - Owned Units	217510	847168	851764	1725107	1737567
集体经济	Collective - owned Units	22956	183012	114168	33364	22162
股份有限公司	Share - holding Corporation Units		218284	338919	329555	425099
其他有限责任公司	Other Limited Liability Corporations			396570	136601	284645
外商投资经济	Foreign Investment		286467	240209	334024	732502
港澳台投资经济	HongKong, Macao&Taiwan Funded		108184	182093	127595	295599
其他经济	Others		2313	22338	81295	196662
按隶属关系分	**By Administrative Relationship**					
#中央	Central Government	115093	228657	652378	443816	415732
省	Province		34759	22159	25088	139805
省辖市	Municipalities Directly Under the Province Government		648427	807374	825255	965664
县(市)、区	Counties and Districts		622599	522504	1178120	1643027
其他	Others		148654	165253	295262	530017
按建设性质分	**By Type of Construction**					
#新建	New Construction	77976	317035	578267	1113489	1841063
扩建	Expansion	113221	373068	880534	970124	1154805
改建	Reconstruction	31697	215599	196393	397150	477114
其他	Others	17572	777394	494163	286778	221263
按构成分	**By Use of Funds**					
#建筑工程	Construction	111951	893840	925463	1330834	1893389
安装工程	Installation	21373	72422	192718	190343	231589
设备工器具购置	Purchase of Equipment and Instruments	87094	299939	585251	611532	832059
其他费用	Others	20048	416859	445925	634832	737208
按资金来源分	**By Source of Funds**					
#国家预算内投资	State Budget	8501	5292	64399	224245	235895
国内贷款	Domestic Loans	48625	476376	592102	602367	883532
利用外资	Foreign Investment	31742	246328	338061	218753	425631
自筹资金	Fund Raising	82431	721069	947068	1539439	2074698

4-13 部分年份建筑业生产经营及主要财务情况

Satatistics and Financial Conditions of Construction in Partial Years

单位:万元 (10000 yuan)

项目	Item	1995	1998	2002	2003
企业个数(家)	**Number of Enterprises**	**126**	**529**	**504**	**569**
建筑业总产值	**Gross Output Value of Construction**	**773104**	**1402423**	**3353941**	**4746787**
建筑工程	Construction	685907	1198412	2826545	3965161
安装工程	Installation	76422	177996	422029	593325
其他	Building Repair and Maintenance	885	10444	105367	188301
竣工产值	Output Value of Buildings Completed	453042	1110779	2344889	3492787
房屋建筑施工面积(万平方米)	Floor Space of Buildings Under Construction (10000 sq.m)	1476	1721	4202	62444625
房屋建筑竣工面积	Floor Space of Buildings Completed	516	747	1778	2468
机械设备年末总台数(台)	Number of Machinery and Equipment(year-end)(unit)	24787	55866	73887	84189
机械设备年末总功率(万千瓦)	Total Power of Machinery and Equipment(10000kw)	32	67	87	96
机械设备净值	Net Value of Machinery and Equipment	52299	130868	209882	223335
年平均人数(万人)	Average Employed Persons (10000 person)	11	18	29	39
年末资产负债	**Asset and Liabilities at Year-end**				
流动资产	Circulating Assets	511192	1025510	1675115	2278206
固定资产小计	Fixed Assets	103728	249329	366091	443737
固定资产原价	Original Value of Fixed Assets	132659	328652	523916	561804
累计折旧	Accumulative Total Depreciation	30424	82366	165932	173387
资产总计	Total Assets	653756	1347721	2164590	2890272
流动负债	Liquid Liabilities	494629	919616	1323702	1860574
长期负债	Long-term Liabilities	19421	47961	66409	55683
所有者权益	Creditors' Equity	139886	380144	774488	974015
损益及分配	**Expenditure, Income and Distribution**				
工程结算收入	Revenue of Project Settlement Accounts	581186	1075887	3031823	4163598
工程结算成本	Costs of Project Settlement Accounts	518080	943698	2705512	3754114
工程结算税金及附加	Taxes and Extra Charges on Project Settlement Accounts	17407	36784	95926	131181
工程结算利润	Profits of Project Settlement Accounts	45699	95405	230385	278303
工资、福利费	**Wages and Welfare Expenses**				
本年应付工资总额	Total Wages Payable in this Year	94576	193658	446777	587995
本年应付福利费总额	Total Welfare Expenses Payable in this Year	6416	16039	62922	76035
建筑业增加值	**Value-added of Construction**	**175035**	**296170**	**753182**	**990020**

注:1995年为城镇以上建筑业企业。
Note: Data in this table refer to above urban collective-owned units in 1995.

4－14　建筑业企业生产情况

(2003)

项目	Item	企业个数(家) Number of Enterprises (unit)	建筑业总产值(万元) 总计 Total	建筑工程 Construction
总计	**Total**	**569**	**4746787**	**3965161**
国有及国有控股企业	State－owned and State Holding Enterprises	39	713361	517304
按注册登记类型分	**By Registered Type**			
内资企业	Domestic Funded Enterprises	563	4742786	3964344
国有企业	State－owned Enterprises	19	388442	207724
集体企业	Collective－oened Enterprises	16	74332	18605
股份合作企业	Share－holding Cooperative Enterprises	16	395458	378730
有限责任公司	Limited Liability Corporations	137	1104614	984243
#国有独资公司	State－owned Sole Investment	2	7983	7983
其他有限责任公司	Other Limited Liability Corporations	135	1096631	976260
股份有限公司	Share－holding Corporations Ltd.	19	1445279	1225222
私营企业	Private Enterprises	356	1334661	1149820
#私营有限责任公司	Private Limited Liability Corporations	341	1207578	1035135
港澳台投资企业	HongKong, Macro & Taiwan Funded	3	1482	739
外商投资企业	Enterprises with Foreign Investment	3	2519	78
按国名经济行业分组	**By Sector**			
房屋和土木工程建筑业	Building and Civil Engineering	253	4051461	3651362
房屋工程建筑业	Building	151	3109434	2900466
土木工程建筑业	Civil Engineering	102	942027	750896
铁路、道路、隧道和桥梁工程建筑	Railways, Tunnels, Highways and Bridges	44	584451	574452
水利和港口工程建筑	Water Conservancy and Port	18	133511	132976
架线和管道工程建筑	Line Installstion and Pipeline	22	187053	16482
其他土木工程建筑	Others Civil Engineering	18	37012	26986
建筑安装业	Equipment Installation	78	432113	128196
建筑装饰业	Building Decoration	214	193327	125759
其他建筑	Others	24	69886	59844

Statistics on Production of Construction Enterprises

Gross Output Value of Construction		竣工产值（万元）Output Value of Buildings Completed (10000yuan)	承包工程完成产值情况(万元) Gross Output Value of Contract the Project			
安装工程 Installation	其他 Building Repair and Maintenance		直接从建设单位承揽工程 Contract Project from Construction Unit Directly	自行完成 Finish by Oneself	分包出去 Resolve and Contract	从建设单位以外承揽工程 Contract ProjectOutside Construction Unit
593325	**188301**	**3492787**	**4675372**	**4593094**	**82278**	**153693**
124012	72045	560267	708376	692159	16217	21202
590141	188301	3489922	4671371	4589093	82278	153693
110760	69958	357163	386196	377324	8872	11118
50272	5455	66331	81939	74132	7807	200
16728		255337	394238	366408	27830	29050
107789	12582	749718	1064887	1056447	8440	48167
		5043	7983	7983		
107789	12582	744675	1056904	1048464	8440	48167
164883	55174	1037157	1439123	1413050	26073	32229
139709	45132	1024216	1304988	1301732	3256	32929
131022	41421	898183	1179251	1175995	3256	31583
743		992	1482	1482		
2441		1873	2519	2519		
302995	97104	2884789	3999391	3932682	66709	118779
133687	75281	2234284	3096042	3033583	62459	75851
169308	21823	650505	903349	899099	4250	42928
7687	2312	441021	561919	560763	1156	23688
130	405	63808	121812	118718	3094	14793
158095	12476	106305	186429	186429		624
3396	6630	39371	33189	33189		3823
243758	60159	403223	428511	413082	15429	19031
41270	26298	154193	186321	186181	140	7146
5302	4740	50582	61149	61149		8737

4－14 续表

项目	Item	房屋建筑施工面积（万平方米）Floor Space of Buildings Under Construction (10000sq.m)	#本年新开工 Beginning Projects in this Year	#投标承包面积 Floor Space of Biding System
总计	**Total**	**62444625**	**36618823**	**52754352**
国有及国有控股企业	State－owned and State Holding Enterprises	3433635	1951547	3116563
按注册登记类型分	**By Registered Type**			
内资企业	Domestic Funded Enterprises	62444625	36618823	52754352
国有企业	State－owned Enterprises	240234	63656	59004
集体企业	Collective－oened Enterprises	196518	98457	117893
股份合作企业	Share－holding Cooperative Enterprises	6613910	3853918	6543535
有限责任公司	Limited Liability Corporations	13319153	7810214	11426518
#国有独资公司	State－owned Sole Investment			
其他有限责任公司	Other Limited Liability Corporations	13319153	7810214	11426518
股份有限公司	Share－holding Corporations Ltd.	20507870	10371752	19817307
私营企业	Private Enterprises	21566940	14420826	14790095
#私营有限责任公司	Private Limited Liability Corporations	20324766	13629427	13997766
港澳台投资企业	HongKong, Macro & Taiwan Funded			
外商投资企业	Enterprises with Foreign Investment			
按国名经济行业分组	**By Sector**			
房屋和土木工程建筑业	Building and Civil Engineering	62090964	36419520	52608626
房屋工程建筑业	Building	59889485	35379546	50953880
土木工程建筑业	Civil Engineering	2201479	1039974	1654746
铁路、道路、隧道和桥梁工程建筑	Railways, Tunnels, Highways and Bridges	1727272	752061	1549057
水利和港口工程建筑	Water Conservancy and Port	64218	13908	15872
架线和管道工程建筑	Line Installstion and Pipeline	65412	53314	17712
其他土木工程建筑	Others Civil Engineering	344577	220691	72105
建筑安装业	Equipment Installation	353661	199303	145726
建筑装饰业	Building Decoration			
其他建筑	Others			

continued

# 本年新开工 Beginning Projects in this Year	房屋建筑竣工面积 Floor Space of Buildings Completed	机械设备年末总台数（台） Number of Machinery and Equipment (year-end)(unit)	机械设备年末总功率（万千瓦） Total Power of Machinery and Equipment (10000kw)	# 施工机械功率 Power of Construction Machines	机械设备净值（万元） Net Value of Machinery and Equipment (10000yuan)	企业总产值 Total Gross Output Value	年末人数（万人） Employed Persons at Year-end (10000person)	年平均人员（万人） Average Employed Persons (10000person)
30686403	**24683376**	**84189**	**962047**	**845896**	**223335**	**4950363**	**378462**	**393269**
1830815	1166949	5659	130674	111995	35388	731268	44674	42963
30686403	24683376	83908	961442	845330	222994	4946362	378101	392847
54406	112149	2503	60227	52251	22793	400799	22503	22414
87997	93489	1414	23746	22607	3594	74332	6596	7147
3852998	1845633	6205	37474	35197	8187	396470	38637	39185
7024355	4913668	19979	292343	269139	61410	1126626	91144	91629
		226	8064	8064	1105	8355	965	955
7024355	4913668	19753	284279	261075	60305	1118271	90179	90674
9832382	7982251	17917	236700	190583	44811	1593068	89608	102873
9834265	9736186	35890	310952	275553	82199	1355067	129613	129599
9251042	9266674	34306	287367	261991	76653	1215212	120409	119655
		2	13	13	25	1482	168	180
		279	592	553	316	2519	193	242
30549677	24535301	66124	843976	736761	191347	4247699	328935	337837
30391232	23655343	52659	526351	457357	113036	3247732	259402	268667
158445	879958	13465	317625	279404	78311	999967	69533	69170
126831	587417	7876	208048	183195	46538	630502	41688	42706
10708	15072	2027	68310	63726	19047	134191	12990	11075
13114	56207	2835	27589	20346	8870	198260	12121	12546
7792	221262	727	13678	12137	3856	37014	2734	2843
136726	148075	6629	66676	62378	18074	435581	25371	29493
		10433	24450	22104	8180	193531	19997	21400
		1003	26945	24653	5734	73552	4159	4539

4－15 建筑业企业财务情况

单位:万元　　(2003)

项目	Item	年末资产负债		
		流动资产合计 Circulating Assets	存货 Stocks	长期投资 Long－term Investment
总计	**Total**	**2278206**	**663695**	**110413**
国有及国有控股企业	State－owned and State Holding Enterprises	369016	65547	24420
按注册登记类型分	**By Registered Type**			
内资企业	Domestic Funded Enterprises	2274475	662909	110407
国有企业	State－owned Enterprises	208206	44164	16786
集体企业	Collective－oened Enterprises	52149	17377	2647
股份合作企业	Share－holding Cooperative Enterprises	106965	74775	4637
有限责任公司	Limited Liability Corporations	635030	167051	28426
#国有独资公司	State－owned Sole Investment	16417	332	5577
其他有限责任公司	Other Limited Liability Corporations	618613	166719	22849
股份有限公司	Share－holding Corporations Ltd.	541158	139987	37247
私营企业	Private Enterprises	730967	219555	20664
#私营有限责任公司	Private Limited Liability Corporations	643081	214671	19841
港澳台投资企业	HongKong, Macro & Taiwan Funded	1044	508	6
外商投资企业	Enterprises with Foreign Investment	2687	278	
按国名经济行业分组	**By Sector**			
房屋和土木工程建筑业	Building and Civil Engineering	1888338	551935	88276
房屋工程建筑业	Building	1253614	427673	61010
土木工程建筑业	Civil Engineering	634724	124262	27266
铁路道路隧道桥梁	Railways, Tunnels, Highways and Bridges	364334	63805	11417
水利和港口工程建筑	Water Conservancy and Port	67576	7958	2474
架线和管道工程建筑	Line Installstion and Pipeline	180305	48177	13054
其他土木工程建筑	Others Civil Engineering	22509	4322	321
建筑安装业	Equipment Installation	230207	62633	19301
建筑装饰业	Building Decoration	115360	31880	1332
其他建筑	Others	44301	17247	1504

Major Financial Indicators of Construction Enperprises

(10000 yuan)

Total Assets and Liabilities at Year－end					
固定资产合计 Fixed Assets	固定资产原价合计 Original Value of Fixed Assets	生产经营用 Use for Production And Management	累计折旧 Accumulative Total Depreciation	本年折旧 Depreciation in this year	资产合计 Total Assets
443737	**561804**	**475691**	**173387**	**32940**	**2890272**
105824	155238	124719	57253	5997	516344
443116	561017	474968	173144	32894	2885895
70506	104225	79914	37663	3747	302751
11552	10529	8756	2957	673	67387
18680	17994	14529	4596	870	131861
117487	150486	132178	48365	8746	799056
4389	2111	2111	715	124	26494
113098	148375	130067	47650	8622	772562
78186	110579	100141	36092	7964	666462
146705	167204	139450	43471	10894	918378
131627	146257	122276	35458	8398	808326
219	281	232	65	16	1280
402	506	491	178	30	3097
348401	443937	372056	140081	25950	2373015
199741	238182	209153	64681	15435	1542400
148660	205755	162903	75400	10515	830615
72611	103422	88183	41001	7190	456217
30197	42656	35802	17494	1209	101980
37375	50276	31755	14300	1743	239704
8477	9401	7163	2605	373	32714
56815	75156	68885	22377	4529	310967
22767	26116	19576	6764	1679	143945
15754	16595	15174	4165	782	62345

单位:万元

4-15 续表1

项目	Item	流动负债合计 Liquid Liabilities	长期负债合计 Long-term Liabilities	所有者权益 Creditors' Equity
总计	**Total**	**1860574**	**55683**	**974015**
国有及国有控股企业	State-owned and State Holding Enterprises	314478	19129	182737
按注册登记类型分	**By Registered Type**			
内资企业	Domestic Funded Enterprises	1857947	55683	972265
国有企业	State-owned Enterprises	173623	9792	119336
集体企业	Collective-oened Enterprises	45428	214	21745
股份合作企业	Share-holding Cooperative Enterprises	86535	654	44672
有限责任公司	Limited Liability Corporations	506994	27073	264989
#国有独资公司	State-owned Sole Investment	11287	7891	7316
其他有限责任公司	Other Limited Liability Corporations	495707	19182	257673
股份有限公司	Share-holding Corporations Ltd.	472725	2949	190788
私营企业	Private Enterprises	572642	15001	330735
#私营有限责任公司	Private Limited Liability Corporations	493289	12883	302154
港澳台投资企业	HongKong, Macro & Taiwan Funded	658		622
外商投资企业	Enterprises with Foreign Investment	1969		1128
按国名经济行业分组	**By Sector**			
房屋和土木工程建筑业	Building and Civil Engineering	1575102	51610	746303
房屋工程建筑业	Building	1054978	19564	467858
土木工程建筑业	Civil Engineering	520124	32046	278445
铁路道路隧道桥梁	Railways, Tunnels, Highways and Bridges	286683	20167	149367
水利和港口工程建筑	Water Conservancy and Port	60378	778	40824
架线和管道工程建筑	Line Installstion and Pipeline	157418	11095	71191
其他土木工程建筑	Others Civil Engineering	15645	6	17063
建筑安装业	Equipment Installation	177895	2769	130303
建筑装饰业	Building Decoration	72242	591	71112
其他建筑	Others	35335	713	26297

continued 1 (10000 yuan)

实收资本 Actual Capital Hold	损益及分配 Expenditure, Income and Distribution					
	工程结算收入 Revenue of Project Settlement Accounts	工程结算成本 Costs of Project Settlement Accounts	工程结算税金及附加 Taxes and Extra Charges on Project Settlement Accounts	工程结算利润 Profits of Project Settlement Accounts	其他业务利润 Other Profits from Business	管理费用 Management
553636	**4163598**	**3754114**	**131181**	**278303**	**21071**	**140277**
99085	700005	636054	16591	47360	2114	34269
552299	4159831	3750803	131072	277956	20960	139896
66834	395190	357747	7028	30415	1106	21188
13557	70828	56161	2236	12431	714	4156
22786	293831	266877	9071	17883	384	5736
156478	1004092	905650	33396	65046	10501	37750
1550	7983	6733	263	987	43	575
154928	996109	898917	33133	64059	10458	37175
77430	1248694	1134303	39063	75328	4182	31361
215214	1147196	1030065	40278	76853	4073	39705
203249	1019873	912329	35938	71606	1446	35125
377	1248	1099	26	123	95	173
960	2519	2212	83	224	16	208
410775	3514031	3196238	114344	203449	18065	97225
265482	2587158	2368884	85926	132348	7283	54679
145293	926873	827354	28418	71101	10782	42546
74864	588764	539345	18361	31058	3496	17719
28084	117085	100114	3677	13294	224	9420
31879	186273	157917	5387	22969	6918	13458
10466	34751	29978	993	3780	144	1949
81495	417244	361285	8487	47472	1450	26781
46994	180384	152806	6576	21002	220	12553
14372	51939	43785	1774	6380	1336	3718

单位:万元　　4-15 续表2

项目	Item	财务费用 Financial Expenditures	利润总额 Total Profits	应交所得税 Income Taxes Payable
总计	**Total**	**12020**	**151294**	**45490**
国有及国有控股企业	State - owned and State Holding Enterprises	1025	16273	5597
按注册登记类型分	**By Registered Type**			
内资企业	Domestic Funded Enterprises	11992	151247	45480
国有企业	State - owned Enterprises	567	10560	3810
集体企业	Collective - oened Enterprises	50	8777	2157
股份合作企业	Share - holding Cooperative Enterprises	106	12905	3946
有限责任公司	Limited Liability Corporations	3251	36379	10010
# 国有独资公司	State - owned Sole Investment	110	356	117
其他有限责任公司	Other Limited Liability Corporations	3141	36023	9893
股份有限公司	Share - holding Corporations Ltd.	2353	47634	15513
私营企业	Private Enterprises	5665	34992	10044
# 私营有限责任公司	Private Limited Liability Corporations	5026	32309	9093
港澳台投资企业	HongKong, Macro & Taiwan Funded	12	31	4
外商投资企业	Enterprises with Foreign Investment	16	16	6
按国名经济行业分组	**By Sector**			
房屋和土木工程建筑业	Building and Civil Engineering	10530	116918	36347
房屋工程建筑业	Building	7595	79158	23825
土木工程建筑业	Civil Engineering	2935	37760	12522
铁路道路隧道桥梁	Railways, Tunnels, Highways and Bridges	1376	16310	5795
水利和港口工程建筑	Water Conservancy and Port	612	3618	1050
架线和管道工程建筑	Line Installstion and Pipeline	862	15950	5264
其他土木工程建筑	Others Civil Engineering	85	1882	413
建筑安装业	Equipment Installation	289	22612	5855
建筑装饰业	Building Decoration	755	7539	2446
其他建筑	Others	446	4225	842

continued 2　　(10000 yuan)

应付利润 Total Profits Payable	工程福利费 Wages and Welfare Expenses 本年应付工资总额 Total Wages Payable in this Year	本年应付福利费总额 Total Welfare Expenses Payable in this Year	建筑业增加值 Value - added of Construction	亏损企业个数 Deficits Enterprises (unit)	亏损额 Total Deficits
67294	**587995**	**76035**	**990020**	**25**	**-628**
8570	65430	8951	115282	1	-3
67231	587444	75956	989170	24	-599
5134	34058	4752	61007		
4294	7524	1002	20755		
2351	57494	7974	88328	1	-14
20212	126760	16965	225208	6	-86
238	1230	170	2269		
19974	125530	16795	222939	6	-86
17076	182661	21332	299992		
18164	178947	23931	293880	17	-499
16691	169148	22684	272869	16	-456
56	132	19	234	1	-29
7	419	60	616		
48058	515951	66148	847480	6	-35
31205	419977	52896	658768	4	-18
16853	95974	13252	188712	2	-17
4895	59922	8299	111451		
1822	13762	1855	24583		
9460	18952	2654	45462		
676	3338	444	7216	2	-17
12269	40552	5731	83113	4	-68
4701	25342	3353	45774	15	-525
2266	6150	803	13653		

4-16 新增生产能力或效益

Newly Increase Production Capacity or Benefit

(2003)

项目		Item		本年新增 Added at This Year
石油加工:催化重整设备能力	(万吨/年)	Processing for Petroleum:Capacity of Distilling Sets	(ten thousand ton handled/year)	100
油罐容量	(万立方米)	Oilcan Capacity	(10000 stere)	6.5
冷加工钢材	(万吨/年)	Steel to Cold Working	(ten thousand ton/year)	8
薄钢板	(万吨/年)	Steel Sheet	(ten thousand ton/year)	8
输电线路长度(11万伏及以上)	(公里)	Length of Electric Wire(above 110000V)	(km)	340.48
变电设备能力(11万伏及以上)	(万千伏安)	Power Transform Capacity(above 110000V)	(10000 kva)	111
水泥	(万吨/年)			250
塑料树脂及共聚物	(吨/年)	Plastic Resin & Copolymer	(ton/year)	40000
服装	(万件/年)	Garments	(10000 suits/year)	59
家用空气调节器	(万台/年)	Household Air - conditioners	(10000 sets/year)	10
新建公路	(公里)	Newly Built Highways	(km)	136.5
改建公路	(公里)	Reconstructed Highways	(km)	287.5
新(扩)建港口码头(年吞吐量)	(万吨)	Newly Built or Expanded Ports (Annual Handling Capairty)	(10000 tons)	581
泊位	(个)	Number of Berths	(unit)	7
船舶购置(艘)	(艘)	Shipping Purchased	(unit)	1
船舶购置(载重量:吨位)	(吨位)	Shipping Purchased(Loading Capacity)	(ton/year)	13
船舶购置(载客量:客位)	(客位)	Shipping Purchased(Seats)	(seats)	28
水库容量(总库容)	(亿立方米)	Capacity of Reservoirs	(100 million cu.m)	
粮食仓库(容量)	(万公斤)	Grain Warehouse(Capacity)	(10000 kg)	1650
粮食仓库(面积)	(平方米)	Grain Warehouse(Area)	(sq.m)	5654
高等院校:学生席位	(个)	Seats for Student in High Education Institutions	(unit)	17212

4－16续表 continued

项目		Item		本年新增 Added at This Year
建筑面积	（平方米）	Floor Space of Construction	（sq.m）	188377
中等学校:学生席位	（个）	Seats for Student in Secondary Schools	（unit）	27720
建筑面积	（平方米）	Floor Space of Construction	（sq.m）	266203
小学校:学生席位	（个）	Seats for Student in Primary Schools	（unit）	14510
建筑面积	（平方米）	Floor Space of Construction	（sq.m）	119496
其他学校:学生席位	（个）	Seats for Student in Others Schools	（unit）	605
建筑面积	（平方米）	Floor Space of Construction	（sq.m）	8808
公共图书馆:藏书量	（万册(件)）	Public Libraries:Total Collections	（10000 volumes）	30
阅览室座	（个）	Seating Capacity of Reading Rooms	（seat）	350
建筑面积	（平方米）	Floor Space	（sq.m）	8000
医院病床	（张）	Number of Hospital Beds	（bed）	836
宾馆、旅馆、招待所客	（间）	Guest Room of Hotels,Restaurants & Hotels	（room）	208
宾馆、旅馆、招待所客	（平方米）	Area of Guest Room of Hotels,Restaurants & Hotels	（sq.m）	13000
城市自来水供水能力	（万吨/日）	Capacity of Tap Water Supply in Urban District	（10000 tons/day）	10
城市供热能力:蒸汽	（吨/小时）	Capacity of Heat Supply in Urban District:Steam	（ton/hour）	75
城市供热能力:热水	（兆瓦/小时）	Capacity of Heat Supply in Urban District: Hot Water	（megawatt/hour）	64
城市公共交通车辆购置	（辆）	Automobile Purchased for Public Transit	（unit）	722
城市道路扩建长度	（公里）	Length of Expanded in Urban Areas Roads	（km）	8.07
城市道路扩建面积	（万平方米）	Area of Expansion in Urban Areas Roads	（10000 sq.m）	40.1
市排水管道铺设长度	（公里）	Length of Paved Drain Pipes in Urban Areas	（km）	5.2

4-17 本年完成建筑业总产值前10位企业

The First 10 Enterprises Of Completed Total Output Value For Constructi on Industry

(2003)

企业名称 Name of Enterprises	资质等级 Grade of Natural Endowments
龙元建设集团股份有限公司 Longyuan Construction Group Ltd.	房屋建筑工程施工总承包一级 Whole Contract To Project of BuildingConstruction by First Grade
浙江中达建设集团股份有限公司 Zhejiang Zhongda Construction Group Ltd.	房屋建筑工程施工总承包一级 Whole Contract To Project of BuildingConstruction by First Grade
宁波华丰建设集团股份有限公司 Ningbo Huafeng Construction Group Ltd.	房屋建筑工程施工总承包一级 Whole Contract To Project of BuildingConstruction by First Grade
浙江省电力建设总公司 Zhejiang Power Construction Head Corp.	电力工程施工总承包特级 Whole Contract To Power Construction by SpecialGrade
宏润建设集团股份有限公司 Hongrun Construction Group Ltd.	市政公用工程施工总承包一级 Whole Contract To Municipal EngineeringConstruction by First Grade
浙江省中兴建设有限责任公司 Zhejiang Zhongxing Construction Ltd.	房屋建筑工程施工总承包一级 Whole Contract To Project of BuildingConstruction by First Grade
浙江建安实业集团股份有限公司 ZhejiangJian' an Industry Group Ltd.	房屋建筑工程施工总承包一级 Whole Contract To Project of BuildingConstruction by First Grade
宁波建工集团股份有限公司 Ningbo Construction And Industry Group Ltd.	房屋建筑工程施工总承包一级 Whole Contract To Project of BuildingConstruction by First Grade
宁波市建设集团股份有限公司 Ningbo Construction Group Ltd.	房屋建筑工程施工总承包一级 Whole Contract To Project of BuildingConstruction by First Grade
宁波市政工程建设集团股份有限公司 Ningbo Municipal Engineering Construction Group Ltd.	市政公用工程施工总承包一级 Whole Contract To Municipal Engineering Construction by First Grade

4－18 1、2级资质等级房地产开发经营企业

Enterprises for Real Estate Developing & Managing with Certificate in First, Second Grade of Natural Endowments

(2003)

企业名称 Name of Enterprises	资质等级 Grade of Natural Endowments
宁波房地产股份有限公司 Ningbo Real Estate Co., Ltd.	1
宁波永和建设开发股份有限公司 Ningbo Yonghe Construction Development Co., Ltd.	1
宁波中房置业股份有限公司 Ningbo Zhongfang Real Estate Co., Ltd.	1
宁波华能房地产开发公司 Ningbo Huaneng Real Estate Developing Corp.	1
宁波华泰股份有限公司 Ningbo Huatai Co., Ltd.	1
宁波宁兴房地产开发有限公司 Ningbo Ningxing Real Estate Developing Co., Ltd.	1
宁波联合建设开发有限公司 Ningbo Lianhe Construction Developing Co., Ltd.	1
宁波中建房地产开发公司 Ningbo Zhongjian Real Estate Co., Ltd.	2
宁波安居住房股份有限公司 Ningbo Setting－In House Co., Ltd.	2
宁波市江东东城房屋开发有限公司 Ningbo Jiangdong Dongcheng House Development Ltd.	2
宁波市甬城房地产总公司 Ningbo Yongchneg Real Estate General Corp.	2
宁波信用房地产开发有限公司 Ningbo Xinyong Real Estate Co., Ltd.	2
宁波东方建设开发有限公司 Ningbo Dongfang Construction Development Co., Ltd.	2
慈溪市房屋建设开发公司 Cixi House Construction Development Corp.	2
象山房地产开发有限公司 Xiangshan Real Estate Developing Co., Ltd.	2
宁波市交通房地产有限公司 Ningbo Jiaotong Real Estate Co., Ltd.	2
慈溪市住宅经营公司 Cixi House Managing Corp.	2
南光雅戈尔(宁波)置业有限公司 Nanguang Yonger (Ningbo) Real Estate Co., Ltd.	2
余姚市房地产开发经营公司 Yuyao Real Estate Developing & Managing Corp.	2

主要指标解释

【全社会固定资产投资】 固定资产投资是社会固定资产再生产的主要手段。通过建造和购置固定资产的活动，国民经济不断采用先进技术装备，建立新兴部门，进一步调整经济结构和生产力的地区分布，增强经济实力，为改善人民物质文化生活创造物质条件。这对我国的社会主义现代化建设具有重要意义。

固定资产投资额是以货币表现的建造和购置固定资产活动的工作量，它是反映固定资产投资规模、速度、比例关系和使用方向的综合性指标。全社会固定资产投资按经济类型可分为国有、集体、个体、联营、股份制、外商、港澳台商、其他等。按照管理渠道，全社会固定资产投资总额分为基本建设、更新改造、房地产开发投资和其他固定资产投资四个部分。

【基本建设投资】 基本建设指企业、事业、行政单位以扩大生产能力或工程效益为主要目的的新建、扩建工程及有关工作。其综合范围为总投资50万元以上(含50万元，下同)的基本建设项目。具体包括：(1)列入中央和各级地方本年基本建设计划的建设项目，以及虽未列入本年基本建设计划，但使用以前年度基建计划内结转投资(包括利用基建库存设备材料)在本年继续施工的建设项目；(2)本年基本建设计划内投资与更新改造计划内投资结合安排的新建项目和新增生产能力(或工程效益)达到大中型项目标准的扩建项目，以及为改变生产力布局而进行的全厂性迁建项目；(3)国有单位既未列入基建计划，也未列入更新改造计划的总投资在50万元以上的新建、扩建、恢复项目和为改变生产力布局而进行的全厂性迁建项目，以及行政、事业单位增建业务用房和行政单位增建生活福利设施的项目。

【更新改造投资】 更新改造指企业、事业单位对原有设施进行固定资产更新和技术改造，以及相应配套的工程和有关工作(不包括大修理和维护工程)。其综合范围为总投资50万元以上的更新改造项目。具体包括：(1)列入中央和各级地方本年更新改造计划的投资单位(项目)和虽未列入本年更新改造计划，但使用上年更新改造计划内结转的投资在本年继续施工的项目；(2)本年更新改造计划内投资与基本建设计划内投资结合安排的对企、事业单位原有设施进行技术改造或更新的项目和增建主要生产车间、分厂等其新增生产能力(或工程效益)未达到大中型项目标准的项目，以及由于城市环境保护和安全生产的需要而进行的迁建工程；(3)国有企、事业单位既未列入基建计划也未列入更新改造计划，总投资在50万元以上的属于改建或更新改造性质的项目，以及由于城市环境保护和安全生产的需要而进行的迁建工程。

【房地产开发投资】 指房地产开发公司、商品房建设公司及其他房地产开发法人单位和附属于其他法人单位实际从事房地产开发或经营的活动单位统一开发的包括统代建、拆迁还建的住宅、厂房、仓库、饭店、宾馆、度假村、写字楼、办公楼等房屋建筑物和配套的服务设施，土地开发工程(如道路、给水、排水、供电、供热、通讯、平整场地等基础设施工程)的投资；不包括单纯的土地交易活动。

【其他固定资产投资】 指全社会固定资产投资中未列入基本建设、更新改造和房地产开发投资的建造和购置固定资产的活动。具体包括：

⑴国有单位按规定不纳入基本建设计划和更新改造计划管理，计划总投资(或实际需要总投资)在50万元以上的以下工程：①用油田维护费和石油开发基金进行的油田维护和开发工程；②煤炭、铁矿、森工等采掘采伐业用维简费进行的开拓延伸工程；③交通部门用公路养路费对原有公路、桥梁进行改建的工程；④商业部门用简易建筑费建造的仓库工程。

⑵城镇集体固定资产投资：指所有隶属城市、县城和经国务院及省、自治区、直辖市批准建制的镇领导的集体单位(乡镇企业局管理的除外)建造和购置固定资产计划总投资(或实际需要总投资)在50万元以上的项目。

⑶除上述以外的其他各种企、事业单位、个体建造和购置固定资产总投资在50万元以上的、未列入基本建设计划和更新改造计划的项目。

【城镇和工矿区私人建房投资和农村个人投资】 城镇和工矿区私人建房包括市、县城、镇、工矿区所辖范围内的全部私人建房，不论其房主是否系本地的常住户口均应包括。农村个人投资包括农村个人建房及购置生产性固定资产的投资。

【农村非农户投资】 农村非农户建造和购置固定资产投资计划固定资本形成总额在5万元以上的项目，农村非农户包括以下二大类：

第一类为企业单位，分成(1)集体企业，包括集体直接经营及集体所有租赁给个人的企业；(2)股份合作企业；(3)联营企业；(4)有限责任公司(5)股份有限公司；(6)私营企业(7)与港澳台商合资、合作企业；(8)中外合资、合作企业；(9)其他企业。

联营和合资企业按其是否由农村集体与个人相对控股或绝对控股，或由农村集体、个人实际管理来确定是否纳入农村固定资产投资统计范围，其投资额按实际发生额全额统计；个体工商户外雇从业人员8人以上(含8人)的按企业统计。

第二类为乡镇行政事业单位及社会群众团体。**【新增固定资产】** 指通过投资活动所形成的新的固定资产价值。包括已经建成投入生产或交付使用的工程价值和达到固定资产标准的设备、工具、器具的价值及有关应摊入的费用。它是以价值形式表示的固定资产投资成果的综合性指标，可以综合反映不同时期、不同部门、不同地区的固定资产投资成果。

【建筑业统计单位】 指从事房屋、构筑物建造和设备安装活动的法人企业。建筑业法人企业应同时具备的条件是:①依法成立,有自己的名称、组织机构和场所,能够承担民事责任;②独立拥有和使用资产,承担负债,有权与其他单位签订合同;③独立核算盈亏,能够编制资产负债表。

【建筑业总产值(即自行完成施工产值)】 指建筑业企业或附属施工单位自行完成的按工程进度计算的建筑安装生产总值。施工产值包括:

①建筑工程产值:指列入建筑工程预算内的各种工程价值。

②设备安装工程产值:指设备安装工程价值。

③房屋、构筑物修理产值:指房屋、构筑物修理所完成的价值,但不包括被修理房屋、构筑物本身的价值和生产设备的修理价值。

④非标准设备制造产值:指加工制造没有定型的、非标准的生产设备的加工费和原材料价值,不论是现场还是附属加工厂为本单位承建工程制造的非标准设备的价值,都应计算产值。

【房屋建筑施工面积】 指报告期内施工的全部房屋建筑面积。包括本期新开工的面积、上期跨入本期继续施工的房屋面积、上期停缓建在本期恢复施工的房屋面积、本期竣工的房屋面积及本期施工后又停缓建的房屋面积。

【房屋建筑竣工面积】 指在报告期内房屋建筑按照设计要求已全部完工,达到住人和使用条件,经验收鉴定合格,正式移交使用单位的建筑面积。

【自有机械设备年末总台数】 指归本企业(或单位)所有,属于本企业固定资产的生产性机械设备年末总台数。包括施工机械、生产设备、运输设备以及其他设备。

【自有机械设备年末总功率】 指本企业(或单位)自有施工机械、生产设备、运输设备以及其他设备等列为在册固定资产的生产性机械设备年末总功率,按设定能力或查定能力计算。包括机械本身的动力和为该机械服务的单独动力设备,如电动机等。计算单位用千瓦,动力换算可按 1 马力 = 0.735 千瓦折合成千瓦数。电焊机、变压器、锅炉不计算动力。

【工程结算收入】 指企业(或单位)按工程的分部分项自行完成的建筑产品价值并已与甲方在报告期内办理结算手续的工程价款收入,以及向甲方收取的除工程价款以外的按规定列作营业收入的各种款项,如临时设施费、劳动保险费、施工机械调迁费等以及向甲方收取的各种索赔款。

【工程结算利润】 指已结算工程实现的利润。如为亏损以“ - ”号表示。其计算公式为:

工程结算利润 = 工程结算收入 - 工程结算成本 - 工程结算税金及附加

Explanatory Notes on Main Statistical Indicators

[Total Investment in Fixed Assets in the Whole Country] Investment in fixed assets is the essential means for social reproduction of fixed assets. By means of construction and purchase of fixed assets, more advanced technologies and equipment are adopted in the national economy, and new sectors are established, which promote the adjustment of economic structure and the regional distribution of productive forces and enhance the economic strengths so as to provide the material conditions for improving people's livelihood. This is significant for speeding up the drive of socialist modernization in China.

Amount of investment in fixed assets refers to the volume of activities in construction and purchases of fixed assets in monetary terms. It is a comprehensive indicator which shows the size, pace, proportional relations and use orientation of the investment in fixed assets. Total investment in fixed assets in the whole country includes, by registration type of ownership, the investment by the state – owned units, collective units, individuals, joint ownership units, share – holding units, as well as investment by businessmen from foreign countries and from Hong Kong, Macao and Taiwan, and by other units. According to China's current management system, the investment in fixed assets in the whole country is classified into the following four parts: investment in capital construction, investment in innovation, investment in real estates development and other investment in fixed assets.

[Investment in Capital Construction] Capital construction refers to the new construction projects or extension projects and the related work of the enterprises, institutions or administrative units mainly for the purpose of expanding production capacity or improving project efficiency covering only projects each with a total investment of 500,000 RMB yuan and over. It includes: (1) projects listed in the capital construction plan of the current year of the central government and the local governments at various levels as well as the projects, though not listed in the capital construction plan of the current year, but continued to be constructed in this year, using the investment listed in the plan of capital construction of previous years and carried forward to this year (also using the equipment and materials kept in stock of the capital construction); (2) new construction projects arranged both in the plan of capital construction and the plan of innovation; extension projects with the newly increased production capacity (or project efficiency) up to the standard of a large and medium – sized project; and the projects of moving the whole factory to a new site so as to improve the distribution of productive forces; (3) new construction projects, extension projects or restoration projects with the total investment of 500,000 RMB yuan and over by the state – owned units, though listed neither in the plan of capital construction nor in the plan of innovation; the projects in the state – owned units of moving the whole factory to a new site so as to improve the distribution of productive forces; and the projects of building additional business houses by the administrative units and institutions and building welfare facilities by the administrative units.

[Investment in Innovation] Innovation refers to the renewal of fixed assets and technological innovation of the original facilities by the enterprises and institutions as well as the corresponding supplementary projects and the related work (excluding major overhaul and maintenance projects) covering only projects each with a total investment of 500,000 RMB yuan and over. It includes: (1) projects listed in the innovation plan of the current year of the central government and the local governments at various levels as well as the projects, though not listed in the innovation plan of the current year, but continued to be constructed in this year, using the investment listed in the plan of innovation of previous years and carried forward to this year; (2) projects of technological innovation or renewal of the original facilities, arranged both in the plan of innovation and in the plan of capital construction; extension projects (main workshops or a branch of the factory) with the newly increased production capacity (or project efficiency) not up to the standard of a large and medium – sized project; and the projects of moving the whole factory to a new site so as to meet the requirements of urban environmental protection or safe production; (3) projects of reconstruction or technological innovation with the total investment of 500,000 RMB yuan and over by the state – owned units, though listed neither in the plan of capital construction nor in the plan of innovation; the projects in the state – owned units of moving the whole factory to a new site so as to meet the requirements of urban environmental protection or safe production.

[Investent in Real Estate Development] It includes the investment by the real estate development companies, commercial buildings construction companies and other real estate development units of various types of ownership in the construction of house buildings, such as residential buildings, factory buildings, warehouses, hotels, guesthouses, holiday villages, office buildings, and the complementary service facilities and land development projects, such as roads, water supply, water drainage, power supply, heating, telecommunications, land leveling and other projects of infrastructure. It excludes the activities in simple land transactions.

[Other Investment in Fixed Assets] refers to the construction and purchases of fixed assets not listed in the investment in capital construction, investment in innovation and investment in real estate development. It includes:

A)The following projects of the state – owned units with the total planned (or actually needed) investment of 500,000 yuan and over, which are not included in the plan of capital construction and the plan of innovation: (1)projects of oil fields maintenance and exploitation with the oil fields maintenance funds and petroleum development funds; (2)opening and extending projects with the maintenance funds in coal, ore and other mining enterprises and logging enterprises; (3)project of reconstruction of the original highways and bridges with the highway maintenance funds in the department of communication; (4)projects of construction of warehouses with the funds of simple construction in the commercial department.

B)The investment in fixed assets by urban collective units: refer to projects of construction and purchases of fixed assets with the planned total investment of 500,000 yuan and over by all collective units in cities and county towns and in townships which are approved by the State Council or provincial governments, excluding investment by collective units under township enterprise administration offices.

C)The projects of construction and purchases of fixed assets by the enterprises, institutions or individuals other than those mentioned above with total investment of 500,000 yuan and over, which are not included in the plan of capital construction and the plan of innovation.

【Private Investment in House Construction in Urban Areas, Industrial and Mining Areas and Individual Investment in Rural Areas】 The private house construction in the urban areas and industrial and mining areas includes all the private house construction under the jurisdiction of cities, counties, towns and industrial and mining areas, no matter whether the owner of the house is registered as the permanent resident in the locality or not. The individual investment in the rural areas includes the investment in house construction and purchase of productive fixed assets by the individuals in the rural areas.

【non – agricultural investment in rural areas】 refers to the project which the estimated total investment amount of its fixed assets built or bought by the non – agriculture units in rural areas is over 50000 yuan. The non – agricultural units include two kinds as below:

I. enterprises. 1. Collective Co. (including companies both directly managed by collective leadership and rent to the private), 2. Stock – hoiding cooperation, 3. Joint Ownership Enterprises, 4. Limited liability Corporations, 5. Share – holding corporations Ltd., 6. Private enterprises, 7. Joint ventures or Cooperative Operation with Hong kong, Macao and Taiwan, 8. Foreign joint ventures or Cooperative Operation Enterprises, 9. other Enterprises whether the associated companies and the joint ventures should be considered as the rural fixed assets depends on whether they are actually possessed or managed by rural communities or privates. Their investment amounts refer to the capital which had been actually invested into the enterprises. Private businesses which employ 8 or more workers should be considered as enterprises in statistics

II. public undertakings and public communities in rural areas.

【Newly Increased Fixed Assets】 refer to the newly increased value of fixed assets through investment, including the value of projects completed and put into production, the value of equipment, tools, and vessels considered as fixed assets, as well as the relevant expenses as investment in fixed assets . This is a comprehensive indicator of investment in fixed assets, reflecting the achievements of investment in fixed assets in different periods, different sect ors, and different regions.

【Statistical units in construction industries】 refers to the legal enterprises which build architectures or install equipments. The legal enterprises should meet all the demands as follows, 1. being formed legally with own name, organizational structure and working place. Can fully bear civil responsibilities. 2. possessing and using its own assets independently, which means it should be able to incur liabilities and has right to make contracts with other enterprises. 3. should be an independent accounting unit which can draw balance sheet.

【Gross Output Value of Construction(Output Value of Projects Under Construction)】 refers to total of construction products, expressed in money terms, completed by construction and installation enterprises during a given period of time. It includes:

(1)Output value of construction projects, that is the value of projects covered by the project budgets;

(2)Output value of installation projects, that is the value of the installation of equipment, (excluding the value of the equipment to be installed);

(3)Output value of repair of buildings and structures, that is the value created through the repairs of buildings or structures, but does not include the value of buildings or structures being repaired and the value of the repair of production equipment;

(4)Output value of manufactured non – standard equipment, that is the value of no-standard production equipment(including raw materials and manufacturing cost)made for the construction project, and the equipment manufactured by subsidiary workshops.

【Floor Space under Construction】 refers to total floor space of all buildings under construction during the reference period, including floor space of newly started buildings during the reference period, floor space of construction extended from the previous period to the current period, floor space of construction suspended during the previous period and resumed in the current period, floor space of construction completed in the current period, and floor space of construction started and then suspended in the current period.

【Floor Space of Buildings Completed】 refers to the floor space of buildings completed in the reference period, which have come up to the designed standards and have been put into use.

【Total Number of Machinery and Equipment Owned by the Construction Enterprises】 refers to the number of machines and equipment owned by the enterprises (or units, and listed as the fixed assets of the enterprises(or units) by the end of the year, including machinery and equipment for construction, production and transportation.

【Total Power of Machinery and Equipment Owned by the Construction Enterprises】 refer to the total power of machinery and equipment owned by the enterprises(or units), and listed as the fixed assets of the enterprises (or units) by the end of the year, including machinery and equipment for construction, production and transportation. The power of the machinery is calculated on basis of the designed or verified capacity, covering the power of the machinery/equipment and the separate power equipment serving the machinery/equipment (such as electric motors), but excluding welders, transformers and boilers. The unit use for the calculation of power is kilowatt, with horsepower converted to kilowatt by 1horsepowe = 0.735 kilowatt.

【Income from Settlement of Projects】 refers to the income received by the construction enterprise/unit from the completed portion of the project through settlement procedures with the contracted during the reference period, and other charges to the contracted as operational costs, such as facility fee, labor insurance premium, moving cost of construction unit, as well as various types of claims to the contracted.

【Profit from Settlement of Projects】 refers to profit realized through settled projects. It is calculated with the following formula:

Profit from Settlement of Projects = Income from Settlement of projects – Settled Cost – Settled Taxes and Other Cost.

5

港口、交通运输、邮电

CHAPTER 5 PORT，TRANSPORTATION，POSTAL AND TELECOMMUNICATION SERVICE

港口、交通、运输、邮电
Port, Transportations, Post and Telecommunications

主要统计指标
Major Statistics Indicators

2003 年全社会客运量	Total Passenger Traffic	24938	万人	10000 persons
比上年增长	Increase Over Last Year	5.0	%	
2003 年全社会货运量	Total Freight Traffic	13919	万吨	10000 tons
比上年增长	Increase Over Last Year	12.0	%	
2003 年港口货物吞吐量	Cargo Handled at Ports	18543	万吨	10000 tons
比上年增长	Increase Over Last Year	20.4	%	
2003 年集装箱吞吐量	Container Handled at Ports	277.2	万标箱	10000 TEU
比上年增长	Increase Over Last Year	49.1	%	
2003 年公路交通工具拥有量	Number of Means of Transportation Through Highway	200271	辆	unit
比上年增长	Increase Over Last Year	30.0	%	
2003 年固定电话用户	Number of Local Telephone Subscribers	240	万户	10000 subcribers
比上年增长	Increase Over Last Year	17.9	%	

5-1 主要年份港口、交通、邮电基本情况

Basic Statistics on Port, Transportation and Telecommunications in Main Year

年份 Year	港口货物吞吐量 (万吨) Cargo Handled at Ports (10000 tons)	集装箱吞吐量 (万标箱) Container Handled at Ports (10000 TEU)	货运量 (万吨) Freight Traffic (10000 tons)	客运量 (万人) Passenger Traffic (10000 persons)	固定电话用户 (万户) Number of Local Telephone Subscribers (10000 subscribers)	电话普及率 (部/百人) Number of Telephone Sets Owned Per 100 Persons (set/100 persons)
1978	214		1385	2966	1.07	0.49
1979	236		1430	3369	1.19	0.54
1980	326		1562	4156	1.36	0.61
1981	349		1496	4654	1.53	0.66
1982	371		1617	5192	1.71	0.74
1983	483		1641	5652	1.86	0.82
1984	597		1810	6026	2.22	0.94
1985	1040		2015	6527	2.60	1.13
1986	1797		3204	7373	2.91	1.25
1987	1940		3745	7473	3.55	1.50
1988	2002		5408	7277	4.64	1.85
1989	2209		4570	7686	5.37	2.15
1990	2554	2.2	4763	7378	6.19	2.41
1991	3390	3.6	5070	8757	8.05	2.79
1992	4367	5.3	6492	9773	12.22	3.52
1993	5321	7.9	7583	11224	18.59	5.03
1994	5850	12.5	8711	17776	27.86	8.12
1995	6853	16.0	9577	19705	41.78	12.43
1996	7638	20.2	10460	21152	53.33	15.36
1997	8220	25.7	10547	21719	67.75	19.21
1998	8707	35.3	10317	21736	83.74	23.88
1999	9660	60.1	10344	22211	104.13	29.16
2000	11547	90.2	10819	22736	130.15	37.09
2001	12852	121.3	11283	23225	163.21	45.18
2002	15398	185.9	12429	23752	203.58	52.20
2003	18543	277.2	13919	24938	242.00	68.54

5－2 港口吞吐情况

Statistics On Cargo Handled at Ports

单位:万吨,万人　　　　(2003)　　　　(10000 tons,10000 persons)

项目	Item	吞吐量 Capacity		出口量 For Export		进口量 For Import	
		总计 Total	外贸 Foreign Trade	合计 Total	外贸 Foreign Trade	合计 Total	外贸 Foreign Trade
货物吞吐量	**Ports Cargo Handling Capacity**	**18543**	**8213**	**7424**	**1420**	**11118**	**6792**
#转口货物	Cargo of Transfer	8062	3259	4050	20	4012	3239
货物分类	**Type of Cargo**						
煤碳及制品	Coal and Coke And Its Products	2271	106	342		1929	106
石油及制品	Petroleum And Its Products	5400	2811	2198	166	3203	2645
金属矿石	Metal Ores	4810	2733	2075		2735	2733
钢铁	Steel and Iron	184	77	17	1	167	76
矿建材料	Mineral Building Materials	111	1	5	1	106	
水泥	Cement	131	17			131	17
木材	Timber	53	11	1		52	11
非金属矿石	Nonmetal Ores	36	19	14	13	22	5
化肥及农药	Chemical Fertilizers and Pesticides	34	29	8	5	26	24
盐	Salt	24	10			24	10
粮食	Grain	173	129	32	5	141	124
机械设备	Machinery Equipment	3172	512	1574	266	1598	246
化工原料及制品	Industrial Chemicals And Its Products	256	202	32	2	224	199
轻工、医药	Products of Leight Industry and Medicine	1793	1524	1071	954	722	570
农林牧渔业产品	Products of Farming, Forestry, Animal Husbandry And Fishery	40	25	9		32	25
其他	Others	55	7	46	7	8	
旅客进出口人数	**Number of Passenger In－And Out**	**637**		**320**		**317**	

5－3　港口国际集装箱吞吐量

International Container Handled At Ports

航线	Shipping Lines	箱数(箱) Number of Containers		重量(吨) Weight (ton)			
				合计 Total		货重 Weight of Cargo	
		2002	2003	2002	2003	2002	2003
总计	**Total**	**1858688**	**2772214**	**15415062**	**22688321**	**11384348**	**17036445**
#进口	of Witch: Import	922593	1383290	6979391	9441274	4979032	6643417
出口	Export	936095	1388924	8435671	13247047	6405316	10393028
国际航线合计	**International Lines**	**1567540**	**2392799**	**12646086**	**18949505**	**9227991**	**14081175**
台湾省	Taiwan, China	13903	12994	171019	84785	140672	58168
香港	Hongkong, China	48730	181347	548886	1454562	450047	1089589
日本	Japan	156717	213674	1344280	2009206	1027490	1542850
南朝鲜	Korea Rep	220898	16318	2202161	230683	1639827	199135
东南亚	Southeast Asia	40299	469295	410324	3673224	313434	2717769
中东	Mideast	258961	120519	2120523	1213741	1508305	954099
欧洲	Europe	511283	6832	3813018	46141	2768533	32455
美国	United States	306016	530812	1977794	3570584	1343406	2532586
俄罗斯	Russia	1779	779049	11774	6088686	8214	4503705
内支线合计	**Total of Domestic Sub－Line**	**93994**	**114715**	**750177**	**1003969**	**556204**	**767279**
上海	Shanghai	60396	66870	483449	588513	358275	450106
台州(海门)	Taizhou (Haimen)	6653	12583	62314	104314	48702	79117
温州	Wenzhou	22250	25030	175446	209369	129793	157562
青岛	Qingdao	2436	1756	12618	12383	7669	8768
广州	Guangzhou	809	3533	5349	33844	3707	26521
国内航线合计	**Total of Domestic Lines**	**197154**	**264700**	**2018799**	**2734847**	**1600153**	**2187991**

5-4 主要年份客运量

Passenger Traffic in Main Years

单位:万人 (10000 persons)

年份 Year	合计 Total	铁路 Railway	公路 Highway	水路 Waterway	航空 Civil Aviation
1978	2966	105	2311	550	
1979	3369	122	2692	555	
1980	4156	317	3241	598	
1981	4654	351	3714	598	
1982	5192	366	4277	549	
1983	5652	411	4737	504	
1984	6026	480	5073	473	
1985	6527	502	5575	450	
1986	7373	482	6472	418	1.2
1987	7473	497	6536	438	2
1988	7277	536	6339	399	3.1
1989	7686	527	6790	366	3.2
1990	7378	462	6611	299	6
1991	8757	445	8006	295	11
1992	9773	414	9076	268	14
1993	11224	435	10523	245	21
1994	17776	486	16993	265	32
1995	19705	506	18870	283	45
1996	21152	405	20432	262	53
1997	21719	342	21101	222	55
1998	21736	300	21199	182	55
1999	22211	278	21734	146	53
2000	22736	288	22255	133	59.7
2001	23225	349	22700	115	61
2002	23752	393	23160	135	64
2003	24938	438	24320	115	65

5-5 主要年份货运量

Freight Traffic in Main Years

单位:万吨 (10000 tons)

年份 Year	合计 Total	铁路 Railway	公路 Highway	水路 Waterway	航空(吨) Civil Aviation (ton)	管道 Pipeline
1978	1385	45	625	715		
1979	1430	67	681	682		
1980	1562	167	709	686		
1981	1496	170	714	612		
1982	1617	186	788	643		
1983	1641	217	810	614		
1984	1810	234	883	693		
1985	2015	284	955	776		
1986	3204	310	1910	984	237	
1987	3745	337	2576	832	371	
1988	5408	380	4196	832	567	
1989	4570	398	3443	729	500	
1990	4763	355	3800	608	800	
1991	5070	302	4143	625	1600	
1992	6492	429	5328	710	2200	25
1993	7583	428	6255	868	3262	32
1994	8711	455	7113	1112	4000	31
1995	9577	527	7843	1173	4900	34
1996	10460	573	8509	1233	5200	44
1997	10547	551	8642	1314	5400	41
1998	9952	569	8195	1143	6900	44
1999	10344	609	8154	1534	9000	46
2000	10819	682	8219	1829	11000	88
2001	11283	725	8300	2156	10000	101
2002	12429	980	8630	2716	12500	102
2003	13919	1158	9070	3568	13812	122

5－6 部分年份全社会旅客周转量和货物周转量

Total Turnover Volume of Passengers and Turnover Volume of Freight Traffic in Partial Years

单位:万人公里,万吨公里 （10000 tons－km,10000 persons－km）

年份 Year	旅客周转量 Turnover Volume of Passengers			货物周转量 Turnover Volume of Freight Traffic			
	总计 Total	公路 Highway	水路 Waterway	总计 Total	公路 Highway	水路 Waterway	管道 Pipeline
1985	147863	135273	12590	132890	34369	98521	
1986	176321	163351	12970	219594	86541	133053	
1987	182877	168280	14597	294320	130907	163413	
1988	191911	176853	15058	271187	89321	181865	
1989	193779	180061	13718	319319	135845	183474	
1990	202868	190057	12811	308099	134299	173800	
1991	229727	215573	14154	438528	187032	251496	
1992	270125	258068	12057	608363	242989	365157	217
1993	324919	314471	10448	777570	262057	515229	284
1994	623257	610761	12496	1243892	448457	795435	
1995	699514	685120	14394	1450892	495929	954674	289
1996	735912	721653	14259	1742582	523495	1218722	365
1997	755941	740381	15560	1853782	533382	1320018	382
1998	752757	741848	10909	1887113	491380	1395325	408
1999	771393	764287	7106	2311376	481555	1829381	440
2000	800193	794858	5335	2367484	482518	1884241	723
2001	822326	818704	3622	2727939	492170	2231435	4335
2002	870546	867830	2716	3342614	492170	2844927	5517
2003	921901	919900	2001	4559749	553005	4002654	4090

5－7 公路运输工具拥有量

Number of Means of Transportation Through Highway

(2003)

项目	Item	单位	Unit	总计 Total	营业性 Business 合计 Total	营业性 Business 个体 Individual	非营业性 Non－business
总计	**Total**	**辆**	**unit**	**200271**	**58291**	**35043**	**141980**
汽车	**Automobile**	**辆**	**unit**	**182480**	**40500**	**17480**	**141980**
载客汽车	Buses And Cars	辆	unit	119233	9217	1899	110016
		客位	seat	788390	128833	12129	659557
#大型	Large－Sized	辆	unit	1618	891		727
		客位	seat	69133	35159		33974
中型	Middle－Sized	辆	unit	5690	3599	235	2091
		客位	seat	109567	68454	4081	41113
载货汽车	Trucks	辆	unit	63247	31283	15581	31964
		吨位	ton	194842	133314	42014	61528
①普通载货汽车	Ordinary Trucks	辆	unit	59306	27367	15489	31939
		吨位	ton	142189	80930	41174	61259
#大型	of Witch：Large－Space	辆	unit	10352	8077	3605	2275
		吨位	ton	73591	52694	23168	20897
重型	within：Heavy	辆	unit	2997	2040	738	959
		吨位	ton	35712	22257	8298	13455
中型	Middle	辆	unit	3234	1193	852	2041
		吨位	ton	9241	3592	2265	5649
②专用载货汽车	Trucks for Special Purpose	辆	unit	3941	3916	92	25
		吨位	ton	52653	52384	840	269
集装箱车	within：Container Trucks	辆	unit	2718	2718		
		TEU	TEU	4660	4660		
其他机动车	**Other Motor Vehicles**	**辆**	**unit**	**313**	**313**	**313**	
货运机动车	Motor Vehicles for Freight	辆	unit	313	313	313	
		吨位	ton	352	352	352	
轮胎式拖拉机	**Tyre－style Tractors**	**辆**	**unit**	**17211**	**17211**	**17206**	
		吨	ton	17674	17674	17669	
载货挂车	**Trailers**	**辆**	**unit**	**267**	**267**	**44**	

5－8　水路运输工具拥有量

Number of Means Transportation Through Waterway

(2003)

项目	Item	单位	Unit	总计 Total	交通部门 Transportation Department	非交通部门 Non－Transportation Department 合计	个体
总计	**Total**	**艘**	**unit**	**572**	**21**	**551**	**19**
机动船	**Motor Vessels**	**艘**	**unit**	**567**	**21**	**546**	**19**
净载重量	Dead Weight	吨位	ton	1100767	433143	667624	2421
载客量	Passenger Capacity	客位	seat	6176	779	5397	
标准箱位	Standard Container Space	TEU	TEU	1061	608	453	
功率	Power	千瓦	kw	396790	106856	289934	1533
客船	Passenger Ships	艘	unit	44	3	41	
载客量	Passenger Capacity	客位	seat	4097	779	3318	
功率	Power	千瓦	kw	24755	8440	16315	
客货船	Passenger－cargo Vessels	艘	unit	10		10	
净载重量	Dead Weight	吨位	ton				
载客量	Passenger Capacity	客位	seat	2079		2079	
功率	Power	千瓦	kw	2498		2498	
货船	Cargo Ships	艘	unit	511	18	493	19
净载重量	Dead Weight	吨位	ton	1100767	433143	667624	2421
标准箱位	Standard Container Space	TEU	TEU	1061	608	453	
功率	Power	千瓦	kw	368790	98416	270374	1533
#①油船	Tanker	艘	unit	61		61	
净载重量	Dead Weight	吨位	ton	131362		131362	
功率	Power	千瓦	kw	52139		52139	
②集装箱船	Container Ships	艘	unit	2	2		
净载重量	Dead Weight	吨位	ton	15165	15165		
标准箱位	Standard Container Space	TEU	TEU	608	608		
功率	Power	千瓦	kw	7281	7281		
拖船	Tugboats	艘	unit	2		2	
功率	Power	千瓦	kw	747		747	
驳船	**Barges**	**艘**	**unit**	**5**		**5**	
净载重量	Dead Weight	吨位	ton	4090		4090	
载客量	Passenger Capacity	客位	seat				

5－9 部分年份运输线路里程长度

Length of Transportation Routes in Partial Years

单位:公里 (km)

项目	Item	1995	1997	2001	2002	2003
公路总里程	**Overal Length For Highway**	**4049**	**4430**	**5291**	**5506**	**5519**
按技术等级分:	Divided by Grade					
①等级公路	Highway Grade	3335	3843	5210	5427	5455
高速公路	Express Way			184	184	184
一级公路	Highway Grade 1	11	38	382	443	460
二级公路	Highway Grade 2	451	573	544	597	616
三级公路	Highway Grade 3	801	961	1241	1264	1293
四级公路	Highway Grade 4	2072	2271	2860	2939	2902
②等外公路	Highway Without Grade	714	586	80	79	64
按路面等级分:	Divided by Road Surface					
高级路面	High Grade Road Surface			2204	2422	2605
次高级路面	Sub－High Grade Road Surface			1115	1131	1108
中级路面	Medium Grade Road Surface			1962	1943	1796
低级路面	Lower Grade Road Surface			10	10	10
按行政等级分:	Divided by Adminitrative Level					
国道	State Way	138	138	321	321	321
省道	Province Way	680	645	673	673	672
县道	County Way	1800	1980	2292	2380	2384
乡道	Township Way	1342	1567	1939	2061	2070
专用道	Special Use Way	87	100	67	71	72
内河通航里程	**Length of Navigable Inland Waterways**	**1367**	**1238**	**1262**	**1262**	**1207**
#水深一米以上	Depths of One Meter and Over	605	512	395	395	395

5-10 主要年份电信业主要指标
Main Indicators of Telecommunications Services in Main Years

年份 Year	固定电话用户（万户） Number of Local Telephone Subscribers（10000 subcribers）	#农话（万户） Rural Telephone Subscribers（10000 subscribers）	移动电话（万户） Number of Subscribers of Mobile Telephone（10000 subscribers）	电话普及率（部/百人） Number of Telephone Sets Owned Per 100 persons set/100 persons	国际互联网用户（户） User of International Computer Network（user）
1978	1.07	0.49		0.49	
1979	1.19	0.53		0.54	
1980	1.36	0.58		0.61	
1981	1.53	0.64		0.66	
1982	1.71	0.70		0.74	
1983	1.86	0.76		0.82	
1984	2.22	0.89		0.94	
1985	2.60	1.05		1.13	
1986	2.91	1.14		1.25	
1987	3.55	1.35		1.50	
1988	4.64	1.68		1.85	
1989	5.37	1.92		2.15	
1990	6.19	2.15		2.41	
1991	8.05	2.88		2.79	
1992	12.22	4.92	0.14	3.52	
1993	18.59	7.49	0.80	5.03	
1994	27.86	11.60	1.92	8.12	
1995	41.78	17.80	4.71	12.43	
1996	53.33	23.10	9.05	15.36	
1997	67.75	31.14	16.44	19.21	
1998	83.74	41.40	25.72	23.88	4248
1999	104.13	54.39	56.75	29.16	37334
2000	130.15	72.69	117.92	37.09	70928
2001	163.21	90.13	195.65	45.18	93208
2002	203.58	91.52	256.86	52.20	104293
2003	242.00	107.20	379.31	68.54	835674

5-11　部分年份邮政业务情况
Basic Statistics on Post Services in Partial Years

项目		Item		1998	2001	2002	2003
邮政局、所数	（处）	Number of Post Offices	（unit）	163	370	376	379
#在农村的	（处）	Rural Area	（unit）	108	313	315	316
邮路总长度(单程)	(公里)	Lengh of Postal Routes	（km）	15860	21639	18796	17725
农村投递路线	（公里）	Rural Delivery Routwes	（km）	13330	13833	15476	15715
邮政业务总量	（万元）	Business volume of Post Services	（10000 yuan）		39514.56	42733.17	47170.51
函件	（万件）	Number of Letters	（10000 pcs）	4740.67	4793.62	11162.08	4906.94
#国际函件	（万件）	International Letters	（10000 pcs）	87.27	35.74	19.94	20.90
国内函件	（万件）	Domestic Letters	（10000 pcs）	4653.40	4757.87	11142.14	4886.03
邮政储蓄年未余额	(万元)	Balance of Postal Deposits	（10000 yuan）	174283	424895	572070	706876
特快专递	（万件）	Pieces of Express Mail Services	（10000 pcs）	74.56	152.18	152.39	175.41
集邮业务	（万枚）	Philately	（10000 pcs）	2778.31	3484.96	2894.71	2082.45
报纸期发份数	（万份）	Newspaper Issued	（10000 copies）	83.49	97.34	88.75	84.02
杂志期发份数	（万份）	Magazine Issued	（10000 copies）	62.61	62.38	52.70	70.49
订销报纸累计份数	(万份)	Number of Newspaper Circulation	（10000 copies）	16589.1	20518.04	21096.68	21765.96
订销杂志累计份数	(万份)	Number of Magazine Circulation	（10000 copies）	1038.67	1127.82	976.99	1051.39

注：邮电业务总量从2001年开始按2000年不变价格计算。
Business volume of post were calculated at constant price of 2000 since 2001.

主要指标解释

【公路里程】 指在一定时期内实际达到《公路工程技术标 JTJ01－88》规定的等级公路，并经公路主管部门正式验收交付使用的公路里程数。其计算单位为:公里。它包括大中城市的郊区公路以及通过小城镇街道部分的公路里程，也包括桥梁、渡口的长度，但不包括大中城市的街道、厂矿、林区生产用道和农业生产用道的里程。两条或多条公路共同经由同一路段，只计算一次，不得重复计算里程长度。公路里程是反映公路建设发展规模的重要指标，也是计算运输网密度等指标的基础资料。

【货(客)运量】 指在一定时期内，各种运输工具实际运送的货物(旅客)数量。是反映运输业为国民经济和人民生活服务的数量指标，也是制定和检查运输生产计划，研究运输发展规模和速度的重要指标。货运按吨计算，客运按人计算。货物不论运输距离长短，货物类别，均按实际重量统计;旅客不论行程远近或票价多少，均按一人一次作为客运量统计。半价票、小孩票也按一人统计。

【货物(旅客)周转量】 指在一定时期内，由各种运输工具运送的货物(旅客)数量与其相应运输距离的乘积之总和，是反映运输业生产总成果的重要指标，也是编制和检查运输生产计划，计算运输效率、劳动生产率以及核算运输单位成本的主要基础资料。通常以吨公里和人公里为计算单位。计算货物周转量通常按发出站与到达站之间的最短距离，也就是计费距离计算。

【港口货物吞吐量】 指由水运进出港区范围，并经过装卸的货物数量，包括邮件及办理托运手续的行李、包裹以及补给运输船舶的燃、物料和淡水。其计量单位为吨。货物吞吐量的货种分类及其主要流向流量，反映了港口在国内外物资交流和对外贸易运输中的地位和作用。吞吐量可以分为进口、出口，又可以分为国内贸易和对外贸易。

【邮电业务总量】 指以货币表现的邮电部门用于传递信息和提供其他邮电服务的总数量。它综合反映了一定时期邮电工作的总成果，是研究邮电业务量构成和发展趋势的重要指标。根据邮电管理体制不同，分为中央国营业务总量和地方国营业务总量。它用各种邮电分类业务量，如函件件数、电报份数、长话张数、市内电话和农村电话的年均户数、订销报刊累计份数等，分别乘以相应的平均单价(不变价)，加总后再加上出租电路和设备的收入、代用户维护电话交换机和线路等设备的收入、其他业务收入求得。

Explanatory Notes on Main Statistical Indicators

【Length of Highways】 refers to the length of highways which are built in conformity with the grades specified by the highway engineering standard formulated by the Ministry of Communications, and have been formally checked and accepted by the departments of highways and put into use. The length of highways includes that of the suburb highways at large and medium-sized cities, highways passing through streets at small cities and towns, and also the length of bridges and ferries. It does not include the length of streets in big and medium-sized cities and highways built for the production purpose at factories, mines, forest areas and agricultural areas, If two or more highways go the same section of the way, the length of the section is only calculated for once and no duplication is allowed. The length of highways is an important indicator to show the development of the highway construction and to provide essential information to calculate the transport network density.

【Freight(Passenger) Traffic】 refers to the volume of freight (passenger) transported with various means. Freight transport is calculated in to ns and passenger traffic is calculated in the number of persons. Despite the type of freight and traveling distance, the freight transport is calculated by the principle that one person can be counted only once in one travel. The passenger who travel with a half price ticket or a child ticket is also calculated as one person. The freight (passenger) traffic provides a quantitative measure to show how the transport industry serves the national economy and people, and is also an important indicator for planning the transport industry and for studying the development scale and speed of the transport industry.

【Freight Ton – kilometers(Passenger – kilometers)】 refers to the sum of the products of the volume of transported cargo(passengers) multiplying by the transport distance, usually using ton-kilometer and passenger-kilometer as units for measurement. Normally, the shortest distance between the departure station and the destination station(i.e., the payable distance) is the basis to calculate the freight ton – kilometers. This is an important indicator to show the total results of the transport industry, to prepare and examine the transport plan and to measure the efficiency, the labor productivity and the unit cost of transport.

【Volume of Freight Handled】 refers to the volume of cargo passing in and out the harbor area of the major coastal ports and having been loaded and unloaded. The volume includes that of the coastal matters, registered luggage and fuels, materials and fresh water as supplies of the ships. The volume of freight dandled maybe classified as import, export, or as domestic trade and foreign trade. The volume of freight handled by type of cargo and by main flow direction reflects he position and function of the ports in the inflow of Chinese and foreign commodities and in the transportation of foreign trade.

【Business Volume of Post and Telecommunications】 refers to the total amount of the information delivered and other post and telecommunications services provided by the post and telecommunications departments for the customers. It is derived by first multiplying the business volume of different types, such as number of letters, telegrams, long distance calls, city and rural telephone subscribers and accumulated number of newspapers and journals subscribed and sold, etc. by their respective average unit price (fixed price) and then adding these products together: plus the income from maintenance of telephone exchanges and lines, and the income from other business operations. The business volume of post and telecommunications indicates the total achievements made by the post and telecommunications department during a given period of time in a comprehensive way, and is an important indicator to study the composition and development of the post and telecommunications business.

6

贸易、餐饮业

CHAPTER 6 DOMESTIC TRADE AND CATERING TRADE

国内贸易、餐饮
Domestic Trade and Catering Trade

主要统计指标
Major Statistics Indicators

2003年社会消费品零售总额	Total Retail Sales of Consumer Goods	5215347	万元	10000 yuan
比上年增长	Increase Over Last Year	12.6	%	
2003年限额以上批发零售贸易企业购进总额	Total Purchases of Enterprises Above Designated Size in Wholesale and Retail Trades	11346400	万元	10000 yuan
比上年增长	Increase Over Last Year	74.6	%	
2003年限额以上批发零售贸易企业销售总额	Total Sales of Enterprises Above Designated Size in Wholesale and Retail Trades	11553495	万元	10000 yuan
比上年增长	Increase Over Last Year	69.6	%	
2003年限额以上批发零售贸易企业利润总额	Total Profits of Enterprises Above Designated Size in Wholesale and Retail Trades	177270	万元	10000 yuan
比上年增长	Increase Over Last Year	39.8	%	
2003年个体工商户	Number of Individual Industry and Commerce	215690	户	Households
比上年增长	Increase Over Last Year	0.5	%	
2003年私营企业个数	Number of Private Enterprises	62515	户	unit
比上年增长	Increase Over Last Year	15.0	%	

6－1 主要年份社会消费品零售总额

Total Retail Sales of Consumer Goods in Main Years

单位:万元 (10000 yuan)

年份 Year	全市 Total	市区 Urban District	县(市)合计 Total County
1978	70663	26175	44488
1979	87628	32386	55242
1980	111793	40368	71425
1981	130182	47157	83025
1982	139809	50056	89753
1983	156913	55343	101570
1984	187876	66573	121303
1985	253306	99210	154096
1986	304587	117850	186737
1987	354706	133444	221262
1988	490453	191994	298459
1989	528158	215768	312390
1990	549750	232255	317495
1991	633841	273167	360674
1992	794007	335769	458238
1993	1182147	522124	660023
1994	1634110	666060	968050
1995	2268195	919410	1348785
1996	2591764	1011445	1580319
1997	2885811	1154527	1731284
1998	3133608	1211018	1922590
1999	3457632	1321484	2136148
2000	3892920	1459537	2433383
2001	4141801		
2002	4628655		
2003	5215347		

6－2　部分年份分行业社会消费品零售总额

Total Retail Sales of Consumer Goods of Partial Years by Sector

单位:万元　　(10000 yuan)

年份 Year	社会消费品零售总额 Total Retail Sales of Consumer Goods	#市的零售额 City	按行业分 Grouped by Sector 批发和零售贸易业 Wholesale and Retail Sale Trades	餐饮业 Catering Trade	其他 Others
1990	549750				
1991	633841				
1992	794007				
1993	1182147				
1994	1634110				
1995	2268195	1320420	1628556	125442	514198
1996	2591764	1555917	1929652	159592	502520
1997	2885811	1703928	2104330	199683	581798
1998	3133608	1792796	2356047	187135	590426
1999	3457632	2018154	2599967	276889	580776
2000	3892920	2247696	2965818	378127	548975
2001	4141801	2401013	3124797	442042	574962
2002	4628655	2737749	3442080	570221	616354
2003	5215347	3084765	4434412	672047	108888

6－3　新型业态

New Status of Retails Industy

(2003)

项目	Item	法人单位数(个) Units of Legal Person (unti)	销售合计(万元) Total Sale (10000 yuan)	其中 of Witch 批发 Wholesale	零售 Retail Sale
零售企业合计	**Total Retail Sale Enterprise**	**110**	**1722936**	**317000**	**1405936**
按经营方式分:	**Grouped by Management Method**				
独立商店	Sole Shop	65	1026932	294580	732352
连锁总店	Chain General Shop	17	364226	3036	361190
连锁分店	Chain Shop	17	298521	16397	282124
其他	Others	11	33257	2987	30270
按零售业态分:	**Grouped by Retail Sale Line**				
百货商店	Department Store	20	374908	113247	261661
超级市场	Super Market	19	513624	5142	508482
专业(专卖)店	Special (Special Sale) Shop	57	793757	191542	602215
其他	Others	14	40647	7069	33578

6－4　部分年份批发零售贸易及餐饮业总额表

Total Sales of Wholesale, Retail Sale Trades and Catering Trades Enperprises in Partial Years

单位:万元　　(10000 yuan)

项目	Item	1999	2000	2001	2002	2003
批发零售贸易业合计	**Total Volume in Wholesale and Retail Trade**					
销售总额	**Total Sale**	**9039836**	**10204196**	**11321821**	**14280444**	**20073262**
#批发	Wholesale	6680979	7185306	8185125	10767039	15475233
零售	Retail Sale	2358857	3018891	3136697	3513405	4598029
限额以上	Above Designated Size					
#批发	Whole Sale	4026173	4587480	4865091	5622135	9867288
零售	Retail Sale	687685	852407	912527	1188188	1686206
限额以下	Under Designated Size					
#批发	Wholesale	1151673	1180325	1379238	2893001	5607945
零售	Retail Sale	290757	580082	690570	568028	2911823
个体商业	Individual Commerce					
#批发	Whole Sale	1503133	1417501	1940795		
零售	Retail Sale	1380415	1586402	1533600		
餐饮业合计	**Total Catering Service**					
营业总收入	**Total Service Income**	**294268**	**385005**	**450405**	**570221**	**683505**
#零售	Retail Sale	278379	378127	444854	570221	683505
限额以上	Above Designated Size					
营业总收入	Total Service Income	59746	90852	128049	158580	192265
#零售	Retail Sale	58389	90033	127979	158580	192265
限额以下	Under Designated Size					
营业总收入	Total Service Income	50928	58108	64648	411641	491240
#零售	Retail Sale	49203	57532	64339	411641	491240
个体餐饮业	Individual Catering Service					
营业总收入	Total Service Income	183594	236045	257708		
#零售	Retail Sale	170787	230561	252537		

6-5 个体工商业情况表

Basic Statistics of Individual Industry and Commerce

(2003)

项目	Item	全市期末实有 Total at The End of This Year	本期开业 Openning for This Term	城镇 Districts
户数(户)	**Number of Households(unit)**	**215690**	**49525**	**76919**
农、林、牧、渔业	Farming, Forestry, Animal Husbandry and Fishery	966	540	126
采掘业	Mining and Quarrying Industry	319	90	16
制造业	Manufacturing Industry	40933	10458	10570
建筑业	Construction	558	383	64
交通运输业、仓储业	Traffic And Transportation, Warehousing	18611	3358	4750
批发零售贸易业、餐饮业	Wholesale and Retail Trade, Catering Service	126633	27389	49963
社会服务业	Social Services	26328	6794	11126
其它行业	Others	1342	513	304
从业人员(人)	**Emplyment Personnel(person)**	**380925**	**89210**	**124552**
农、林、牧、渔业	Farming, Forestry, Animal Husbandry and Fishery	2070	1090	214
采掘业	Mining and Quarrying Industry	1786	874	64
制造业	Manufacturing Industry	125418	30572	27916
建筑业	Construction	2583	1001	191
交通运输业、仓储业	Traffic And Transportation, Warehousing	23028	4590	5739
批发零售贸易业、餐饮业	Wholesale and Retail Trade, Catering Service	181622	38965	71880
社会服务业	Social Services	41968	11358	18105
其它行业	Others	2450	760	443
注册资金(万元)	**Registered Capital (10000 Yuan)**	**591742**	**178939**	**182331**
农、林、牧、渔业	Farming, Forestry, Animal Husbandry and Fishery	7361	3253	545
采掘业	Mining and Quarrying Industry	2927	1028	255
制造业	Manufacturing Industry	240771	67833	53995
建筑业	Construction	4414	2737	624
交通运输业、仓储业	Traffic And Transportation, Warehousing	106991	22203	21118
批发零售贸易业、餐饮业	Wholesale and Retail Trade, Catering Service	175537	46824	81647
社会服务业	Social Services	49687	18605	23230
其它行业	Others	4054	16456	917

6－6 私营企业基本情况表

Basic Statistics on Private Enterprises

(2003)

项目	Item	全市期末实有 Total at The End of This Year	本期开业 Openning for This Term	城镇 Districts
户数(户)	**Number of Households (unit)**	**62515**	**15917**	**29878**
农、林、牧、渔业	Farming, Forestry, Animal Husbandry and Fishery	549	201	119
采掘业	Mining and Quarrying Industry	124	48	28
制造业	Manufacturing Industry	36231	7790	10980
建筑业	Construction	1243	458	774
交通运输业、仓储业	Traffic And Transportation, Warehousing	1120	418	769
批发零售贸易业、餐饮业	Wholesale and Retail Trade, Catering Service	16820	4740	12840
社会服务业	Social Services	5275	1821	3884
其它行业	Others	1153	441	484
雇工人数(人)	**Number of Employed Persons(Persons)**	**1018688**	**175585**	**331073**
农、林、牧、渔业	Farming, Forestry, Animal Husbandry and Fishery	5268	1770	1119
采掘业	Mining and Quarrying Industry	1652	510	380
制造业	Manufacturing Industry	772000	84149	154598
建筑业	Construction	26237	9284	16889
交通运输业、仓储业	Traffic And Transportation, Warehousing	10168	3133	6011
批发零售贸易业、餐饮业	Wholesale and Retail Trade, Catering Service	142073	59753	107137
社会服务业	Social Services	45752	12998	32955
其它行业	Others	15538	3988	11984
注册资金(万元)	**Registered Capital(10000 Yuan)**	**5367054**	**1312349**	**2445989**
农、林、牧、渔业	Farming, Forestry, Animal Husbandry and Fishery	44003	12696	11590
采掘业	Mining and Quarrying Industry	8304	4696	1636
制造业	Manufacturing Industry	3008430	576532	914943
建筑业	Construction	425413	91579	227189
交通运输业、仓储业	Traffic And Transportation, Warehousing	67166	26303	35966
批发零售贸易业、餐饮业	Wholesale and Retail Trade, Catering Service	1213100	367517	861101
社会服务业	Social Services	265038	88606	190885
其它行业	Others	335600	144420	202679

6－7 限额以上批发、零售贸易企业购进、销售、库存总额

单位:万元 (2003)

项目	Item	法人企业数(个) Number of Corporatio Unit (unit)	活动单位数(个) Number of Activities Units (unit)
总计	**Total**	**359**	**956**
批发业	**Wholesale Trade**	**249**	**609**
#国有及国有控股	State－owned and State－holding Enterprises	81	262
按注册类型分	**Grouped by Registration Status**		
内资企业	Domestic Funded Enterprises	248	687
国有企业	State－Owned Enterprises	30	113
集体企业	Collective－Owned Enterprises	12	23
股份合作企业	Share Cooperative Enterprises	7	19
联营企业	Joint－owned Enterprises	3	4
有限责任公司	Limited Liability Corporations	119	338
股份有限公司	Share－holding Corporations Ltd.	8	24
私营企业	Private Enterprises	69	86
其他企业	Others Enterprises		
港、澳、台商投资企业	Hongkong, Macao and Taiwan Funded		1
外商投资企业	Enterprises with Foreign Investment	1	1
按行业分	**Grouped by Sector**		
农畜产品批发	Agricultural and Animal Products	6	12
食品、饮料及烟草制品批发	Food, Beverages and Tobaccos	35	145
#米、面制品及食用油批发	Rice, Wheaten Food and Edible Oil	4	32
烟草制品批发	Tobacco	9	72
纺织、服装及日用品批发	Textile, Garments and Daily Use Articles	43	56
#服装批发	Garments	9	9
文化、体育用品及器材批发	Culture, Sports and Equipments	9	9
医药及医疗器材批发	Medical and Medical Appliance	14	97

Total Purchases, Sale and Inventory of Wholesale and Retail Trade Above Designated Size

(10000 yuan)

从业人数(人) Total Employees (person)	购进总额 Total Purchases	进口 Imports	销售总额 Total Sales 合计 Total	批发 Wholesale	出口 Exports	零售 Retail Sale	年末库存总额 Inventory (Year-end)
34641	**11346400**	**1370792**	**11553495**	**9867288**	**4214268**	**1686206**	**584411**
15517	**9663580**	**1356016**	**9830558**	**9550289**	**4100672**	**280270**	**410198**
7608	3770702	709728	3863405	3687990	1841863	175415	173615
15429	9636917	1356016	9801459	9521189	4100525	280270	403554
3050	1285234	178059	1310566	1292023	589236	18543	52423
919	135203	3946	138284	133484		4800	16151
848	410027		313107	305293	51875	7813	4610
53	56594		56948	56008		940	1344
7176	4929933	703655	5071188	4925222	2383187	145967	227163
1488	1672372	458930	1743993	1676949	839637	67044	39378
1895	1147555	11426	1167374	1132211	236590	35163	62486
45	9213		9213	9213	147		6594
43	17451		19887	19887			50
450	371646	64701	381788	381788	322526		26539
3823	776801	6011	907605	875203	232831	32402	44105
600	26719		29848	29635		214	3074
1568	324475	30	427237	419690		7548	29115
1948	2428127	591502	2531488	2518453	1880436	13035	19171
350	868431	328309	872313	867513	526160	4800	1754
235	237919	5087	242641	242641	166476		2634
2483	295361	29	315419	149689		165730	49232

单位:万元

6-7 续表1

项目	Item	法人企业数(个) Number of Corporatio Unit (unit)	活动单位数(个) Number of Activities Units (unit)
矿产品、建材及化工产品批发	Mineral Products, Building Materials and Chemical Products	76	196
#煤炭及制品批发	Coal and Coal Products	7	11
石油及制品批发	Petroleum and Related Products	14	18
金属及金属矿批发	Metal and Metallic Ore	35	39
建材批发	Building Materials	4	11
化肥批发	Chemical Fertilizer	2	101
机械设备、五金交电及电子产品批发	Machine Equipments, Hardware and Electrical Appliance, Electronic Products	48	55
#汽车、摩托车及零配件批发	Motor Vehicles, Motorcycles and Related Spares and Fittings	5	6
家用电器批发	Household Appliances	7	8
计算机、软件及辅助设备批发	Computer, Software and Auxiliary Equipment	1	1
贸易经纪与代理	Trade Manager and Agency		
其他批发	Others	18	40
零售业	**Retail Trade**	**110**	**347**
#国有及国有控股	State - owned and State - holding Enterprises	20	78
按注册类型分	**Grouped by Registration Status**		
内资企业	Domestic Funded Enterprises	109	343
国有企业	State - Owned Enterprises	9	36
集体企业	Collective - Owned Enterprises	1	2
股份合作企业	Share Cooperative Enterprises	5	5
联营企业	Joint - owned Enterprises	4	4
有限责任公司	Limited Liability Corporations	41	172
股份有限公司	Share - holding Corporations Ltd.	9	35
私营企业	Private Enterprises	40	89
其他企业	Others Enterprises		

continued 1

(10000 yuan)

从业人数（人）Total Employees (person)	购进总额 Total Purchases		销售总额 Total Sales				年末库存总额 Inventory (Year－end)
		进口 Imports	合计 Total	批发 Wholesale	出口 Exports	零售 Retail Sale	
3428	2300008	247213	2165898	2145706	370704	20193	76483
578	39625		41208	40729		479	2080
1040	667988	6390	604218	584936	9093	19282	11624
804	676309	721	670773	670758		15	45078
303	94913	2983	92336	92190		146	5274
167	39017		36142	36142			4596
2733	2982726	439603	3004725	2955818	1027683	48907	184604
96	22466		22957	17763		5194	1043
731	378422	8831	393279	392335	108049	944	62486
170	10896		11680			11680	445
417	270992	1871	280994	280991	100017	3	7432
19124	**1682821**	**14775**	**1722936**	**317000**	**113597**	**1405936**	**174213**
2096	161238		178151	46946	934	131205	18865
18502	1629172	14775	1667698	317000	113597	1350697	170011
642	32457		29997	8198		21799	8759
59	3309		3782			3782	329
254	28627		28737	5168		23569	3088
157	22865		23844			23844	1082
11008	672551		666663	41017		625645	82680
3055	352926	8193	376087	141699	78722	234388	19813
3327	516437	6583	538588	120917	34874	417671	54259

单位:万元

6-7 续表2

项目	Item	法人企业数(个) Number of Corporatio Unit (unit)	活动单位数(个) Number of Activities Units (unit)
港、澳、台商投资企业	Hongkong, Macao and Taiwan Funded		1
外商投资企业	Enterprises with Foreign Investment	1	3
按行业分	**Grouped by Sector**		
综合零售	General Retail	37	175
百货零售	Department Store	18	52
超级市场零售	Super Market	16	111
食品、饮料及烟草制品专门零售	Food, Beverages and Tobaccos	7	25
纺织、服装及日用品专门零售	Textile, Garments and Daily Use Articles	3	5
服装零售	Garments	1	3
文化、体育用品及器材专门零售	Culture, Sports and Equipments	9	36
体育用品零售	Sports Goods		
图书零售	Books	8	35
医药及医疗器材专门零售	Medical and Medical Appliance	6	55
药品零售	Medicines	6	55
汽车、摩托车、燃料及零配件专门零售	Motor Vehicles, Motorcycles Fuels and Related Spares and Fittings	30	33
汽车零售	Motor Vehicles	24	27
机动车燃料零售	Motor Vehicle Fuels	2	2
家用电器及电子产品专门零售	Household Appliances and Electronic Products	14	14
家用电器零售	Household Appliances	10	10
计算机、软件及辅助设备零售	Computer, Software and Auxiliary Equipment	3	3
通信设备零售	Communication Equipment	1	1
五金、家具及室内装修材料专门零售	Hardware, Furniture and Decoration Materials		
无店铺及其他零售	Others	4	4
邮购及电子销售	Mail – order and Electron Sold		

continued 2 (10000 yuan)

从业人数（人）Total Employees (person)	购进总额 Total Purchases	进口 Imports	销售总额 Total Sales 合计 Total	批发 Wholesale	出口 Exports	零售 Retail Sale	年末库存总额 Inventory (Year－end)
150	4980		3315			3315	1410
472	48668		51924			51924	2792
14014	831292	796	866069	132066	78722	734003	90330
5482	365300	796	399002	131255	78722	267747	28950
8110	460262		461267	811		460456	60947
505	19279		23525	7508		16018	2674
376	74972		68051	56651	34874	11399	7677
234	68982		61330	56651	34874	4678	7397
608	27987		26211	4418		21793	7965
571	26668		24602	4418		20184	7337
1123	48135		48987	5004		43984	8695
1123	48135		48987	5004		43984	8695
1063	487072	13979	524213	92933		431280	32772
899	423605	7397	459513	87029		372484	29952
46	10074		10539	5904		4635	166
1329	187596		158700	18421		140279	23958
955	163985		133861	18421		115440	22091
154	11025		12450			12450	1231
220	12586		12389			12389	637
106	6488		7181			7181	142

6－8　限额以上批发、零售贸易企业主要财务指标

单位:万元　　(2003)

项目	Item	企业数(个) Number of Enterprises (unit)	#亏损企业(个) Loss Making Enterprises (unit)
总计	**Total**	**359**	**49**
批发业	**Wholesale Trade**	**249**	**25**
#国有及国有控股	State－owned and State－holding Enterprises	81	10
按注册类型分	**Grouped by Registration Status**		
内资企业	Domestic Funded Enterprises	248	25
国有企业	State－Owned Enterprises	30	1
集体企业	Collective－Owned Enterprises	12	4
股份合作企业	Share Cooperative Enterprises	7	
联营企业	Joint－owned Enterprises	3	1
有限责任公司	Limited Liability Corporations	119	12
股份有限公司	Share－holding Corporations Ltd.	8	1
私营企业	Private Enterprises	69	6
外商投资企业	Enterprises with Foreign Investment	1	
外资企业	Foreign Funded	1	
按行业分	**Grouped by Sector**		
农畜产品批发	Agricultural and Animal Products	6	1
食品、饮料及烟草制品批发	Food, Beverages and Tobaccos	35	2
#米、面制品及食用油批发	Rice, Wheaten Food and Edible Oil	4	
烟草制品批发	Tobacco	9	
纺织、服装及日用品批发	Textile, Garments and Daily Use Articles	43	2
#服装批发	Garments	9	
文化、体育用品及器材批发	Culture, Sports and Equipments	9	
医药及医疗器材批发	Medical and Medical Appliance	14	3
矿产品、建材及化工产品批发	Mineral Products, Building Materials and Chemical Products	76	5

Main Financial Indicators of Wholesale and Retail Enperprises Above Designated Size

(10000yuan)

年末资产负债 Total Assets and Liabilities at the Year - end							
流动资产小计 Circulating Funds	存货 Inventories	长期投资 Long - Term Investment	固定资产小计 Total Fixed Assets	固定资产原价 Original Value of Fixed Assets	累计折旧 Accumulative Total Depreciation	#本年折旧 Depreciation in this year	资产合计 Total Asset
3101024	**585655**	**200583**	**326260**	**397521**	**90142**	**19688**	**3734595**
2624747	**406888**	**142926**	**171193**	**211420**	**49454**	**11188**	**3008413**
980999	135228	78806	100069	123362	30770	5462	1179858
2624295	406777	142926	171193	211420	49454	11188	3007960
385652	44994	57717	51709	62234	14919	2855	507656
52890	16084	5531	9128	12163	3095	458	79259
32006	4544	319	2316	2668	399	132	37981
9054	1291		436	621	185	43	9494
1434446	220628	51967	59404	75561	19577	5057	1577255
370146	60713	17431	29621	36283	7176	1243	421486
340102	58524	9962	18580	21890	4101	1402	374829
453	111						453
453	111						453
141593	26738	2220	9336	11845	2568	388	166881
236674	26828	46707	54390	65871	16175	3221	356807
12162	6873	219	5050	8561	3511	204	17658
124155	12599	43972	34815	37931	7510	1942	212798
817278	53577	25146	25918	33047	7131	1892	876018
237888	19849	11886	5646	6574	929	354	257522
83422	2659	938	1686	1890	452	166	86579
90483	31721	7252	23690	27985	5744	1237	124004
486860	97691	38087	23569	30842	7675	2810	568053

项目	Item	企业数（个）Number of Enterprises (unit)	# 亏损企业（个）Loss Making Enterprises (unit)
# 煤炭及制品批发	Coal and Coal Products	7	1
石油及制品批发	Petroleum and Related Products	14	
金属及金属矿批发	Metal and Metallic Ore	35	1
建材批发	Building Materials	4	1
化肥批发	Chemical Fertilizer	2	1
机械设备、五金交电及电子产品批发	Machine Equipments, Hardware and Electrical Appliance, Electronic Products	48	8
# 汽车、摩托车及零配件批发	Motor Vehicles, Motorcycles and Related Spares and Fittings	5	3
家用电器批发	Household Appliances	7	1
计算机、软件及辅助设备批发	Computer, Software and Auxiliary Equipment	1	
其他批发	Others	18	4
零售业	**Retail Trade**	**110**	**24**
# 国有及国有控股	State – owned and State – holding Enterprises	20	
按注册类型分	**Grouped by Registration Status**		
内资企业	Domestic Funded Enterprises	109	24
国有企业	State – Owned Enterprises	9	
集体企业	Collective – Owned Enterprises	1	
股份合作企业	Share Cooperative Enterprises	5	
联营企业	Joint – owned Enterprises	4	
有限责任公司	Limited Liability Corporations	41	16
股份有限公司	Share – holding Corporations Ltd.	9	2
私营企业	Private Enterprises	40	6
外商投资企业	Enterprises with Foreign Investment	1	
按行业分	**Grouped by Sector**		

continued 1 (10000 yuan)

年末资产负债 Total Assets and Liabilities at the Year – end							
流动资产小计 Circulating Funds	存 货 Inventories	长期投资 Long – Term Investment	固定资产小计 Total Fixed Assets	固定资产原价 Original Value of Fixed Assets	累计折旧 Accumulative Total Depreciation	# 本年折旧 Depreciation in this year	资产合计 Total Asset
8910	1976	269	1397	2140	764	86	11863
70019	11464	16533	6053	8179	2467	1379	104653
194508	43235	5076	6347	7991	1646	586	208461
22412	5236	50	894	1119	226	20	26250
16565	4980	4232	3332	4430	1126	236	24400
700894	160371	18251	27378	34034	8445	1097	752304
3278	967		271	303	32	15	3830
169457	80542	1111	3298	3629	758	134	173965
2520	1534		59	62	3	3	2578
67543	7303	4324	5227	5906	1263	376	77767
476277	**178767**	**57657**	**155067**	**186101**	**40689**	**8499**	**726183**
55473	12427	20351	40741	49500	10076	1449	119618
475027	178332	57657	154857	185801	40598	8415	724635
15025	5262	53	6942	7983	2050	318	22222
358	72		196	263	122	6	696
6455	2677	21	899	1103	262	87	7764
2551	898		2251	3326	1134	204	5238
171458	53405	18844	57689	62895	12522	2981	265740
165782	82720	31217	62425	82132	20110	3228	263323
113398	33301	7522	24455	28099	4399	1593	159653
1250	435		210	300	90	84	1547

项目	Item	企业数(个) Number of Enterprises (unit)	#亏损企业(个) Loss Making Enterprises (unit)
综合零售	General Retail	36	11
#百货零售	Department Store	18	4
超级市场零售	Super Market	15	7
食品、饮料及烟草制品专门零售	Food, Beverages and Tobaccos	8	1
纺织、服装及日用品专门零售	Textile, Garments and Daily Use Articles	3	1
#服装零售	Garments	1	
文化、体育用品及器材专门零售	Culture, Sports and Equipments	9	1
#图书零售	Books	8	
医药及医疗器材专门零售	Medical and Medical Appliance	6	1
#药品零售	Medicines	6	1
汽车、摩托车、燃料及零配件专门零售	Motor Vehicles, Motorcycles Fuels and Related Spares and Fittings	30	3
#汽车零售	Motor Vehicles	24	1
机动车燃料零售	Motor Vehicle Fuels	2	
家用电器及电子产品专门零售	Household Appliances and Electronic Products	14	5
家用电器零售	Household Appliances	10	4
计算机、软件及辅助设备零售	Computer, Software and Auxiliary Equipment	3	1
通信设备零售	Communication Equipment	1	
无店铺及其他零售	Others	4	1
按经营形式分	**Grouped by Management Method**		
百货商店	Department Store	20	4
超级市场	Supermarket	19	8
专业(专卖)店	Specialized Shop	57	10
其他	Others	14	2

continued 2 (10000 yuan)

年末资产负债 Total Assets and Liabilities at the Year – end							
流动资产小计 Circulating Funds	存货 Inventories	长期投资 Long – Term Investment	固定资产小计 Total Fixed Assets	固定资产原价 Original Value of Fixed Assets	累计折旧 Accumulative Total Depreciation	#本年折旧 Depreciation in this year	资产合计 Total Asset
257724	120577	45211	112075	135628	30965	5760	432624
190574	88194	32233	81982	105953	24409	3034	313368
66173	31910	12979	29545	29033	6461	2663	117561
8672	3522	817	4255	4840	893	269	14829
25030	6305	5226	7946	9198	1591	418	38643
24279	6018	5205	3806	4443	638	270	33536
19223	7325	253	7035	8161	2135	306	26749
12971	3875	53	6811	7800	1998	303	20037
10831	4002	351	6049	6636	895	307	18224
10831	4002	351	6049	6636	895	307	18224
89926	23842	4059	12414	14767	2576	992	121421
81780	21245	2751	10531	11843	1500	800	108943
1425	216	524	1399	2087	721	111	3479
63349	13019	1044	3869	4499	629	284	69017
57140	10452	1044	2834	3256	423	144	61496
3332	1231		999	1201	202	140	4608
2877	1337		37	42	5	1	2913
1523	175	696	1424	2373	1005	163	4676
179305	87111	32367	76199	97857	22096	2764	296525
75964	36115	550	32543	32165	6904	2865	118156
212153	53453	23377	41796	49285	9411	2374	294715
8856	2089	1363	4529	6794	2278	496	16786

单位:万元　　6－8 续表 3

项目	Item	年末资产 Total Assets and Liabilities	
		负债合计 Total Liabilities	所有者权益合计 Creditors' Equity
总计	**Total**	**2962643**	**771953**
批发业	**Wholesale Trade**	**2442283**	**566130**
#国有及国有控股	State－owned and State－holding Enterprises	863999	315859
按注册类型分	**Grouped by Registration Status**		
内资企业	Domestic Funded Enterprises	2442824	565136
国有企业	State－Owned Enterprises	320262	187394
集体企业	Collective－Owned Enterprises	58384	20875
股份合作企业	Share Cooperative Enterprises	32334	5647
联营企业	Joint－owned Enterprises	8326	1168
有限责任公司	Limited Liability Corporations	1372514	204741
股份有限公司	Share－holding Corporations Ltd.	332677	88809
私营企业	Private Enterprises	318327	56502
外商投资企业	Enterprises with Foreign Investment	－541	994
外资企业	Foreign Funded	－541	994
按行业分	**Grouped by Sector**		
农畜产品批发	Agricultural and Animal Products	155693	11188
食品、饮料及烟草制品批发	Food, Beverages and Tobaccos	192495	164311
#米、面制品及食用油批发	Rice, Wheaten Food and Edible Oil	17849	－191
烟草制品批发	Tobacco	67190	145607
纺织、服装及日用品批发	Textile, Garments and Daily Use Articles	780145	95873
#服装批发	Garments	225679	31844
文化、体育用品及器材批发	Culture, Sports and Equipments	76859	9721
医药及医疗器材批发	Medical and Medical Appliance	89013	34991
矿产品、建材及化工产品批发	Mineral Products, Building Materials and Chemical Products	449784	118269

continued 3 (10000 yuan)

负债 at the Year－end	损益与分配 Profit, Loss and Distribution						
实收资本 Total Capital Hold	商品销售收入净额 Net Value of Sales Revenue	商品销售成本 Cost of Sales	经营费用 Operating Expense	商品销售税金及附加 Sales Taxes and Extra Charges	商品销售利润 Sales Profits	代购代销收入 Revenue of Agent Purchase & Agent Sale	主营业务利润 Profits of Major Business
333152	**9954115**	**9384151**	**256385**	**10986**	**302593**	**4550**	**307143**
210748	**8541493**	**8103346**	**193786**	**7387**	**236974**	**4550**	**241524**
94508	3155853	2949378	67770	4246	134459	3872	138331
210748	8524495	8087343	193786	7387	235980	4550	240530
17859	1261645	1130064	31154	3212	97216	142	97357
7703	133509	126476	3121	117	3796	224	4020
1858	116875	112230	2942	35	1669		1669
1155	48891	47929	525	33	404		404
91951	4390563	4195558	102548	3335	89122	3715	92837
53101	1474272	1420834	28885	276	24277	468	24745
37121	1098740	1054251	24612	380	19497	1	19498
	16997	16003			994		994
	16997	16003			994		994
3757	398542	391420	5061	70	1990	59	2050
18607	747162	637611	21554	1983	86014	3640	89654
1910	26560	24965	763		831		831
4452	364911	273804	10808	1712	78586		78586
43008	2441661	2354935	46248	278	40201	722	40923
15670	811500	786031	16050	49	9370	469	9838
3917	238155	226022	7331	53	4750	3	4753
20759	273115	254840	6583	749	10943		10943
56943	1852363	1756195	51003	2104	43061	27	43087

单位:万元　　6－8 续表 4

项目	Item	年末资产 Total Assets and Liabilities 负债合计 Total Liabilities	所有者权益合计 Creditors' Equity
#煤炭及制品批发	Coal and Coal Products	9923	1939
石油及制品批发	Petroleum and Related Products	65142	39511
金属及金属矿批发	Metal and Metallic Ore	176063	32399
建材批发	Building Materials	21539	4712
化肥批发	Chemical Fertilizer	12014	12386
机械设备、五金交电及电子产品批发	Machine Equipments, Hardware and Electrical Appliance, Electronic Products	632462	119842
#汽车、摩托车及零配件批发	Motor Vehicles, Motorcycles and Related Spares and Fittings	3207	623
家用电器批发	Household Appliances	158968	14998
计算机、软件及辅助设备批发	Computer, Software and Auxiliary Equipment	2051	528
其他批发	Others	65831	11936
零售业	**Retail Trade**	**520360**	**205823**
#国有及国有控股	State – owned and State – holding Enterprises	55958	63659
按注册类型分	**Grouped by Registration Status**		
内资企业	Domestic Funded Enterprises	519340	205296
国有企业	State – Owned Enterprises	12418	9803
集体企业	Collective – Owned Enterprises	652	44
股份合作企业	Share Cooperative Enterprises	6046	1718
联营企业	Joint – owned Enterprises	3889	1349
有限责任公司	Limited Liability Corporations	205865	59875
股份有限公司	Share – holding Corporations Ltd.	168444	94879
私营企业	Private Enterprises	122025	37628
外商投资企业	Enterprises with Foreign Investment	1020	528
按行业分	**Grouped by Sector**		

continued 4 (10000 yuan)

负债 at the Year - end	损益与分配 Profit, Loss and Distribution						
实收资本 Total Capital Hold	商品销售收入净额 Net Value of Sales Revenue	商品销售成本 Cost of Sales	经营费用 Operating Expense	商品销售税金及附加 Sales Taxes and Extra Charges	商品销售利润 Sales Profits	代购代销收入 Revenue of Agent Purchase & Agent Sale	主营业务利润 Profits of Major Business
1164	37275	34771	1931	50	523		523
15823	347975	321507	12955	1726	11787		11787
17360	608850	582730	14307	231	11583	13	11596
3208	75725	73864	1438	5	418		418
5141	41726	39335	917	1	1473		1473
56830	2306743	2209014	49686	2044	46000	98	46098
608	20509	20026	366	14	104		104
2459	354849	337371	13936	22	3520	2	3522
500	9893	9365	402	12	115		115
6928	283751	273310	6320	107	4015	1	4016
122404	**1412623**	**1280805**	**62600**	**3599**	**65620**		**65620**
35183	156520	137543	7224	501	11252		11252
121854	1407212	1276273	62288	3555	65096		65096
2010	26400	21009	2189	81	3122		3122
66	1343	1295		1	47		47
1572	24731	23503	451	19	758		758
750	23917	22028	481	407	1001		1001
35146	543411	489377	29942	1181	22912		22912
60281	338904	304104	15138	1239	18423		18423
22029	448508	414959	14088	627	18834		18834
550	5411	4532	311	44	523		523

单位:万元　　　　6-8 续表 5

项目	Item	年末资产 Total Assets and Liabilities	
		负债合计 Total Liabilities	所有者权益合计 Creditors' Equity
综合零售	General Retail	299487	133137
#百货零售	Department Store	213008	100360
超级市场零售	Super Market	84931	32630
食品、饮料及烟草制品专门零售	Food, Beverages and Tobaccos	11378	3452
纺织、服装及日用品专门零售	Textile, Garments and Daily Use Articles	30272	8371
#服装零售	Garments	26008	7529
文化、体育用品及器材专门零售	Culture, Sports and Equipments	16376	10373
#图书零售	Books	10440	9598
医药及医疗器材专门零售	Medical and Medical Appliance	12020	6204
#药品零售	Medicines	12020	6204
汽车、摩托车、燃料及零配件专门零售	Motor Vehicles, Motorcycles Fuels and Related Spares and Fittings	86587	34833
#汽车零售	Motor Vehicles	77704	31238
机动车燃料零售	Motor Vehicle Fuels	2597	882
家用电器及电子产品专门零售	Household Appliances and Electronic Products	61605	7412
家用电器零售	Household Appliances	56466	5030
计算机、软件及辅助设备零售	Computer, Software and Auxiliary Equipment	2762	1846
通信设备零售	Communication Equipment	2378	536
无店铺及其他零售	Others	2635	2041
按经营形式分	**Grouped by Management Method**		
百货商店	Department Store	196170	100355
超级市场	Supermarket	101455	16702
专业(专卖)店	Specialized Shop	212087	82628
其他	Others	10648	6139

continued 5 (10000 yuan)

负债 at the Year－end	损益与分配 Profit, Loss and Distribution						
实收资本 Total Capital Hold	商品销售收入净额 Net Value of Sales Revenue	商品销售成本 Cost of Sales	经营费用 Operating Expense	商品销售税金及附加 Sales Taxes and Extra Charges	商品销售利润 Sales Profits	代购代销收入 Revenue of Agent Purchase & Agent Sale	主营业务利润 Profits of Major Business
78014	657190	581182	39230	2146	34632		34632
67338	352122	313028	15086	1485	22523		22523
10316	300103	263878	23087	643	12494		12494
2359	50557	45953	2682	490	1432		1432
5730	63759	53196	5051	84	5430		5430
4850	58015	48477	4453	65	5019		5019
2710	22710	17394	2349	162	2805		2805
1610	21101	16147	2081	77	2796		2796
4930	39289	32763	3021	89	3417		3417
4930	39289	32763	3021	89	3417		3417
20629	434654	413530	5836	428	14861		14861
17958	374825	357308	4805	312	12400		12400
600	10075	9262	270	21	522		522
6247	138088	130885	4336	182	2685		2685
4497	123245	117617	3775	129	1725		1725
1250	12365	10915	498	52	901		901
500	2478	2354	64		60		60
1787	6376	5902	95	21	359		359
67438	331944	294513	13758	1292	22381		22381
8593	364651	325793	26206	1144	11508		11508
41940	670967	619783	20028	1047	30109		30109
4433	45062	40716	2608	116	1622		1622

单位:万元

6-8 续表6

项目	Item	损益与分配	
		其他业务利润 Profits of Other Business	管理费用 Overhead Expenses
总计	**Total**	**33421**	**137478**
批发业	**Wholesale Trade**	**13856**	**91560**
#国有及国有控股	State - owned and State - holding Enterprises	6911	53560
按注册类型分	**Grouped by Registration Status**		
内资企业	Domestic Funded Enterprises	13856	91560
国有企业	State - Owned Enterprises	756	28749
集体企业	Collective - Owned Enterprises	1148	3446
股份合作企业	Share Cooperative Enterprises	337	1114
联营企业	Joint - owned Enterprises	34	599
有限责任公司	Limited Liability Corporations	5064	39634
股份有限公司	Share - holding Corporations Ltd.	4043	10209
私营企业	Private Enterprises	2475	7810
外商投资企业	Enterprises with Foreign Investment		
外资企业	Foreign Funded		
按行业分	**Grouped by Sector**		
农畜产品批发	Agricultural and Animal Products	216	2242
食品、饮料及烟草制品批发	Food, Beverages and Tobaccos	1336	25828
#米、面制品及食用油批发	Rice, Wheaten Food and Edible Oil	10	1272
烟草制品批发	Tobacco	183	16379
纺织、服装及日用品批发	Textile, Garments and Daily Use Articles	3300	20458
#服装批发	Garments	779	3146
文化、体育用品及器材批发	Culture, Sports and Equipments	547	2318
医药及医疗器材批发	Medical and Medical Appliance	443	7593
矿产品、建材及化工产品批发	Mineral Products, Building Materials and Chemical Products	2845	15967

continued 6 (10000 yuan)

Profit, Loss and Distribution					工资福利与税金 Wages, Welfare and Tax		
财务费用 Financial Expenses	利息支出 Interest Expenditure	营业利润 Operating Profits	补贴收入 Subsidy Revenue	利润总额 Total Profits	本年应付工资总额 Total Wages Payable in This Year	本年应付福利费总额 Total Welfare Funds Paybale in This Year	本年应交增值税总额 Value-added Taxes Payable in This Year
40697	**31421**	**142420**	**22633**	**177270**	**81249**	**10649**	**167207**
32471	**24127**	**116142**	**21469**	**146255**	**57359**	**7576**	**149560**
10840	8458	79784	9810	88805	31868	4264	108887
32471	24127	116142	21469	145261	57359	7576	149334
2849	2001	67799	4214	71837	17965	2276	18144
960	965	903	108	2163	1857	233	923
541	359	359	94	443	578	80	306
131	127	-292	70	-270	85	10	303
17228	11372	29482	12881	44898	26314	3541	30258
6390	6345	8975	2843	14248	6272	863	85605
4373	2958	8917	1259	11940	4289	575	13795
				994			226
				994			226
2405	2199	-2148	2926	596	1353	92	582
1102	619	62944	3604	67268	15328	1868	32391
294	294	-1719	2004	1056	835	114	249
-1005	-1007	63590	115	63637	10741	1215	16417
14587	10290	9961	8433	20543	11475	1775	2143
4595	4436	2877	2674	6587	2852	323	361
1115	915	1734	431	2248	951	145	207
1488	1338	2460	13	2710	4822	869	2792
4988	4382	23961	1364	33019	10495	1278	19636

单位:万元　　6－8 续表 7

项目	Item	损益与分配 其他业务利润 Profits of Other Business	管理费用 Overhead Expenses
#煤炭及制品批发	Coal and Coal Products	842	1439
石油及制品批发	Petroleum and Related Products	150	1699
金属及金属矿批发	Metal and Metallic Ore	727	3603
建材批发	Building Materials	343	421
化肥批发	Chemical Fertilizer	59	1231
机械设备、五金交电及电子产品批发	Machine Equipments, Hardware and Electrical Appliance, Electronic Products	4217	15290
#汽车、摩托车及零配件批发	Motor Vehicles, Motorcycles and Related Spares and Fittings	38	283
家用电器批发	Household Appliances	229	2398
计算机、软件及辅助设备批发	Computer, Software and Auxiliary Equipment	157	217
其他批发	Others	952	1866
零售业	**Retail Trade**	**19566**	**45918**
#国有及国有控股	State – owned and State – holding Enterprises	1031	8645
按注册类型分	**Grouped by Registration Status**		
内资企业	Domestic Funded Enterprises	19566	45495
国有企业	State – Owned Enterprises	330	2910
集体企业	Collective – Owned Enterprises		25
股份合作企业	Share Cooperative Enterprises	81	693
联营企业	Joint – owned Enterprises	147	731
有限责任公司	Limited Liability Corporations	10628	22628
股份有限公司	Share – holding Corporations Ltd.	6039	10560
私营企业	Private Enterprises	2341	7947
外商投资企业	Enterprises with Foreign Investment		424
按行业分	**Grouped by Sector**		

continued 7 (10000 yuan)

Profit, Loss and Distribution					工资福利与税金 Wages, Welfare and Tax		
财务费用 Financial Expenses	利息支出 Interest Expenditure	营业利润 Operating Profits	补贴收入 Subsidy Revenue	利润总额 Total Profits	本年应付工资总额 Total Wages Payable in This Year	本年应付福利费总额 Total Welfare Funds Paybale in This Year	本年应交增值税总额 Value - added Taxes Payable in This Year
139	129	- 238	87	- 60	718	91	372
217	355	9042	12	13724	990	133	15516
1483	1483	6695	44	7603	2031	254	2017
154	142	176		173	356	30	41
372	370	70	80	365	336	43	12
5062	3339	15715	3733	17339	11445	1303	91272
12	11	- 153	3	- 162	152	18	74
923	783	203	451	824	3903	179	72
12	1	42		41	183	26	- 50
1724	1047	1515	966	2532	1489	247	538
8226	**7294**	**26277**	**1164**	**31016**	**23890**	**3074**	**17647**
877	710	2750	234	4901	4576	722	3016
8194	7266	26210	1164	30964	23556	3027	17637
- 21	- 29	562	51	627	1342	288	832
		22		2	10		2
49	51	97	60	140	389	58	111
149	26	442	- 5	436	429	31	240
1487	1571	7703	244	7941	10218	1334	7728
4657	4044	6047	658	10789	5329	581	5089
1875	1604	11337	157	11030	5839	733	3636
32	28	68		52	335	47	10

单位:万元　　6-8 续表 8

项目	Item	损益与分配	
		其他业务利润 Profits of Other Business	管理费用 Overhead Expenses
综合零售	General Retail	15094	27320
#百货零售	Department Store	5971	19190
超级市场零售	Super Market	8511	8015
食品、饮料及烟草制品专门零售	Food, Beverages and Tobaccos	770	1702
纺织、服装及日用品专门零售	Textile, Garments and Daily Use Articles	159	1908
#服装零售	Garments	9	1474
文化、体育用品及器材专门零售	Culture, Sports and Equipments	329	2677
#图书零售	Books	329	2608
医药及医疗器材专门零售	Medical and Medical Appliance	445	3190
#药品零售	Medicines	445	3190
汽车、摩托车、燃料及零配件专门零售	Motor Vehicles, Motorcycles Fuels and Related Spares and Fittings	1451	5483
#汽车零售	Motor Vehicles	1274	4704
机动车燃料零售	Motor Vehicle Fuels	10	216
家用电器及电子产品专门零售	Household Appliances and Electronic Products	1053	3228
家用电器零售	Household Appliances	1021	2502
计算机、软件及辅助设备零售	Computer, Software and Auxiliary Equipment	17	710
通信设备零售	Communication Equipment	15	16
无店铺及其他零售	Others	265	410
按经营形式分	**Grouped by Management Method**		
百货商店	Department Store	5003	18225
超级市场	Supermarket	9528	9071
专业(专卖)店	Specialized Shop	3989	16576
其他	Others	1046	2047

continued 8 (10000 yuan)

Profit, Loss and Distribution					工资福利与税金 Wages, Welfare and Tax		
财务费用 Financial Expenses	利息支出 Interest Expenditure	营业利润 Operating Profits	补贴收入 Subsidy Revenue	利润总额 Total Profits	本年应付工资总额 Total Wages Payable in This Year	本年应付福利费总额 Total Welfare Funds Paybale in This Year	本年应交增值税总额 Value - added Taxes Payable in This Year
6212	5456	11034	783	14833	13474	1567	10918
5770	5087	3570	633	7519	7798	821	5973
418	346	7378	145	7227	5424	710	4790
186	118	498	161	774	1674	134	599
509	502	3166	106	2918	1728	236	849
332	332	3223	106	2972	1479	207	701
77	66	380	51	448	1303	283	909
- 29	- 36	546	51	614	1254	276	832
138	189	774		596	1111	246	784
138	189	774		596	1111	246	784
994	698	9819	33	10843	2111	277	2180
810	597	8154	38	9279	1808	233	1715
59	57	247		235	67	11	130
97	247	406	31	313	2369	316	1349
- 20	139	262	31	188	1743	238	1279
113	109	93		74	598	74	68
3	- 1	52		52	28	4	3
14	17	200		290	119	15	58
5683	5013	3513	442	7211	7478	812	5917
683	447	6744	145	6575	6680	866	5428
1785	1749	15485	416	16338	8323	1242	5724
75	85	536	161	892	1410	155	578

主要指标解释

【社会消费品零售额】 指各种经济类型的批发零售贸易业、餐饮业、制造业和其他行业对城乡居民和社会集团的消费品零售额。这个指标反映通过各种商品流通渠道向居民和社会集团供应的生活消费品来满足他们生活需要，是研究人民生活，社会消费品购买力、货币流通等问题的重要指标。社会消费品零售额包括：(1)售给城乡居民作为生活用的商品和修建房屋用的建筑材料；(2)售给社会集团的各种办公用品和公用消费品(3)售给 机关、团体、学校、部队、企业、事业单位的职工食堂和旅店(招待所)附设专门供本店旅客食用，不对外营业的食堂的各种食品、燃料；企业、单位和国营农场直接售给本单位职工和职工食堂的自已生产的产品；(4)售给部队干部、战士生活用的粮食、副食品、衣着品、日用品、燃料；(5)售给来华的外国人、华侨、港澳(台)同胞的消费品；(6)居民自费购买的中、西药品、中药材及医疗用品；(7)报社、出版社直接售给居民和社会集团的报纸、图书、杂志、集邮公司出售的新、旧纪念邮票、特种邮票、首日封、集邮册、集邮工具等；(8)旧货寄售商店自购、自销部分的商品；(9)煤气公司、液化石油气站售给居民和社会集团的煤气灶具和罐装液化石油气；(10)农民售给非农业居民和社会集团的商品。不包括售给国民经济各部门企业、事业单位(包括国有经济的农场) 生产经营用的各种原材料、燃料、设备、工具等和售给批发零售贸易业、餐饮业作为转卖用的商品、旧货寄售商店受托寄售卖出的商品、服务业的营业收入、邮局出售邮票的收入、自来水、电力、煤气生产(供应)单位的产品供应收入，也不包括农民之间的商品销售。

【限额以上批发企业】 指年销售额在 2000 万元及以上，并且年末从业人员在 20 人及以上的批发贸易企业。

【限额以上零售企业】 指年销售额在 500 万元及以上，并且年末从业人员在 60 人及以上的零售企业。

【限额以上餐饮企业】 指年销售额在 200 万元及以上，并且年末从业人员在 40 人及以上的餐饮企业。

【批发零售贸易业商品购、销、存总额】 指以各种经济类型的批发、零售贸易业(不包括个体)为总体的商品购、销、存。

【商品购进总额】 指从本企业(单位)以外的单位和个人购进(包括从国外直接进口)作为转卖或加工后转卖的商品。这个指标反映批发零售贸易业从国内、国外市场上购进商品的总量。商品购进总额包括：(1)从工农业生产者购进的商品；(2)从出版社、报社的出版发行部门购进的图书、杂志和报纸；(3)从各种经济类型的批发零售贸易企业(单位)购进的商品；(4)从其他单位购进的商品，如从机关、团体、企业单位购进的剩余物资，从餐饮业、服务业购进的商品，从海关、市场管理部门购进的缉私和没收的商品，从居民收购的废旧商品等；(5)从国(境)外直接进口的商品。不包括企业(单位)为自身经营用，和未通过买卖行为而收入的商品以及销售退回、商品升溢等。

【商品销售总额】 指对本企业(单位)以外的单位和个人出售(包括对国(境)外直接出口)的商品。这个指标反映批发零售贸易业在国内市场上销售商品以及出口商品的总量。商品销售总额包括：(1)售给城乡居民和社会集团消费用的商品；(2)售给工业、农业、建筑业、运输邮电业、批发零售贸易业、餐饮业、服务业等作为生产、经营使用的商品；(3)售给批发零售贸易业作为转卖或加工后转卖的商品；(4)对国(境)外直接出口的商品。不包括：出售本企业(单位)自用的废旧包装用品，未通过买卖行为付出的商品，经本单位介绍，由买卖双方直接结算，本单位只收取手续费的业务，购货退出的商品以及商品损耗和损失等。

Explanatory Notes on Main Statistical Indicators

【Total Retail Sales of Consumer Goods】 refer to the sum of retail sales of consumer goods by the establishments in wholesale trade, retail sale trade, catering trade, manufacturing industry and other industries of different types of ownership, to urban and rural residents and social groups. This indicator is used to show the supply of consumer goods through various channels to households and institutions to meet their demands, and is therefore very important for the study of the issues on people's livelihood, on the purchasing power of consumer goods and on the circulation of money. The retail sales of consumer goods include: (1) commodities sold to urban and rural residents for residential use and building materials sold to them for the construction or repair of houses; (2) food and fuels sold to canteens of institutions, enterprises, schools, military units and to canteens of hotels and hostels that only serve their guests, and commodities produced by enterprises, institutions or state farms and sold directly to their employees or their canteens; (3) grain and non – staple food, clothing, daily articles and fuels sold to military personnel; (4) consumer goods sold to foreigners, overseas Chinese, and Chinese compatriots from Taiwan, Hong Kong and Macao during their stay in the mainland of China; (5) Chinese an d western medicines, herbs and medical facilities purchased by residents; (6) newspapers, books and magazines directly sold to residents and social groups by publishers, new and old commemorative stamps, special stamps, first day covers, stamp albums and other stamp collection articles sold by stamp companies; (7) consumer goods purchased and then sold by second – hand shops; (8) stoves and other heating facilities and liquified gas sold by gas companies to households and institutions; (9) commodities sold by farmers to non – agricultural residents and social groups. Excluded under this heading are: raw materials, fuels, equipment, tools sold to enterprises, institutions and state farms for production purpose; commodities sold to trade establishments for re – selling; commissioned sales at second – hand shops; operational income of urban public utilities; stamps sold at post offices; income of water, power, gas production and supply establishments from the supply of their products; and sales of commodities among farmers.

【Enterprises of Over – norm Wholesale Volume】 refers to wholesale trade enterprises that register an annual sales volume of over 20 million yuan RMB and a total year-end staff of more than 20.

【Enterprises of Over – norm Retail Sales Volume】 refers to those that register an annual sales volume of over 5 million yuan RMB and a total year – end staff of more than 60.

【Catering Enterprises of Over – norm Sales Volume】 refers to those that register an annual sales volume of over 2 million yuan RMB and a total year – end staff of more than 40.

【Purchase, Sales and Stock of Commodities by Wholesale and Retail Trade】 refer to the purchase, sales and stock of commodities by wholesale and retail establishments of different ownership (excluding individual sellers).

【Total Purchases of Commodities】 refer to the purchases of commodities by the establishments from other establishments or individuals (including direct import from abroad) for the purpose of re – selling, either with or without further processing of the commodities purchased. This indicator is used to show the total value of purchases of commodities by wholesale and retail establishments from domestic and overseas markets. The total purchases include: (1) agricultural and industrial products purchased from producers; (2) books, magazines and newspapers purchased from distribution departments of the publishers; (3) commodities purchased from wholesale and retail establishments; (4) commodities purchased from other units, such as surplus materials purchased from government agencies, enterprises or institutions, commodities purchased from catering and service establishments, confiscated goods purchased from customs authorities or market management agencies, second – hand goods and wastes purchased from residents; and (5) commodities directly imported from abroad. Excluded are commodities purchased by establishments (units) for use in their own business operation, commodities obtained without buying or selling procedures, rejected commodities, etc.

【Total Sales of Commodities】 refer to selling of commodities by the establishments to other establishments and individuals (including direct export). This indicator is used to show the total value of sales of commodities at domestic markets and export. The total sales include: (1) commodities sold to urban and rural residents and social groups for their consumption; (2) commodities so ld to establishments in industry, agriculture, construction, transportation, post and telecommunications, wholesale and retail trades, catering trade and public utility for their production and operation; (3) commodities sold to wholesale an d retail establishments for re – selling, with or without further processing; and (4) commodities for direct export to other countries. Excluded are selling of waste packaging materials used by the establishments (units) themselves, commodities transferred without buying or selling procedures, commission income from brokerage in transactions whose settlement is directly handled by buyers and sellers, rejected commodities in the purchase, loss in commodities, etc.

7

对外经济、旅游

CHAPTER 7 FOREIGN TRADE AND TOURISM

对外经济、旅游
Foreign Trade and Tourism

主要统计指标
Major Statistics Indicators

2003 年自营进出口总额	Total Direct Import and Export	1880934	万美元	USD 10000
比上年增长	Increase Over Last Year	53.3	%	
2003 年自营出口总额	Total Exports	1207370	万美元	USD 10000
比上年增长	Increase Over Last Year	47.9	%	
2003 年新签合同数	Number of Projects of Signed Contracts	1209	个	unit
比上年增长	Increase Over Last Year	18.9	%	
2003 年实际利用外资金额	Value of Foreign Captial Actually Used	172727	万美元	USD 10000
比上年增长	Increase Over Last Year	38.5	%	
2003 年接待境外旅游者人数	Number of Received Foreign Tourists	221546	人	person
比上年增长	Increase Over Last Year	7.9	%	
2003 年旅游创汇收入	Foreign Exchange Earnings	9976	万美元	USD 10000
比上年增长	Increase Over Last Year	12.9	%	
2003 年国内旅游总收入	Earning From Domestic Tourism	155.83	亿元	100 million yuan
比上年增长	Increase Over Last Year	8.0	%	

7－1　主要年份对外经济情况

Basic Statistics on Foreign Economy and Trade in Main Years

单位:万美元　　　　(USD 10000)

年份 Year	外商直接投资情况 Foreign Direct Investments			自营进出口情况 Directive Import and Export Situation		口岸进出口情况 Import and Export situation of port	
	新批项目数(个) Number of Projects(unit)	协议利用外资 Foreign Investments of Agreements	实际利用外资 Foreign Investments Actually Used	进出口 Total Imports and Exports	出口 Total Exports	进出口 Total Imports and Exports	出口 Total Exports
1980	1	5	5				
1981							
1982						14917	10963
1983						17683	12173
1984	8	850	21			26336	16102
1985	11	682	359	1029	389	45474	23521
1986	7	447	500	2079	540	54690	34432
1987	13	4341	429	2061	791	52493	29999
1988	62	4002	689	14766	11458	78717	39155
1989	64	6295	1758	22024	18005	110175	53615
1990	89	5624	2197	29840	27962	125527	63253
1991	184	17460	2680	57339	47532	219638	87101
1992	636	156725	11497	99072	78389	260387	101699
1993	1015	107152	34455	169434	110824	328871	120138
1994	680	77149	35812	251462	174992	375919	168340
1995	496	114630	39909	385335	226825	521501	232789
1996	322	87838	50162	418573	233003	586140	252248
1997	260	45849	55408	460896	293332	663807	311848
1998	281	51198	50329	421237	296386	610109	339904
1999	364	65660	52035	500898	347721	774194	411200
2000	550	95151	62186	754065	516781	1372547	703357
2001	806	195519	87446	889202	624500	1613794	869768
2002	1017	320024	124696	1227343	816304	2145755	1232723
2003	1209	344382	172727	1880934	1207370	3394193	1888206

注:2003 年起,利用外资统计口径有变动。
Note: From 2003, the Statstistical Standard which will utilize the foreign capitals willhave changes.

7-2　按企业性质分进出口总值

Total Value of Imports and Exports in Foreign Trade by Registered Type of Enterprises

单位:万美元　　(2003)　　(USD 10000)

企业性质	Grouped by Registered Type	进出口 Total Imports and Exports		出口 Exports		进口 Imports	
		贸易额 Value	增长率(%) Rate of Increase	贸易额 Value	增长率(%) Rate of Increase	贸易额 Value	增长率(%) Rate of Increase
合计	**Total**	**1880934**	**53.25**	**1207370**	**47.91**	**673564**	**63.87**
国有企业	State - Owned Enterprises	680168	33.41	445705	28.71	234463	43.36
三资企业	Foreign Funded Enterprises	664262	55.83	355629	46.87	308633	67.61
#合作	Cooperative Operation Enterprises	18401	91.46	10236	65.66	8165	137.91
合资	Joint VentureEnterprises	395626	54.31	216481	46.68	179145	64.65
独资	Foreign - funded Sole Enterprises	250235	56.13	128912	45.87	121323	68.75
集体企业	Collective Owned Enterprises	309111	64.04	230409	55.84	78702	93.92
个体企业	Individual Enterprises	227386	121.20	175627	119.48	51759	127.24
其他企业	Others						7

7-3　按贸易方式分进出口总值表

Total Value of Imports and Exports by Trade Property

单位:万美元　　(2003)　　(USD 10000)

贸易方式	Trade Property	进出口 Total Import and Exports		出口 Exports		进口 Imports	
		贸易额 Value	增长率(%) Rate of Increase	贸易额 Value	增长率(%) Rate of Increase	贸易额 Value	增长率(%) Rate of Increase
总额	**Total**	**1880934**	**53.25**	**1207370**	**47.91**	**673564**	**63.87**
一般贸易	General Trade	1438023	51.95	988523	47.29	449500	63.29
来料加工	Processing by Supplied Material	58813	69.69	28419	61.48	30394	78.16
进料加工	Processing by Import Material	263302	43.35	185799	48.26	77503	32.80
保税仓储转口货物	Transit Goods in Protective Tariff Zone	21169	54.59	1112	64.74	20057	54.06
外资企业进口设备	Equipments of Foreign - funded Enterprises Import	85449	103.85			85449	103.85
保税仓库进出境货物	Import & Export Commodities in Protective Tariff Zone	12169	106.57	3434	117.34	8735	102.62
其他	Others	2010	83.39	83		1927	76.47

7-4 分洲别及主要国家(地区)进出口总值表

Total Value of Exports and Imports by Continent and Country

单位:万美元 (2003) (USD 10000)

地区 Region	进出口 Total Imports and Exports		出口 Exports		进口 Imports	
	贸易额 Value	增长率(%) Rate of Increase	贸易额 Value	增长率(%) Rate of Increase	贸易额 Value	增长率(%) Rate of Increase
合计 Totle	**1880934**	**53.25**	**1207370**	**47.91**	**673564**	**63.87**
亚洲 Asia	846420	46.55	449577	40.73	396843	53.74
#东盟 The Association of Southeast Asian Nations	110435	51.72	66323	51.18	44112	52.54
中国香港 HongKong, China	81560	58.73	64850	54.99	16710	75.16
日本 Japan	249565	42.57	146042	28.44	103523	68.76
韩国 Republic of Korea	139389	25.78	39374	19.02	100015	28.66
中国台湾 Taiwan, China	95528	41.02	15909	32.37	79619	42.89
非洲 Africa	84864	82.85	62422	71.51	22442	124.04
欧洲 Europe	502784	63.77	361031	57.37	141753	82.70
#欧盟 Eurpoean Free Trade Association	406468	60.54	291990	55.59	114478	74.73
南美洲 South America	84010	56.81	63403	44.37	20607	113.37
北美洲 North America	309466	53.08	230336	44.28	79130	86.14
#美国 USA	275841	53.65	210245	43.57	65596	98.27
大洋洲 Oceania	53392	31.40	40602	47.73	12790	-2.72

7－5 部分年份按各大洲分的进出口分类表

Total Value of Exports and Imports by Continent in Partial Years

单位:万美元 (USD 10000)

项目	Item	1999	2000	2001	2002	2003
进出口总额	**Total Value of Export & Import**	**500898**	**754065**	**889202**	**1227343**	**1880934**
亚洲	Asia	248798	374313	420604	577572	846420
非洲	Africa	23376	28247	35525	46412	84864
欧洲	Europe	112556	166983	213274	306999	502784
# 欧盟	Eurpoean Free Trade Association	98804	147177	179487	253184	406468
南美洲	South America	21871	38753	44841	53574	84010
北美洲	North America	75488	118359	145054	202154	309466
大洋洲	Oceania	18807	27410	29903	40632	53392
出口	**Export**	**347721**	**516781**	**624500**	**816304**	**1207370**
亚洲	Asia	154251	227207	257149	319454	449577
非洲	Africa	14992	22748	30808	36395	62422
欧洲	Europe	92462	134370	169716	229412	361031
# 欧盟	Eurpoean Free Trade Association	81611	118157	142427	187667	291990
南美洲	South America	17660	32772	40407	43916	63403
北美洲	North America	57067	83141	106501	159643	230336
大洋洲	Oceania	11288	16544	19919	27484	40602
进口	**Import**	**153177**	**237284**	**264702**	**411039**	**673564**
亚洲	Asia	94547	147106	163455	258118	396843
非洲	Africa	8384	5500	4717	10017	22442
欧洲	Europe	20094	32613	43558	77587	141753
# 欧盟	Eurpoean Free Trade Association	17193	29020	37060	65517	114478
南美洲	South America	4211	5981	4434	9658	20607
北美洲	North America	18421	35218	38553	42511	79130
大洋洲	Oceania	7519	10866	9984	13148	12790

7－6 利用外资按投资方式分基本情况

Utilization of Foreign Capital by Way

单位:万美元 (2003) (USD 10000)

项目	Item	项目数(个) Projects (unit)	协议利用外资 Foreign Investment Contracted	实际利用外资 Actual Utilization of Foreign Capital
总计	**Total**	**1209**	**344382**	**172727**
对外借款	**Foreign Loans**			
外国政府贷款	Foreign Government Loans			
国际金融组织贷款	Loans from International Financial Organization			
外国银行商业贷款	Commercial Loans from Foreign Banks			
其他	Others			
外商直接投资	**Foreign Direct Investment**	**1209**	**344382**	**172727**
合资经营	Joint Venture Enterprises	520	97446	50535
合作经营	Cooperative Operation Enterprises	14	2566	9827
独资企业	Foreign－funded Sole Enterprises	674	243830	112104
外商投资股份制	Share－system Enterprises	1	540	261
外商其他投资	**Other Foreign Investment**			

7－7 部分年份按投资方式分利用外资基本情况

Utilization of Foreign Capital by Way in Partial Years

单位:万美元 (USD 10000)

项目	Item	1999	2000	2001	2002	2003
协议利用外资	**Foreign Investment Contracted**	**65660**	**95151**	**195519**	**320024**	**344382**
对外借款	Foreign Loans					
外商直接投资	Foreign Direct Investment	65660	95151	195519	320024	344382
合资经营	Joint Venture Enterprises	21862	19137	64708	57113	97446
合作经营	Cooperative Operation Enterprises	5795	12365	1571	8181	2566
独资企业	Foreign－funded Sole Enterprises	38004	63649	129852	254730	243830
实际利用外资	**Actual Utilization of Foreign Capital**	**58456**	**62708**	**87916**	**124696**	**172727**
对外借款	Foreign Loans	6421	522	470		
外商直接投资	Foreign Direct Investment	52035	62186	87446	124696	172727
合资经营	Joint Venture Enterprises	26382	23932	35584	42132	50535
合作经营	Cooperative Operation Enterprises	7078	10746	5779	5627	9827
独资企业	Foreign－funded Sole Enterprises	18575	27508	46083	76937	112104

7-8 外商直接投资分行业情况

单位:万美元

项目	Item
总计	**Total**
农、林、牧、渔业	Farming, Forestry, Animal Housbandry and Fishery
#农业	Farming
制造业	Manufacturing
#纺织业	Textile Industry
纺织服装、鞋、帽制造业	Textile Clothing. Shoes. Cap Manufacturing
文教体育用品制造业	Cultural. Educational and Sports Goods Manufacturing
化学原料及化学制品制造业	Raw Chemical Materials and Chemical Products
塑料制品业	Plastic Products
金属制品业	Metal Products
通用设备制造业	General Equipment Manufacturing
专用设备制造业	Special Equipment
交通运输设备制造业	Transport Equipment Manufacturing
电气机械及器材制造业	Electric Equipment and Machinery Manufacturing
通信设备、计算机及其他电子设备制造业	Communication Equipment. Computer and Other Electronic Equipment Manufacturing
仪器仪表及文化、办公用机械制造业	Instruments. Meters. Cultural and Office Machinery
电力、煤气及水的生产和供应业	Electricity, Gas and Water Production and Supply
建筑业	Construction
交通运输、仓储及邮政业	Transport, Storage and Post
批发和零售贸易、餐饮业	Wholesale and Retail Sale Trade
餐饮业	Catering Trade
房地产业	Real Estate Trade
居民服务和其他服务业	Resident Service and Other Service Industries
其他行业	Others

注:2002 年利用外资数据按 2003 年新口径调整。

Foreign Direct Investments by Sector

(USD 1000)

新批项目数(个) Number of Newly Projects(unit)		协议利用外资 Total Investments of Agreements		实际利用外资 Foreign Investment Actually Used	
2002	2003	2002	2003	2002	2003
1017	**1209**	**217146**	**344382**	**110300**	**172727**
10	8	2278	298	242	168
4	5	203	93	170	56
875	1082	179928	319755	89430	153248
46	57	8569	12876	4632	7057
132	125	11732	25769	5457	11542
32	55	5559	8623	2511	4038
32	32	13835	23653	8514	15127
73	58	10138	11172	3712	5383
104	134	14056	50250	8868	10086
80	105	15066	22320	7917	10756
23	36	8869	11601	4877	6012
36	76	7307	33580	4093	8378
87	129	15685	36793	7239	11034
99	82	46861	31197	19004	29323
20	31	2950	7846	1592	3751
2	4	5629	-1090	1611	4044
4	6	5128	1070	2914	2981
5	8	737	2535	978	791
64	45	4147	2830	6380	2345
7	4	101	1097	138	358
12	14	4384	10256	3791	4858
35	34	10412	5997	1966	2395
3	4	4402	1634	2850	1539

Note: Utilization of foreign capitals data in 2002 are adjusted according to the Statistical Standard in 2003.

7-9 按国别(地区)分的外商直接投资情况

Foreign Direct Investment by Country and Region

单位:万美元 (USD 10000)

国别、地区	Country, Region	新批项目数(个) New Projects (unit)		协议利用外资 Foreign Investment Contracted		实际利用外资 Actual Utilization of Foreign Capital	
		2003	2002	2003	2002	2003	2002
总计	**Total**	**1209**	**1017**	**344382**	**217146**	**172727**	**110300**
#香港	Hongkong, China	447	335	142220	74985	67556	34877
台湾省	Taiwan, China	170	178	30233	37597	13888	10031
日本	Japan	59	89	16104	11539	8925	11546
韩国	Korea Rep	27	25	4096	2795	2773	2006
印度尼西亚	Indonesia	15	11	5710	3491	1316	361
新加坡	Singapore	13	25	39	-6868	1318	3445
文莱	Brunei	4	1	4506	120	885	100
马来西亚	Malaysia	4	10	632	1386	531	958
泰国	Thailand	7	5	354	514	110	149
阿拉伯联合酋长国	United Arab Emirates	5	3	2220	111	233	20
毛里求斯	Mauritius	7	2	2263	200	1424	972
英国	United Kingdom	13	8	2418	4386	412	1087
德国	Germany	16	11	2023	747	502	358
法国	France	13	14	2170	1517	1348	654
意大利	Italy	13	6	3299	379	1336	371
荷兰	Netherlands	10	6	2689	-1603	989	446

注:2002年利用外资数据按2003年新口径调整。

单位:万美元　　7－9 续表　continued　　(USD 10000)

国别、地区	Country, Region	新批项目数(个) New Projects (unit)		协议利用外资 Foreign Investment Contracted		实际利用外资 Actual Utilization of Foreign Capital	
		2003	2002	2003	2002	2003	2002
比利时	Belgium	5	1	636	2	40	
西班牙	Spain	7	12	990	2825	706	534
瑞典	Sweden	8	2	3335	500	543	
瑞士	Switzerland	2	1	626	1000	261	10
俄罗斯	Russia	7	4	2779	400	738	211
巴哈马	The Bahamas	2	1	18	－1380	431	1295
巴西	Brazil	2		1310		10	21
开曼群岛	Cayman Islands	12	7	17009	25735	19137	7025
乌拉圭	Uruguay	1		945			
英属维尔京群岛	US Virgin Islands	81	50	41539	21644	25359	16385
加拿大	Canada	27	18	1600	2057	815	258
美国	United States	145	134	36977	18352	13401	9503
澳大利亚	Australia	30	28	3486	2559	1140	900
库克群岛	The Cook Islands	1		600			363
新西兰	New Zealand	16	6	862	933	375	298
萨摩亚	Samoa	12	12	8104	4560	3697	3222

Note: Utilization of foreign capitals data in 2002 are adjusted according to the Statistical Standard in 2003.

7－10　旅游业简况

Basic Statistic on Tourism Department

项目		Item		2001	2002	2003
国际旅行社(含分社)	(家)	International Tour Agencies	(unit)	7	9	12
国内旅行社	(家)	Domestic Tour Agencies	(unit)	87	98	120
旅游星级饭店	(家)	Star－rated Hotel	(unit)	100	122	130
国内旅游总人数	(万人次)	Number of Domestic Tourism	(10000 persons－times)	1384	1600	1720
旅游总收入	(亿元)	Income of Toursim	(100 million yuan)	130.6	151.4	164.06
#旅游创汇	(万美元)	Foreign Exchange Earnings	(USD 1000)	7125	8835	9976
国内旅游总收入	(亿元)	Earning From Domestic Tourism	(100 million yuan)	124.8	144.32	155.83

7－11　接待国际旅游者情况

Number of International Tourists

项目		Item		2001	2002	2003
接待过夜国际旅游者人数	**(人)**	**Total International Tourism**	**(person)**	**160901**	**205402**	**221546**
外国人	(人)	Foreigner	(person)	86674	118977	136435
台湾同胞	(人)	Taiwan, China	(person)	46254	54132	48325
香港同胞	(人)	Hongkong, China	(person)	20271	25394	30003
澳门同胞	(人)	Macao, China	(person)	7702	6899	6783
接待过夜国际旅游者人天数	**(人天)**	**Total International Person－day**	**(person－day)**	**352759**	**465386**	**526230**
外国人	(人天)	Foreigner	(person－day)	197878	275332	331631
台湾同胞	(人天)	Taiwan, China	(person－day)	95588	117019	113740
香港同胞	(人天)	Hongkong, China	(person－day)	39976	53135	58347
澳门同胞	(人天)	Macao, China	(person－day)	19317	19900	22512

7－12　接待外国旅游者分国别(地区)情况

Number of Foreign Tourists in Partial Years

单位:人　　　　(person)

国家(地区)	Country(Region)	2000	2001	2002	2003
总计	**Total**	**69081**	**86674**	**118977**	**136475**
亚洲小计	**Total of Asia**	**38768**	**54748**	**78432**	**81678**
#日本	Japna	22138	30467	43639	44205
韩国	Korea Rep	4039	10464	14967	15684
印度尼西亚	Indonesia	666	1018	1743	2096
马来西亚	Malaysia	1440	1813	2983	3402
新加坡	Singapore	2131	3368	5254	4149
泰国	Thailand	1095	1014	1873	1962
印度	India	1392	2003	2549	3407
欧洲小计	**Total of Europe**	**14332**	**15323**	**19714**	**27927**
#英国	United Kingdom	2140	2688	3262	4453
法国	France	1848	2248	2861	4188
德国	Germany	2107	2603	3126	4985
意大利	Italy	1462	1728	2231	3085
俄罗斯	Russia	798	793	1661	1837
美州小计	**Total of America**	**10266**	**10711**	**14083**	**17876**
#美国	United States	7005	7985	11240	14059
加拿大	Canada	1350	1729	2104	2681
大洋州小计	**Total of Oceania**	**2713**	**2951**	**3818**	**5259**
#澳大利亚	Australia	1649	2047	2725	3854
非州小计	**Total of Africa**	**797**	**1160**	**1593**	**2164**
其他小计	**Others**	**2305**	**1781**	**1337**	**1571**

7－13　宁波市前十名出口企业

The Order Table of Frist 10 Enterprises For Export In Ningbo

(2003)

企业名称 Name of Enterprise	排名 Seating Arrangement
宁波市慈溪进出口股份有限公司 Ningbo Cixi Import & Expirt Company Ltd.	1
中基宁波对外贸易股份有限公司 Chian – Base Ningbo Comercio Exterior Company Ltd..	2
宁波维科联合进出口有限公司 Ningbo Veken United Import & Export Company Ltd.	3
宁波海田国际贸易有限公司 Ningbo Haitian Internnatioanl Trade Company Ltd.	4
宁波市鄞县对外贸易有限责任公司 Ningbo Yinxian Foreign Trade Company Ltd.	5
宁波联合集团进出口股份有限公司 Ningbo United Group Import & Export Company Ltd.	6
宁波市工艺品进出口公司 Ningbo Arts & Crafts Imp. & Exp. Corp	7
浙江远大进出口有限公司 Zhejiang Yuanda Import & Export Company Ltd.	8
宁波申洲世通针织有限公司 Ningbo Shenzhou Shitong Weaving Group Company Ltd.	9
中化宁波进出口有限公司 China Chemicals Import & Export Company Ltd. Ningbo Branch	10

7－14　宁波市前十名进口企业

The Order Table of First 10 Enterprises For Import In Ningbo

(2003)

企业名称 Name of Enterprise	排名 Seating Arrangement
宁波波导股份有限公司 Ningbo Bird Company Ltd.	1
宁波宝新不锈钢有限公司 Ningbo Baoxin Stainless Steel Company ltd.	2
浙江远大进出口有限公司 Zhejiang YuandaImport & Export Company Ltd.	3
中基宁波对外贸易股份有限公司 Chian－Base Ningbo Comercio Exterior S.A.	4
中国石化镇海炼油化工股份有限公司 Sinopec Zhenhai Refining & Chemical Company Ltd.	5
宁波乐金甬兴化工有限公司 Ningbo Lejin Yongxing Chemical Industry Company Ltd.	6
宁波华东 BP 液化石油有限公司 Ningbo East China BP LPG Co.	7
宁波中华纸业有限公司 Ningbo Zhonghua Paper Company Ltd.	8
宁波宁兴集团公司 Ningbo Ningxing Group Corp	9
宁波市工艺品进出口公司 Ningbo Arts & Crafts Import & Export Corp	10

主要指标解释

【进出口总额】 海关进出口总额是指实际进出我国国境的货物总金额。包括对外贸易实际进出口货物,来料加工装配进出口货物,国家间、联合国及国际组织无偿援助物资和赠送品,华侨、港澳台同胞和外籍华人捐赠品,租赁期满归承租人所有的租赁货物,进料加工进出口货物,边境地方贸易及边境地区小额贸易进出口货物(边民互市贸易除外),中外合资经营企业、中外合作经营企业、外商独资经营企业进出口货物和公用物品,到、离岸价格在规定限额以上的进出口货样和广告品(无商业价值、无使用价值和免费提供出口的除外),从保税仓库提取在中国境内销售的进口货物以及其他进出口货物。进出口总额用以观察一个国家在对外贸易方面的总规模。我国规定出口货物按离岸价格计算,进口货物按到岸价格计算。

【利用外资】 指我国各级政府、部门、企业和其他经济组织通过对外借款、吸收外商直接投资以及用其他方式筹措的境外现汇、设备、技术等。

【对外借款】 是我国利用外资的主要部分。包括我国通过外国政府贷款,国际金融组织贷款,外国银行商业贷款,出口信贷以及对外发行债券,股票等方式,从境外筹措的资金。

【外商直接投资】 是指外国企业和经济组织或个人(包括华侨、港澳台胞以及 我国在境外注册的企业)按我国有关政策、法规,用现汇、实物、技术等在我国境内开办外 商独资企业、与我国境内的企业或经济组织共同举办中外合资经营企业、合作经营企业或作 合作开发资源的投资(包括外商投资收益的再投资)以及经政府有关部门批准的项目投资总 额内,企业从境外借入的资金。

【外商其他投资】 指除对外借款和外商直接投资以外的各种利用外资的形式。包括企业在境内外股票市场公开发行的以外币计价的股票(目前主要是在香港证券市场发行的 H 股和在境内证券市场发行的 B 股)发行价总额,国际租赁进口设备的应付款,补充贸易中外商提供的进口设备、技术、物料的价款,加工装配贸易中外商提供的进口设备、物料的价款。

【旅游人数】 包括入境国际旅游者人数、出境居民人数和国内旅游者人数。

⑴入境国际旅游者人数:指来中国参观、访问、旅行、探亲、访友、休养、考察、参加会议和从事经济、科技、文化、教育、宗教等活动的外国人、港澳和台湾同胞的人数。不包括外国在我国的常驻机构,如使领馆、通讯社、企业办事处的工作人员;来我国常住的外国专家、留学生以及在岸逗留不过夜人员。

⑵出境居民人数:指大陆居民因公务活动或私人事务短期出境的人数。公务活动出境居民人数包括在国际交通工具上的中国服务员工,因私出境居民人数不包括在国际交通工具上的中国服务员工。

⑶国内旅游者人数:指我国大陆居民和在我国常住 1 年以上的外国人、港澳台同胞离开常住地在境内其他地方的旅游设施内至少停留一夜,最长不超过 6 个月的人数。

【国际旅游(外汇)收入】 指入境旅游的外国人、华侨、港澳台同胞在中国大陆旅游过程中发生的一切旅游支出,对国家来说就是国际旅游(外汇)收入。

Explanatory Notes on Main Statistical Indicators

【Total Imports and Exports】 refer to the value of commodities imported into and exported from the boundary of China. They include the actual imports and exports through foreign trade, imported and exported goods under the processing and assembling trades and materials, supplies and gifts as aid given gratis between government and by the United Nations and other international organizations, and contributions denoted by overseas Chinese, compatriots in Hong Kong, Macao and Taiwan and Chinese with foreign citizenship, leasing commodities owned by tenants at the expiration of leasing period, the imported and exported commodities processed with imported materials, commodities trading, imported and exported small value trading goods in border areas (excluding mutual change goods), the imported and exported commodities and articles for public use of the Sino – foreign joint ventures, Sino – foreign cooperative enterprises and ventures exclusively with foreign own investment. They also included import and export of samples and advertising goods for those CIF or FOB value are beyond the permitted ceiling (excluding goods of no trading or no use value and free commodities for export), imported goods sold in China from bonded warehouse and other imported and exported goods. The indicator of total imports and exports at customs can be used to observe the total size of external trade in a country. In accordance with the stipulation of the Chinese government, imports are calculated at CIF, while exports are calculated at FOB.

FOB refer to Free on Board.

CIF refer to Cost Insurance and Freight.

【Utilization of Foreign Capital】 refers to remittance, equipment and technology financed from abroad, by loans, foreign direct investment and other forms undertaken by the Chinese governments at all levels, by various departments, enterprises and other economic units.

【Foreign Loans】 a major part of China's utilization of foreign capital, refer to funds borrowed from abroad, including loans of foreign governments, loans of international financial institutions, commercial loans of foreign banks, export credit, and funds raised by Chinese bonds and shares issued abroad.

【Direct Investment by Foreign Entrepreneurs】 refers to the investments inside China by foreign enterprises and economic organizations or individuals (including overseas Chinese, compatriots from Hong Kong and Macao, and Chinese enterprises registered abroad), following the relevant policies and laws of China, for the establishment of ventures exclusively with foreign own investment, Sino – foreign joint ventures and cooperative enterprises or for cooperative exploration of resources with enterprises or economic organizations in China. It includes the re – investment of the foreign entrepreneurs with the profits gained from the investment and the funds that enterprises borrow from abroad in the total investment of projects which are approved by the relevant department of the government.

【Other Overseas Investments】 refer to all kinds of investments except the foreign loan and the FDI. They include: the total value(in foreign currency) of the stocks of one enterprises distributed publicly both at home and abroad(now mainly refer to H.shares at HK bond market, and B.shares at China mainland bond market); the rent charges of the foreign equipments; the total value of Technology, raw material and foreign equipment provided by foreign investors in supplemental trades, and value of foreign raw material, equipment in the trade of assemble machining.

【tourists number】 is a sum of overseas tourists, local residents going abroad and domestic tourists. overseas tourists number. Which refers to the number of foreigners and residents from Hongkong, Macao and Taiwan who come to China to go sightseeing, travel, visit relatives and friends, spend holidays, inspect, attend conferences and to do activities in economics, science, education, religious etc. Personnel as below are not taken into calculation, office workers in Chinese standing bodies at abroad, such as in embassies, news agencies, oversea offices of companies. Foreign experts and students living in China and foreigners who enter China only for voyage transferring are also not calculated. number of local residents going abroad. Which refers to the number of mainland China residents who go abroad either for official business or for private affairs. Number of Chinese workers who serve in the international transportation vehicles are included in those who exit for official business, but not in those for private affairs. domestic tourists. Which refers to the number of people who leave their living places to stay in the tourism facilities for at least one night but no more than 6 months, including mainland China residents, foreigners, residents from HK, Macao and TW who lived in China for more than one year.

【Foreign Exchange Earnings from International Tourism】 refer to the total expenditures of the foreigners, overseas Chinese, compatriots from HongKong, Macao and Taiwan in the process of their tourism in the mainland of China. Their expenditures mentioned above are foreign exchange earnings to China.

8

科学技术

CHAPTER 8 SCIENCE AND TECHNOLOGY

科学技术
Science and Technology

主要统计指标
Major Statistics Indicators

2003年科技成果进步奖	Scientific and Technological Progress Prizes	73	个	unit
比上年增长	Increase Over Last Year	-32.4	%	
2003年授权专利数	Number of Patent Applications Approved	3414	个	unit
比上年增长	Increase Over Last Year	22.8	%	
2003年高中级技术职称人员数	Number of Personnel with Senior and Medium Qualification	7074	人	person
比上年增长	Increase Over Last Year	7.5	%	
2003年科技活动经费筹集额	Funding for Scientific and Technological Activities	286538	万元	10000 yuan
比上年增长	Increase Over Last Year	33.6	%	
2003年科技活动经费支出	Expenditures of Scientific and Technological Activities	230131.2	万元	10000 yuan
比上年增长	Increase Over Last Year	31.0	%	
2003年研究与试验发展经费支出	Expenditure of R&D	94795.8	万元	10000 yuan
比上年增长	Increase Over Last Year	44.6	%	

8－1 市级以上科技成果鉴定、获奖、专利权情况

Basic Statistics on Verification, Award－Winning and Patent Right of Above City Level

项目	Item	2001	2002	2003
科技成果鉴定	Scientific and Technological Assessment of Results	280	285	310
科技进步奖	Scientific and Technological Progress Prizes	115	108	73
省级	Province Level	22	26	5
市级	Municipal Level	93	82	68
授权专利数	Number of Patent Applications Approved	2148	2780	3414
# 发明	Inventions	34	44	78
实用新型	Utility Models	689	728	890
外观设计	Designs	1425	2008	2446

8－2 科协系统情况

The Status of Science and Technology Associations

项目	Item	2001	2002	2003
基本情况	**Basic Situation**			
科技机构数(个)	Insitutions of Science and Technology(unit)	74	77	77
科学家与工程师(人)	Scientist and Engineer (person)	180	143	157
活动情况	**Activity Situation**			
学术交流会参加人数(人)	Participants of Academic Seminar(person)	12736	16032	9192
论文数(篇)	Papers Presented (paper)	4363	4007	1148
学术报告会参加人数(人)	Participants of Academic Symposium(person)	45575	16365	3623
科普讲座参加人数	Particapants of Activities for Popular Science	102481	122181	188636
青少年科技竞赛参加人数	Teenagers Particapants in Scinece－technology Competitions	36396	184850	
科技培训班参加人数	Particapants of Scinece－technology Training	6499	58289	56950
科技咨询服务完成合同数(个)	Scinece－technology Consultative Contratcs Completed (kind)	828	852	1298
实现金额 (万元)	Revenue for Fulfillment of Contract (10000 yuan)	1017	2663	1545

8－3　科技活动单位主要指标综合表

(2003)

项目		Item	
单位数	(个)	Number of Enterprises	(unit)
#有科技活动	(个)	Number of Enterprises with Scientific and Technical Activities	(unit)
科技活动人员合计	(人)	Number of Persons Engaged in Scientific and Technical Activities	(person)
科技活动经费筹集额	(万元)	Funds for Scientific and Technical Activities	(10000) yuan)
科技活动经费支出	(万元)	Expenditures for Scientific and Technical Activities	(10000 yuan)
#内部支出	(万元)	Internal Expenditures	(10000 yuan)
#R&D经费	(万元)	R&D	(10000 yuan)
用于科研基建经费支出	(万元)	Expenditures for Capital Construction of Research	(10000 yuan)
全部科技项目数	(项)	Total Number of Scientific and Technical Projects	(unit)
全部项目参加人员合计	(人)	Number of Persons Engaged in All Projects	(person)
全部项目内部支出经费	(万元)	Internal Expenditures for All Projects	(10000 yuan)
#R&D经费	(万元)	R&D	(10000 yuan)
技术引进经费支出	(万元)	Expenditures of Technical Introduce	(10000 yuan)
#引进设计图纸工艺配方专利的支出	(万元)	Expenditures for Introduce Design drawing and Technology Fills a Prescription	(10000 yuan)
购买国内技术经费支出	(万元)	Expenditures for Purchases of Domestic Technologies	(10000 yuan)
单位办科技机构数	(个)	Number of Scientific and Technological Institutions Run by Enterprises	(unit)
机构中科技活动人员	(人)	Personnel of Scientific and Technological Research Institutions	(person)
科技机构科技经费内部支出	(万元)	Internal Expenditures Scientific and Technological Research Institutions	(10000 yuan)

Main Indicators of Enterprises with Scientific and Technical Activities

全部调查单位 Total Enterprises	农业企事业单位 Agricultural Enterprises and Institutions	全部工业单位 Industrial Enterprises	#大中型 Large - sized and Medium sized	#规模以上小型 Small - sized above Designated Sized	软件开发单位 Software Development Enterprises	排重后的民营科技企业(单位) Private Scientific and Technological Enterprises
1147	55	1021	401	576	57	6
913	54	798	216	540	50	3
20769	471	18870	9836	8737	372	25
288345.0	5726.2	274008.0	166945.9	104404.1	1790.6	117.6
232141.2	4908.4	219063.6	129480.4	87119.8	1752.7	76.8
215644.5	4884.1	202724.5	119788.9	80531.2	1747.4	76.8
94795.8	1382.1	87229.6	56276.7	30423.8	737.8	76.8
28887.5	1269.7	27614.3	15056.1	11809.2		
2085	168	1822	678	1088	68	8
17666	460	15873	7735	7857	280	22
198372.0	4735.2	186776.0	113805.3	70698.0	1348.6	76.8
90245.0	1379.8	82810.4	55757.6	26525.7	664.8	76.8
60147.1	325.0	59816.3	43549.2	16215.1	5.8	
5143.0		5142.5	3910.6	1205.4	0.5	
3577.7		3569.7	2203.3	1366.4	8.0	
373	14	354	141	212	3	1
9558	80	9431	5295	4128	23	15
109020.9	836.6	107620.3	72719.6	34888.7	456.4	17.6

8－4　科技活动单位人员基本情况

单位：人　　(2003)

项目	Item	企业数（个）Number of Units (unti)	有科技活动企业数 With Scientific & Technological Activties
总计	**Total**	**1147**	**913**
按国民经济行业大类分组	Group by Sector		
农、林、牧、渔服务业	Farming, Forestry, Animal Husbandary and Fisgery Services	12	11
农副食品加工业	Agricultural Non－staple Food Processing	18	11
食品制造业	Food Manufacturing	11	8
饮料制造业	Beverage Manufacturing	6	4
纺织业	Textile Industry	51	20
纺织服装、鞋、帽制造业	Textile Clothing, shoes, cap Manufacturing	35	10
文教体育用品制造业	Cultural, Educational and Sports Goods	32	21
化学原料及化学制品制造业	Chemical Raw Materials and Chemical Products	37	36
医药制造业	Medical and Pharmaceutical Products	19	19
化学纤维制造业	Chemical Fiber	13	9
橡胶制品业	Rubber Products	11	9
塑料制品业	Plastic Products	45	31
非金属矿物制品业	Nonmetal Mineral Products	13	11
黑色金属冶炼及压延加工业	Smelting and Pressing of Ferrous Metals	10	6
有色金属冶炼及压延加工业	Smelting and Pressing of Nonferrous Metals	16	12
金属制品业	Metal Products	39	31
通用设备制造业	General Equipment Manufacturing	170	146
专用设备制造业	Equipment Manufacturing for Special Purpose	55	51
交通运输设备制造业	Transport Equipment Manufacturing	89	80
电气机械及器材制造业	Electric Equipment and Machinery	188	153
通信设备、计算机及其他电子设备	Communication Equipment, Computer and Other Electric Equipment Manufacturing	74	65
仪器仪表及文化、办公用机械制造业	Instruments, Meters, Cultural and Office Machinery	40	36
计算机服务业和软件业	Computer Services and Software	58	51
国家机构	Government Agencies	25	25

Basic Statistics on Persons Engaged in Scientific & Technological Activties Units

(person)

专业技术人员 Specialized Technical Personnel	# 工程技术人员 Engineering	科技活动人员合计 Total of Scientific & Technical Personnel	# 全时人员 Full - time Personnel	# 高中级技术职称人员 Personnel with Senior and Medium Qualification	无高级职称的大本及以上学历人员 Personnel without Senior and Medium but with or Over University Education	# 研究与试验发展人员 Personnel for Research & Development
48047	**24027**	**20769**	**13443**	**6764**	**6561**	**9093**
106	66	79	56	30	5	33
465	198	123	60	51	38	42
240	101	115	81	35	57	52
310	164	40	23	7	27	27
2375	1101	420	222	164	111	122
4518	685	428	360	81	131	162
1603	667	445	297	102	140	106
801	546	442	326	130	171	172
519	305	237	170	89	69	112
438	259	102	41	33	12	58
220	150	213	129	65	82	104
981	450	539	377	146	187	322
247	126	158	80	72	39	42
318	170	116	21	50	43	5
559	273	388	227	86	149	248
783	386	429	300	165	114	175
4992	3311	3389	2278	981	973	1232
1671	976	1224	854	364	327	488
2895	1553	1806	1210	548	648	696
6774	3951	3433	1961	956	1025	1267
4809	2613	2650	2254	769	1212	1507
1890	973	1234	985	309	424	589
405	175	382	352	72	156	121
244	30	210	121	82	27	66

8－5　科技活动单位科技活动经费筹集及支出情况

单位:万元　　(2003)

项目	Item	科技活动经费筹集总额 Funding for Scientific and Technological Activities	企业资金 Funds Self Raised by Enterprises
总计	**Total**	**288345.0**	**241262.0**
按国民经济行业大类分组	Group by Sector		
农、林、牧、渔服务业	Farming, Forestry, Animal Husbandary and Fisgery Services	1570.6	36.0
农副食品加工业	Agricultural Non－staple Food Processing	2678.5	1641.0
食品制造业	Food Manufacturing	2414.0	2076.0
饮料制造业	Beverage Manufacturing	853.9	297.0
纺织业	Textile Industry	6933.4	6886.2
纺织服装、鞋、帽制造业	Textile Clothing, shoes, cap Manufacturing	9526.4	8153.4
文教体育用品制造业	Cultural, Educational and Sports Goods	3923.7	3168.0
化学原料及化学制品制造业	Chemical Raw Materials and Chemical Products	4702.1	3625.3
医药制造业	Medical and Pharmaceutical Products	3026.3	2691.4
化学纤维制造业	Chemical Fiber	1505.6	1049.6
橡胶制品业	Rubber Products	3657.1	3357.1
塑料制品业	Plastic Products	6828.8	6230.8
非金属矿物制品业	Nonmetal Mineral Products	4579.3	3900.3
黑色金属冶炼及压延加工业	Smelting and Pressing of Ferrous Metals	3145.1	3145.1
有色金属冶炼及压延加工业	Smelting and Pressing of Nonferrous Metals	7902.1	7602.1
金属制品业	Metal Products	6648.2	4568.6
通用设备制造业	General Equipment Manufacturing	50532.9	37467.1
专用设备制造业	Equipment Manufacturing for Special Purpose	19854.2	18153.3
交通运输设备制造业	Transport Equipment Manufacturing	29949.0	25807.3
电气机械及器材制造业	Electric Equipment and Machinery	43465.2	38202.4
通信设备、计算机及其他电子设备	Communication Equipment, Computer and Other Electric Equipment Manufacturing	30591.7	26679.1
仪器仪表及文化、办公用机械制造业	Instruments, Meters, Cultural and Office Machinery	9454.8	8681.8
计算机服务业和软件业	Computer Services and Software	1790.6	1292.6
国家机构	Government Agencies	2091.8	3.0

Funding and Expenditures for Scientific & Technological Activities Units

(10000 yuan)

金融机构贷款 Bank Loans	来自政府部门的资金 Funds from Government	科研活动经费支出总额 Expenditures of Scientific and Technological Activities	内部支出合计 Internal Expenditure	#研究与试验发展经费支出 Expenditure of R&D	#新产品开发经费支出 Expenditure of New Products	外部支出合计 External Expenditure	用于科研基建经费支出 Expenditures for Capital Construction of Research
26317.0	**13664.5**	**232141.2**	**215644.5**	**94795.8**	**138316.7**	**16496.7**	**28887.5**
	609.7	873.1	868.3	190.5		4.8	553.5
700.6	336.0	2293.7	2269.1	817.2	886.1	24.6	131.0
200.0	138.0	2362.0	2329.5	292.5	1960.0	32.5	720.0
370.0	11.0	831.9	831.9	90.5	305.0		
	47.2	5801.9	5663.3	1495.8	3192.6	138.6	450.8
403.0	970.0	4755.2	4492.4	1175.9	2215.6	262.8	475.4
600.0	155.7	4060.5	3900.4	1134.2	3073.6	160.1	1734.7
554.0	250.8	4617.6	4157.1	1471.1	3127.9	460.5	443.5
40.0	294.9	2912.4	2417.2	1101.0	1131.8	495.2	50.0
150.0	16.0	1220.1	1201.1	990.0	860.3	19.0	280.0
100.0		2321.1	2311.1	630.5	1959.9	10.0	
230.0	88.0	6243.4	6118.0	3472.0	4769.9	125.4	1417.7
510.0	143.0	2697.6	2672.2	366.0	2494.7	25.4	
		3200.9	3200.9	15.2	2758.3		
250.0		7819.0	7819.0	6515.6	2957.6		150.2
1905.0	74.6	5358.0	3149.3	1060.2	2523.5	2208.7	748.7
7848.7	3023.3	33545.0	32198.2	11500.5	22371.7	1346.8	4580.5
1070.0	556.2	17350.2	16190.9	10432.8	11131.4	1159.3	3223.2
3447.7	336.0	19329.3	18594.6	8431.7	15128.3	734.7	4247.4
4217.0	531.8	40529.7	37241.3	13286.9	24571.0	3288.4	3694.0
3071.0	783.2	25499.1	24580.1	15949.2	20079.8	919.0	3250.5
305.0	140.0	9400.8	8061.8	3885.1	5356.8	1339.0	1195.7
5.0	33.0	1832.0	1826.7	805.1		5.3	
	1695.9	2066.2	2056.7	433.7		9.5	

8－6 科技活动单位科技成果及技术引进、改造和吸收情况

单位：万元　　(2003)

项目	Item	专利申请数（件）Patents Submitted for Examination (unit)	拥有发明专利（件）Patents Granted (unit)
总计	**Total**	**1820**	**378**
按国民经济行业大类分组	Group by Sector		
农、林、牧、渔服务业	Farming, Forestry, Animal Husbandary and Fisgery Services		
农副食品加工业	Agricultural Non－staple Food Processing	5	2
食品制造业	Food Manufacturing	3	
饮料制造业	Beverage Manufacturing		
纺织业	Textile Industry		
纺织服装、鞋、帽制造业	Textile Clothing, shoes, cap Manufacturing		
文教体育用品制造业	Cultural, Educational and Sports Goods	538	1
化学原料及化学制品制造业	Chemical Raw Materials and Chemical Products	7	2
医药制造业	Medical and Pharmaceutical Products	2	1
化学纤维制造业	Chemical Fiber	14	4
橡胶制品业	Rubber Products	123	4
塑料制品业	Plastic Products	60	21
非金属矿物制品业	Nonmetal Mineral Products	2	
黑色金属冶炼及压延加工业	Smelting and Pressing of Ferrous Metals	3	2
有色金属冶炼及压延加工业	Smelting and Pressing of Nonferrous Metals	22	6
金属制品业	Metal Products	96	26
通用设备制造业	General Equipment Manufacturing	135	66
专用设备制造业	Equipment Manufacturing for Special Purpose	28	8
交通运输设备制造业	Transport Equipment Manufacturing	23	14
电气机械及器材制造业	Electric Equipment and Machinery	538	113
通信设备、计算机及其他电子设备	Communication Equipment, Computer and Other Electric Equipment Manufacturing	94	53
仪器仪表及文化、办公用机械制造业	Instruments, Meters, Cultural and Office Machinery	79	38
计算机服务业和软件业	Computer Services and Software	4	
国家机构	Government Agencies		1

Results and Expenditures for Technical Introduce, Innovations and Absorption of Scientific and Technological Activities Units

(10000 yuan)

全部科技项目(项) Total Number of Scientific and Technical Projects (unit)	# 新产品开发项目(项) Development for Newly Products (unit)	全部科技项目参加人员合计(人) Number of Persons Engaged in All Projects	技术改造经费支出 Expenditures of Technical Innovation	技术引进经费支出 Expenditures of Technical Introduce	引进设计图纸工艺配方专利支出 Expenditures for Introduce Design drawing and Technology Fills a Prescription	消化吸收经费支出 Expenditures for Technical Absorption	购买国内技术经费支出 Expenditures for Purchases of Domestic Technologies
2085	**1464**	**17666**	**324962.5**	**60147.1**	**5143.0**	**2437.0**	**3577.7**
25		78					
27	11	114	1569.0	1330.0			
12	11	105	4300.0				
5	5	34					
36	25	381	21967.3	3950.3		4.0	
19	18	203	1588.0	60.9			
39	37	408	3934.5	92.5	29.0	192.0	37.1
65	54	431	2376.0	1069.7	52.0	220.0	30.0
45	39	197	778.0	775.0	5.0		
9	6	97	148.5	0.2	0.2	10.0	27.1
10	10	208	2461.4	1040.0	7.2		
72	60	522	1407.4	338.5	109.5	59.5	92.5
14	12	142	525.6	592.6	20.0		
24	5	114	56.2	1057.8	1057.8		
22	15	320	6821.0	97.1	14.0		25.0
55	49	381	2750.6	1456.9	3.0		
286	235	2927	51654.5	10446.3	482.6	737.0	817.3
123	111	933	8684.8	2406.3	2190.2	39.5	68.0
157	134	1610	8050.3	6367.5	270.4	230.8	147.2
377	344	3095	39186.4	4796.0	632.5	398.5	1794.6
208	137	1993	6480.4	9042.8	136.9	15.7	176.2
140	110	911	10054.6	3486.5	127.2	527.0	54.7
69		290	14.5	5.8	0.5	3.0	8.0
92		200					

8－7　科技活动单位与科技机构基本情况

(2003)

项目	Item	机构数（个）Number of Institutions (unit)
总计	**Total**	**373**
按工业企业规模分组	**Grouped by Size of Enterprises**	
大型企业	Large－Size	20
中型企业	Medium－Size	121
小型企业	Small－Size	213
按登记注册类型分组	**Grouped by Registration Status**	
内资企业	Domestic Funds	290
港、澳、台商投资公司	Enterprises with Investment form Hongkong, Macao and Taiwan	40
外商投资企业公司	Enterprises with Foreign Investment	43
按学科分组	**Grouped by Discipline**	
自然科学	Natural Science	16
农业科学	Agricultural Science	18
医药科学	Medicinal Science	10
工程与技术科学	Project and Technological Sciences	324
人文与社会科学	Humanity and Social Science	5
按机构组成类型分组	**Grouped by Operate Jointly Way**	
与境外机构合办	With the Abroad Organization	8
与国内高校合办	With the Domestic University	21
与国内独立研究机构合办	With the Domestic Independent Research Institution	9
与境内注册外商独资企业合办	With Registering Solely Foreign－owned Enterprise within the Border	4
与境内注册其他企业合办	With Registering Other Enterprises within the Border	6
单位自办	Instituions Run by Enterprises	307
其他	Others	18
按机构运营状况分组	**Grouped by Running the Status**	
有经常性开发任务	Having Regular Development Tasks	334
有稳定经费来源	Having Stabilize Source of Funds	332
有一定的测试条件	Having Certain Test Conditions	347
参与新产品市场调查或生产销售	Participate Market Survey or Production and Sales of New Products	340

Basic Statisitcs on Scientific and Technological Activities Units and Institutions

参加项目人员合计（人） Number Persons of Engaged in Projects (person)	#高中级技术职称人员 Personnel with Senior and Medium Qualification	无高级职称的大本及以上学历人员 Personnel without Senior and Medium but with or Over University Education	#研究与试验发展人员 Personnel for Research & Development	科技经费内部支出（万元） Internal Expenditures for Scientific and Technological Activities (10000 yuan)	#研究与试验发展经费 Expenditure for R&D
9558	**3147**	**3154**	**4014**	**109020.9**	**48030.7**
1141	568	406	736	22084.5	11290.2
4154	1206	1482	1669	50635.1	21613.8
4136	1306	1241	1525	34900.7	14202.9
7686	2582	2596	3253	83968.3	36882.5
995	327	288	427	14009.5	8007.2
877	238	270	334	11043.1	3141.0
350	139	106	175	9181.1	5444.6
124	61	24	72	1764.3	1187.2
162	70	44	66	1812.6	692.9
8853	2868	2960	3686	95828.9	40560.5
69	9	20	15	434.0	145.5
184	88	79	128	4491.7	2345.4
602	225	230	385	5534.1	3926.1
172	67	62	21	1828.1	255.4
118	43	43	48	1379.8	140.0
93	27	17	57	611.2	370.1
8202	2642	2678	3305	93816.5	40108.4
187	55	45	70	1359.5	885.3
8957	3005	2962	3921	103733.5	45647.2
8909	2944	3028	3883	101699.4	45182.7
9295	3064	3099	3985	107210.0	47724.5
9002	2955	3030	3809	101082.9	44293.0

8－8　计量标准质监情况

项目		Item		全市 Total
计量验收情况		**Measuring Implements Test**		
已开展强制检定数	(项)	Measurement Implement Tested Compulsively	(kind)	81
开展强制检定种数	(种)	The Kind of Measurement Implement Tested Compulsively	(kind)	113
强制检定实际检出数	(件)	Actual Quantity Checked by Compulsively Examined Out	(piece)	142080
计量仪器实际检出数	(件)	Actual Quantity Checked by Messurement Implement Tested	(piece)	386504
质监情况		**Qualtiy Supervision**		
国家监督抽查批次	(批次)	Batch of supervises and Check by Country	(batch. time)	245
#合格批次	(批次)	Regular Batch	(batch. time)	197
批次合格率	(%)	Ratio of Regular by Batch	(%)	80.40
省定期监督抽查企业数	(个)	Number of Enterpriese of Periodic Supervises and Check by Province	(unit)	2159
省定期监督抽查批次	(批次)	Batch of Periodic supervises and Check by Province	(batch. time)	2328
#合格批次	(批次)	Regular Batch	(batch. time)	2015
批次合格率	(%)	Ratio of Regular by Batch	(%)	86.60
宁波市质量指数	(%)	Index of Product Quality about NingBo	(%)	93.60

市区 Urban District	# 鄞州 Yinzhou	余姚市 Yuyao	慈溪市 Cixi	奉化市 Fenghua	象山县 Xiangshan	宁海县 Ninghai
28	8	13	3	8	8	5
44	14	21	8	13	18	9
110523	6500	15346	6266	1678	7197	1070
275828	43842	49288	26141	3096	10351	21800
107	31	37	75	6	5	15
88	25	33	52	6	4	14
82.89	80.65	89.19	69.33	100.00	80.00	93.33
885	332	480	469	167	77	81
931	354	506	540	177	80	94
857	323	412	451	147	62	86
93.00	91.20	81.40	83.50	83.10	77.50	91.50
99.66	93.00	87.99	94.80	96.30	92.40	99.50

主要指标解释

【从事科技活动人员】 指单位在报告期内，从事科技开发活动的时间(不包括加班时间)占全年工作时间 10%及以上的专业技术人员、管理人员、辅助人员及其他人员。

【全时人员】 指报告年内从事科技活动的时间占全年工作时间 90%及以上的人员数。

【非全时人员】 指报告年内从事科技活动的时间占全年工作时间 10%(含 10%)~90%(不含 90%)的人员数。

【从事研究与发展活动人员】 指报告期参与研究与发展项目(课题)研究、管理和辅助工作的人员，具体包括直接参加研究与发展项目(课题)人员，直接参与上述项目(课题)的行政管理人员和直接为上述项目(课题)活动提供服务的辅助人员。包括从事基础研究、应用研究、实验发展的人员。

【科技活动经费筹集总额】 指报告年内调查单位从各种渠道筹集到的科技活动经费(含科技基建费)总额。具体包括单位自筹资金、银行贷款、上级拨款和其他。

【科技活动经费支出总额】 指报告期内单位用于科技活动的全部实际支出。包括劳务费、科研业务费、科研管理费、非基建投资购建的固定资产、科研基建支出以及其他用于科技活动的支出。包括内部支出和外部支出，不包括生产性活动支出及归还贷款支出。

【科技活动经费内部支出】 指单位在报告年度用于内部开展科技活动实际支出的费用，包括外协加工费。不包括委托研制或合作研制而支付外单位的经费。科技活动经费内部支出按用途分为科技活动人员劳务费、原材料费、购买与自制设备支出、其他支出。

【研究与发展经费支出】 指报告期内本单位用于研究与发展活动的经费内部支出。具体包括研究与发展项目(课题)经费支出，从事研究与发展项目(课题)的科技人员与管理人员劳务费以及其他非研究与发展项目(课题)经费而用于研究与发展活动的各项经费支出。

【劳务费(含工资)】 指单位当年以货币或实物形式直接或间接支付给从事科技活动人员从事科技活动期间的劳动报酬及各种费用。包括各种形式的工资(补助工资)、津贴、奖金、福利、离退休人员费用、人民助学金等。

【原材料费】 单位当年用于科技活动实际消耗的原材料、辅助材料、备用配件、外购半成品、燃料、动力、包装物以及其他材料等。

【外部支出合计】 指单位委托外单位或与外单位合作进行的科技活动而拨给对方的科技活动经费支出合计。

【单位办科技机构】 指单位自办、或与外单位合办、管理上同生产系统相对独立的，或单独核算的专门技术开发机构(如办研究所、开发中心、开发部等专门技术开发机构)。

【科技机构从业人员年末数】 指在报告期的最后一天，在科技机构中工作并取得劳动报酬或经营收入的全部从业人员数。

【对外转让科技成果收入】 指报告年内本单位对外转让本单位科学研究和技术开发成果的收入。

【专利申请数】 指当年单位向专利管理机关提出专利申请并被受理的件数。

【购买国内技术支出】 指本单位在报告年内为发展本单位的生产经营，而购买国内(其它单位)技术成果的经费支出，包括购买设计图纸、工艺、配方、关键设备等所支付的经费额。

Explanatory Notes on Main Statistical Indicators

【Science and Technology Personnel】 refers to the professional experts, managerial personnel, auxiliary persons who spend 10% or more of their total working time for science and technology researches with in a year.

【Full – Time Personnel】 refers to the persons who spend 90% or more of their total working time for science and technology researches with in a year.

【Non – Full – Time Personnel】 refers to the persons who spend 10%(included) – – 90%(not included) of their total working time for science and technology researches with in a year.

【Personnel in Research and Development Activities】 refers to personnel who directly work for the research and development of a certain project (subject), who directly manage the project (subject) and who directly provide supplement service to it. Include the basic research staff, applied research staff and the development staff.

【The Total Collection of The S&T Fund】 refers to the total amount of the fund for S&T which raised by the investigation unit from varies of ways in a reporting year, including self – collected fund, bank loans, allocations and others. Note: S&T is short form of science and technology, same as follows.

【The Total Expenditures of The S&T Fund】 refers to total actual expenditure for science and technology activities of a unit in a reporting period. Including remuneration, researching fee, managing fee of the research, fixed assets of non – fundamental investment, fundamental investment and other expenditure both inside and outside the unit for science and technology activities. Regular expenditures for productive activities and returning of the loans are excluded.

【Internal Expenditures of the S&T Fund】 refer to the actual expenditures of a unit for internal science and technology activities in a reporting year, including 外协加工费。Fees paid to the other units for their works and co – operations in the researches are excluded. To serve the different purposes, the internal expenditures can be classified as the remunerations for science and technology staffs, cost of raw materials, expenditures for buying and making of the equipments, other expenditures.

【Expenditures for Research and Development】 refers to the internal expenditures of a unit for research and development. Including the expenditures for research and development of a project (subject) itself, remunerations for researching and managing staffs and all other expenditures for project (subject) related activities.

【Remunerations(Including Wages)】 refers to the rewards paid directly or indirectly to the science and technology staffs either in forms of currency or in form of materials by the unit. Including all kinds of wages (subsidies), allowance, bonus, welfares, pensions, people's stipend etc.

【Cost of Raw Materials】 refers to the raw materials, supplemental materials, spare fittings, purchased semi – finished articles, fuel, power, packages and other materials which had been actually consumed by a unit in science and technology activities.

【Total External Expenditure】 refers to the total amount of expenditures which one unit pays to other units for their works or co operations in S&T activities.

【S&T Organizations Run by the Unit】 refers to the professional technology developing organizations separately run by a certain unit or jointly managed by several units, which have comparatively independent managerial systems and productive systems, or have self – accounting status. Those organizations include research institutions, developing centers, developing departments etc.

【Year – end Number of Employees in S&T Organizations】 refers to the total number of employees in S&T organizations who acquire remunerations or business profits at the last day of the reporting period.

【Profits Gained from the Public Transactions of S&T Achievements】 refers to the profits one unit gained from the transactions of its S&T achievements to the others in a reporting year.

【Applied Number of Patents】 refers to the number of patent applied by a unit to the patent office and then accepted in a reporting year.

【Expenditures for Purchasing Technology Achievements in Domestic Market】 refers to the expenditures of a unit for purchasing the technology achievements from other units in domestic market in a reporting year, in order to develop its own business. Those achievements include blueprint of designs, industrial technology, formulas, key equipment, etc.

9

文教、卫生、体育

CHAPTER 9 CULTURE，EDUCATION，PUBLICHEALTH AND SPORTS

文教、卫生、体育
Culture, Education, Public Health and Sports

主要统计指标
Major Statistics Indicators

2003 年公共图书馆	Number of Public Libraries	9	个	unit
2003 年电影观众人次	Number of Spectator	123.4	万人次	10000 persons – times
2003 年各类学校数	Number of Various School	2669	所	unit
2003 年各类学校招生人数	Number of New Students Enrollment of Various Schools	258331	人	person
2003 年各类学校在校学生数	Number of Students Enrollment of Various Schools	1870642	人	person
2003 年各类学校毕业人数	Number of Graduates by Various Schools	889703	人	person
2003 年专任教师数	Number of Full – time Teacher	56133	人	person
2003 年高等学校在校生人数	Number of Students Enrollmentin Institutions of Higher Education	78886	人	person
2003 年医疗机构床位数	Number of Beds in Health Institutions	15279	张	bed
2003 年卫生技术人员数	Number of Medical Technical Personnel	21473	人	person
2003 年医生数	Number of Doctors	10630	人	person
2003 年学生国家体标达标率	Number of Persons Reaching National Standard	95.32	%	person
2003 年参赛获奖数	Number of Obtain Awards by Athletic Competition	361	枚	unit
2003 年有线电视用户数	Number of User Terminal for Cable TV Station	127.50	万户	10000 users

9－1 部分年份文化事业单位、机构、人员及活动情况

Basic Statistics of Cultural Institutions and Personnel in Partial Years

项目		Item		1999	2000	2001	2002	2003
艺术表演团体	**（个）**	**Art Performance Troupes**	**(unit)**	**8**	**9**	**9**	**8**	**6**
机构人员数	（人）	Persons of Institutions	(person)	327	312	316	312	309
国内演出场次	（场次）	Internal Performances	(times)	1011	934	1112	844	917
国内观众人次	（千人次）	Internal Spectator	(1000 persons times)	1131	1087	1102	1301	1234
艺术表演场所	**（所）**	**Art Performance Places**	**(unit)**	**10**	**10**	**10**	**10**	**9**
机构人员数	（人）	Persons of Institutions	(person)	248	245	232	219	203
演出场次	（场次）	Performances	(times)	6949	4230	3157	1874	1184
观众人次	（千人次）	Spectator	(1000 persons times)	61826	389	431	350	316
公共图书馆	**（个）**	**Public Libraries**	**(unit)**	**9**	**9**	**9**	**9**	**9**
机构人员数	（人）	Persons of Institutions	(person)	199	196	195	195	208
总藏量	（万册）	Total Collections	(10000 volumes)	165.9	177.0	185.0	193.2	204.5
古籍	（千册）	Ancient Books	(1000 volumes)	165.0	166.0	166.5	167.0	167.6
图书	（万册）	Books	(10000 volumes)	124.9	131.0	137.0	145.0	155.0
群艺馆、文化馆	**（个）**	**Mass Art Center and Cultural Center**	**(unit)**	**13**	**12**	**12**	**12**	**12**
机构人员数	（人）	Persons of Institutions	(person)	332	323	280	275	276
文化站	**（个）**	**Cultural Center**	**(unit)**	**165**	**166**	**151**	**11**	**11**
机构人员数	（人）	Persons of Institutions	(person)	604	574	444	121	82
文化教育机构	**（个）**	**Institutions of Cultural & Education**	**(unit)**	**1**	**1**	**1**	**1**	**1**
机构人员数	（人）	Persons of Institutions	(person)	32	37	35	37	34
文物单位		**Historical Relic Protection Units**						
文物保护管理机构	（个）	Historical Relic Protection Institutions	(unit)	17	17	19	13	13
国家级文保单位	（个）	Historical Relic Protection Units of State Level	(unit)	5	5	5	5	5
博物馆、纪念馆	（个）	Museums, Memorial Hall	(unit)	5	7	8	6	6
文物商店	（个）	Historical Relic	(unit)	3	2	2	1	1
电影放映单位		**Film Projecting Units**						
放映管理机构	（个）	Projecting Management Institutions	(unit)	7	8	7	8	5
电影院	（个）	Movie House	(unit)	53	50	47	43	20
放映队	（个）	Projecting Teams	(unit)	164	184	138	153	166
电影放映场次	（万场）	Projecting Performance	(10000 times)	3.00	2.60	2.20	2.75	1.95
电影观众人次	（万人次）	Spectator	(10000 persons times)	288.00	204.00	187.00	297.40	89.84

9－2 分地区文化事业单位、机构、人员及活动情况

(2003)

项目		Item		全市 Total
艺术表演团体	(个)	**Art Performance Troupes**	(unit)	**6**
机构人员数	(人)	Persons of Institutions	(person)	309
国内演出场次	(场次)	Internal Performances	(times)	917
国内观众人次	(千人次)	Internal Spectator	(1000 persons times)	1234
艺术表演场所	(所)	**Art Performance Places**	(unit)	**9**
机构人员数	(人)	Persons of Institutions	(person)	203
演出场次	(场次)	Performances	(times)	1184
观众人次	(千人次)	Spectator	(1000 persons times)	316
公共图书馆	(个)	**Public Libraries**	(unit)	**9**
机构人员数	(人)	Persons of Institutions	(person)	208
总藏量	(万册)	Total Collections	(10000 volumes)	204.5
古籍	(千册)	Ancient Books	(1000 volumes)	167.6
图书	(万册)	Books	(10000 volumes)	155.0
群艺馆.文化馆	(个)	**Mass Art Center and Cultural Center**	(unit)	**12**
机构人员数	(人)	Persons of Institutions	(person)	276
文化站	(个)	**Cultural Center**	(unit)	**11**
机构人员数	(人)	Persons of Institutions	(person)	82
文化教育机构	(个)	**Institutions of Cultural & Education**	(unit)	**1**
机构人员数	(人)	Persons of Institutions	(person)	34
文物单位		**Historical Relic Protection Units**		
文物保护管理机构	(个)	Historical Relic Protection Institutions	(unit)	13
国家级文保单位	(个)	Historical Relic Protection Units of State Level	(unit)	5
博物馆.纪念馆	(个)	Museums, Memorial Hall	(unit)	6
文物商店	(个)	Historical Relic	(unit)	1
电影放映单位		**Film Projecting Units**		
放映管理机构	(个)	Projecting Management Institutions	(unit)	5
电影院	(个)	Movie House	(unit)	20
放映队	(个)	Projecting Teams	(unit)	166
电影放映场次	(场)	Projecting Performance	(times)	19513
电影观众人次	(万人次)	Spectator	(10000 persons times)	89.84

Basic Statistics of Cultural Institutions and Personnel by Region

市区 Urban District	#鄞州 Yinzhou	余姚市 Yuyao	慈溪市 Cixi	奉化市 Fenghua	象山县 Xiangshan	宁海县 Ninghai
4	**2**	**1**				**1**
255	57					54
483	162	234				200
701	257	233				300
6		**1**			**1**	**1**
77		94			23	9
517		537			6	124
104		163			6	43
4	**1**	**1**	**1**	**1**	**1**	**1**
113	14	27	23	16	15	14
114.4	15.5	24.2	21.8	12.5	16.5	15.1
102.6	1.9	35.7	5.4		0.9	23.0
84.8	13.1	18.2	17.4	11.1	14.4	9.2
7	**1**	**1**	**1**	**1**	**1**	**1**
170	22	22	25	26	16	17
6	**1**	**1**	**1**	**1**	**1**	**1**
27	17	15	17	9	14	
1						
34						
8	1	1	1	1	1	1
3	1	1	1			
4	2	1	1			
1						
2	1	1	1	1		
14	1	2	1	1		2
47	45	35	44	11	11	18
16518	1112	1869	436	320	50	320
46.54	10.33	34.59	1.66	4.50	1.50	1.05

9－3 分地区各类学校数

单位:所 (2003)

项目	Item	全市 Total	市区 Urban District
各类学校校所情况	**Information of Various School**	**2669**	**939**
高等学校	Institutions of Higher Education	12	12
#大专	Junior Colleges	9	9
中等专业学校	Specialized Secondary Schools	10	7
技工学校	Technical Schools	14	14
普通中学	Regular Secondary Schools	303	114
#完(高)中	Senior Secondary Schools	80	35
职业中学	Vacational Secondary Schools	51	18
普通小学	Primary Schools	790	268
特殊教育学校	Special Education Schools	7	3
幼儿园	Kindergarten	1496	517
成人学校合计	**Basic Statistics for Adult Education**	**2067**	**781**
成人高校数	Number of Higher Education for Adult	2	2
成人中等学校	Secondary Education for Adult	74	30
#中专	Specialized Secondary Schools for Adult	18	11
中学	Secondary Schools for Adult	56	19
成人技术培训学校	Technical Training Schools for Adult	1917	729
成人初等学校	Primary Schools for Adult	74	20

Number of Various Schools by Region

(unit)

# 鄞州 Yinzhou	余姚市 Yuyao	慈溪市 Cixi	奉化市 Fenghua	象山县 Xiangshan	宁海县 Ninghai
374	**432**	**492**	**212**	**310**	**284**
2	1	1	1		
40	50	51	23	33	32
10	10	13	6	6	10
7	7	10	4	6	6
113	156	142	77	61	86
1	1	1		1	1
211	217	287	107	209	159
715	**338**	**42**	**313**	**257**	**336**
11	5	22	1	7	9
1	2	2	1	1	1
10	3	20		6	8
684	314	20	312	248	294
20	19			2	33

9-4 分地区各类学校学生情况

单位:人,%　　(2003)

项目	Item	全市 Total	市区 Urban District
各类学校招生人数	**New Students Enrollment of Various Schools**	**258331**	**138355**
研究生	Postgraduates	130	130
普通高校	Institutions of Higher Education	30571	30571
#大专	Junior Colleges	16280	16280
中等专业学校	Specialized Secondary Schools	6283	5622
技工学校	Technical Schools	3412	3412
普通中学	Regular Secondary Schools	106766	44429
职业学校	Secondary Vacational Schools	30098	12506
普通小学	Primary Schools	69320	30001
特殊教育学校	Special Education Schools	69	42
成人高校	Higher Education for Adult	12126	12126
#电大	Radio and TV Universities	229	229
成人中等学校	Secondary Education for Adult	2968	2928
#中专	Specialized Secondary Schools for Adult	2968	2928
各类学校在校学生数	**Students Enrollment of Various Schools**	**1870642**	**710022**
研究生	Postgraduates	222	222
普通高校	Institutions of Higher Education	79886	79886
#大专	Junior Colleges	36796	36796
中等专业学校	Specialized Secondary Schools	18863	16093
技工学校	Technical Schools	9025	9025
普通中学	Regular Secondary Schools	309875	124438
#高中	Senior Schools	85669	32179
职业中学	Vacational Secondary Schools	65150	26628
普通小学	Primary Schools	452560	185268
特殊学校	Special Education Schools	675	415
成人高校	Higher Education for Adult	35853	35853
#电大	Radio and TV Universities	1347	1347
成人中等学校	Secondary Education for Adult	13284	8905
#中专	Specialized Secondary Schools for Adult	6317	6111
中学	Secondary Schools for Adult	6967	2794

Basic Statistics on Student of Various Schools by Region

(person, %)

# 鄞州 Yinzhou	余姚市 Yuyao	慈溪市 Cixi	奉化市 Fenghua	象山县 Xiangshan	宁海县 Ninghai
32163	**31346**	**40100**	**13995**	**15534**	**19001**
925	118	234	309		
15735	16186	21491	6161	8489	10010
4778	5068	5532	1786	1749	3457
10714	9952	12838	5739	5291	5499
11	22	5			
				5	36
				5	35
263244	**355670**	**388105**	**82814**	**149472**	**184559**
2335	278	627	1865		
44652	47050	60150	22509	25487	30241
9782	12109	15671	7516	8153	10041
8757	10514	11158	4414	3706	8730
67788	70114	85751	37900	34331	39196
133	100	94			66
1438	867	1900		858	754
				111	95
1438	867	1900		747	659

项目	Item	全市 Total	市区 Urban District
成人技术培训学校	Technical Training Schools for Adult	727462	168278
成人初等学校	Primary Schools for Adult	855	112
幼儿院在院人数	Persons of Kindergarten	165957	63924
各类学校毕业人数	**Graduates by Various Schools**	**889703**	**222012**
高等学校	Institutions of Higher Education	12118	12118
#大专	Junior Colleges	5432	5432
中等专业学校	Specialized Secondary Schools	7604	6797
技工学校	Technical Schools	3021	3021
普通中学	Regular Secondary Schools	102905	36882
#高中	Senior Schools	21554	7831
职业中学	Vacational Secondary Schools	13431	5304
普通小学	Primary Schools	70909	29954
特殊教育学校	Special Education Schools	64	29
成人高校	Higher Education for Adult	10812	10812
#电大	Radio and TV Universities	640	640
成人中等学校	Adult Secondary Schools	8412	4506
#中专	Specialized Secondary Schools for Adult	3145	3110
中学	Secondary Schools for Adult	5267	1396
成人技术培训学校	Technical Training Schools for Adult	662458	115530
成人初等学校	Primary Schools for Adult	990	80
学生入.升学毕业情况	**Percentage for Enrollment and Graduation of Students**		
小学学龄儿童入学率	Enrollment Rate for Children of School Age	100.1	100.1
小学毕业升学率	Graduation Rate for Pupils	100.0	100.0
初中毕业升学率	Graduation Rate for Students of Secondary School	90.3	96.4
升入普通高中人数	Number of Enrolling Senior School	34697	13200
升学率	Rate of Enrolling Senior School	42.6	51.9
升入职业高中人数	Number of Enrolling Vacational Senior School	28437	10048
升学率	Rate of Enrolling Vacational Senior School	34.9	30.1
升入中专技校人数	Number of Enrolling Technical Secondary School	10341	4139
升学率	Rate of Entrolling Technical Secondary School	13.7	17.9

continued (person, %)

# 鄞州 Yinzhou	余姚市 Yuyao	慈溪市 Cixi	奉化市 Fenghua	象山县 Xiangshan	宁海县 Ninghai
111985	203720	191011	5041	70535	88877
112	150			5	588
26044	22877	37414	11085	14550	16107
88268	**174624**	**270445**	**22690**	**86421**	**113511**
496	55	124	628		
13286	16948	20653	8606	8474	11342
2378	3035	3444	2140	2375	2729
1595	1439	2563	824	1145	2156
11035	11011	14557	3431	5724	6232
	11	10		3	11
829	372	2302		689	543
					35
829	372	2302		689	508
60947	144661	230236	9201	70381	92449
80	127			5	778
99.9	99.9	99.8	100	99.8	98.7
100.0	100.0	100.0	100.0	100.0	100.0
90.8	89.9	86.4	86	89.5	89.1
4119	5035	7261	2662	2821	3718
37.8	36.2	42.2	41.2	46.1	43.2
4778	5778	5786	1880	1963	2982
43.8	41.5	33.6	29.1	32.1	34.6
1005	1699	1813	1017	697	976
9.2	12.2	10.5	15.7	11.4	11.3

9－5　分地区各类学校教职工情况

单位:人　　　　(2003)

项目	Item	全市 Total	市区 Urban District
各类学校教职工人数	**Number of Teachers and Staff of Various Schools**	**74631**	**35406**
高等学校	Institutions of Higher Education	6604	6604
#大专	Junior Colleges	3024	3024
中专学校	Specialized Secondary Schools	2167	555
普通中学	Regular Secondary Schools	23011	9597
职业中学	Vacational Secondary Schools	3010	1164
普通小学	Primary Schools	21581	9079
特殊教育学校	Special Education Schools	198	121
成人高校	Higher Education for Adult	551	551
#电大	Radio and TV Universities	431	431
成人中等学校	Secondary Education for Adult	955	496
#中专	Specialized Secondary Schools for Adult	450	239
中学	Secondary Schools for Adult	505	257
成人技术培训学校	Technical Training Schools for Adult	2555	852
成人初等学校	Primary Schools for Adult	41	
幼儿园	Kindergarten	13958	6387
各类学校专任教师人数	**Number of Full－time Teachers of Various Schools**	**56133**	**26380**
高等学校	Institutions of Higher Education	4225	4225
#大专	Junior Colleges	1974	1974
中专学校	Specialized Secondary Schools	782	350
普通中学	Regular Secondary Schools	18258	7655
#高中	Senior Secondary Schools	5693	2341

Basic Statistics on Teachers and Staff of Various Schools by Region

(person)

# 鄞州 Yinzhou	余姚市 Yuyao	慈溪市 Cixi	奉化市 Fenghua	象山县 Xiangshan	宁海县 Ninghai
9217	**11498**	**11437**	**4743**	**5794**	**5753**
154	1233	255	124		
3150	3808	3925	1708	2054	1919
343	407	533	252	256	398
2717	3491	3378	1553	2102	1978
30	35	24			18
258	75	210	42	98	34
59	29	59	42	62	19
199	46	151		36	15
581	696	151	321	220	315
	30			2	9
1984	1723	2961	743	1062	1082
7215	**6887**	**9454**	**3828**	**4617**	**4967**
115	92	230	110		
2531	2540	3373	1456	1599	1668
725	769	1013	456	505	609

单位:人　　9-5 续表

项目	Item	全市 Total	市区 Urban District
职业中学	Vacational Secondary Schools	2336	919
普通小学	Primary Schools	18490	7841
特殊教育学校	Special Education Schools	139	84
成人高校	Higher Education for Adult	370	370
#电大	Radio and TV Universities	302	302
成人中等学校	Secondary Education for Adult	692	395
#中专	Specialized Secondary Schools for Adult	297	161
中学	Secondary Schools for Adult	395	234
成人技术培训学校	Technical Training Schools for Adult	1383	616
成人初等学校	Primary Schools for Adult	19	
幼儿园	Kindergarten	9439	3958
各类学校兼任教师人数	**Number of Part-time Teachers of Various Schools**	**6932**	**3579**
普通中学	Regular Secondary Schools	192	171
职业中学	Vacational Secondary Schools	187	71
普通小学	Primary Schools	36	31
成人高校	Higher Education for Adult	522	522
成人中等学校	Secondary Education for Adult	927	337
#中专	Specialized Secondary Schools for Adult	234	198
中学	Secondary Schools	693	139
成人技术培训学校	Technical Training Schools for Adult	4952	2437
成人初等学校	Primary Schools for Adult	116	10

continued (person)

# 鄞州 Yinzhou	余姚市 Yuyao	慈溪市 Cixi	奉化市 Fenghua	象山县 Xiangshan	宁海县 Ninghai
242	269	466	111	214	357
2335	2538	3080	1468	1735	1828
23	22	17			16
224	46	130	32	60	29
34	16	28	32	45	15
190	30	102		15	14
414	189	102	131	185	160
	12			2	5
1331	1179	2056	520	822	904
2128	**691**	**999**	**311**	**532**	**820**
66	5	8		8	
11	18	19	21	7	51
26	4		1		
56	35	486	12	27	30
	19		12	2	3
56	16	486		25	27
1959	567	486	277	490	695
10	62				44

9－6 部分年份高等学校基本情况

Basic Statistics on Institutions of Higher Education in Partial Years

单位:人 (person)

项目	Item	1995	1997	1998	2001	2002	2003
学校数(所)	Number of Institutions(unit)	4	3	3	11	11	12
在校学生数	Student Enollment	9764	11548	12473	43417	62044	79886
招生人数	New Student Enollment	3169	3919	3956	19277	26124	30571
毕业学生数	Number of Graduates	2521	2724	2815	4172	6152	12118
教职员工数	Number of Teachers and Staff	2268	2337	2358	4881	5553	6604
#专任教师	Full－time Teachers	1079	1078	1104	2758	3523	4225

9－7 部分年份中等学校基本情况

Basic Statistics on Specialized Secondary Schools in Partial Years

单位:人 (person)

项目	Item	1995	1997	1998	2001	2002	2003
学校数(所)	Number of Institutions(unit)	22	21	23	11	10	10
在校学生数	Student Enollment	19617	23248	25497	22656	19232	18863
招生人数	New Student Enollment	8228	8504	9202	5616	5643	6283
毕业学生数	Number of Graduates	4481	6032	6855	7432	6932	7604
教职员工数	Number of Teachers and Staff	2035	2017	2085	1245	1054	2167
#专任教师	Full－time Teachers	1089	1072	1139	742	737	782

9－8 部分年份技工学校基本情况

Basic Statistics on Technical Schools in Partial Years

单位:人 (person)

项目	Item	1995	1997	1998	2001	2002	2003
学校数(所)	Number of Institutions(unit)	14	15	15	14	14	14
在校学生数	Student Enollment	7341	7223	8369	8510	9114	9025
招生人数	New Student Enollment	3903	3092	3612	2825	3308	3412
毕业学生数	Number of Graduates	2069	2085	2387	2902	2981	3021
教职员工数	Number of Teachers and Staff	1150	1057	1054	898	854	
#专任教师	Full－time Teachers	524	622	631	742	694	

9－9　部分年份普通中学基本情况

Basic Statistics on Regular Secondary Schools in Partial Years

单位:人　　　　(person)

项目	Item	1995	1997	1998	2001	2002	2003
学校数(所)	Number of Institutions(unit)	389	369	365	321	305	303
在校学生数	Student Enollment	257376	262154	247393	295971	308627	309875
招生人数	New Student Enollment	98278	79236	82525	98468	103792	106766
毕业学生数	Number of Graduates	75190	81705	92166	78516	88196	102905
教职员工数	Number of Teachers and Staff	16444	17866	18028	21286	22073	23011
#专任教师	Full－timeTeachers	12869	14341	14247	16622	17309	18258

9－10　部分年份职业中学基本情况

Basic Statistics on Vocational Secondary Schools in Partial Years

单位:人　　　　(person)

项目	Item	1995	1997	1998	2001	2002	2003
学校数(所)	Number of Institutions(unit)	87	99	104	92	55	51
在校学生数	Student Enollment	31876	37104	42599	45151	50919	65150
招生人数	New Student Enollment	14272	17544	18906	17590	22560	30098
毕业学生数	Number of Graduates	9218	12575	11079	14558	14265	13431
教职员工数	Number of Teachers and Staff	2873	3168	3407	3871	3884	3010
#专任教师	Full－time Teachers	1969	2240	2473	2737	2908	2336

9－11　部分年份小学基本情况

Basic Statistics on Primary Schools in Partial Years

单位:人　　　　(person)

项目	Item	1995	1997	1998	2001	2002	2003
学校数(所)	Number of Institutions(unit)	1945	1664	1454	964	901	790
在校学生数	Student Enollment	412902	431436	439116	422357	445482	452560
招生人数	New Student Enollment	76547	74009	68740	68698	77402	69320
毕业学生数	Number of Graduates	84157	61354	61249	73891	74269	70909
教职员工数	Number of Teachers and Staff	18599	19462	19759	20586	21177	21581
#专任教师	Full－time Teachers	16818	17683	17789	17800	18241	18490

9－12　成人教育基本情况

Basic Statistics on Adult Education in Partial Years

单位:人　　　　　　　　(person)

项目	Item	1995	1997	1998	2001	2002	2003
学校数(所)	Number of Institutions(unit)	3106	3727	3543	2968	2535	2067
在校学生数	Student Enollment	388392	494710	606186	469962	494233	777454
招生人数	New Student Enollment	376405	590171	613444	611715	675442	15094
毕业学生数	Number of Graduates	247577	395766	446132	458590	452180	682672
教职员工数	Number of Teachers and Staff	3583	5004	4239	4085	3947	4102
#专任教师	Full－time Teachers	1561	2035	2024	2317	2235	2464

注:成人学校包括成人高等学校、中等学校、技术学校、初等学校。
Note:Schools for adult include Higher Education,Secondary Education, Technical Training Schools and Primary Schools.

9－13　平均每一专任教师负担的学生数

The Ratio of Student Enrollment and Full－time Teachers in Partial Years

单位:人　　　　　　　　(person)

项目	Item	1995	1997	1998	2001	2002	2003
高等学校	Institutions of Higher Education	9.1	10.7	11.3	15.7	17.6	18.9
中等专业学校	Specialized Scendary Schools	18.0	21.7	22.4	30.5	26.1	24.1
技工学校	Technical Schools	14.0	11.6	13.3	11.5	13.1	
普通中学	Regular Secondary Schools	20.0	18.3	17.4	17.8	17.8	17.0
职业中学	Vocational Secondary Schools	16.2	16.6	17.2	16.5	17.5	27.9
小学	Primary Schools	24.6	24.2	24.7	23.7	24.4	24.5

9－14　平均每万人口在校学生数

Student Enrollment Per 10000 Populations in Partial Years

单位:人　　　　　　　　(person)

项目	Item	1995	1997	1998	2001	2002	2003
大学学生	University and College Students	18.6	21.6	23.3	79.9	113.6	145.5
中专学生	Specialized Scendary Schools Students	37.3	43.6	47.6	41.7	35.2	34.4
技校学生	Technical Schools Students	14.0	13.5	15.6	15.7	16.7	16.4
中学学生	Regular Secondary Schools Students	489.1	491.6	462.2	544.7	565.1	564.4
职校学生	Vocational Secondary Schools Students	60.6	69.6	79.6	83.1	93.2	118.7
小学学生	Primary Schools Students	784.7	809.0	820.4	777.3	815.6	824.2

9－15 主要年份教育事业主要指标

Basic Statistics on Education in Main Years

单位:万人 (10000 persons)

年份 Year	在校教职工 Teachers and Staff	# 教师 Teachers	在校学生 Students Enrollment 大学生 Higher Education	中专生 Secondary Specialized Schools	中学生 Secondary Schools	小学生 Primary Schools
1978	4.15	3.55	0.10	0.29	27.16	59.11
1979	4.01	3.53	0.21	0.28	23.04	57.85
1980	4.28	3.48	0.25	0.27	20.99	56.39
1981	4.13	3.23	0.20	0.26	19.36	52.02
1982	3.31	2.75	0.15	0.30	18.77	46.67
1983	3.72	3.06	0.16	0.36	19.48	41.71
1984	3.73	3.00	0.21	0.45	21.42	38.50
1985	3.94	3.16	0.27	0.55	23.47	36.43
1986	4.09	3.28	0.34	0.67	24.35	36.90
1987	4.21	3.34	0.39	0.74	23.48	36.41
1988	4.32	3.47	0.45	0.86	20.34	38.69
1989	4.45	3.56	0.49	0.90	18.75	41.84
1990	4.24	3.34	0.49	0.90	19.65	42.70
1991	4.34	3.39	0.48	0.95	22.01	41.62
1992	4.37	3.47	0.53	1.05	24.39	40.16
1993	4.59	3.61	0.66	1.36	25.03	40.40
1994	4.75	3.76	0.83	1.60	26.76	41.92
1995	5.00	4.01	0.98	1.96	28.93	41.29
1996	5.12	4.17	1.04	2.51	30.07	41.80
1997	5.27	4.32	1.15	2.32	29.93	43.14
1998	5.44	4.40	1.25	2.55	29.00	43.91
1999	6.16	4.81	1.68	2.73	25.12	43.36
2000	6.59	5.17	2.59	2.51	27.98	42.40
2001	6.86	5.12	4.34	2.27	29.60	42.24
2002	7.05	5.27	6.21	1.92	30.86	44.55
2003	7.46	5.61	7.99	1.88	30.99	45.26

注:在校教职工包括幼儿园。
Note:The number of teachers and staff include kinder－gardens.

9－16　各县(市)区卫生事业单位机构情况

单位:个　　(2003)

项目	Item	全市 Total
卫生事业机构数	**Number of Health Care Intitiutions**	**1297**
1.医院合计	Total Hospitals	55
综合医院	omprehensive Hospitals	31
中医医院	Hospitals of Chinese Medicine	7
专科医院	Specialized Hospitals	17
口腔医院	Stomatological Hospitals	5
眼科医院	Ophthalmology Hospitals	1
妇产(科)医院	Obstetrics and Gynecology Hospitals	1
精神病医院	Mental Hospitals	5
传染病医院	Infectious Disease Hospitals	1
骨科医院	Orthopedist Hospitals	3
其他专科医院	Others Specialized Hospitals	1
2.疗养院	Sanatoriums	1
3.社区卫生服务中心	Community Sanitation Service Sites	17
4.卫生院	Local Hospitals	217
街道卫生院	Subdistric Local Hospitals	11
乡镇卫生院	Town and Township Local Hospitals	206
中心卫生院	Center Locale Hospitals	42
乡卫生院	Towhship Locale Hospitals	164
5.门诊部合计	Clinics	116
6.急救中心(站)	First－aid Centre(Stations)	1
7.采供血机构	Blood Collecting and Supplying Organization	1
8.妇幼保健院(所、站)	Maternity and Child Care Centers or Stations	11
9.专科疾病防治院(所、站)	Specialized Prevention and Treatment Centers or Stations	2
10.疾病预防控制中心(防疫站)	Center for Disease Control and Prevention	12
11.卫生监督所	Health Supervision Centers	12
12.卫生监督检验(监测、检测)所	Health Supervised and Examined Centers	1
13.医学科学研究机构	Research Institution of Medicine	3
14.在职培训机构	Institution of On－the－job Training	7
15.诊所、卫生保健所、医务室社区卫生服务站合计	Clinique, Stations for Sanitation and Health, Clinics	831
16.其他卫生机构	Others Health Care Institutions	10

Basic Statistics on Health Care Institutions by Region

(unit)

市区 Urban District	# 鄞州 Yinzhou	余姚 Yuyao	慈溪 Cixi	奉化 Fenghua	象山 Xiangshan	宁海 Ninghai
729	**154**	**150**	**102**	**115**	**106**	**95**
33	4	5	5	6	4	2
19	2	3	2	2	4	1
2		1	1	1	1	1
10	2	1	2	3	1	
4	1			1		
1						
1						
1		1	1	1	1	
1						
	1		1	1		
1						
1						
17						
74	43	21	22	27	28	45
6		3	2			
68	43	18	20	27	28	45
14	7	6	6	3	7	6
54	36	12	14	24	21	39
25		29	54	1	7	
1						
1						
6	1	1	1	1	1	1
1	1		1			
7	1	1	1	1	1	1
7	1	1	1	1	1	1
1						
3						
2		1	1	1	1	1
545	103	91	15	76	62	42
5			1	1	1	2

9－17 各县(市)区卫生事业人员、床位情况

(2003)

项目	Item	全市 Total
从业人员总计(人)	**Total Employment(person)**	**25403**
卫生技术人员	Medical Technical Personnel	21473
医生数	Number of Doctors	10630
执业医师	Medical Practitioner	8546
执业助理医师	Assistant Medical Practitioner	2084
注册护士	Register Nurse	6253
药剂人员	Pharmacists	1661
检验人员	Laboratory Technicians	1103
其他	Others	1826
其他技术人员	Other Technical Personnel	881
管理人员	Manager	1450
工勤人员	Logistics Workers	1599
每千人拥有卫生技术人员	Number of Medical Technical Personnel Per 1000 Persons	3.91
每千人拥有医生	Number of Doctors Per 1000 Persons	1.94
每千人拥有护师、护士	Number of Junior Nurses and Senior Nurses Per 1000 Persons	1.14
卫生事业床位数(张)	**Number of Beds (bed)**	**15279**
医院床位	Beds of Hospitals	10654
社区卫生服务中心床位	Beds of Health Service Center of Communities	541
卫生院床位	Beds of Local Hospitals	3406
妇幼保健院(所、站)床位	Beds of Maternity and Child Care Centers	184
专科疾病防治院(所、站)床位	Beds of Specialized Prevention Stations	44
其他卫生机构床位	Beds of Others Health Care Institutions	270
#精神病管理所床位	Beds of Mental Hospitals	270
每千人拥有总床位	Total Beds of Per 1000 Persons	2.78
每千人拥有医院卫生院床位	Beds of Hospitals and Local Hospitals Per 1000 Persons	2.66

Number of Health Care Personnel and Beds by Region

市区 Urban District	#鄞州 Yinzhou	余姚 Yuyao	慈溪 Cixi	奉化 Fenghua	象山 Xiangshan	宁海 Ninghai
14090	**2813**	**2567**	**3085**	**1938**	**1655**	**2068**
11712	2434	2251	2599	1639	1441	1831
5784	1296	1221	1261	846	671	847
4874	936	955	934	677	509	597
910	360	266	327	169	162	250
3569	610	582	688	464	411	539
829	198	171	201	148	137	175
651	123	92	143	68	68	81
879	207	185	306	113	154	189
487	118	82	126	115	43	28
984	87	84	157	62	52	111
907	174	150	203	122	119	98
5.66	3.22	2.73	2.58	3.40	2.74	3.14
2.80	1.71	1.48	1.25	1.76	1.27	1.45
1.72	0.81	0.71	0.68	0.96	0.78	0.93
8202	**1314**	**1544**	**1881**	**1723**	**980**	**949**
6132	648	1063	836	1493	642	488
541						
1152	666	481	801	230	338	404
27			100			57
			44			
270						
270						
3.96	1.74	1.87	1.87	3.58	1.86	1.63
3.78	1.74	1.87	1.63	3.58	1.86	1.53

9－18 各级医院工作情况

(2003)

项目	Item	门诊人次合计 (万人) Out－patients (10000 persons)
全市总计	**Total**	**2553.88**
1.医院合计	Total Hospitals	1118.49
综合医院	Comprehensive Hospitals	776.19
省辖市属医院	Urban Hospitals administered by Province	237.81
#市第一医院	The No.1 Hospital of Ningbo	86.74
市第二医院	The No.2 Hospital of Ningbo	42.15
市第三医院	The No.3 Hospital of Ningbo	39.68
市李惠利医院	Li Huili Hospital of Ningbo	57.22
市保黎医院	Bao Li Hospital of Nnningbo	12.02
中医医院	Hospitals of Chinese Medicine	191.38
#市中医院	Hospital of Chinese Medicine of Ningbo	47.97
专科医院	Specialized Hospitals	150.91
口腔医院	Stomatological Hospitals	17.62
眼科医院	Ophthalmology Hospitals	0.70
精神病医院	Mental Hospitals	19.59
#市康宁医院	Kangning Hospital of Ningbo	6.80
妇产(科)医院	Obstetrics and Gynecology Hospitals	79.17
#市妇儿医院	Hospital for Maternity and Child of Ningbo	79.17
骨科医院	Orthopedist Hospitals	22.45
传染病医院	Infectious Disease Hospitals	10.09
2.社区卫生服务中心	Health Service Center of Communities	232.67
3.卫生院	Local Hospitals	1069.62
4.门诊部	Clinics	34.31
5.妇幼保健院(所、站)	Maternity and Child Care Centers or Stations	86.80
6.专科疾病防治院	Specialized Prevention and Treatment Centers or Stations	11.98

Medical Treatment of Various Hospitals

本年入院人数（万人）in This Year（10000 persons）	平均住院日（天）Average Day In－patients（day）	住院病人治愈率（%）Recovering Rate of In－patients（%）	好转率（%）Effcetive Cure Rate of In－patients（%）	期末实有病床数（张）Factual Beds at The Year－end（bed）	平均开放病床数（张）Average Openning Bed（bed）
31.93	**11.73**	**59.72**	**34.87**	**14924**	**13237**
25.08	12.66	55.72	38.26	10654	9434
19.71	12.00	55.16	38.22	7311	6994
6.72	13.87	49.79	42.58	2460	2433
1.64	14.48	51.99	41.72	625	625
2.01	13.23	56.35	36.77	610	610
0.94	15.06	62.19	32.24	405	405
1.78	13.43	57.64	35.44	620	593
0.35	13.72	34.62	54.08	200	200
2.21	13.88	49.68	45.95	1040	953
0.46	21.00	37.95	55.81	300	300
3.17	15.94	63.44	33.17	2303	1488
				20	
0.18	9.88	96.98	3.02	70	48
0.27	65.06	16.26	80.12	1270	578
0.16	74.48	0.84	97.17	340	318
2.09	9.12	68.85	28.73	490	437
2.09	9.12	68.85	28.73	490	437
0.30	8.54	80.90	19.10	143	115
0.33	26.90	36.70	49.41	310	310
0.51	15.58	63.38	33.80	541	497
5.40	7.69	73.93	22.63	3406	3126
				100	
0.93	6.42	86.97	11.61	179	130
				44	50

9－19 居民病伤死亡原因

(2003)

项目	Item	死亡人数(人) 合计 Total
宁波市总计	**Total in Ningbo**	**35702**
市区总计	**Total in Urban Destricts**	**12377**
十种死因合计	Main 10 Causes of Death	34182
1.恶性肿瘤	Malignant Tumour	10297
2.脑血管病	Cerebral Vascular Disease	6097
3.呼吸系病	Respiratory Disease	7531
4.损伤和中毒	Trauma and Toxicosis	3505
5.心脏病	Cardiopathy	2253
6.诊断不明	Unable to Be Diagnosed	1711
7.内分泌等疾病	Internal System Disease	700
8.传染病(不包括肺结核)	Infectious Disease(Phthisic not Included)	845
9.消化系统疾病	Digestive Disease	726
10.精神病	Digestive Disease	517
十种死因合计	Main 10 Causes of Death	11342
1.恶性肿瘤	Malignant Tumour	3769
2.脑血管病	Cerebral Vascular Disease	2257
3.呼吸系病	Respiratory Disease	2148
4.损伤和中毒	Trauma and Toxicosis	1228
5.心脏病	Cardiopathy	694
6.内分泌等疾病	Internal System Disease	384
7.消化系统疾病	Digestive Disease	259
8.精神病	Digestive Disease	206
9.传染病(不包括肺结核)	Infectious Disease(Phthisic not Included)	240
10.泌尿生殖系统病	Urinary Disease	157

Main 10 Diseases of Death in Urban Residents

Number of Death (person)		死因构成(%) Composition of Death (%)	死亡专率(/10万) Death Rate (per 0.1 million persons)		
男 Male	女 Female		合计 Total	男 Male	女 Female
19936	**15766**	**100.00**	**651.93**	**719.41**	**582.81**
6798	**5579**	**100.00**	**603.29**	**661.34**	**544.99**
19154	15028	95.74	624.17	691.20	555.53
6986	3311	28.84	188.03	252.10	122.40
3105	2992	17.08	111.33	112.05	110.60
3624	3907	21.09	137.52	130.78	144.43
2132	1373	9.82	64.00	76.94	50.75
1154	1099	6.31	41.14	41.64	40.63
710	1001	4.79	31.24	25.62	37.00
281	419	1.96	12.78	10.14	15.49
579	266	2.37	15.43	20.89	9.83
383	343	2.03	13.26	13.82	12.68
200	317	1.45	9.44	7.22	11.72
6349	4993	91.32	552.91	617.67	487.76
2533	1236	30.45	183.71	246.42	120.74
1125	1132	18.24	110.01	109.45	110.58
1031	1117	17.35	104.70	100.30	109.12
704	524	9.92	59.86	68.49	51.19
343	351	5.61	33.83	33.37	34.29
151	233	3.10	18.72	14.69	22.76
129	130	2.09	12.62	12.55	12.70
71	135	1.66	10.04	6.91	13.19
166	74	1.94	11.70	16.15	7.23
96	61	1.27	7.65	9.34	5.96

9-20 主要年份卫生事业主要指标

Basic Statistics on Health Care in Main Years

年份 Year	卫生机构数(个) Total Number of Health Institutions (unit)	#医院 Hospitals	卫生机构床位(张) Total Number of Beds in Health Institutions (bed)	#医院 Hospitals	卫生技术人员 (万人) Number of Medical technical (10000 persons)	#医生 Doctors
1978	949	400	5989	5549	0.93	0.36
1979	1013	398	6618	5871	0.99	0.36
1980	1032	397	6948	6368	1.06	0.38
1981	1077	394	7537	7015	1.13	0.44
1982	1100	400	8130	7230	1.19	0.48
1983	1107	396	8372	7525	1.24	0.50
1984	1117	396	8823	7954	1.28	0.53
1985	1123	311	9067	8250	1.30	0.54
1986	1181	320	9436	8605	1.34	0.56
1987	1199	327	9922	9057	1.41	0.60
1988	1259	330	10447	9629	1.46	0.73
1989	1293	331	11073	10067	1.53	0.74
1990	1301	344	11449	10522	1.58	0.75
1991	1313	345	11731	10816	1.66	0.76
1992	1270	303	12175	11259	1.69	0.78
1993	1262	300	12529	11633	1.70	0.80
1994	1257	345	12976	12090	1.76	0.84
1995	1257	345	13193	12316	1.74	0.87
1996	1123	297	13012	12299	1.78	0.88
1997	1678	296	13654	8849	1.83	0.92
1998	1407	296	13689	9481	1.86	0.91
1999	961	54	13795	9364	1.89	0.93
2000	929	56	14535	9968	1.92	0.95
2001	921	57	14393	10246	1.96	0.97
2002	1263	58	14653	10292	2.01	0.99
2003	1297	55	15279	10654	2.14	1.06

9－21 全市体育工作情况

Basic Statistics on Physical Culture Schools and Sports

(2003)

项目		Item		1997	2001	2002	2003
各类体校情况		**Various Physical Culture and Sports School**					
体育运动学校数	(个)	Physical Education and Sports School	(unit)	1	1	2	1
在校学生数	(人)	Student Enrollment	(person)	247	490	670	631
专职教练员	(人)	Full－time Coaches	(person)	9	26	42	39
业余体校个数	(个)	Sparetime Sports Schools	(unit)	7	10	4	4
#重点业余体校	(个)	Emphatic Sparetime Sports School	(unit)	3	3	4	4
业余体校在校学生数	(人)	Student Enrollment in Sparetime Sports Schools	(person)	2251	2000	320	728
业余体校送入优秀运动队	(人)	Number of Persons from Sparetime Sports School Enrolling Excelent Sports Team	(person)	11	9	28	32
业余体校考入高等院校	(人)	Number of Persons Admitted to Institutions Higher Education from Sparetime Sports School	(person)	12	8	10	9
传统项目布局情况		**Distribution on Traditional Events**					
分布学校数	(个)	Number of Distributing Schools	(unit)	177	225	62	63
#中学	(个)	Secondary Schools	(unit)	82	93	5	10
小学	(个)	Primary Schools	(unit)	95	132	57	53
国家体标达标学生比率	**(%)**	**Rate of Persons Reaching National Standard**	**(%)**				**95.32**
中学达标学生	(%)	Students Reaching National Standard at Secondary School	(%)				99.24
小学达标学生	(%)	Pupils Reaching National Standard at Primary School	(%)				99.24
市区健身设施	(套)	Health－care Facilities in Urban Districts	(set)			466	680
传统项目活动情况		**Statistics on Traditional Events**					

9－21 续表 continued

项目		Item		1997	2001	2002	2003
参加活动学生人数	（人）	Number of Participants in Student	(person)	10870	111575	2546	6162
参加田径学生	（人）	Track and Field	(person)	7530	64497	1162	3900
参加游泳学生	（人）	Swimming	(person)	587	4930	150	350
参加射击学生	（人）	Shoot	(person)	192	532	65	65
参加蓝球学生	（人）	Basketball	(person)	670	20035	356	406
参加排球学生	（人）	Volleyball	(person)	328	3660	202	250
参加足球学生	（人）	Football	(person)	736	4250	240	400
参加乒乓排球学生	（人）	Pingpong	(person)	416	5621	220	220
参加羽毛球学生	（人）	Badminton	(person)	411	8050	151	171
游泳池情况(体育系统)		**Swimming Pool Managed by Sports Commission**					
游泳池个数	（个）	Number of Swimming Pools	(unit)	8	9	62	66
#室内游泳池	（个）	Indoor	(unit)	4	4	28	28
游泳池活动场次	（场次）	Number of Running Swimming Pool	(times)	1853	2230	14400	13140
#室内游泳池	（场次）	Indoor	(times)	1305	1690	11200	10220
参赛获奖数	**（枚）**	**Number of Obtain Awards by Athletic Competition**	**(unit)**			**116**	**361**
#省级及以上金牌	（枚）	Number of Gold Medals Won in Procincial Competitions	(unit)			38	142
省级及以上银牌	（枚）	Number of Silver Medals Won in Procincial Competitions	(unit)			35	111
省级及以上铜牌	（枚）	Number of Bronze Medals Won in Procincial Competitions	(unit)			43	108

9-22 广播电视基本情况

Basic Statisits on Broadcasting and Television

项目		Item		1997	2001	2002	2003
广播电视机构		**Institutions**					
电台和转播台	(座)	Broadcasting and Relaying Stations	(set)	4	4	4	4
电视台和转差台	(座)	TV and Transfer Stations	(set)	21	10	8	8
卫星地面站	(个)	Ground Satellite Stations	(unit)	406	386	352	451
乡镇广播站	(个)	Broadcasting Statioons in Township	(unit)	149	135	134	124
平均播音时间		**Average Broadcasting Hours**					
广播播音时间(每日)	(时:分)	Daily Broadcasting Hours	(hour:minute)	50:20	195:25	182:45	16:30
#自办时间	(时:分)	Time of Self - Producting Programs	(hour:minute)	46:50	163:25	162:40	13:40
电视播出时间(每周)	(时:分)	Weekly Hours Through TV Broadcasting	(hour:minute)	377:30	880:08	963:10	84:00
#自办时间	(时:分)	Time of Self - Producting Programs	(hour:minute)	329:37	827:43	926:15	80:00
有线广播喇叭		**Wired Broadcasting Loudspeaker**					
广播喇叭数	(万只)	Number of Broadcasting Loudspeaker	(10000 units)	105.80	98.40	98.41	95.58
喇叭入户率	(%)	Percentage for Households - owned	(%)	74.74	50.98	64.87	63.00
有线广播专线传输杆路	**杆公里)**	**Lines for Wired Broadcasting Transfer**	**(km pole)**	**6941**	**4766**	**4489**	**4453**
行政村	(个)	Administrative Village	(unit)	5054	3963	3870	3826
通广播村	(个)	Village Through Transferring Broadcasting	(unit)	4920	3963	3783	3826
通村率	(%)	Rate of Transferred Broadcasting Village	(%)	97.62	100	97.75	100
电视频道	**(个)**	**TV Channel**	**(set)**	**33**	**20**	**20**	**6**
发送功率		**Transfer Power**					
中波功率	(千瓦)	Middle - Wave Power	(kw)	27	27	27	25
调频功率	(千瓦)	Frequency Modulation Power	(kw)	13.30	23.30	23.30	18.85
电视功率	(千瓦)	TV Power	(kw)	28.23	26.4	26.43	25.63
有线电视台.站		**Cable TV Station**					
台.站数	(个)	Number of Stations and Center	(unit)	2	1	1	1
用户终端数	(万户)	Number of User Terminal	(10000 users)	31.47	121.23	124.39	127.50

9-23 各县市电视基本情况

Basic Statistics on TV Broadcasting by Region

(2003)

地区	Region	电视台和转差台（座）TV and Transfer Stations (set)	电视播出时间(每周)（时:分）Weekly Hours Through TV Broadcasting (hour:minute)	# 自办时间 Time of Self-Producting Programs	电视频道（个）TV Channel (unit)	有线电视用户终端数（万户）Number of User Terminal with Cable TV (10000 users)
全市	Total	8	84:00	80:00	6	127.50
市区	Urban District	3	122:30	122:00	3	28.55
# 鄞州	Yinzhou	1	85:33	82:03	1	22.46
余姚	Yuyao	1	43:30	40:00	1	15.69
慈溪	Cixi	1	77:00	73:30		25.00
奉化	Fenghua	1	105:00	101:30		9.70
象山	Xiangshan	1	119:00	114:20	1	13.10
宁海	Ninghai	1	36:50	33:20	1	13.00

9-24 各县市广播基本情况

Basic Statistics on Broadcasting by Region

(2003)

地区	Region	电台和转播台（座）Broadcasting and Relaying Stations (set)	乡镇广播站（个）Broadcasting Statioons in Township (unit)	广播播音时间（每日）（时:分）Daily Broadcasting Hours (hour,minute)	# 自办时间 Time of Self-Producting Programs	广播喇叭数（万只）Number of Broadcasting Loudspeaker (10000 units)
全市	Total	4	124	16:30	13:30	95.58
市区	Urban District	2	40	21:00	20:10	12.51
# 鄞州	Yinzhou		20	16:00	13:00	19.02
余姚	Yuyao		19	12:00	9:55	17.40
慈溪	Cixi		20	17:10	15:10	21.50
奉化	Fenghua		16	16:10	13:20	9.75
象山	Xiangshan	1	13	16:30	14:00	8.50
宁海	Ninghai	1	16	17:30	10:30	6.90

主要指标解释

【艺术表演团体】 指从事戏曲、音乐、舞蹈、杂技等专业艺术表演，有独立帐 户，实行单独核算的团体。不包括半工半艺、半农半艺和民间职业剧团。

【艺术表演观众人数(人次)】 指售票、包场演出或民族地区免费演出的艺术表演观众人次数。不包括彩排审查和内部观摩演出的观众人次数。

【电影放映单位】 指具有放映机器设备、固定或不固定的放映场所与专职或兼职的放映技术人员，经有关部门登记批准，经常为一定的观众对象放映电影的机构。包括经批准对外开放进行营业，并与电影发行放映管理机构分帐的专用放映单位和军委系统租片单位。

【普通高等学校】 指按照国家规定的设置标准和审批程序批准举办，通过国家统一招生考试，招收高中毕业生为主要培养对象，实施高等教育的全日制大学、独立设置的学院和高等专科学校、短期职业大学。

【成人高等学校】 指按照国家有关规定审批，招收通过全国成人高教统一招生 考试的具有高中毕业或同等学历的在职从业人员利用脱产、半脱产、业余或函授等多种形式 对其实施高等学历教育，培养高等教育专科或本科毕业水平的专门人才，修业年限、课程设 置和总学时数均按高等学历教育要求付诸实施的学校。包括广播电视大学、职工高等学校、农民高等学校、管理干部学院、教育学院、独立设置的函授学院等。

【小学学龄儿童入学率】 指调查范围内已入小学学习的学龄儿童占校内外学龄儿童总数(包括弱智儿童在内，但不包括盲聋哑儿童)的比重。计算公式为：

小学学龄儿童入学率 = 已入学的小学学龄儿童数 × 100%

校内外小学学龄儿童总数

【医院】 指名称为医院，设有固定床位能收容病人住院并能为病人提供医疗、护理服务的医疗机构。包括县及县以上医院、农村乡卫生院、其他医院三部分。按所属性质分为卫生部门、工业及其他部门，集体经济单位三类。其中县及县以上医院按业务性质分为 综合医院和专科医院。

【卫生技术人员】 指卫生事业机构支付工资的全部固定职工和合同制职工中现任职务为卫生技术工作的专业人员。包括中医师、西医师、中西医结合高级医师、护师、中 药师、西药师、检验师、其他技师、中医士、西医士、护士、助产士、中药剂士、西药剂士、检验士、其他技士、其他中医、护理员、中药剂员、西药剂员、检验员，其他初级卫生技术人员。

【医生】 指经卫生部门审查合格，从事医疗工作的专业人员。分为中医医生和西医医生。包括卫生技术人员中的中医师、西医师、中西结合高级医师、中医士、西医士和其他中医。

Explanatory Notes on Main Statistical Indicators

【Art Troupe】 refers to the troupe which is engaged in drama, opera, music, dance, acrobatics or other art performance, opens independent accounts with banks and has self – supporting accounting system; excluding the troupes which h are engaged partly in industrial or agricultural activities, partly in art performance and the professional troupes organized by the people.

【Number of Sectors at Art Performance】 refers to the number of attendants at commercial shows completely booked shows or free shows given in minority national areas, and does not include the number of spectators at rehearsals for examination and initial shows for study.

【Film Projection Units】 refer to units with film projection equipment, full or part time projectionists, permanent or nonpermanent places, approved by related administrative departments to show films regularly for certain groups of audience, including those film projection units which have been approved to give commercial shows and run business with independent accounting system as well as those film-renting units of the military system.

【Regular Institutions of Higher Learning】 refer to educational establishments set up according to the government evaluation and approval procedures, enrolling graduates from senior secondary schools and providing higher education courses and training for senior professionals. They include full – time universities, colleges, high professional schools and short – term professional universities.

【Institutions of Higher Learning for Adults】 refer to educational establishments, set up in line with relevant rules approved by the government, enrolling staff and workers with senior secondary school or equivalent education, and providing higher education courses in many forms of full – time, part – time, spare – time, or correspondence for adults. Professionals thus trained receive a qualification equivalent to graduates studying regular courses at regular universities, colleges and professional colleges. Institutions of higher learning for adults include Radio and TV universities, schools of high education for staff and workers and peasants, colleges for management cadres, pedagogical colleges, independent correspondence colleges.

【Enrollment Rate of Primary School – age Children】 refers to the proportion of school – age children enrolled at schools to the total number of school – age both in and outside schools (including retarded children, but excluding blind, deaf and mute children). The formula is:

Enrollment Rate of Primary School – age Children = Total Primary School – age Children at Schools × 100%

Total Primary School – age Children at and Outside Schools

【Hospitals】 refer to medical institutions named as "hospital" with permanent hospital beds, which are able to take in patients and provide them with medical and nursing services. Hospitals are classified into three categories : hospitals at or above the county – level, hospitals of rural townships, and other hospitals. According to their ownership, hospitals can be classified into three categories: hospitals under the public health departments, hospitals under industrial and other departments and collective – owned hospitals. Hospitals at or above county level are divided into comprehensive and specialized hospitals.

【Medical Technical Personnel】 refers to all permanent medical staff and workers employed by medical institutions, including doctors of Chinese and Western medicine, senior doctors who integrate traditional Chinese therapeutics with Western therapeutics in practice, senior nurses, pharmacists of Chinese and Western medicine, laboratory specialists, other specialists, paramedics of Chinese and Western medicine, nurses, midwives, druggists in Chinese and Western medicine, laboratory technicians, other technicians, other practitioners of Chinese medicine, nursing attendants, pharmacological workers of Chinese and Western medicine, laboratory workers, and other primary medical personnel.

【Doctors】 refer to qualified professional medical workers approved to practice by public health departments. They are classified into doctors of Chinese medicine, doctors of Western medicine, senior doctors who integrate traditional Chinese therapeutics with Western therapeutics in practice, paramedics of Chinese medicine and Western medicine, and other specialists of Chinese medicine.

10

财政、金融、保险

CHAPTER 10 FINANCE，BANKING AND INSURANCE

财政、金融、保险
Finance, Banking and Insurance

主要统计指标
Major Statistics Indicators

2003 年全市财政总收入	Total Financial Revenue	330.03	亿元	100 million yuan
比上年增长	Increase Over Last Year	25.9	%	
2003 年全市财政一般预算收入	Total Financial Budgetary Revenue	325.01	亿元	100 million yuan
比上年增长	Increase Over Last Year	25.8	%	
2003 年地方财政一般预算收入	Total Local Financial Budgetary Revenue	139.42	亿元	100 million yuan
比上年增长	Increase Over Last Year	32.4	%	
2003 年财政支出	Total Financial Expenditure	187.09	亿元	100 million yuan
比上年增长	Increase Over Last Year	24.6	%	
2003 年金融机构存款余额	Deposits of Financial Institutions at Year – end	2629.03	亿元	100 million yuan
比上年增长	Increase Over Last Year	37.9	%	
2003 年城乡居民储蓄存款余额	Urban and Rural Residents Saving Balance at Year – end	1059.63	亿元	100 million yuan
比上年增长	Increase Over Last Year	22.9	%	
2003 年金融机构贷款余额	Loans Balance of Financial Institutions at Year – end	2102.78	亿元	100 million yuan
比上年增长	Increase Over Last Year	42.1	%	

10－1　主要年份财政收入及支出

Total Financial Budgetary Revenue and Expenditure in Main Year

单位:万元　　　　(10000 yuan)

年份 Year	一般预算财政收入 Financial Budgetary Revenue		财政支出 Financial Expenditure	
	全市 Total	市区 Urban District	全市 Total	市区 Urban District
1978	49697	29662	11176	4672
1979	48860	29536	11803	4252
1980	56290	34924	15712	6956
1981	65432	41157	14585	5812
1982	71546	44574	14689	5331
1983	80801	49130	18873	7747
1984	93318	58817	25544	12148
1985	91237	46963	34610	17449
1986	102264	50872	48978	27413
1987	113351	55227	41655	19490
1988	133395	66580	70336	38395
1989	152751	74892	89355	50141
1990	158910	75725	97133	54389
1991	177875	86733	106961	58704
1992	198354	96918	119133	62758
1993	282429	137495	180622	92931
1994	420202	244253	250553	145946
1995	531135	328458	353700	231321
1996	659529	424052	453292	306509
1997	750412	485289	549989	364757
1998	876351	572222	646089	417522
1999	1039976	679852	740516	477550
2000	1431511	937655	892345	566103
2001	1903064	1209606	1219330	759071
2002	2583984	1869395	1501556	1039828
2003	3250078	2287641	1870929	1268421

10-2 部分年份财政收入主要指标

Main Indicators of Financial Revenue in Partial Years

单位:万元 (10000 yuan)

项目	Item	1998	2001	2002	2003
财政收入	**Financial Revenue**	**923588**	**1942928**	**2621808**	**3300291**
中央收入	**Revenue of Central Government**	**458776**	**911972**	**1465616**	**1855916**
#消费税	Consumption Tax	111072	230988	301939	333966
增值税	Value-added Tax	341193	680984	841878	1019939
地方财政收入	**Local Financial Revenue**	**464812**	**1030956**	**1156192**	**1444375**
一般预算收入	**Budgetary Revenue**	**417575**	**991092**	**1118368**	**1394162**
增值税	Value-added Tax	113729	226994	280626	339982
营业税	Operation Tax	139736	230545	319215	413150
企业所得税	Enterprise's Income Tax	65840	399262	232835	241704
个人所得税	Individual Income Tax	30744	115043	90562	97403
资源税	Resources Tax	115	125	121	163
固定资产投资方向调节税	Tax on Adjustment of the Orientation of Investment in Fixed Assets	7272	234	20	-17
城市维护建设税	Tax on Urban Construction and Maintenance	36190	65084	82352	93991
房产税	Tax on Real Estates	14655	24611	29586	33449
印花税	Stamp Tax	3729	7233	10029	13631
城镇土地使用税	Tax on Use of Urban Land	2072	2594	3067	3781
土地增值税	Land Value Added Tax	382	366	948	6781
车船使用税	Tax on the Use of Vehicles and Ships	1302	1848	2256	3174
屠宰税	Slaughter Tax	555	830	250	4
农业税	Agriculture Tax	8840	6981	5967	5066
农业特产税	Tax on Special Agricultural Products	1926	1691	1606	14
耕地占用税	Tax on the Occupancy of Cultivated Land	3344	11324	22024	30504
契税	Contract Tax	13749	32883	65697	92395
国有企业计划亏损补贴	Subsidies to Loss-suffering State-owned Enterprises	-58282	-212589	-132653	-90973
罚没收入	Fine & Confiscatory Revenue	10389	27477	35708	36779
专项收入	Special Revenue	19076	34438	41040	48269
其他收入	Other Revenue	2212	2283	3457	2520
基金收入	**Fund Revenue**	**47237**	**39864**	**37824**	**50213**

10－3　部分年份财政支出主要指标

Main Indicators of Financial Expenditure in Partial Years

单位:万元　　(10000 yuan)

项目	Item	1998	2001	2002	2003
财政支出	**Financial Expenditure**	**646089**	**1219330**	**1501556**	**1870929**
一般预算支出	**Ordinary Budgetary Expenditure**	**607332**	**1162797**	**1452639**	**1802545**
#基本建设支出	Expenditure for Capital Construction	34048	154353	196152	241430
企业挖潜改造支出	Expenditure for Innovation Enterprises	100731	169875	176127	195346
科技三项费用	Expenditure for Science and Technology Promotion	5447	19347	25929	33561
农林水利气象等部门的事业费	Expenditure for Operating Expenses of Agriculture, Forestry, Wate Conservancy and Meteorology	25811	26552	31295	104662
工业交通等部门的事业费	Expenditure for Operating Expenses of Departments of Industry & Transportation	7567	7748	9498	10444
文体广播事业费	Expenditure for Operating Expenses of Department of Culture, Sport & Broadcasting	16017	24759	29879	37694
教育事业费	Expenditure for Operating Expenses of Education	80333	154172	184553	217807
科学事业费	Expenditure for Operating Expenses of Department of Science	2004	3834	5030	5103
卫生经费	Expenditure for Public Health	35745	48681	57345	75527
其他部门的事业费	Expenditure for Operating Expense of Others Departments etc.	30837	77617	111890	160901
抚恤和社会福利救济费	Expenditure for Pensions and Relief Funds for Social Welfare	8758	14492	21371	32908
行政事业单位离退休经费	Expenditure for Retired Persons in Administrative Department	416	441	1071	1787
社会保障补助支出	Expenditure on Subsidies to Social Security Programs	5403	20004	41529	59609
国防支出	Expenditure for National Defence	525	1053	1215	2712
行政管理费	Expenditure for Government Administration	41515	74633	103865	141406
外交外事支出	Expenditure for Foreign Affairs	570	760	1167	2501
武装警察部队支出	Expenditure for Armed Police Troops	790	1350	1988	2629
公检法司支出	Expenditure for Public Security Agency, Procuratorial Agency and Court of Justice	33580	78848	93211	118870
城市维护费	Expenditure for City Maintenance	94355	142845	193665	220981
政策性补贴支出	Expenditure for Price Subsidies	2980	4353	3426	3792
支援不发达地区支出	Expenditure for supporting Underdeveloped Area	126	163	171	4789
专项支出	Special Expenditure	18023	34720	38502	44253
其他支出	Other Expenditure	42658	57775	69961	80646
基金支出	**Fund Expenditure**	**38757**	**56533**	**48917**	**68384**

10-4 各县(市)财政收入与支出情况

单位:万元

(2003)

项目	Item
财政总收入	**Total Financial Revenue**
中央收入	**Revenue of Central Government**
地方财政收入	**Local Financial Revenue**
一般预算收入	**Budgetary Revenue**
#增值税	Value - added Tax
营业税	Operation Tax
企业所得税	Enterprise's Income Tax
个人所得税	Individual Income Tax
城市维护建设税	Tax on Urban Construction and Maintenance
农业四税	Total Agriculture Tax
国有企业计划亏损补贴	Subsidies to Loss - suffering State - owned Enterprises
罚没收入	Fine & Confiscatory Revenue
专项收入	Special Revenue
其他收入	Other Revenue
基金收入	**Fund Revenue**
财政支出	**Financial Expenditure**
一般预算支出	**Ordinary Budgetary Expenditure**
#基本建设支出	Expenditure for Capital Construction
企业挖潜改造支出	Expenditure for Innovation Enterprises
科技三项费用	Expenditure for Science and Technology Promotion
农业林业水利和气象支出	Expenditure for Agriculture, Forestry, Water Conservancy and Meteorology
教育事业费	Expenditure for Operating Expenses of Education
科学事业费	Expenditure for Operating Expenses of Department of Science
卫生经费	Expenditure for Public Health
其他等部门的事业费	Expenditure for Operating Expense of Others Departments etc.
社会保障补助支出	Expenditure on Subsidies to Social Security Programs
公检法司支出	Expenditure for Public Security Agency, Procuratorial Agency and Court of Justice
行政管理费	Expenditure for Government Administration
城市维护费	Expenditure for City Maintenance
基金支出	**Fund Expenditure**

Basic Statistics on Financial Revenue and Expenditure by Region

(10000 yuan)

全市 Total	市区 Urban District	# 市本级 Directly Under Municipality	# 鄞州 Yinzhou	余姚 Yuyao	慈溪 Cixi	奉化 Fenghua	象山 Xiangshan	宁海 Ninghai
3300291	**2322854**	**1018430**	**376639**	**269416**	**355611**	**114374**	**107651**	**130385**
1855916	**1327932**	**663046**	**200587**	**142407**	**181863**	**68833**	**60450**	**74431**
1444375	**994922**	**355384**	**176052**	**127009**	**173748**	**45541**	**47201**	**55954**
1394162	**959709**	**339228**	**171373**	**119876**	**168195**	**44055**	**46678**	**55649**
339982	214825	73169	47741	34784	42972	16884	12875	17642
413150	290449	101356	54534	30508	50977	11648	13226	16342
241704	177732	68591	21091	16598	22361	7479	9999	7535
97403	63558	20107	14015	8579	12358	3299	4475	5134
93991	71631	33696	7286	5487	7888	3601	2533	2851
127979	79299	3732	17323	13998	21735	4409	4408	4130
- 90973	- 56607	- 27228	- 6080	- 7036	- 5502	- 9185	- 7642	- 5001
36779	17698	5893	4932	3370	6424	3067	2972	3248
48269	39498	25468	3682	3057	2952	1064	786	912
2520	2094	1494	167	145	149	31	64	37
50213	**35213**	**16156**	**4679**	**7133**	**5553**	**1486**	**523**	**305**
1870929	**1268421**	**448299**	**219203**	**163788**	**203843**	**69983**	**79532**	**85362**
1802545	**1220526**	**417481**	**215520**	**157319**	**196946**	**68004**	**76440**	**83310**
241430	164509	55020	43716	26064	39819	5742	3077	2219
195346	157360	19942	35459	4088	24184	2785	3416	3513
33561	21288	4802	5749	3040	6268	1134	600	1231
104662	37621	9547	10494	15026	23864	6370	11436	10345
217807	116034	42907	24111	22858	29635	13697	16476	19107
5103	4414	3757	224	185	304	52	87	61
75527	46149	22249	9398	8810	6995	3598	5731	4244
160901	108851	24752	14323	12064	15866	7173	6877	10070
59609	50408	22309	16799	3109	3377	1117	986	612
118870	72153	36248	7273	14817	12258	6130	6372	7140
141406	78128	28495	12720	22249	10571	11021	8652	10785
220981	193811	71942	5276	9656	11384	1730	2200	2200
68384	**47895**	**30818**	**3683**	**6469**	**6897**	**1979**	**3092**	**2052**

10－5 主要年份金融机构存贷款与现金收支情况

Savings Deposits and Loans Balances of Financial Institutions & Cash Revenue and Expenditures in Main Years

单位:万元 (10000 yuan)

年份 Year	存款余额 Deposits Balance	#城乡居民储蓄 Urban and Rural Savings Deposits	贷款余额 Loans Balance	现金收入 Cash Income	现金支出 Cash Expenditure	货币投放(＋)回笼(－) Currency Issues (＋) or Cash Withdrawal(－)
1978	48358	15190	65015	73808	82932	
1979	61699	20612	74688	93147	103768	
1980	83670	28781	97127	116500	130884	
1981	100998	34418	106366	134891	145646	
1982	124092	46298	121746	152004	163021	
1983	146331	60536	135140	187097	198487	
1984	182683	81558	222276	239421	275813	
1985	243288	109853	270853	346161	386016	39855
1986	318036	149451	371124	427346	466049	38703
1987	385955	199095	435067	558362	623683	65321
1988	521275	215357	645506	812913	929145	116210
1989	639108	317572	764912	929399	1000287	70888
1990	901290	461221	974358	1043951	1102544	58593
1991	1180588	605796	1227009	1321356	1401416	80060
1992	1605229	792466	1603689	1957225	2099612	142387
1993	2012813	979740	2116122	3295921	3441608	145687
1994	2972601	1468634	2671174	4949086	5199010	249924
1995	4546806	2094162	3892271	7121857	7452530	330682
1996	5879170	2840023	4936543	9312625	9789622	476997
1997	7172242	3644769	5747533	12202712	12646470	443758
1998	8552754	4596343	6700817	19733593	20136905	403312
1999	10080232	5296350	7734820	24090235	24591240	501005
2000	11729401	5860592	8831213	30467325	31088353	621028
2001	14445304	6994639	10515601	36286694	37062049	775355
2002	19062373	8623908	14794723	49240318	50379541	1139223
2003	26290346	10596339	21027772	68390220	69703625	1313405

10－6　金融机构信贷资金主要指标(资金来源)

Main Indicators of Credit Funds of Financial Institutions – Sources of Funds

(年末余额)单位:万元　　(year – end)(10000　yuan)

项目	Item	1998	2001	2002	2003
资金来源合计	**All Sources**	**7151851**	**11499747**	**16177221**	**23229994**
各项存款	**Deposits**	**8552754**	**14445304**	**19062373**	**26290346**
企业存款	Deposits of Enterprise	3197506	6134533	7857053	11262310
#活期存款	Circulating – term Deposits	2192770	4457291	5897154	8005297
定期存款	Fixed – term Deposits	1004736	1677242	1959899	3257013
财政存款	Deposits of Finance	46566	76196	117629	161830
机关团体存款	Deposits of Government Agencie Organizations	87794	185618	405365	818148
储蓄存款	Savings Deposits	4596343	6994639	8623908	10596339
#活期存款	Circulating – term Deposits	727480	1815173	2566803	3427008
定期存款	Fixed – term Deposits	3868863	5179466	6057105	7169331
农业存款	Agricultural Deposits	294099	536070	777298	1141187
信托存款	Trusted Deposits	149096	1746	491	288
委托存款	Commissiom Deposits	60221	8309	12243	79125
其他存款	Other Deposits	121129	508193	1268386	2231119
金融债券	**Bonds**	**106**	**41**	**37**	**– 85707**
应付及暂收款	**Payment and Temporary Receipts**		**160088**	**237277**	**371447**
同业往来	**Exchanges of Financial Institutions**		**594013**		**219851**
各项准备	**Every Provision**		**53321**	**84384**	**103851**
所有者权益	**Creditors Equity**	**109240**	**156469**	**203844**	**371515**
#实收资本	Capital Obtained	175288	130007	82434	101605
当年结益	Balance	– 79235	60831	86920	207573
其他	**Others**	**– 1567009**	**– 3389237**	**– 3410694**	**– 4041309**

10-7 金融机构信贷资金主要指标(资金运用)

Main Indicators of Credit Funds of Financial Institutions - Use of Funds1

(年末余额)单位:万元 (year - end)(10000 yuan)

项目	Item	1998	2001	2002	2003
资金运用合计	**All Uses**	**7151851**	**11499747**	**16177221**	**23229994**
各项贷款	**Loans**	**6700817**	**10515601**	**14794723**	**21027772**
短期贷款	Short - term Loans	5035128	7204200	9640296	13165387
工业贷款	Industrial Loans	981214	1315507	1728500	2556164
商业贷款	Commercial Loans	1432813	1459475	1897762	2308090
建筑业贷款	Construction Loans	122522	315759	566947	492629
农业贷款	Agricultural Loans	211715	321904	437332	670755
乡镇企业贷款	Loans to Township Enterprises	1290106	1638497	1858957	2338104
三资企业贷款	Loans to Sino - foreign Joint Venture and Cooperative Enterprises and Foreign - funded Enterprises	301609	510236	578247	630358
私营企业及个体贷款	Loans to Private Enterprises and Individuals	58391	148268	335601	519811
其他短期贷款	Other Short - term Loans	636758	1494554	2236950	3649476
中期流动资金贷款	Medium - term Circulating Funds Loans	54615	219348	497401	714558
中长期贷款	Medium - term&Long - term Loans	1106715	2750438	3633548	5734436
基本建设贷款	Capital Construction	664305	1566125	2006634	3027414
技术改造贷款	Technical Innovation	283776	242369	99396	152346
其它中长期贷款	Other Medium - term&Long - term Loans	158634	941944	1527518	2554676
信托贷款	Trusted Loans	112342	12757	1836	691
委托贷款	Commission Loans	59857	7623	13028	85027
票据融资	Circulating Funds of Bills		305889	987970	1297059
各项垫款	Paying in advance		15277	13569	13026
有价证券及投资	**Securities & Investment**	**256214**	**662562**	**1085294**	**1214546**
应收及预付款	**Receivables and Advance Payment**		**140916**	**128741**	**157505**
同业往来	**Exchanges of Financial Institutions**		**54512**		**36082**
委托投资	**Consigned Investments**	**21577**	**1107**	**1107**	**50831**
金银占款	**Purchase of Gold & Silver**	**2002**	**3314**	**8**	**35**
外汇占款	**Purchase of Foreign Exchanges**	**77130**	**2346**	**27779**	**25933**
库存现金	**Storage Cash**	**71126**	**124444**	**139569**	**171490**

10－8　金融机构现金收入与支出主要指标

Main Indicators Cash income and Cash Expenditures of Financial Institutions

单位:万元　　(10000 yuan)

项目	Item	1998	2001	2002	2003
收入合计	**Total Income**	**19733593**	**36286694**	**49240318**	**68390220**
商业销售收入	Commodity Sales	3419873	5486736	6753852	8879479
服务业收入	Service Trade	995542	1685501	2073957	2493709
税款收入	Taxes	111215	197720	220197	316852
城乡个体经营收入	Urban and Rural Individual Business	887687	1778172	2383331	3286639
储蓄存款收入	Savings Deposits	12009108	22153851	31508129	45032522
其他金融机构收入	Other Financial Institutions	203407	363814	322141	206943
居民归还贷款收入	Repayment of Loans by Residents	217220	465715	564649	839281
汇兑收入	Remittances	355621	764123	741863	827628
有价证券收入	Securities	178677	268637	222985	313840
其他收入	Other Income	1355243	3122425	4449214	6193327
支出合计	**Total Expenditure**	**20136905**	**37062049**	**50379541**	**69703625**
工资性支出	Wages	1997446	2714757	3239342	4516036
农副产品采购支出	Purchases of Agricultural and Sideline Products	318542	1002707	1226815	1610430
工矿及其他产品采购支出	Purchases of Dustrial and MineralProducts		843288	1039274	1711575
行政企事业管理费支出	Government and Enterprises Overhead	1521696	2572612	3130413	4093456
城乡个体经营支出	Individual Business	1436605	2762552	3651823	4707277
储蓄存款支出	Savings Deposits	11674060	22620064	31699253	44563119
其他金融机构支出	Other Financial Institutions	125716	300666	364645	318517
居民提取贷款支出	Loans by Residents	192094	401023	483180	715908
汇兑支出	Remittances	266658	335325	371091	375586
有价证券支出	Securities	221806	232975	227881	215810
其他支出	Other Expenditure	1582147	3276080	4945824	6875911
投放(＋)回笼(－)	**Monetary Issues(＋)Cash Withdrawn(－)**	**403312**	**775355**	**1139223**	**1313405**

10－9 部分年份保险业务情况

Conditions of Insurance Business in Partial Year

单位:亿元 (100 million yuan)

项目	Item	1995	1997	2001	2002	2003
承保额	Insurance Value	1950.43	2171.80	5072.30	5508.31	9927.47
保费收入	Premiums	7.51	13.38	26.95	31.47	38.36
#财产险	Property Insurance	5.63	6.85	9.73	11.51	13.35
#人身险	Life Insurance	1.88	6.53	17.22	19.96	25.01
赔付支出	Indemnity Expenditure of the Year	2.98	6.76	6.35	7.96	9.45

10－10 分地区保险业务情况

Conditions of Insurance Business by Region

单位:万元 (2003) (10000 yuan)

地区	Region	承保额 Total Insurance	保费 Premium	#财产险 Property	#人身险 Life	已决赔款 Indemnity Expenditure
全市	Total	99274700	383646	133498	250148	94512
市区	Urban District	73969600	243628	83017	160611	55265
#鄞州	Yinzhou	10533000	34240	11429	22810	11380
余姚	Yuyao	6184800	33736	13329	20407	10156
慈溪	Cixi	9331800	51616	19710	31906	14011
奉化	Fenghua	4119900	19846	6069	13777	5471
象山	Xiangshan	2968300	17738	4817	12921	4570
宁海	Ninghai	2700300	17082	6556	10526	5040

主要指标解释

【财政收入】 国家财政参与社会产品分配所取得收入，是实现国家职能的财力保证。财政收入包括的内容几经变化，目前主要包括：

(1)各项税收 包括增值税、营业税、消费税、土地增值税、城市维护建设税、资源税、城市土地使用税、印花税、固定资产投资方向调节税、个人所得税、企业所得税、关税、农牧业税和耕地占用税等。

(2)专项收入 包括征收排污费、征收城市水资源费收入，教育费附加收入等。

(3)其他收入 包括基本建设贷款归还收入、国家能源交通重点建设基金收入、国家预算调节基金等。

(4)国有企业计划亏损补贴 这项为负收入，冲减财政收入。

【财政支出】 国家财政将筹集起来的资金进行分配使用，以满足经济建设和各项事业的需要，主要包括：

(1)基本建设支出

(2)企业挖潜改造资金

(3)地质勘探费用

(4)科技三项费用

(5)支援农村生产支出

(6)农林水利气象等部门的事业费用

(7)工业交通商业等部门的事业费

(8)文教科学卫生事业费

(9)抚恤和社会福利救济费

(10)国防支出

(11)行政管理费

(12)价格补贴支出

【存款】 企业、机关、团体或居民根据可以收回的原则，把货币资金存入银行或其他信用机构保管并取得一定利息的一种信用活动形式。根据存款对象的不同可划分为企业存款、财政存款、机关团体存款、基本建设存款、城镇储蓄存款、农村存款等科目。它是银行信贷资金的主要来源。

【贷款】 银行或其他信用机构根据必须归还的原则，按一定利率，为企业、个人等提供资金的一种信用活动形式。我国银行贷款分为流动资金贷款、固定资产贷款、城乡个体工商户贷款以农业贷款等科目。

【承保额】 又叫保险金额。它是保险人员对被保险人负提损失补偿或约定给付的金额。它是保险合同上的最高责任额，也是计算保费的依据。

【保费】 又叫保险费。是保险人根据保险合同的有关规定，为被保险人取得因约定危险事故发生所造成的经济损失补偿(或给付)权利，付给保险人的代价。包括财产险和人身险储金收入。

【赔款】 保险事故发生后，经查证确属保险责任范围以内的保险标的损失，保险人根据保险合同的规定履行赔偿义务，给与被保险人的款项叫做赔款。赔款可以分为已决赔款和未决赔款两种。

Explanatory Notes on Main Statistical Indicators

【Government Revenue】 refers to the revenue of government finance by means of participating the distribution of the social products, which is the financial resources for ensuring the government to function. The contents of government revenue have been changed several times. Now it includes the following main items:

(1) Various tax revenue, including value added tax, business tax, consumption tax, land value added tax, tax on city maintenance and construction, resources tax, tax on the urban land, stamp tax, tax on the adjustment of orientation of investment in the fixed assets, personal income tax, tariff, tax on agriculture and animal husbandry and tax on occupation of cultivated land, etc.

(2) Special revenues, including revenue collected from imposing fee on sewage treatment, revenue collected from imposing fee on urban water resources, and extra – charges for educations, etc.

(3) Other revenues, including revenue from the re – payment of capital construction loan, the funds for the state key construction projects in energy industry and transportation, and the funds for state budget adjustment, etc.

(4) Planned subsidies for the losses of the state – = owned enterprises. This is an item of negative revenue, used to eat up part of the government revenue.

【Government Expenditure】 refers to the distribution and use of the funds the government finance has raised, so as to meet the need s of economic construction and various causes. It included the following main items:

(1) Expenditure for capital construction

(2) Innovation funds of the enterprises

(3) Geological prospecting expenses

(4) Expenditures for science and technology promotion

(5) Expenditure for supporting rural production

(6) Operating Expenses of departments of farming, forestry, water conservancy and meteorology etc.

(7) Operating expenses of departments of industry, transport and commerce

(8) Operating expenses of departments of culture, education, science and public health

(9) Pension for the disabled or the families of the bereaved and relief funds for social welfare

(10) Expenditures for national defense

(11) Administrative expenses

(12) Expenditure for price subsidies

【Deposit】 is a form a of credit by which enterprises, institutions, organizations or residents can put money into banks and other credit institutions for safekeeping and interest earning under the principle of free withdrawal. According to different depositors, deposits are divided into enterprise deposits, deposits of government agencies and institutions, capital construction deposits, urban savings deposits, rural deposits and other deposits. Deposits are major sources of the credit funds of banks.

【Loan】 is a form a of credit by which banks and other institutions provide funds at a certain interest rate to enterprise sand individuals in light of the principle of unconditional re – payment. Loans from Chinese banks include circulating capital loans, fixed assets loans, loans to urban and rural individuals engaged in industrial and commercial business and agricultural loans.

【Amount Insured】 refers to the amount of compensation for loss or agreed sum of money to be paid by the insurer to the insurant. It is the maximum amount of liabilities written in the insurance contract and is also used as a basis to calculate the premium.

【Premium】 is the fee paid by the insurant based on a proportion of the benefit he or she may get from the insurance plus the insurance value. It includes the income from the deposit of property insurance and personal insurance.

【Settled Claim】 is the compensation paid by the insurer to the insurant in accordance with the insurance contract for the loss which has been checked and found to be in the range of liability of insurance after an accident has happened to the insured property or to a person who has insured for his life. It is further divided into settled and unsettled claim.

11

劳动工资、劳保福利、从业人员

CHAPTER 11 WAGES, WELFARE AND EMPLOYMENT

劳动工资，劳保福利，从业人员
Wages, Welfare and Employment

主要统计指标
Major Statistics Indicators

2003 年劳动力资源总数	Total Labor Force Resource at The Year – end	484.7	万人	10000 persons
2003 年城镇集体以上从业人员数	Number of Employed Personnel at The Year – end Above Town Level	65.34	万人	10000 persons
2003 年城镇集体以上在岗职工数	Number of Staff and Workers at Work Above Town Level	61.29	万人	10000 persons
2003 年城镇集体以上在岗职工平均工资	Average Wage of Staff and Workers at Work Above Town Level	23690	元	yuan
2003 年城镇集体以上在岗职工中研究生人数	Number of Postgraduates in Staff ans Workers at Work Above Town Level	3060	人	person
2003 年城镇集体以上在岗职工中大学本科人数	Number of Regular Collage in Staff and Workers at Work Above Town Level	60678	人	person
2003 年城镇集体以上在岗职工中大专生人数	Number of Junior College in Staff and Workers at Work Above Town Level	87009	人	person
2003 年末登记失业人员数	Number of Registered Unemployment at the Year – end	41029	人	person
2003 年保险福利费总额	Total Insurance and Welfare Funds	3089250	万元	10000 yuan
2003 年退休金总额	Total Living Expenses for Resignation Allowances	2724519	万元	10000 yuan

11－1 城乡劳动力资源配置情况

Sources and Distribution of Urban and Rural Labor Force

单位:万人　　(2003)　　(10000 persons)

项目	Item	城乡合计 Total	城镇 Urban	乡村 Rural
年末人口数	**Total Population at The Year－end**	**614.3**	**258**	**356.3**
年末16岁以上全部人口数	Total Population Above 16 Ages at the Year－end	508.9	172	336.9
#不计入劳动力资源的人数	Non labor Force Resource	24.2	13.6	10.6
年末劳动力资源总数	**Total Labor Force Resource at The Year－end**	**484.7**	**158.4**	**326.3**
经济活动人口	**Economic Activity Population**	**390.3**	**113.1**	**277.2**
从业人员	Employmed Person	386.2	109.0	277.2
按就业身份分组	Group by Employment Identity			
城镇单位从业人员	Urban Collective－Owned and Above	65.3	65.3	
私营业主	Private Owner	13.2	6.4	6.8
个体户主	Individual Householder	21.6	7.7	13.9
私营企业和个体从业人员	Employed Persons in Private and Individual Units	118.4	27.9	90.5
乡镇企业从业人员	Employed Persons in Township Enterprises	75.2		75.2
乡村农业劳动力	Rural Labor Force	87.0		87.0
其他	Others	5.5	1.7	3.8
按登记注册类型分组	Group by Registered Type			
国有单位	State－Owned Units	23.3	23.3	
集体单位	Collective－Owned Units	162.3	4.3	158.0
股份合作单位	Share－holding Cooperative Units	1.9	1.9	
联营单位	Joint Ownership Units	0.2	0.2	
有限责任公司	Limited Liability Corporations	11.0	11.0	
股份有限公司	Share－holding Corporations Ltd.	12.3	12.3	
私营单位	Private Enterprises	115.1	27.3	87.8
其他	Others	1.6	1.6	
港、澳、台商投资单位	HongKong, Macao and Taiwan Funded	7.9	7.9	
外商投资单位	Enterprises with Foreign Investment	4.3	4.3	
个体	Individual Enterprises	46.3	14.9	31.4

单位:万人　　11－1续表　continued　　(10000 persons)

项目	Item	城乡合计 Total	城镇 Urban	乡村 Rural
按国民经济行业分组	Group by Sector			
农、林、牧、渔业	Framing, Forestry, Animal Husbandry and Fishery	88.1	0.3	87.8
采掘业	Mining and Quarrying	0.4		0.4
制造业	Manufacuring	183.6	32.6	151.0
电力煤气及水的生产和供应业	Electric Power, Gas and Water Production and Supply	1.3	1.3	
建筑业	Construction	13.1	11	2.1
交通运输、仓储业及邮政业	Transportation, Storage and Post Industries	7.2	4.8	2.4
信息传输、计算机服务和软件业	Information Transmission, Computer Service and Software Industries	1.0	1.0	
批发和零售业	Wholesale & Retail Industries	34.7	15.3	19.4
住宿和餐饮业	Hotel and Catering Trade	7.2	4.8	2.4
金融业	Financial Industries	3.0	3.0	
房地产业	Real Estate Industries	1.4	1.4	
租赁和商务服务业	Leasing and Business Service Industries	1.5	1.5	
科学研究、技术服务和地质勘察业	Scientific Research, Technology Service and Geological Prospecting	1.0	1.0	
水利、环境和公共设施管理业	Water Conservancy, Environment and Public Facility Management Industries	1.0	1.0	
居民服务和其他服务业	Resident Service and Other Service IndustuiesOthers	23.1	11.4	11.7
教育	Education	8.3	8.3	
卫生、社会保障和社会福利业	Health Care, Social Security and Social Welfare	3.8	3.8	
文化、体育和娱乐业	Culture, Sports and Entertainment	1.7	1.7	
公共管理和社会组织	Public Administration and Social Organizations	4.8	4.8	
国际组织	International Organizations			
城镇失业人员	Unemployed Persons in Urban			
城镇登记失业人员	Registered Unemployed Persons in Urban	4.1	4.1	
非经济活动人口	Not the Economic Activity Population	94.4	45.3	49.1
#16岁以上在上在校学生	Student Enrollment Above 16 Ages	24.6	14.2	10.4
家务劳动者	House Work Labourer	56.1	22.5	33.6

11－2　部分年份城镇集体以上在岗职工平均工资

Avergae Wage of Staff and Workers at Work Above Town Level in Partial Year

单位:元　　(yuan)

项目	Item	2001	2002	2003
总计	**Total**	**19089**	**21122**	**23690**
按企业、事业、机关分组	**Grouped by Enterprises, Institutions and Agencies**			
企业	Enterprises	17134	19050	20946
事业	Institutions	22595	24745	29018
机关	Agencies	28325	30713	37068
按国民经济行业分组	**Grouped by Sector**			
农、林、牧、渔业	Framing, Forestry, Animal Husbandry and Fishery	16163	19061	22500
采掘业	Mining and Quarrying	11416	11796	11708
制造业	Manufacuring	14120	15315	16572
电力、煤气及水的生产和供应业	Electric Power, Gas and Water Production and Supply	28971	32223	36213
建筑业	Construction	16728	17873	18606
地质勘查业、水利管理业	Geological Prospecting and Water Conservancy	18607	22696	27934
交通运输、仓储及邮电通信业	Transportation, Storage, Post and Telecommunications	26115	29835	35474
批发和零售贸易、餐饮业	Wholesale & Retail Trade and Catering Services	16428	19099	22576
金融、保险业	Banking and Insurance	24010	28419	34582
房地产业	Real Estate Trade	22859	25470	28967
社会服务业	Social Services	16505	18062	19574
卫生、体育和社会福利业	Health Care, Sports and Social Welfare	24231	26364	29649
教育、文化艺术及广播电视业	Education, Culture and Arts, Radio, Film and Television	22134	24294	28872
科学研究和综合技术服务业	Scientific Research and Polytechnical Services	24965	28668	38522
国家机关、政党机关和社会团体	Government Agencies, Party Agencies and Social Organization	28282	30673	37040
其他行业	Others	29002	26667	33891
按经济类型分	**Group by Type of Ownership**			
国有单位合计	State－Owned Units	23576	26381	31817
城镇集体单位合计	Collective Owned Units	14357	16820	18688
其他单位合计	Others Units	16159	17594	18986

11－3 全市城镇集体以上从业人员和劳动报酬情况

(2003)

项目	Item	单位从业人员年末人数（人）Number of Employed Personnel at The Year－end (person)	女性 Female	在岗职工合计 Staff and Workers at Work
总计	**Total**	**653362**	**248816**	**612933**
按企业、事业、机关分组	**Grouped by Enterprises, Institutions and Agencies**			
企业	Enterprises	483773	175754	449956
事业	Institutions	124215	62391	118972
机关	Agencies	45374	10671	44005
按国民经济行业分组	**Grouped by Sector**			
农、林、牧、渔业	Framing, Forestry, Animal Husbandry and Fishery	2506	782	2475
采掘业	Mining and Quarrying	254	29	245
制造业	Manufacuring	207386	106780	203212
电力、煤气及水的生产和供应业	Electric Power, Gas and Water Production and Supply	13077	3007	12636
建筑业	Construction	121068	7641	104240
地质勘查业、水利管理业	Geological Prospecting and Water Conservancy	2751	565	2696
交通运输、仓储及邮电通信业	Transportation, Storage, Post and Telecommunications	34402	9050	33487
批发和零售贸易、餐饮业	Wholesale & Retail Trade and Catering Services	36462	17312	34393
金融、保险业	Banking and Insurance	30193	16307	24172
房地产业	Real Estate Trade	8299	2590	7169
社会服务业	Social Services	39791	15135	36829
卫生、体育和社会福利业	Health Care, Sports and Social Welfare	29253	18327	28161
教育、文化艺术及广播电视业	Education, Culture and Arts, Radio, Film and Television	70175	37195	67441
科学研究和综合技术服务业	Scientific Research and Polytechnical Services	6391	1711	6047
国家机关、政党机关和社会团体	Government Agencies, Party Agencies and Social Organization	45740	10809	44348
其他行业	Others	5614	1576	5382
按经济类型分	**Group by Type of Ownership**			
国有单位合计	State－Owned Units	232511	92499	222728
城镇集体单位合计	Collective Owned Units	42963	19534	41077
其他单位合计	Others Units	377888	136783	349128

Employed Personnel and Remuneration Payment Above Town Level

专业技术人员 Speciallzed Technical Personnel	年末人数中：职工人数（人） Number of Staff and Workers (person)	平均人数(人) Average Employed Personnel (person)			劳动报酬和生活费(万元) Remuneration Payment and Liging Experses (10000 yuan)				
		单位从业人员 Employed Personnel	在岗职工 Staff and Workers at Work	职工人数 Staff and Workers	单位从业人员报酬 Remuneration Payment to Employed Personnel	在岗职工工资总额 Wages of Staff and Workers at Work	劳动报酬和生活费中：职工工资总额 Wages of Staff and Workers	在岗职工平均工资（元） Average Wage of Staff and Workers at Work (yuan)	职工平均工资（元） Average Wage of Staff and Workers (yuan)
169614	**624349**	**636631**	**598830**	**611482**	**15102994**	**14186352**	**14361566**	**23690**	**23486**
84353	459041	469934	438566	448859	10012547	9186065	9306211	20946	20733
85261	120236	121900	116820	118094	3462282	3389924	3410289	29018	28878
	45072	44797	43444	44529	1628165	1610363	1645066	37068	36944
842	2618	2514	2483	2638	56050	55867	57229	22500	21694
11	246	280	271	272	3305	3173	3188	11708	11721
25292	207809	199816	195912	201396	3365307	3246619	3302877	16572	16400
3965	12699	13022	12605	12661	469543	456471	457184	36213	36110
13674	105035	115152	100676	101623	2331319	1873133	1883863	18606	18538
1286	3010	2732	2675	2999	75682	74724	78192	27934	26073
8524	34845	34644	33832	35258	1217505	1200157	1225681	35474	34763
8082	35453	36162	34109	35248	795731	770050	779502	22576	22115
15527	24806	30351	24045	24613	966071	831526	841074	34582	34172
2677	7313	8072	6938	7086	220189	200974	202740	28967	28611
6143	37256	39417	36442	36913	751292	713298	719802	19574	19500
22461	28253	28455	27416	27503	831350	812856	814588	29649	29618
55063	67767	68950	66327	66658	1956418	1914989	1921760	28872	28830
3995	6170	6258	5905	6027	234016	227470	229301	38522	38046
96	45457	45143	43767	44900	1639001	1621120	1656320	37040	36889
1976	5612	5663	5427	5687	190215	183925	188265	33891	33104
102209	228555	230094	220508	226560	7162757	7015916	7118657	31817	31421
12331	42148	42982	41055	42275	787941	767223	780354	18688	18459
55074	353646	363555	337267	342647	7152296	6403213	6462555	18986	18861

11－4　职工素质情况表

单位：人　　　　(2003)

项目	Item	在岗职工 Staff and Workers at Work	研究生 Postgraduates
总计	**Total**	**612933**	**3260**
按企业、事业、机关分组	**Grouped by Enterprises, Institutions and Agencies**		
企业	Enterprises	449956	940
事业	Institutions	118972	1682
机关	Agencies	44005	638
按国民经济行业分组	**Grouped by Sector**		
农、林、牧、渔业	Framing, Forestry, Animal Husbandry and Fishery	2475	2
采掘业	Mining and Quarrying	245	
制造业	Manufacuring	203212	385
电力、煤气及水的生产和供应业	Electric Power, Gas and Water Production and Supply	12636	35
建筑业	Construction	104240	65
地质勘查业、水利管理业	Geological Prospecting and Water Conservancy	2696	5
交通运输、仓储及邮电通信业	Transportation, Storage, Post and Telecommunications	33487	71
批发和零售贸易、餐饮业	Wholesale & Retail Trade and Catering Services	34393	123
金融、保险业	Banking and Insurance	24172	121
房地产业	Real Estate Trade	7169	20
社会服务业	Social Services	36829	80
卫生、体育和社会福利业	Health Care, Sports and Social Welfare	28161	205
教育、文化艺术及广播电视业	Education, Culture and Arts, Radio, Film and Television	67441	1307
科学研究和综合技术服务业	Scientific Research and Polytechnical Services	6047	158
国家机关、政党机关和社会团体	Government Agencies, Party Agencies and Social Organization	44348	648
其他行业	Others	5382	35
按经济类型分	**Group by Type of Ownership**		
国有单位合计	State－Owned Units	222728	2582
城镇集体单位合计	Collective Owned Units	41077	46
其他单位合计	Others Units	349128	632

Basic Statistics on Quality Situation of Staff and Workers

(person)

在岗职工按文化程度分 Group by Educational Background of Personnel					在岗职工中人才资源 Number of Trained Personnel Resources	在岗职工中专业技术人员 Specialized Technical Personnel
大学本科 Regular Collage	大专 Junior College	中专 Specialized Secondary Schools	中技及职高 Vocational Secondary Schools & Technical Schools	初中及以下 Junior Secondary Schools Nand Below		
60678	**87009**	**76649**	**142770**	**242567**	**256054**	**169614**
21451	41434	41791	123555	220785	125224	84353
28125	29100	29162	12402	18501	94593	85261
11102	16475	5696	6813	3281	36237	
206	245	354	504	1164	976	842
	5	3	27	210	14	11
7036	12734	18158	54302	110597	45454	25292
1312	2189	1318	4767	3015	5195	3965
2407	4496	4724	24809	67739	17367	13674
305	362	492	622	910	1457	1286
2460	5455	3450	11049	11002	12522	8524
1644	4443	4403	11599	12181	12641	8082
3947	7616	5852	4559	2077	18981	15527
638	1538	971	2017	1985	3640	2677
1574	3797	3472	10681	17225	10406	6143
3850	5102	12196	2944	3864	23956	22461
21371	19833	14109	5371	5450	59225	55063
2138	1418	700	935	698	4718	3995
11165	16593	5754	6882	3306	36499	96
625	1183	693	1702	1144	2978	1958
45188	56375	39030	39744	39809	153073	102209
1247	4057	7328	10232	18167	15608	12331
14343	26577	30291	92794	184591	87373	55074

11－5　各县(市)、城镇就业和失业人员变化情况

单位:人　　(2003)

项目	Item	全市 Total	市区 Urban District
本期失业人员总数	**Total Unemployment at the Year－end**	**90829**	**64623**
上期末结转的失业人数	From the Previous Year	39453	28831
本期增加的失业人员	Newly Added in This Year	51376	35792
#女性	Female	25203	17640
由就业转失业	Reemployed to Unemployed	28514	19740
本期失业人员就业人数	**Unemployed to Reemployed at This Year**	**47277**	**32764**
#女性	Female	23769	16620
除就业外其它原因减少的失业人员	Unemployment Reduced for Other Reasons	2523	1762
期末实有登记失业人数	**Registered Unemployment at the Year－end**	**41029**	**30097**
#女性	Female	20238	14820
长期失业者	Long－term Unemployment	16743	13162
本期末从业人员总数	**Total Employed Persons at the Year－end**	**979000**	**624266**
失业率(%)	**Unemployment Rate (%)**	**4.02**	**4.60**

Number of Being Employed and Being Unemployed by Region

(person)

# 鄞州 Yinzhou	余姚 Yuyao	慈溪 Cixi	奉化 Fenghua	象山 Xiangshan	宁海 Ninghai
4877	**3156**	**4838**	**4300**	**7734**	**6178**
2159	1529	2775	1735	3005	1578
2718	1627	2063	2565	4729	4600
1611	822	916	1011	2453	2361
1310	1323	1454	987	1068	3942
2087	**1654**	**2142**	**1528**	**4650**	**4539**
1022	848	899	867	2381	2154
590		51	492	210	8
2200	**1502**	**2645**	**2280**	**2874**	**1631**
1288	760	1159	1235	1513	751
1096	488	891	1045	246	911
65700	**54700**	**107905**	**66000**	**81037**	**45092**
3.24	**2.67**	**2.39**	**3.34**	**3.43**	**3.49**

11－6 各县(市)、区城镇就业和失业人员基本情况

单位:人 (2003)

项目	Item	全市 Total	市区 Urban District
总计	**Total**	**41029**	**30097**
年龄(周岁)和性别	**Group by Age and Sex**		
16－－25周岁	Between 15 to 25 Years Old	10280	7042
#女性	Female	4900	3301
26岁及以上	26 Years Old and Above	30749	23055
#女性	Female	15338	11519
失业时间	**Group by Unemployment Time**		
六个月以下	Below 6 Months	24286	16935
#女性	Female	11807	8120
六个月以上	6 Months and Above	16743	13162
#女性	Female	8431	6700
文化程度	**Group by Education Background**		
大专及以上	Junior College Degree and Above	1920	967
#女性	Female	900	469
中专和高中	Special Secondary school and Senior Secondary Schools Degree	15934	11938
#女性	Female	7106	5310
初中及以下	Junior Secondary Schools Degree and Below	23175	17192
#女性	Female	12232	9041

注:失业时间以办理失业登记时间开始计算。

Basic Statistics on Unemployed Persons in Urban Areas by Region

(person)

# 鄞州 Yinzhou	余姚 Yuyao	慈溪 Cixi	奉化 Fenghua	象山 Xiangshan	宁海 Ninghai
2200	**1502**	**2645**	**2280**	**2874**	**1630**
592	216	347	1042	821	812
391	127	146	575	412	339
1608	1286	2298	1238	2053	819
897	633	1013	660	1101	412
1104	1014	1754	1235	2628	720
653	513	785	656	1418	315
1096	488	891	1045	246	911
635	247	374	579	95	436
202	63	53	504	72	261
98	26	24	234	26	121
907	574	872	717	821	1012
479	288	368	326	316	598
1091	865	1720	1059	1981	358
711	446	767	675	1171	132

Note: Unemployment time begins to calculate with the time of applying for unemployment registration.

11－7 全市离休退休退职人员人数及保险福利费用构成情况

(2003)

项目	Item	离退休退职人员(人)Number of Retired		
		合计 Total	女性 Female	离休人员 Retire Veterans
总计	**Total**	**225521**	**115970**	**3333**
企业	Enterprises	180614	96025	1512
内资企业	Internal Funds Enterprises	173250	93046	1499
国有企业	State－Owned Enterprises	34855	18830	669
集体企业	Collective－Ownwed Enterprises	27991	15139	109
其他企业	Other Enterprises	110404	59077	721
港、澳、台商投资企业	Hongkong, Macao and Taiwan Funded	3886	1534	10
外商投资企业	Enterprises with Foreign Investment	3478	1445	3
事业	Institutions	35294	17544	779
机关	Agencies	9613	2401	1042

Composition of Social Insunrance and Welfare Funds for Tetired and Resigned Persens

and Resigned Persons (person)		保险福利费(万元)Insurance and Welfare Funds (10000 yuan)					
退休人员 Retire Persons	领生活费的退职人员 Resigned Persons Receiving Regular Livin Expense Allowances	合计 Total	离休金 Pensions for Retired Veterans	退休金 Pensions for Retired Persons	退职人员生活费 Living Expenses for Resignation Allowances	医疗卫生费 Expenses for Medical Care	其他 Others
216003	**6185**	**3089250**	**88990**	**2724519**	**50635**	**90359**	**134747**
173496	5606	2038521	35457	1829304	44599	49785	79376
166375	5376	1953458	35167	1752512	42810	47195	75774
32693	1493	399654	15997	345353	11797	10494	16013
26614	1268	314760	2509	281399	10048	8309	12495
107068	2615	1239044	16661	1125760	20965	28392	47266
3736	140	44905	223	40539	1098	1306	1739
3385	90	40158	67	36253	691	1284	1863
33988	527	806976	20436	709493	5351	32989	38707
8519	52	243753	33097	185722	685	7585	16664

主要指标解释

【单位从业人员】 各单位的从业人员是指在各级国家机关、政党机关、社会团体及企业、事业单位中工作,并取得劳动报酬的全部人员。包括:在岗职工、再就业的离退休人员、民办教师以及在各单位中工作的外方人员和港澳台方人员、兼职人员、聘用的外单位下岗人员、借用的外单位人员和第二职业者。不包括离开本单位仍保留劳动关系的职工。

【在岗职工】 指在本单位工作并由单位支付劳动报酬的职工。包括由单位派出学习、劳务及病伤产假且仍由单位支付劳动报酬的人员。

【离开本单位仍保留劳动关系的职工】 指由于各种原因,已经离开本人的生产或工作岗位、并已不在本单位从事其他工作,但仍与用人单位保留劳动关系的职工。包括内部退养人员、停薪留职人员、借给外单位使用人员、下岗职工。

【内部退养职工】 指接正常退休年龄但因各种原因退出工作岗位,并办理了内退手续,在正式办理退休手续前由单位按月发给一定生活费的职工。

【长期职工】 指用工期限在一年以上(含一年)的职工。包括原固定工、合同工、长期临时工和使用期一年以上的原计划外用工。

【临时职工】 指用工期限不超过一年的职工。包括签订一年以内的劳动合同或使用期不超过一年的临时性、季节性用工。

【专业技术人员】 指从事专业技术和从事专业技术管理工作的人员。统计对象为事业、企业单位中已经聘任专业技术职务从事专业技术工作的人员,以及未聘任专业技术职务,现在专业技术岗位上工作的具有中专以上学历的人员。

【人才资源】 指具有初级及以上专业技术职务(职称)或中专以上学历的人员。

【职工受教训培训人员】 指在报告期内纳入单位培训计划,已接受各级各类教育和培训累计五十学时以上的职工人数,以及取得自学考试合格证书的人数。不包括全民普法教育,经常性政治学习和党团活动等。一人参加两项以上学习的按一人计算。

Explanatory Notes on Main Statistical Indicators

【Employees of the Unit】 refers to the personnel who work in the government offices, political parties, social communities, enterprises and public undertakings and get paid. Including: on – the – job employees, reemployed retirees, teachers in schools run by the local people, personnel from abroad or HK, Macao, TW who work in the unit, persons on part time, laid – off personnel from other units, hands borrow ed from other units and concurrent employees. Employees who had left their units but still retain labor contracts with them are excluded.

【Full Employed Staff and Workers】 refers to the employees who work for the unit and get paid by it, including those who are leave because of illness, injuries and pregnancies.

【Left Employees Who Still Retain Labor Contracts with the Unit】 refers to the personnel who had stop working in the unit but still retain labor contracts with the unit. Include pre – retirees, personnel on temporary leave without pays, helping hands borrowed from other units, laid – off personnel.

【Pre – retirees】 refers to the employees who retired a little earlier than their regular retiring ages after had gone though the pre – retiring formalities. These personnel can still get certain amount of living expense monthly from the unit until they formally retire.

【Long – term Employees】 refer to the personnel who had been employed by one unit for at least one year. Include permanent employees, contract employees, long – term temporary workers and others.

【Temporary Workers】 refer to the personnel who had been employed by one unit for less than one year. Include any contract employed, temporary and seasonal employed labors for less than one year.

【Specialized Technical Personnel】 refer to the professional technology and administrative personnel. Its statistical targets include personnel who had been employed and given professional posts by the enterprises and pubic under takings, and the personnel who work in the unit have degrees higher than polytechnic school, but not given professional posts.

【Trained Personnel Sesources】 refer to the personnel who have professional posts (ranks) above the primary grade, or have degrees higher than polytechnic school.

【Personnel Who Receive Further Studies and Job Trainings Among the Employees】 refer to the employees who had received at least 50 class hours of varies kinds of studies and trainings according to the unit's training plan, and those who had acquired certificates for self – study examinations in the reporting period. Popular legal knowledge education for the whole nations, regular political studies, Party or League activities are excluded. Person who have more than two trainings are calculated as one.

Explanatory Notes on Main Statistical Indicators

12

物价及人民生活

CHAPTER 12 PRICES AND PEOPLE'S LIVELIHOOD

物价指数和人民生活
Price Index and People's Livelihood

主要统计指标
Major Statistics Indicators

以上年价格为 100	The Price of Preceding Year is Taken as 100			
2003 年市区居民消费价格总指数	General Consumer Price Index of Urban Residents	101.2		
2003 年市区商品零售价价格指数	General Retail Price Index of Commodities in Urbgan Area	101.6		
2003 年全部工业品出厂价格指数	Total Industrial Products Producer Price Index	102.89		
2003 年全部原材料购进价格指数	Total Raw Materials Fuel and Motive Power Purchasing Price Index	108.37		
2003 年房屋销售价格指数	Saling Price Index of Buildings	116.6		
2003 年土地交易价格指数	Land Transcation Price Index	113.2		
2003 年市区城镇居民人均可支配收入	Per Capital Disposable Income of Urban Resident	14277	元	yuan
2003 年市区城镇居民人均消费性支出	Per Capital Living Expenditure for Consumption of Urban Area	10463	元	yuan
2003 年农村居民人均纯收入	Per Capital Net Income of Rural Resident	6221	元	yuan
2003 年农村居民生活消费性支出	Per Capital Living Expenditures for Consumption of Rural Resident	5194	元	yuan

12－1 市区居民消费价格指数及商品零售价格指数(以上年为 100)

Residents Consumer Price Indices and Retail Price Indices of Commodities in Urban Area(Preceding Year = 100)

各年以上年价格为 100 (Preceding Year = 100)

年份 Year	居民消费价格总指数 General Consumer Price Index	#服务项目 Service	商品零售价格总指数 General Retail Price Index of Commodities
1978	100.0		99.6
1985	116.6	113.6	116.9
1986	106.4	106.0	106.4
1987	110.6	105.2	111.1
1988	124.2	123.9	124.2
1989	116.7	111.6	117.1
1990	104.0	113.7	103.2
1991	106.8	111.5	106.4
1992	112.2	119.5	111.4
1993	126.0	149.5	122.8
1994	123.5	129.8	118.0
1995	119.1	129.8	112.6
1996	110.4	122.0	106.3
1997	103.9	119.5	100.8
1998	99.8	108.4	97.6
1999	100.1	117.8	97.3
2000	100.3	114.0	98.3
2001	99.3	105.4	94.8
2002	99.2	100.6	98.6
2003	101.2	101.3	101.6

12－2 市区居民消费价格指数及商品零售价格指数(以不同年份为 100)

Residents Consumer Price Indices and Retail Price Indices of Commodities in Urban Area(Preceding different Years＝100)

以下列不同年份价格为 100 (Preceding of Price with following different Years＝100)

年份 Year	居民消费价格总指数 General Consumer Price Index	#服务项目 Service	商品零售价格总指数 General Retail Price Index of Commodities
1952	773.3	1843.0	518.0
1957	698.9	1622.6	488.8
1965	660.7	1613.7	505.8
1975	665.1	1751.6	457.0
1978	666.4	1677.1	459.9
1980	572.1	1677.1	413.7
1985	451.4	1341.3	309.8
1989	264.7	869.9	189.6
1990	254.4	764.6	183.6
1991	238.2	686.3	172.5
1992	212.4	574.1	155.1
1993	168.5	384.1	126.3
1994	136.4	296.0	107.2
1995	114.6	227.9	95.0
1996	103.8	186.8	89.4
1997	99.9	156.4	88.7
1998	100.1	144.2	90.8
1999	100.0	122.4	93.4
2000	99.7	107.4	95.0
2001	100.4	101.9	100.2
2002	101.2	101.3	101.6

12－3　城市及农村居民消费价格分类指数
Residents Consumer Price Indices by Urban and Rural

（2003）

项目	Item	城市 Urban	农村 Rural
居民消费价格总指数	**General Consumer Price Index**	**101.2**	**101.0**
服务项目价格指数	**Price Index for Service**	**101.3**	**100.8**
一、食品	Food	103.4	102.7
#粮食	Grain	100.7	104.5
肉禽及其制品	Meat, Poultry and Related Products	107.3	105.3
蛋	Eggs	99.5	100.5
水产品	Aquatic Products	106.4	99.1
菜	Vegetables	106.9	106.6
鲜菜	Fresh Vegetables	106.8	107.9
在外用膳食品	Eating Outside	101.0	102.2
二、烟酒及用品	Tobacco. Liquor and Articles	102.8	102.0
三、衣着	Garments	100.4	100.6
四、家庭设备用品及维修服务	Houshold Facilities Articles and Maintenance Services	97.2	99.1
#耐用消费品	Durable Consumer Goods	97.8	98.8
五、医疗保健和个人用品	Medicine, Medical Articles and Personal Goods	102.1	102.1
#医疗保健	Medicine and medical Articles	102.6	102.7
六、交通和通讯	Transportation and Communication	96.4	97.5
#交通	Transportation	97.4	96.5
通信	Communication	95.6	98.8
七、娱乐教育文化用品及服务	Recreation, Education, Stationery Articles and Services	99.8	99.6
#文娱用耐用消费品及服务	Durable Consumer Goods for Recreational Use	93.7	95.4
教育	Education	101.3	100.1
八、居住	Residence	102.0	99.2

12－4　市区商品零售价格分类指数

Urban Retail Price Index By Category of Commodities

(2003)

项目	Item	城市 (以上年为 100) City(Preceding Year = 100)
商品零售价格总指数	**General Retail Price Index**	**101.6**
一、食品类	Food	103.6
#粮食	Grain	101.4
油脂类	Oil or Fat	107.3
肉禽蛋	Meat, Poultry and Eggs	99.6
水产品	Aquatic Products	106.4
鲜菜	Fresh Vegetables	107.6
鲜果	Fresh Fruits	91.1
饮食业	Catering Trade	101.1
二、饮料、烟酒类	Beverages, Tobacco and Liguor	102.4
三、服装、鞋帽类	Garments, Shoes and Hats	99.7
四、纺织品类	Textiles	99.6
五、家用电器及音像器材	Household Appliances and Audio－video Apparatus	97.2
六、文化办公用品	Stationery and Office Goods	95.4
七、日用品	Daily Use Articles	99.0
八、体育娱乐用品	Sports and Recreation Articles	98.6
九、交通、通信用品	Transportation and Communication Articles	92.8
十、家具	Furniture	99.4
十一、化妆品类	Cosmetics	100.1
十二、金银珠宝类	Gold, silver and Jewelry	124.0
十三、中西药品及医疗保健用品类	Traditional Chinese and Western Medicines, Medical Treatment & Health Protection Articles	104.6
十四、书报杂志及电子出版物类	Book, Newspaper, Magazine and Electronic Publication	102.7
十五、燃料类	Fuels	106.5
十六、建筑材料及五金电料类	Building, Hardware and Electrical Equipment Materials	101.6

12－5 工业品出厂价格指数
Ex－Factory Price Indices of Industrial Products

项目	Item	以上年价格为 100(Preceding Year＝100)				
		1990	1995	1998	2002	2003
全部工业品出厂价格指数	**Total Industrial Products Producer Price Index**	**103.10**	**115.40**	**94.35**	**97.53**	**102.89**
#轻工业	Light Industry	102.20	119.00	99.12	97.79	100.69
以农产品为原料	Using Farm Products as Raw Materials	105.60	118.50	99.08	98.04	102.00
以非农产品为原料	Using Non－Farm Products as Raw Materials	99.10	119.40	99.15	96.40	99.12
重工业	Heavy Industry	102.20	111.80	89.60	97.14	107.31
采掘	Mining and Quarrying Industry				101.29	98.59
原料	Raw Material Industry	102.50	117.30	84.93	97.12	111.32
加工	Manufacturing Industry	102.00	109.40	96.07	97.30	102.76
#生产资料	Production Goods	101.70	114.20	89.94	96.77	105.38
采掘	Mining and Quarrying Industry				101.29	98.59
原料	Raw Material Industry	102.00	123.50	85.00	96.81	111.16
加工	Manufacturing Industry	101.60	110.20	96.48	96.78	102.49
生活资料	Means of Subsistence	103.70	115.90	99.95	98.42	99.71
食品	Food	102.00	122.30	97.56	98.87	100.23
衣着	Garments	110.50	115.40	101.56	98.22	99.56
一般日用品	Articles for Daily Use	102.10	119.00	98.93	99.63	99.09
耐用消费品	Durable Consumer Goods	98.50	91.80	88.41	95.34	98.20

12－6　原材料、燃料、动力购进价格指数

General Purchase Price Indices of Raw Mater, Fuels and Power

项目	Item	以上年价格为 100(Preceding = 100)				
		1990	1995	1998	2002	2003
全部原材料购进价格指数	**Total Raw Materials Fuel and Motive Power Purchasing Price Index**	**101.80**	**114.60**	**87.83**	**96.65**	**108.37**
燃料、动力类	Fuels and Energy	104.10	105.50	85.27	101.20	106.68
黑色金属材料类	Ferrous Metals	101.90	104.60	93.62	98.94	115.03
有色金属材料和电线类	Nonferrous Metal Materials and Electric Wire	93.90	95.20	86.74	96.04	108.59
化工原料类	Chemical Raw Materials	95.30	145.90	92.45	96.22	108.13
木材及纸浆类	Wood and Paper Pulps	107.00	132.30	94.71	100.17	101.66
建筑材料及非金属矿类	Building Materials and Nonmetal Minerals		95.70	99.46	99.90	101.96
其它工业原材料及半成品类	Other Industrial Raw Materials and Semi－products			92.61	92.29	102.86
农副产品类	Farm and Sideline Products	105.30	127.30	99.27	95.82	115.09
纺织原料类	Textile Raw Materials	109.70	123.90	84.42	91.76	106.38

12－7 房地产价格指数
Saling Price Index of Real Estate

(2003)

项目	Item	以上年同期为 100(Preceding = 100)				
		一季度 1. Quarter	二季度 2. Quarter	三季度 3. Quarter	四季度 4. Quarter	全年 Year
房屋销售价格指数	**Saling Price Index of Buildings**	**120.6**	**116.4**	**116.1**	**113.4**	**116.6**
商品房	Commercial Houses	116.3	114.4	117.7	114.7	115.8
住宅	Residential Buildings	116.8	114.8	118.3	114.7	116.2
经济适用房	Economy Buildings	100.0	100.0	100.0	100.0	100.0
普通住宅	Common Residence	118.8	115.7	120.0	117.9	118.1
多层住宅	Multilayer Residence	119.2	122.3	121.9	116.7	120.0
高层住宅	Higher Lever Residence	117.1	107.0	119.0	118.7	115.5
豪华住宅	Luxury Buildings	108.1	115.8	107.3	108.9	110.0
别墅	Villas	111.6	115.8	107.3	108.9	110.9
高档公寓	Flats	104.0				104.0
非住宅	Non－residential Buildings	114.6	113.2	115.7	114.6	114.5
写字楼	Office Buildings	109.1	105.1	105.8	111.0	107.8
商业用房	Commercial Buildings	123.3	121.0	119.0	118.1	120.4
其他	Other	128.0	119.2	109.6	109.4	116.6
公房交易	State－owned Housing Transaction	100.0	100.0	103.0	103.0	101.5
#住宅	Residence	100.0	100.0	103.0	103.0	101.5
私有住房	Private Housing	129.8	121.0	114.0	111.7	119.1
住宅	Residence	134.0	123.7	115.5	110.0	120.8
非住宅	Non－residential Buildings	106.3	105.6	105.7	115.9	108.4
房地产租赁价格指数	**Real Estate Leasing Price Index**	**106.3**	**106.2**	**104.4**	**107.0**	**106.0**
土地交易价格指数	**Land Transcation Price Index**	**127.7**	**106.6**	**106.4**	**111.9**	**113.2**

12-8 36个大中城市基本情况

Basic Statistcis on Urban Households of 36 Largeat Cities

(2003)

城市	City	人均可支配收入(元) Per Capital Disposable Income(yuan)	人均消费性支出(元) Per Capital Consumption Expenditure(yuan)	居民消费价格指数(%) General Consumer Price Index(%)	商品零售价格指数(%) General Retail Price Index(%)
36个城市平均	**Average of 36 Cities**	**10445.95**	**8255.18**	**100.7**	**99.2**
北京	Beijing	13882.62	11123.84	100.2	98.2
天津	Tianjin	10312.91	7867.53	101.0	97.4
石家庄	Shijiazhuang	7740.49	6094.00	102.0	99.7
太原	Taiyuan	8264.34	6374.22	101.9	100.9
呼和浩特	Hohhot	8230.44	6332.14	101.7	100.1
沈阳	Shenyang	7960.97	6690.33	100.9	99.7
大连	Dalian	9101.35	7759.90	100.6	99.4
长春	Changchun	7905.32	6765.98	101.0	100.7
哈尔滨	Harbin	7907.03	6228.93	100.1	98.9
上海	Shanghai	14867.49	11040.34	100.1	99.0
南京	Nanjing	10194.24	7723.14	101.4	98.1
杭州	Hangzhou	12892.04	10071.00	99.5	98.1
宁波	Ningbo	14277.27	10462.94	101.2	101.6
合肥	Hefei	7782.01	6233.62	101.2	101.4
福州	Fuzhou	10183.00	7380.39	99.4	97.6
厦门	Xiamen	12915.28	9457.90	101.0	99.0
南昌	Nanchang	7793.15	5078.88	100.5	99.7
济南	Jinan	11012.86	8395.36	99.9	98.0

12－8 续表 Continued

城市	City	人均可支配收入(元) Per Capital Disposable Income(yuan)	人均消费性支出(元) Per Capital Consumption Expenditure(yuan)	居民消费价格指数(%) General Consumer Price Index(%)	商品零售价格指数(%) General Retail Price Index(%)
青岛	Qingdao	10073.88	8055.03	101.4	98.3
郑州	Zhengzhou	8647.47	6127.18	102.0	101.5
武汉	Wuhan	8520.18	7251.55	102.3	100.4
长沙	Changsha	9942.51	8557.60	100.9	99.2
广州	Guangzhou	15002.58	11570.58	100.1	99.1
深圳	Shenzhen	23905.89	17372.03	100.7	100.0
南宁	Nanning	9162.04	7216.87	100.8	99.5
海口	Haikou	8351.90	6608.65	99.8	99.9
重庆	Chongqing	8093.67	7118.06	100.6	99.5
成都	Chengdu	8823.38	7062.58	102.1	100.2
贵阳	Guiyang	7980.02	6324.37	100.8	97.6
昆明	Kunming	7979.43	6471.65	101.6	100.7
拉萨	Lhasa	8765.45	8045.34	100.4	99.9
西安	Xi'an	7749.49	6805.32	100.5	100.0
兰州	Lanzhou	7094.29	5679.21	100.9	99.2
西宁	Xining	7040.24	5519.62	101.8	101.9
银川	Yinchuan	7246.58	6094.07	101.7	99.8
乌鲁木齐	Urumqi	8370.19	6335.24	100.6	100.2

12－9　城镇居民家庭生活基本情况

(2003)

项目	Item	单位	Unit
调查户数	**Number of Households Surveyed**	**户**	**household**
现住房屋总使用面积	**Total Living Space of Buildings**	**平方米/人**	**sq. m/person**
家庭人口	**Persons Per Household**	**人/户**	**person/household**
就业人口数	Employees Per Household	人/户	person/household
负担系数	Persons Supported By Each Employee	人/就业者	person/empolee
家庭总收入	**Total Income per Household**	**元/人**	**yuan/person**
#可支配收入	Disposable Income	元/人	yuan/person
家庭总支出	**Total Expenditure per Household**	**元/人**	**yuan/person**
(一)消费支出	Consumption Expenditure	元/人	yuan/person
#服务性消费支出	Consumption Expenditure for Service	元/人	yuan/person
恩格尔系数	Engel Coeffcient	%	%
1.食品	Food	元/人	yuan/person
2.衣着	Garments	元/人	yuan/person
3.家庭设备用品及服务	Houshold Facilities Articles and Services	元/人	yuan/person
4.医疗保健	Medicine and medical Articles	元/人	yuan/person
5.交通和通信	Transportation and Communication	元/人	yuan/person
6.教育文化娱乐服务	Recreation, Education and Cultural Services	元/人	yuan/person
7.居住	Residence	元/人	yuan/person
8.杂项商品和服务	Miscellaneous Commodities and Service	元/人	yuan/person
(二)购房与建房支出	Expenditure for Houseing	元/人	yuan/person
(三)转移性支出	Expenditure for Transfer	元/人	yuan/person
(四)财产性支出	Expenditure for Property	元/人	yuan/person
(五)社会保障支出	Expenditure for Social Security	元/人	yuan/person

Basic Living Statistics on Urban Households

全市 Total	市区 Urban Districts	余姚 Yuyao	慈溪 Cixi	奉化 Fenghua	象山 Xiangshan	宁海 Ninghai
800	**400**	**50**	**100**	**100**	**50**	**100**
22.61	**17.13**	**21.32**	**32.73**	**31.55**	**35.68**	**42.10**
2.87	**2.88**	**2.98**	**2.74**	**2.70**	**2.90**	**2.86**
1.63	1.63	1.84	1.55	1.48	1.61	1.47
1.76	1.76	1.62	1.77	1.82	1.80	1.95
15220.50	**15909.18**	**13344.24**	**15976.80**	**13467.00**	**14095.56**	**13312.32**
13851.71	14277.27	12018.36	15096.12	12641.52	13294.08	12560.76
14433.77	**14986.60**	**13145.76**	**12930.36**	**14944.68**	**13533.60**	**14179.32**
9984.16	10462.94	8844.48	10006.56	10231.92	8542.56	8242.44
2714.62	2822.42	2166.12	2863.56	2916.12	2317.08	2585.88
37.96	38.09	39.71	39.86	35.52	33.77	37.12
3790.10	3984.99	3512.04	3988.32	3634.80	2885.16	3059.28
865.09	855.78	1065.00	836.04	809.04	841.56	697.68
670.69	731.33	485.16	617.52	809.88	432.60	589.92
579.86	538.59	411.12	829.20	461.76	782.04	834.96
1177.97	1398.43	622.08	1110.60	873.72	739.56	868.44
1497.55	1623.90	1177.56	1443.96	1521.96	1078.32	1316.04
1143.92	1058.10	1337.52	964.08	1902.72	1481.64	635.40
258.97	271.83	233.88	216.84	218.04	301.80	240.60
1824.18	1844.17	1875.48	606.84	2366.40	2095.32	2880.00
1370.53	1223.21	1291.92	1539.24	1535.40	2049.00	1855.44
70.18	27.69	9.72	76.32	81.48	151.44	593.76
1184.72	1428.59	1124.04	701.52	729.60	695.16	607.68

12-10 市区住户基本情况

Basic Data of Urban Districts Households

(2003)

项目	Item	单位	Unit	合计 Total
现住房总建筑面积	**Total Floor Space of Buildings**	**平方米**	**sq.m**	**23.22**
现住房屋总使用面积	**Total Living Space of Buildings**	**平方米**	**sq.m**	**17.13**
住宅配套率	Rate of Housing Complete Unit	%	%	98.25
房屋产权(合计)	**Housing Property Right(Total)**	**%**	**%**	**100.00**
# 租赁公房	Leasing of State - owned Housing	%	%	10.00
租赁私房	Leasing of Private Housing	%	%	1.25
原有私房	Private Housing existed	%	%	2.50
房改私房	Private Housing through Housing Reforming	%	%	58.00
商品房	Commercial Housing	%	%	28.25
其他	Other	%	%	0.00
住宅建筑式样(合计)	**Construction Model of Building (Total)**	**%**	**%**	**100.00**
# 单栋住宅	Single Housing	%	%	0.25
四居室	With Four Rooms	%	%	3.50
三居室	With Three Rooms	%	%	27.00
二居室	With Two Rooms	%	%	64.00
一居室	Only One Rooms	%	%	3.50
普通楼房	Common Building	%	%	1.75
平房及其他	One - Story Housing and Other	%	%	0.00
装修状况(合计)	**Dekoration (Total)**	**%**	**%**	**100.00**
# 有装修	Dekorated	%	%	86.50
未装修	Non - Dekorated	%	%	13.50
饮水情况(合计)	**Drink (Total)**	**%**	**%**	**100.00**
# 自来水	Tap Water	%	%	41.50
矿泉水	Mineral Water	%	%	18.00

12－10 续表　Continued

项目	Item	单位	Unit	合计 Total
纯净水	Clean Water	%	%	40.50
井、河水	Well－Water, River Water	%	%	0.00
用水情况(合计)	**Consumption of Water (Total)**	**%**	**%**	**100.00**
#独用自来水	Separate Using Tap Water	%	%	100.00
公用自来水	Public Using Tap Water	%	%	0.00
井、河水	Well and River Water	%	%	0.00
卫生设备(合计)	**Sanitary Equipment**	**%**	**%**	**100.00**
#无卫生设备	Non－sanitary Equipment	%	%	1.75
有厕所浴室	With Toilet	%	%	94.25
有厕所无浴室	Non－toilet	%	%	3.50
公用	Public Using Tap Water	%	%	0.50
取暖设备(合计)	**Warm Equipment (Total)**	**%**	**%**	**100.00**
#无取暖设备	Non－warm Equipment	%	%	32.25
空调设备	With Air－Condition	%	%	67.75
暖气	With Heating Installation	%	%	0.00
炊用燃料使用情况(合计)	**Consumption of Fuil (Total)**	**%**	**%**	**100.00**
#管道煤气	Piping Gas	%	%	11.00
液化石油气	Liquid Gas	%	%	88.75
煤	Coal	%	%	0.25
其他	Other	%	%	0.00
通信设备使用情况	**Communication Equipment Owned**			
#无电话(合计)	Non－telephone	%	%	0.50
固定电话	Fixed Telephone	百户	100 Households	100.75
移动电话	Auto－mobile	百户	100 Households	132.50

12－11　市区居民家庭生活基本情况

（2003）

项目	Item	单位	Unit
调查家庭所占比重	**Weight of Surveyed Households**	%	
现住房屋总使用面积	**Total Living Space of Buildings**	**平方米/人**	**sq. m/person**
家庭人口	**Persons Per Household**	**人/户**	**person/household**
就业人口数	Employees Per Household	人/户	person/household
负担系数	Persons Supported By Each Employee	人/就业者	person/empolee
家庭总收入	**Total Income per Household**	**元/人**	**yuan/person**
#可支配收入	Disposable Income	元/人	yuan/person
家庭总支出	**Total Expenditure per Household**	**元/人**	**yuan/person**
(一)消费支出	Consumption Expenditure	元/人	yuan/person
#服务性消费支出	Consumption Expenditure for Service	元/人	yuan/person
恩格尔系数	Engel Coeffcient	%	%
1.食品	Food	元/人	yuan/person
2.衣着	Garments	元/人	yuan/person
3.家庭设备用品及服务	Houshold Facilities Articles and Services	元/人	yuan/person
4.医疗保健	Medicine and medical Articles	元/人	yuan/person
5.交通和通信	Transportation and Communication	元/人	yuan/person
6.教育文化娱乐服务	Recreation, Education and Cultural Services	元/人	yuan/person
7.居住	Residence	元/人	yuan/person
8.杂项商品和服务	Miscellaneous Commodities and Service	元/人	yuan/person
(二)购房与建房支出	Expenditure for Houseing	元/人	yuan/person
(三)转移性支出	Expenditure for Transfer	元/人	yuan/person
(四)财产性支出	Expenditure for Property	元/人	yuan/person
(五)社会保障支出	Expenditure for Social Security	元/人	yuan/person

Basic Living Statistics on Urban Districts Households

按可支配收入分组 Group by Disposable Income							
合计 Total	最低收入户 Lowest Income Households	低收入户 Low Income Households	较低收入户 Relatively Low Income Households	中间收入户 Medium Income Households	较高收入户 Medium - high Income Households	高收入户 High Income Households	最高收入户 Highest Income Households
100	**10**	**10**	**20**	**20**	**20**	**10**	**10**
17.13	**12.95**	**14.39**	**15.23**	**16.76**	**18.43**	**20.63**	**23.69**
2.88	**3.04**	**3.02**	**3.01**	**2.85**	**2.81**	**2.78**	**2.63**
1.63	1.41	1.64	1.64	1.68	1.59	1.71	1.75
1.76	2.15	1.84	1.84	1.70	1.76	1.63	1.50
15909.18	**4642.84**	**6872.15**	**9219.11**	**12578.56**	**17035.97**	**24337.44**	**50699.42**
14277.27	3550.43	5872.57	8153.33	11135.65	15202.80	21873.08	47308.42
14986.60	**6118.05**	**7933.96**	**8878.99**	**11976.98**	**21399.34**	**21203.88**	**33694.15**
10462.94	4902.64	6680.24	7383.59	8936.60	13136.11	13416.60	22828.43
2822.42	1101.69	1880.20	1883.92	2284.94	3443.86	4080.90	6565.87
38.09	52.37	46.11	46.66	44.04	34.70	37.16	25.16
3984.99	2567.30	3080.30	3444.99	3936.07	4557.74	4986.11	5743.26
855.78	287.82	435.19	581.59	763.06	1040.32	1220.59	2052.49
731.33	233.53	317.46	391.76	591.58	925.03	1003.38	2169.37
538.59	184.68	308.99	341.28	433.87	568.82	670.78	1690.43
1398.43	432.04	568.24	781.96	965.26	2453.22	1543.93	3422.29
1623.90	398.74	1288.49	1033.53	1371.09	2088.69	2366.18	3556.61
1058.10	719.07	566.06	640.57	640.89	1162.21	1247.99	3456.58
271.83	79.46	115.51	167.90	234.78	340.07	377.64	737.40
1844.17		34.87	20.63	755.26	5038.35	3670.14	3857.14
1223.21	134.59	241.49	429.99	926.99	1580.24	2054.91	4445.57
27.69		1.24	26.15	20.08	40.11	24.49	87.15
1428.59	1080.81	976.13	1018.64	1338.05	1604.53	2037.74	2475.85

12－12　市区每百户居民家庭主要耐用消费品拥有量

Per 100 Urban Households Annual Average Possession of Durable Consumer Goods

(2003)

项目	Item	单位	Unit	每百户 per 100 Hoseholds
摩托车	Motorcycles	辆	unit	13.50
自行车	Bicycles	辆	unit	186.50
助力车	Electric Bicycles	辆	unit	22.25
家用汽车	Homeuse Car	辆	unit	2.00
洗衣机	Washing Machines	台	unit	92.00
电冰箱	Refrigerators	台	unit	98.75
彩色电视机	Color TV Sets	台	unit	166.75
影碟机	Video CD Sets	台	unit	58.50
家用电脑	Micro－Computers	台	unit	49.50
组合音响	Music Centers	套	set	27.50
摄像机	Video Camera	架	unit	1.75
照相机	Cameras	架	unit	55.75
钢琴	Pianos	架	unit	1.75
微波炉	Microwave Ovens	台	unit	54.25
空调器	Air－conditioners	台	unit	117.25
淋浴热水器	Shower Heaters	台	unit	90.50
排油烟机	Range Hoods	台	unit	93.75
消毒碗柜	Disinfecting Case	台	unit	13.00
洗碗机	Dishwasher	台	unit	0.50
饮水机	Drinking Bowl	台	unit	73.75
吸尘器	Dust Catcher	台	unit	18.00
健身器材	Training Equipment	套	set	8.00
普通电话	common Telephone	部	set	100.75
移动电话	Handy	部	set	132.25
传真机	Fax Mashine	部	set	3.00

12－13　主要年份人民生活水平

Civil Livelihood in Main Years

单位:元 平方米　　(yuan sq.m)

年份 Year	市区居民人均可支配收入 Per Capital Annual Disposable Income of Urban Districts Residents	市区居民人均消费性支出 Per Capital Annual Expenditure for Consumption of Urban Districts Residents	农村居民人均纯收入 Per Capital Annual Net Income of Rural Residents	农村居民人均生活消费支出 Per Capital Annual Living Expenditure of Rural Residents	市区居民人均使用面积 Per Capital Floor Space of Urban Districts Residents	农村居民人均住房面积 Per Capital Floor Space of Rural Residents
1978	306	299				
1979	340	332				
1980	429	419	222	183		
1981	481	490	217	274		
1982	509	492	353	338		
1983	530	502	340	375	9.47	
1984	643	561	483	428	9.63	
1985	889	862	627	564	9.71	21.30
1986	1110	1057	735	673	9.69	22.80
1987	1192	1076	871	762	10.08	24.50
1988	1518	1469	1066	964	10.87	26.00
1989	1742	1543	1199	1051	11.49	27.30
1990	1963	1628	1254	1166	11.67	27.70
1991	2182	1854	1441	1221	11.95	29.90
1992	2674	2204	1624	1368	12.00	31.00
1993	3983	3139	2060	1599	12.06	30.20
1994	6008	4442	2685	2215	12.94	33.60
1995	7275	5566	3484	2432	13.06	31.30
1996	8354	6545	4267	3283	12.82	30.75
1997	9069	7189	4568	3483	13.07	39.95
1998	9193	7912	4697	3589	13.66	37.58
1999	9492	7493	4798	3591	14.55	39.78
2000	10921	7997	5069	3929	15.26	41.57
2001	11991	9463	5362	4383	16.15	43.14
2002	12970	9396	5764	4508	16.17	45.77
2003	14277	10463	6221	5194	17.13	46.86

12－14　部分年份农村居民人均总收入和纯收入

Per Capita Annual Total Income and Net Income of Rural Households in Partial Year

单位:元　　　　(yuan)

项目	Item	1999	2000	2001	2002	2003
全年总收入	**Gross Income**	**5618**	**6431**	**6867**	**7320**	**7628**
全年纯收入	**Net Income**	**4798**	**5069**	**5362**	**5764**	**6221**
基本收入	**Basic Income**	**5191**	**5899**	**6291**	**6531**	**6915**
劳动者报酬收入	Laborers' Remuneration	2487	2685	3251	3380	3598
家庭经营收入	Income from Household Business	2705	3214	3040	3151	3317
农业收入	Planting	1326	1004	1011	1134	1184
林业收入	Forestry	21	47	55	42	50
牧业收入	Animal Husbandry	235	458	516	323	389
渔业收入	Fishery	60	50	99	179	144
工业收入	Industry	60	282	371	363	364
建筑业收入	Construction	164	220	192	243	224
交通运输邮电业收入	Transportation, Post and Communications	216	321	315	391	433
批零售贸易餐饮业收入	Wholesale. Retail Sale and Catering Trade	83	209	201	207	248
服务业收入	Service Trade	98	155	153	119	175
其他家庭经营收入	Others	138	146	99	135	105
转移性收入	**Transfer Income**	**280**	**363**	**376**	**717**	**419**
财产性收入	**Property Income**	**146**	**169**	**199**	**52**	**294**
恩格尔系数(%)	**Engel Coeffcient(%)**	**48.5**	**45.2**	**43.5**	**43.1**	**40.1**

12-15 按收入等级分组农村居民人均总收入

Per Capita Annual Total Income and Net Income of Rural Households Grouped by Level of Net Income

单位:元 (2003) (yuan)

项目	Item	按人均纯收入等级分组 Grouped by Level of Net Income				
		低20%收入户 Lower Income Households (20%)	次低20%收入户 Low Income Households (20%)	中等20%收入户 Middle Income Households (20%)	次高20%收入户 High Income Households (20%)	高20%收入户 Higher Income Households (20%)
全年总收入	**Gross Income**	**3666.9**	**4906.7**	**6800.6**	**8670.0**	**15478.7**
工资性收入	**Wage Income**	**1230.6**	**2441.8**	**3556.6**	**4630.6**	**6788.2**
在非企业组织中劳动得到	From Other Orgazination Except Enterprises	151.7	300.1	549.8	842.6	2548.3
在本地企业中劳动得到	From Local Enterprises	619.2	1417.8	2107.4	2501.1	3221.7
#在本地乡镇企业得到	From Local Township Enterprises	416.9	913.1	1393.2	1846.8	2235.2
常住人口外出从业得到	From Permanent Population Outside Work	214.1	292.2	435.9	521.6	384.4
其他	Others	245.6	431.7	463.5	765.4	633.8
家庭经营收入	**Income from Household Business**	**2232.3**	**2032.1**	**2634.0**	**3181.8**	**7065.4**
农业收入	Agriculture	995.4	912.9	888.4	1293.7	1948.2
林业收入	Forestry	59.5	53.6	81.9	28.9	20.6
牧业收入	Animal Husbandy	432.1	117.7	380.1	60.0	1014.9
渔业收入	Fishery	305.8	138.7	87.3	61.4	104.6
工业收入	Industry	107.8	128.0	153.3	263.0	1299.3
建筑业收入	Construction	120.9	234.4	162.4	321.4	305.8
交通、运输和邮电业收入	Transportation. Posts and Telecommunication	36.2	119.1	519.1	615.3	990.8
批发和零售贸易、餐饮收入	Wholesale. Retail Sale and Catering Trade	86.9	159.7	146.0	292.4	617.1
社会服务业收入	Social Serve Trade	35.6	51.0	144.0	148.5	342.6
文教卫生业收入	Culture. Education and Public Health	0.2		3.1	34.5	173.2
其他家庭经营收入	Others	51.3	117.0	64.6	61.9	248.1
财产性收入	**Property Income**	**-43.0**	**92.4**	**257.9**	**375.9**	**893.0**
转移性收入	**Transfer Income**	**247.0**	**340.4**	**352.0**	**481.7**	**732.1**
全年纯收入	**Net Income**	**1871.1**	**4124.0**	**5807.6**	**7645.8**	**12943.1**

12－16　分地区农村住户收入与支出情况

单位:元

(2003)

项目	Item
农村住户总收入与总支出	**Total Gross Income and Total Expenditures of Rural Households**
总收入	**Total Gross income**
工资性收入	Wage Income
在非企业组织中得到收入	Remuneration from Other Organization Except Enterprises
在本地企业中得到收入	From Local Enterprises
常住人口外出从业得到收入	Transfer Income From Family Outside Members
其他	Others
家庭经营收入	Income from Households Business Operation
第一产业	Primary Industry
第二产业	Secondary Industry
第三产业	Tertiary Industry
财产性收入	Porperty Income
转移性收入	Transfer Income
总支出	**Total Expenditures**
家庭经营费用支出	Expenditure for Households Business Operation
第一产业	Primary Industry
第二产业	Secondary Industry
第三产业	Tertiary Industry
购置生产性固定资产支出	Expenditure for Purchasing Productive Fixed Assets
生产性固定资产折旧	Depreciation of Productive Fixed Assets
税费支出	Expenditure for Tax abd Public Expense
生活消费支出	Living Expenditures for Consumption
食品消费支出	Food
衣着消费	Clothing
居住消费	Residence
家庭设备、用品及服务	Household Facilities, Articles and Services
医疗保健	Medicines and Medical Services
交通通讯消费	Transportations and Communications
文教娱乐用品及服务	Cultural, Education, Recreation Articles &Services
其他商品和服务消费	Others Commodities & Services
财产性支出	Prorerty Expenditure
转移性支出	Transfer Expenditure
可支配收入	**Disposable Income**
全年人均纯收入	**Per Capita Annual NetIncome**
恩格尔系数(%)	**Engel Coeffcient(%)**

Per Annsual Total Income and Per Annual Expenditure of Rural Households by Region

(yuan)

全市 total	市区 Urban District	余姚 Yuyao	慈溪 Cixi	奉化 Fenghua	象山 Xiangshan	宁海 Ninghai
7627.98	**7722.97**	**7667.67**	**8224.06**	**7298.29**	**7187.63**	**6799.17**
3597.78	3932.05	3733.95	5560.21	2886.40	2394.95	2491.75
823.63	1255.51	605.61	1111.64	289.90	185.03	130.27
1912.02	2004.84	2255.31	3281.98	1615.85	834.44	1840.28
364.64	240.14	184.99	235.22	296.93	1056.64	372.58
497.49	431.56	688.03	931.37	683.72	318.84	148.62
3317.34	2956.38	3139.22	1582.04	3814.47	4565.64	3774.93
1767.06	1728.64	1815.91	636.58	2527.43	2491.48	1388.45
588.15	331.49	476.41	151.57	556.02	703.21	1272.10
962.13	896.25	846.90	793.89	731.02	1370.95	1114.38
293.53	424.54	283.63	185.25	160.82	38.63	86.42
419.33	410.00	510.87	411.57	436.60	188.14	446.07
7324.05	**7661.61**	**7240.20**	**6304.72**	**7348.69**	**6684.02**	**6178.50**
1026.36	765.12	874.97	324.74	1244.61	1617.09	701.16
783.39	623.55	612.04	179.49	796.22	1433.59	547.53
122.08	62.32	166.54	20.50	327.02	30.12	15.03
120.89	79.25	96.39	124.75	121.37	153.38	138.60
281.54	152.83	302.57	388.26	157.49	138.34	653.91
165.02	158.82	218.41	431.29	209.32	110.07	172.80
47.60	8.95	28.12	8.42	68.74	19.04	195.90
5194.12	5684.10	5558.02	4927.90	5232.38	4385.44	4131.60
2082.71	2253.42	2095.95	2310.91	2124.49	1755.42	1639.21
288.70	344.62	278.83	313.05	212.99	206.99	237.06
975.53	1245.74	1025.09	341.12	1024.83	856.08	741.30
277.03	334.78	339.50	207.89	224.99	208.49	113.85
374.94	341.75	411.24	460.48	432.97	295.02	316.34
489.98	534.42	561.71	744.40	516.45	400.42	350.54
605.69	531.28	724.93	394.17	618.19	630.08	642.36
99.55	98.09	120.79	155.87	77.48	32.95	90.95
30.84	38.01	10.00	13.09	45.01	38.36	16.77
743.58	1012.61	466.52	642.31	600.45	485.83	479.16
5626.51	**5739.80**	**6085.32**	**6319.2**	**5137.12**	**4916.97**	**5314.89**
6220.86	**6665.04**	**6290.50**	**6777.26**	**5592.15**	**5382.39**	**5445.94**
40.10	**39.64**	**37.71**	**46.89**	**40.60**	**40.00**	**39.67**

12－17　部分年份农村居民人均支出情况

Per Capita Annual Expenditure of Rural Households in Partial Years

单位:元　(yuan)

项目	Item	1999	2000	2001	2002	2003
全年总支出	**Total Expenditure**	**4605**	**5577**	**6376**	**6420**	**7324**
家庭经营费用支出	**Expenditure for Household Business**	**640**	**999**	**1089**	**1033**	**1026**
农业生产支出	Framing	288	280	309	369	382
林业生产支出	Forestry	7	10	16	13	19
牧业生产支出	Animal Husbandry	127	380	396	245	299
渔业生产支出	Fishery	17	29	37	120	83
工业生产支出	Industry	10	155	173	115	115
建筑业支出	Construction	5	9	3	8	7
交通运输邮电业支出	Transportation, Post and Communications	55	82	84	103	92
批发和零售贸易餐饮业	Wholesale. Retail Sale and Catering Trade	3	28	23	32	4
服务业支出	Service Trade	5	14	29	10	16
其他经营支出	Others	7	5	8	13	10
生活消费支出	**Living Expenditure for Consumption**	**3591**	**3929**	**4394**	**4508**	**5194**
食品	Food	1742	1777	1909	1944	2083
衣着	Clothing	204	222	249	270	285
居住	Residence	512	586	779	629	976
家庭设备、用品及服务	Household Facilities. Articles and Services	218	182	173	194	277
医疗保健	Medicines and Medical Services	223	263	299	337	375
交通和通讯	Transportations and Communications	213	307	370	399	490
文教娱乐服务	Cultural. Edcational and Recreational Services	358	421	452	519	606
其他商品和服务	Other Commodities and Services	119	170	163	216	100
购置生产用固定资产支出	**Expenditure for Purchasing Productive Fixed Assets**	**48**	**54**	**152**	**43**	**280**
生产用固定资产折旧	**Depreciation of Productive Fixed Assets**		**141**	**154**	**198**	**165**
税费支出	**Expenditure for Taxes and Expenses**	**44**	**47**	**55**	**68**	**48**
财产性支出	**Prorerty Expenditure**		**47**	**79**	**52**	**31**
转移性支出	**Transfer Expenditure**		**500**	**608**	**717**	**744**

12－18 按收入等级分农村居民人均总支出

Per Capita Annual Expenditure of Rural Households Grouped by Level of Net Income

单位:元　　(2003)　　(yuan)

项目	Item	按人均纯收入等级分组 Grouped by Level of Net Income 低20%收入户 Lower Income Households (20%)	次低20%收入户 Low Income Households (20%)	中等20%收入户 Middle Income Households (20%)	次高20%收入户 High Income Households (20%)	高20%收入户 Higher Income Households (20%)
全年总支出	**Gross Expenditure**	**4939.19**	**4952.64**	**6424.15**	**7649.19**	**13682.82**
生活消费支出	**Living Expenditure forConsumption**	**2792.43**	**3694.37**	**4714.08**	**6056.77**	**9506.42**
食品	Food	1388.30	1831.63	2037.23	2374.87	2965.78
#主食	Staple Food	172.54	190.47	191.89	184.53	211.20
副食	Non－staple Food	671.39	860.66	985.30	1106.78	1261.65
其他食品	Other Food	398.20	504.92	615.68	726.68	1010.54
在外饮食	Eating Outside	98.94	241.82	214.62	311.78	458.68
衣着	Clothing	122.12	206.17	280.77	322.05	562.65
居住	Residence	270.19	460.63	669.76	1067.91	2688.31
家庭设备、用品及服务	Houschold Facilitics, Articles and Services	197.74	153.45	273.07	302.61	495.16
医疗保健	Medicines and Medical Services	212.51	257.63	337.90	522.33	594.28
交通和通迅	Transportation and Communications	212.75	295.45	383.03	664.04	990.68
文教娱乐用品及服务	Cultural, Educational and Recreational Articles and Services	331.13	433.46	607.79	713.22	1025.55
其他商品和服务	Other Commodities and Services	57.69	55.97	124.54	89.75	184.00
家庭经营费用支出	**Expenditure ForHousehold Business**	**1510.43**	**476.60**	**683.35**	**662.59**	**1849.57**
农业生产支出	Agriculture	659.75	303.83	218.35	326.23	378.52
林业生产支出	Forestry	31.90	10.58	21.34	9.01	18.30
牧业生产支出	Animal Husbandry	412.72	76.82	265.96	26.32	750.73
渔业生产支出	Fishery	275.95	45.26	36.35	17.16	13.50
工业生产支出	Industry	95.59	0.04	0.01	130.29	384.23
农村居民生产费用现金支出	**Productive Expenditure Pay for Cash of Rural Inhabitant**	**1561.98**	**640.30**	**765.06**	**777.33**	**2721.68**
农村居民生活消费现金支出	**Living Expenditure Pay for Cash of Rural Inhabitant**	**2649.13**	**3570.42**	**4599.15**	**5957.45**	**9405.24**
食品	Food	1249.82	1711.85	1923.91	2277.83	2865.31
#主食	Staple Food	71.92	88.64	96.83	99.94	138.63
副食	Non－Staple Fooc	635.26	844.31	968.71	1097.77	1238.68

12－18 续表 Continued

项目	Item	按人均纯收入等级分组 Grouped by Level of Net Income				
		低20%收入户 Lower Income Households (20%)	次低20%收入户 Low Income Households (20%)	中等20%收入户 Middle Income Households (20%)	次高20%收入户 High Income Households (20%)	高20%收入户 Higher Income Households (20%)
食品加工费	Food Processing	22.84	30.31	23.06	35.30	20.20
衣着	Clothing	122.12	206.17	280.77	322.05	562.65
#服装	Garments	68.61	129.13	178.72	215.99	389.46
衣着材料	Material of Dress	2.98	3.83	7.22	5.70	8.47
居住	Residence	265.37	456.44	668.15	1065.63	2687.61
#住房	Housing	122.32	272.14	474.24	835.98	2408.87
#装饰、装修	Decorating	5.54	30.41	103.51	291.69	247.34
电费	Electricity	60.60	79.74	87.08	101.66	144.38
燃料	Fuel	65.39	65.99	82.02	80.34	92.98
家庭设备、用品及服务	Household Facilities. Articles and Services	197.74	153.45	273.07	302.61	495.16
医疗保健	Medicines and Medical Services	212.51	257.63	337.90	522.33	594.28
#医药卫生保健用品	Medical Articles	115.28	119.02	181.92	245.62	345.38
医疗保健服务费	Medical Services	97.23	138.61	155.98	276.70	248.90
交通和通讯	Transportation and Communications	212.75	295.45	383.03	664.04	990.68
#交通工具	Means of Transportation	33.26	73.70	103.08	237.97	334.99
通讯工具	means of commumitation	16.97	24.12	52.55	77.38	145.05
交通费	Traffic Fare	51.07	59.56	57.94	100.91	139.56
邮电费	Postage	102.65	129.32	150.32	201.35	318.15
文教娱乐用品及服务	Cultural. Educational and Recreational Articles and Services	331.13	433.46	607.79	713.22	1025.55
#文化教育娱乐用品	Cultural. Edcational and Recreational Articles	38.25	43.72	108.18	152.13	238.80
文教娱乐服务	Cultural. Edcational and Recreational Services	292.88	389.73	499.61	561.09	786.76
#学杂费	Tuition Fee	239.96	343.19	370.64	388.01	518.70
技术培训费	Training Fee	7.53	2.06	13.51	26.59	67.05
文娱费	Cultural and Recreational Fee	20.59	17.89	22.57	19.09	32.28
其他商品和服务	Others	57.69	55.97	124.54	89.75	184.00

12－19　部分年份农村居民家庭平均每百户耐用消费品拥有量

Annual Averger Possession of Durable Consumer Goods Per 100 Rual Huoseholds in Partial Year

项目	Item	1998	1999	2000	2001	2002	2003
洗衣机(台)	Washing Machine (unti)	37	39	47	50	48	50
电冰箱	Refrigerator	56	58	65	69	70	73
空调机	Air Conditioner	3	3	6	8	12	21
抽油烟机	Range Hoods	27	32	45	49	51	55
微波炉	Micro－wave Oven			4	6	8	9
热水器	Shower Heaters			28	30	34	37
摩托车(辆)	Motorcycle	14	19	28	35	40	38
汽车(生活用)	Homeuse Car				1	1	1
电话机(部)	Telephone (set)			68	81	88	90
移动电话	Mobile Phone			24	43	63	79
彩色电视机(台)	Color TV Set (unit)	69	80	100	109	117	129
录放像机	Video Tape Recorder	7	7	11	14	15	14
摄像机	Pickup Camera				1	1	2
影碟机	Video CDSets			20	27	27	31
组合音响(套)	Hi－Fi Stereo Component System			12	15	16	16
照相机(架)	Cameras	8	9	11	11	12	11
家用计算机(台)	Micro－Computers			1	4	9	11
中高档乐器(件)	Medium and High Grade Musical Instruments			1	1	2	2

主要指标解释

【居民消费价格指数】 居民消费价格，是指城乡居民支付生活消费品和服务项目消费的价格，是社会产品和服务项目的最终价格。居民消费价格指数，就是反映一定时期内居民消费价格变动趋势和变动程度的相对数。利用居民消费价格指数，可以全面观察居民消费价格变动对居民生活的影响。居民消费价格指数还是反映通货膨胀程度的重要指标。

【商品零售价格指数】 商品的零售价格是商品在流通过程中的最后一个环节的价格，是工业、商业、餐饮业和其他零售企业向城乡居民、机关团体出售生活消费品和办公用品的价格。因此，商品零售价格指数是全面反映市场零售物价总水平变动趋势和程度的相对数。其目的在于掌握零售商品的价格变动状况，为国家制定经济政策、研究城乡市场流通和为国民经济核算提供科学依据。

【工业品出厂价格指数】 工业品出厂价格，是指工业企业向商业(物资)部门或商业企业、其他生产单位、个人出售的或调拨产品的价格，亦称工业生产者价格。它是工业品进入流通领域的最初价格。工业品出厂价格指数是指反映一定时期内工业品出厂价格水平变动趋势及变动程度的相对数，是国民经济核算和计算工业发展速度的一个重要参考指标。

【原材料、燃料和动力购进价格指数】 是反映工业企业作为生产投入，而从物资交易市场和能源、原材料生产企业购买原材料、燃料、动力产品时，所支付的价格水平变动趋势和程度的统计指标，是扣除工业企业物质消耗成本中价格变动影响的重要依据。

【房屋销售价格指数】 房屋销售价格是指房产所有权转移时买卖双方实际成交的价格。它包括商品房销售、旧房交易和公有住房出售三部分。房屋销售价格指数，就是反映一定时期内房屋销售价格变动趋势和变动程度的相对数。

【城镇居民家庭就业人口】 指城镇居民从事社会劳动并取得劳动报酬或经营收入的人口。就业人口包括国家统筹规划和指导由劳动部门介绍就业，自愿组织起来就业合自谋职业等方式，在国有制、集体所有制、中外合资、中外合作、外商在华独资的企事业单位或私营企业单位工作或从事个体劳动又固定性职业或临时性职业的人口。被聘用或留用的离退休人员也计入就业人口。本指标可以反映出城镇人口的就业情况，是计算就业面、负担系数的资料。

【城镇居民家庭总收入】 指调查户中生活在一起的所有家庭成员在调查期得到的工薪收入、经营净收入、财产性收入、转移性收入的总和，不包括出售财物和借贷收入。收入的统计标准以实际发生的数额为准，无论收入是补发还是预发，只要是调查期得到的都如实计算，不作分摊。

【城镇居民家庭可支配收入】 指调查户可用于最终消费支出和其它非义务性支出以及储蓄的总和，即居民家庭可以用来自由支配的收入。它是家庭总收入扣除交纳的所得税、个人交纳的社会保障费以及调查户的记帐补贴后的收入。

【城镇居民家庭消费性支出】 指被调查的居民家庭用于满足家庭日常生活消费需要的全部支出，包括食品、衣着、家庭设备用品及服务、医疗保健、交通与通讯、娱乐教育文化服务、居住、杂项商品及服务支出等八大类。包括用于赠送的商品和劳务，不包括罚没、丢失款和缴纳的各种税款(如个人所得税、牌照税、房产税等)，也不包括个体劳动者生产经营过程中发生的各项费用。

【农村住户纯收入】 是总收入扣除各项费用性支出后，归农民所有的收入。它是用于生产、非生产投资，改善物质文化生活，以及用于再分配和结余的收入。这个指标用来观察农民实际收入水平，以及农民扩大再生产和改善生活的能力。

纯收入＝总收入—家庭经营费用支出—生产用固定资产折旧—税收—上缴集体承包任务—集体提留和摊派—调查补贴。

【农村住户生活消费支出】 是指农村住户年内用于物质生活和精神生生活方面的支出，直接反映出农民的生活水平、研究农民消费结构的基本指标。生活消费支出包括食品、衣着、家庭设备、用品及服务、医疗保险、交通与通讯、娱乐、教育、文化服务、其他商品和服务等消费支出。

【恩格尔系数】 恩格尔(E. ENGEL)是十九世纪德国的统计学家。他根据经验统计资料，对消费结构的变化提出这样一个看法：一个家庭收入越少，家庭收入中或家庭总支出中用来购买食物的支出所占的比例就越大；一个国家越穷，每个国民的平均收入或平均支出中用来购买食物的费用所占比例就越大；随着家庭收入的增加，家庭收入中或家庭支出中用来购买食物的比例将会下降。这就是恩格尔定律。恩格尔系数是根据恩格尔定律而得出的比例数。

即：恩格尔系数＝食物支出金额/总消费支出金额　X 100%

国际上常常用恩格尔系数来衡量一个国家和地区人民生活水平的状况。根据联合国粮农组织提出的标准，恩格尔系数在60%以上为贫困、50－60%为温饱、40－50%为小康、低于40%以下为富裕。

Explanatory Notes on Main Statistical Indicators

【Consumer Price Index】 refers to the consumption price for living necessities and services by people in urban and rural areas. It is the ultimate price of consumer goods and services. Thus it reflects the relative change in prices of consumer goods and services purchased by urban and rural families and can be used to observe and analyse the impact of price changes in consumer goods and services on living expenditure and actual charge in urban and rural households. The index also serves as a key norm in inflation.

【Retail Price Index】 refers to the last price of goods in the circulation. It is the price that industry, commerce, catering trade and other retail enterprises sell consumer goods and appliances to urban and rural residents, institutions and social organizations. The index thus reflects the relative change of the price in retail markets and as a result the index provides basis for the government on the policymaking, studies of market circulation in urban and rural areas, and national economy accounting.

【Ex – factory Price Index of Industrial Products】 It means that the industrial enterprises sell, allocate and transfer the products price from the commercial (or goods and material) departments or commercial enterprises, other manufactures and individuals, it is also called as industrial producers price. It is the initial price that the industrial products enter into circulate domain. The industrial products Ex – factory price index means that it reflects the ex – factory price level alteration trend and the change degree comparative figure for the industrial products within a certain period of time. It is an important reference target for the national economy accounting and calculation industry development speed as well.

【Price Index of the Purchased Materials, Fuel and Power】 refers to the statistical index of the trend and extent of the price fluctuation which industrial enterprises paid in purchasing the raw materials, fuel and power from goods exchange markets and fuel, material manufacturing enterprises for their own production needs. It is an important basis for the industrial enterprises in deducting fluctuant affections of the price from the material consumption cost.

【Price Index of Houses Selling】 houses selling price refers to the actual price paid in the deal between buyer and seller when the proprietary of houses transfers. Include commodity houses sales, second – hand houses transactions and the public – owned houses sales. The price index of house selling reflects the relative figures which indicate the trend and extent of house price fluctuations within a certain period.

【Employment Population in Urban Households】 refers to urban residents engaged in certain work and receiving payment for their labor or income from their business operation, including those who work in state – owned or collective units, joint ventures, foreign – owned units and private with permanent or temporary jobs. The self – employed individuals and re – employed retirees are also included. This indicator reflects the situation of urban employment and is the basic data for calculating employment rate and dependency ratio.

【Total Income of Urban Households】 It means the summation of the salary income, business net income, property income and transferring income obtained from all the family members lived together who were investigated during the period of investigation, it does not include property sale and the income of the debit and credit. The income statistical standard is subjected to the actual occurred amount no matter what complementary or advanced income. So long as the amount obtained during the period of investigation, it should be calculated as what it is, not be calculated by apportionment.

【Disposable Income of Urban Households】 It means that the investigated family can use final consumed expenditure and the other non – obligation expenditure as well as the saving deposit summation that is the income disposed freely by the resident family. It is the income after the paid income tax, individual paid social security fee and billing allowance of which are deducted from the family total income.

【Expenditure for Consumption of Urban Households】 refers to total expenditure of the sample households for consumption in daily life, including expenditure for various commodities and expenses for non – commodity items such as culture and service, etc., but excluding fines and confiscation, loss, tax payments (such as income tax, license tax, real estates tax, etc.) and various expenses by individual laborers for business purposes.

【Net income of Rural Households】 refers to the income owned by peasants after the deduction of various expenses from total income. It's used for productive and non – productive investment, for improvement of material and cultural life, for expenditure and balance in redistribution. This indicator is used to observe the actual income level of peasants, and the peasants' capacity of expanding reproduction and improving livelihood.

Net income = total income – expenditure of household operational expenses – depreciation of fixed assets from production – tax – payment for collective units for contracted tasks – collective reserve and apportion – subsidy from survey.

【Expenditure of Rural Households for Consumption】 refer to total expenditure of rural households on daily life, including expenses on food, clothing, housing, fuel, articles for daily use, and expenditures on daily life and services. This indicator is used to show the actual consumption level of peasants.

【**Engel Coefficient**】 Mr. E. Engel is a German Statistician at the nineteenth century. According to his experience for statistic information, he pointed out such an opinion for the variation of the consumption structure: the lower a family's income is, the higher ratio is for the expenditure used to buy food from the family total expenditure. The poorer the country is, the higher ratio is for the expenditure used to buy food from every civil average income or average expenditure. Along with the family income increasing, the ratio for the expenditure used to buy food from family income or family expenditure will be decreased. This is called as Engel Law. Engel coefficient is the proportion figure obtained according to the Engel Law. That is: Engel coefficient = food expenditures amount / overall consumption expenditures amount X 100 %. Internationally, Engel coefficient is frequently used for evaluating the people's living standard in a country or area. According to the Standard by the Food and Agricultural Organization's of the United Nation, Engel coefficient above 60% deems as poverty, 50% - 60% deems as subsistence level, 40% - 50% deems as fairly well - off level, less than 40% deems as well - riched level.

13

市政、环保、民政、计划生育、政法

CHAPTER 13 CIVIL FACILITIES, ENVIRONMENT, SOCIAL WELFARE, JUDICATURE AND OTHERS

市政、环保、民政、计划生育、政法及其他
Civil Facilities, Environment, Social Welfare, Judicature and Others

主要统计指标
Major Statistics Indicators

2003 年城市人口密度	Population Density of Urban Districts	1260	人/平方公里	person/sq.km
2003 年人均拥有道路面积	Per Capita Area of Paved Roads	14.64	平方米	sq.m
2003 年人均公共绿地面积	Per Capita Public Green Areas	9.29	平方米	sq.m
2003 年废水排放总量	Total Volume of Waste Water Discharged	23244.6	万吨	10000 tons
2003 年环境噪声达标面积	Standardization Areas of Environment Noise	150.49	平方公里	sq.km
2003 年收养性福利单位数	Number of Welfare – Units for Adopting	18	家	unit
2003 年社会救济总人数	Number of Persons Receiving Relief	77517	人	person
2003 年末实有社团机构数	Factual Number of Social Organizations at The Year – end	1281	个	unit
2003 年准予登记结婚数	Number of Registering Marrige Permitted	42075	对	couple
2003 年计划生育率	Rate of Family Planning	98.97	%	%
2003 年律师人数	Number of Lawyers	580	人	person
2003 年办理公证事项	Number of Notarized Documents	97156	件	case
2003 年调解纠纷总件数	Number of Mediating Disputes	25650	件	case
2003 年档案馆数	Number of Archives	13	个	unit

13-1 部分年份市政公用设施水平
Level of Municipal Public Facilities in Partial Years

项目		Item		1997	2001	2002	2003
城市人口密度	（人/平方公里）	Population Density of Urban Districts	(person/sq.km)	1371	1132	1240	1260
人均拥有城市维护建设资金	（元）	Per Capita Fund on Urban Construction and Maintenance	(yuan)	927.60	4104.00	4516.00	4816.00
人均使用面积	（平方米）	Per Capita Using Space	(sq.m)	19.15	22.80	23.60	24.17
人均居住面积	（平方米）	Per Capita Living Space	(sq.m)	12.23	15.12	14.59	15.30
人均日生活用水量	（升）	Per Capita Daily Consumption of Tap Water for Residential Use	(liter)	206.10	290.63	310.64	315.21
用水普及率	（%）	Percentage of Population with Access to Tap Water	(%)	100.00	98.90	99.65	99.78
每万人拥有公共交通车辆	（标台）	Number of Public Transportations Vehicles Per 10000 Persons	(unit)	19.24	12.80	14.23	15.63
燃气普及率	（%）	Percentage of Population with Access to Gas	(%)	99.73	97.34	99.09	99.49
人均拥有道路面积	（平方米）	Per Capita Area of Paved Roads	(sq.m)	11.47	12.70	13.88	14.64
路网密度	（公里/平方公里）	Density of Road Net	(km/sq.km)		1.04	1.19	1.23
排水管道密度	（公里/平方公里）	Density of Drainpipes	(km/sq.km)	9.15	13.90	15.34	14.61
污水处理率	（%）	Percentage of Sewage Disposed	(%)	27.20	36.44	38.92	37.65
人均公共绿地面积	（平方米）	Per Capita Public Green Areas	(sq.m)	4.44	6.26	7.95	9.29
建成区绿地率	（%）	Rate of Afforestation in Developed Area	(%)	20.35	25.37	28.09	27.80
建成区绿化覆盖率	（%）	Coverage Rate of Afforestation in Developed Area	(%)	22.22	30.99	33.43	33.13
垃圾无害化处理率	（%）	Innocuous Disposal Rate of Garbage	(%)	74.40	85.07	88.10	90.52
粪便处理率	（%）	Innocuous Disposal Rate of Night Soil	(%)		90.81	99.52	99.04
水冲公厕比率	（%）	Rate of Public latrine with Water Washes	(%)		93.15	93.76	96.00

13－2　各县(市)城市市政,公用事业情况

(2003)

项目		Item	
人口密度	(人/平方公里)	Population Density of Urban Districts	(person/sq.km)
人均拥有城市维护建设资金	(元)	Per Capita Fund on Urban Construction and Maintenance	(yuan)
人均使用面积	(平方米)	Per Capita Using Space	(sq.m)
人均居住面积	(平方米)	Per Capita Living Space	(sq.m)
人均日生活用水量	(升)	Per Capita Daily Consumption of Tap Water for Residential Use	(liter)
用水普及率	(%)	Percentage of Population with Access to Tap Water	(%)
每万人拥有公共交通车辆	(标台)	Number of Public Transportations Vehicles Per 10000 Persons	(unit)
燃气普及率	(%)	Percentage of Population with Access to Gas	(%)
人均拥有道路面积	(平方米)	Per Capita Area of Paved Roads	(sq.m)
路网密度	(公里/平方公里)	Density of Road Net	(km/sq.km)
排水管道密度	(公里/平方公里)	Density of Drainpipes	(km/sq.km)
污水处理率	(%)	Percentage of Sewage Disposed	(%)
人均公共绿地面积	(平方米)	Per Capita Public Green Areas	(sq.m)
建成区绿地率	(%)	Rate of Afforestation in Developed Area	(%)
建成区绿化覆盖率	(%)	Coverage Rate of Afforestation in Developed Area	(%)
垃圾无害化处理率	(%)	Innocuous Disposal Rate of Garbage	(%)
粪便处理率	(%)	Innocuous Disposal Rate of Night Soil	%
水冲公厕比率	(%)	Rate of Public latrine with Water Washes	(%)

Basic Statistics on Civil Facilities and Public Utilities by Region

全市 Total	市区 Urban District	#鄞州 Yinzhou	余姚 Yuyao	慈溪 Cixi	奉化 Fenghua	象山 Xiangshan	宁海 Ninghai
1260	1005		1181	3561	1499	4697	2550
4816	5343		2816	7544	2383	3030	2525
24.17	22.54		19.09	22.79	29.68	36.20	34.58
15.30	14.27		12.08	14.43	18.79	22.90	21.85
315.21	355.98		206.29	287.82	238.42	321.50	353.92
99.78	100.00	100.00	100.00	100.00	100.00	95.80	100.00
15.63	19.58		7.47	3.97	30.21	11.63	14.88
99.49	100.00	100.00	100.00	98.60	100.00	93.84	100.00
14.61	12.95	25.36	15.46	15.85	9.56	21.75	27.39
1.23	0.88	5.03	0.91	4.01	1.46	6.34	4.97
14.61	19.55	13.45	6.29	9.97	8.81	13.62	13.31
37.65	42.05		36.82	20.33	20.09	25.83	
9.29	10.56	5.98	6.48	8.09	4.75	9.37	12.34
27.80	33.35	27.96	24.49	19.70	27.41	12.73	25.97
33.13	36.53	28.74	32.29	26.70	35.14	18.87	34.00
90.52	83.46	100.00	93.00	93.64	91.11	95.45	100.00
99.04	98.61	100.00	100.00	100.00	100.00	97.06	100.00
96.00	100.00	100.00	100.00	90.10	96.32	100.00	100.00

13－3 各县(市)环境保护,环境卫生情况

(2003)

项目		Item	
废水排放总量	**(万吨)**	**Total Volume of Waste Water Discharged**	**(10000 tons)**
工业废水排放总量	(万吨)	Valume of Industrial Waste Water Discharged	(10000 tons)
废水排放达标量	(万吨)	Volume of Industrial Waste Water Up to the Discharged Standard	(10000 tons)
工业废水中化学需氧排放量	(万吨)	Emission Amount of Chemical Oxygen Demand in Industrial Waste Water	(10000 tons)
工业用水总量	(万吨)	Volume of Water Consumption for Industrial Use	(10000 tons)
工业重复用水率	(%)	Rate of Water Utilized Repeatedly in Industry	(%)
废水治理设施数	(套)	Number of Administration Facility of Waste Water	(set)
生活污水排放量	(万吨)	Emission Amount of Living Sewage	(10000 tons)
工业废气排放量	**(亿标立米)**	**Emission Amount of Industrial Waste Gas**	**(100 million cu.m)**
工业二氧化硫排放量	(吨)	Volume of Industrial Sulphur Dioxide Emission	(ton)
工业烟尘排放量	(吨)	Volume of Industrial Soot Emission	(ton)
工业粉尘排放量	(吨)	Volume of Industrial Dust Emission	(ton)
工业锅炉数	(台)	Number of Boiler for Industrial Use	(unit)
#烟尘排放达标的工业锅炉数	(台)	Soot Emission Up to the Discharged Standard	(unit)
#二氧化硫排放达标的锅炉数	(台)	Sulphur Dioxide Emission Up to the Discharged Standard	(unit)
工业固体废物产生量	**(万吨)**	**Volume of Industrial Solid Waste Produced**	**(10000 tons)**
工业固体废物综合利用量	(万吨)	Volume of Industrial Solid Waste Utilized in a Comprehensiv	(10000 tons)
工业固体废物处理量	(万吨)	Volume of Industrial Solid Waste Treated	(10000 tons)
工业固体废物处置利用率	(%)	Rate of Industrial Solid Waste Treated and Utilized	(%)
工业固体废物排放量	(吨)	Volume of Industrial Solid Waste Discharged	(ton)
工业污染处理本年施工项目数	**(个)**	**Number of Projects Treating Industrial Pollution**	**(unit)**
施工项目本年投资额	(万元)	Investment Amount of Projects in This Tear	(10000 yuan)
环境噪声达标面积	**(平方公里)**	**Standardization Areas of Environment Noise**	**(sq.km)**

注:工业“三废”统计范围为重点调查工业企业与非重点调查单位测算之和。

Basic Statistics on Protection, Enviroment Sanitation by Region

全市 Total	市区 Urban District	# 鄞州 Yinzhou	余姚 Yuyao	慈溪 Cixi	奉化 Fenghua	象山 Xiangshan	宁海 Ninghai
23244.63	**15595.66**	**3478.00**	**2485.40**	**1924.08**	**837.60**	**1392.56**	**1009.33**
11750.63	7916.67	2026.00	1499.40	829.08	309.60	665.56	500.33
11345.22	7687.05	1975.35	1428.32	822.85	303.71	606.73	496.57
14186.94	8482.60	2681.92	3683.30	571.48	274.72	766.24	408.60
512312.45	500103.83	2687.31	3903.91	4784.13	1078.84	989.16	1452.58
23.66	22.90	15.52	57.49	69.27	11.52	16.14	58.35
705	378	72	69	115	58	34	51
11524	7679	1452	986	1095	528	727	509
2071.65	**1786.22**	**18.59**	**180.92**	**66.59**	**8.87**	**15.56**	**13.49**
190070.56	177881.03	2560.55	3670.16	4613.39	1116.35	1772.64	1016.98
22607.29	18811.59	725.83	1579.11	1127.93	204.97	587.67	296.02
5350.65	3910.61		1295.00	129.50		15.54	
534	280	88	53	105	47	17	32
526	275	88	53	102	47	17	32
481	230	66	53	102	47	17	32
354.20	**291.21**	**9.31**	**21.64**	**27.55**	**4.13**	**4.10**	**5.56**
274.59	217.14	8.76	21.64	22.30	4.10	3.95	5.36
79.38	73.91	0.48		5.16	0.02	0.14	0.16
99.94	99.97	99.25	100.00	100.00	99.76	99.76	99.28
500					100		400
161	**64**		**38**	**47**	**7**	**3**	**2**
16820.9	7178.6		5948.0	2885.3	657.0	72.0	80.0
150.49	**112.70**	**11.48**	**20.18**	**9.60**	**4.69**	**3.25**	

Note: Statistical Information of Waste Water, Waste Gas and Waste Residue Collected is calculated data that investigate industrial enterprise especially and non – investigate unit especially.

13－4　各县(市)社会，优抚，救济工作情况

(2003)

项目		Item	
建立社会保障网络数	(个)	**Number of Building Social Security Net**	**(unit)**
年末优抚对象		**Enjoying Favoured Treatment at The Year－end**	
安置下岗人员数	(人)	Setting Unemployed Personnel	(person)
安置军转干部，士兵	(人)	Setting Military Cadres or Soldiers Transferred to Civilian Work	(person)
收养人数	(人)	Number of Adopted Persons	(person)
优待军属户	(人)	Servicemen's Families	(person)
优待总金额	(万元)	Total Amount of Give Special Treatment	(10000 yuan)
在乡复员军人	(人)	Demobilized Soldiers in Hometown	(person)
在乡退伍军人	(人)	Veterans in Hometown	(preson)
抚恤.补助.优待情况		**Comfort and Compensate, Subsidize, Preferential Treatment**	
享受伤残保健金	(万元)	Enjoy the Wounded or Disabled Health Care Money	(10000 yuan)
享受抚恤金人数		Number of Enjoying Pension	
定期抚恤人数	(人)	Number of Persons Receiving Periodical Commiseration	(person)
#烈士家属	(人)	Members of Revolutionary Martyr's Family	(person)
优待总金额	(万元)	Total Amount of Give Special Treatment	(10000 yuan)
年末享受定补人数	(人)	Number of Persons Receiving Periodical Subsidies at The Year－end	(person)

Basic Statistics on Receiving Social Welfare, Subsidy and Commiseration by Region

全市 Total	市区 Urban District	# 鄞州 Yinzhou	余姚 Yuyao	慈溪 Cixi	奉化 Fenghua	象山 Xiangshan	宁海 Ninghai
98	**29**	**20**	**15**	**20**	**6**	**12**	**16**
8673	7629	105		68	198	738	40
3124	1056	464	509	601	302	310	346
1216	374	149	176	353	57	160	96
6299	2042	895	1006	1200	639	675	737
4572.3	2031.9	677.6	609	864.2	356.2	351.0	360.0
5425	1913	1022	763	1201	590	503	455
4272	757	481	630	1570	374	375	566
1323	727	153	165	111	113	99	108
912	187	77	176	256	111	81	101
655	244	118	101	128	67	37	78
322	125	61	57	58	23	16	43
4572.3	2031.9	677.6	609.0	864.2	356.2	351.0	360.0
9697	2670	1503	1393	2771	964	878	1021

13－5 民政部门收养性幼抚事业情况

Statistics on Adopting and Receiving by Institution for Civil Administration Department

(2003)

项目		Item		全市 Total	# 市区 Urban District	光荣院 Homes for Disabled Veterans
收养性福利单位数	**(个)**	**Number of Welfare－Units for Adopting**	**(unit)**	**18**	**11**	**2**
全部职工人数	**(人)**	**Total Numeber Staff and Workers**	**(person)**	**366**	**267**	**14**
# 医务人员	(人)	Doctors And Nurses	(person)	87	80	
年末固定资产原值	**(万元)**	**Original Value of Fixed Assets at The Year－end**	**(10000 yuan)**	**4552.6**	**3892.1**	**123.8**
各院病床数	**(张)**	**Number of Beds in Each Hospital**	**(bed)**	**2628**	**1976**	**62**
年末在院人数	**(人)**	**In－patients at The Year－end**	**(person)**	**2274**	**1724**	**41**
# 优抚人员	(人)	Adopting Persons for Enjoying Favoured Treatment	(person)	97	73	41
"三无"对象人员	(人)	Non Depending on, Non Ability to Labor and Non Income	(person)	624	514	
自费人员	(人)	Persons on Self－expense	(person)	1544	1134	
老年人	(人)	Old People	(person)	1589	1172	
青壮年人员	(人)	Young People	(person)	360	318	
少年儿童	(人)	Juvenile and Child	(person)	284	234	

13－5 续 continued

项目	单位	Iterm	Unit	在总计中 Of Which		
				社会福利院 Social Welfare House	儿童福利院 Welfare Homes for Children	精神病福利院 Welfare Homes for Mental Patients
收养性福利单位数	**(个)**	**Number of Welfare－Units for Adopting**	**(unit)**	**15**	**1**	**1**
全部职工人数	**(人)**	**Total Numeber Staff and Workers**	**(person)**	**278**	**30**	**44**
# 医务人院	(人)	Doctors And Nurses	(person)	65	3	19
年末固定资产原值	**(万元)**	**Original Value of Fixed Assets at The Year－end**	**(10000 yuan)**	**3818.4**	**415.8**	**194.6**
各院病床数	**(张)**	**Number of Beds in Each Hospital**	**(bed)**	**2146**	**220**	**200**
年末在院人数	**(人)**	**In－patients at The Year－end**	**(person)**	**1830**	**213**	**190**
# 优抚人员	(人)	Adopting Persons for Enjoying Favoured Treatment	(person)	56		
"三无"对象人员	(人)	Non Depending on, Non Ability to Labor and Non Income	(person)	344	204	76
自费人员	(人)	Persons on Self－expense	(person)	1430		114
老年人	(人)	Old People	(person)	1528		61
青壮年人员	(人)	Young People	(person)	222	9	129
少年儿童	(人)	Juvenile and Child	(person)	80	204	

13－6　城乡居民最低生活保障情况

Basic Statistics on Minimum Living Standard for Urban and Rural Residents

(2003)

地区	Region	社会救济总人数(人) Number of Persons Receiving Relief (person)	城镇低保人数(人) Number of ①MSLUR (person)	城镇低保家庭数(户) Households of MSLUR ② (household)	城镇低保资金支出(万元) Expenditure for MSLUR (10000 yuan)	农村低保人数(人) Number of MSLRR② and Receiving Relief (person)	农村低保家庭数(户) Households of MSLRR ② (household)	农村低保资金支出(万元) Expenditure for MSLRR② (10000 yuan)
宁波市	Total	77617	18563	9958	3600	59054	39091	3510
市区	Urban District	26355	14860	7554	2915	11495	6807	1146
#鄞州区	Yinzhou	7920	990	610	199	6930	4228	706
余姚市	Yuyao	9371	1361	838	259	8010	5418	608
慈溪市	Cixi	10826	738	655	210	10088	9264	939
奉化市	Fenghua	7883	556	286	90	7327	4180	244
象山县	Xiangshan	8063	550	381	74	7513	5767	195
宁海县	Ninghai	15119	498	244	52	14621	7655	378

①MSLUR　is the short form that means minimum standard of living for urban residents.
②MSLRR　is the short form that means minimum standard of living for rural residents.

13－7　社会收容遣送情况

Basic Statistics on Accepted and Repatriated

(2003)

	遣送站情况 Repatriated Units			本年救助(人次) Relief Person in This Year (Person－time)
	站数(个) Number of Units (unit)	年末职工人数(人) Number of Staff and Workers (person)	年末固定资产原值(万元) Original Value of Fixed Assets (10000 yuan)	
全市总计　Total	3	43	761.2	3618

13－8 各县(市)社会团体机构情况

单位:个 (2003)

项目	Item	全市 Total
上年末实有社团机构数	Number of Social Organizations Last Year－end	1281
本年准予登记社团机构数	Number of Social Organizations Authorized in This Year	99
本年注销社团数	Social Organizations Writed Off in This Year	32
年末实有社团机构数	Factual Number of Social Organizations at The Year－end	1348
年末实有民办非企业数	Factual Number of Civilian－run Non－enterprises at The Year－end	1679
本年批准登记单位	Number of Units Authorized in This Year	308
本年注销及取缔单位	Number of Writed Off and Clampdown in This Year	41

13－9 各县(市)婚姻状况

(2003)

项目		Item		全市 Total
准予登记结婚数	**(对)**	**Number of Registering Marrige Permitted**	**(couple)**	**42075**
#涉外及华侨.港澳台同胞	(人)	Marrige of FOHMT①	(person)	159
(1)国内公民	(人)	Demestic Citizen	(person)	159
#女性	(人)	Female	(person)	152
(2)港澳台同胞	(人)	Chinese of Hong Kong, Macao and Taiwan	(person)	106
(3)华侨	(人)	Overseas Chinese	(person)	8
(4)外国人	(人)	Foreigner	(person)	45
1.初婚人数	(人)	First Marriage	(person)	75735
2.再婚人数	(人)	Remarriage	(person)	8097
3.再婚中恢复结婚	(对)	Resume Marriage	(couple)	394
准予离婚数	**(对)**	**Number of Divorce Approved**	**(couple)**	**5538**

①FOHMT is short form that means Foreigner, Overseas－Chinese and Hong Kong, Macao and Taiwan Compatriot.

Basic Statistics on Social Organizations And Unions by Region

(unit)

市区 Urban District	# 鄞州 Yinzhou	余姚 Yuyao	慈溪 Cixi	奉化 Fenghua	象山 Xiangshan	宁海 Ninghai
733	**103**	**132**	**136**	**102**	**85**	**93**
55	**5**	**3**	**14**	**15**	**1**	**11**
25					5	2
763	108	135	150	117	81	102
660	173	279	207	131	166	236
107	**5**	**50**	**39**	**27**	**26**	**59**
22			**6**		**9**	**4**

Basic Statistics On Marrige by Region

市区 Urban District	# 鄞州 Yinzhou	余姚 Yuyao	慈溪 Cixi	奉化 Fenghua	象山 Xiangshan	宁海 Ninghai
17986	**5889**	**4510**	**6932**	**3656**	**3409**	**5582**
159						
159						
152						
106						
8						
45						
31802	10633	8077	12649	6469	6203	10535
3852	1145	943	1215	843	615	629
208	51	29	70	42	28	17
2616	**654**	**587**	**891**	**558**	**503**	**383**

13-10 各县(市)计划生育情况

(2003)

项目		Item	
计划生育率	(%)	Rate of Family Planning	(%)
年内出生人数	(人)	Number of Birth in This Year	(person)
#女	(人)	Female	(person)
#一孩人数	(人)	One - Child	(person)
#两孩人数	(人)	Two - Child	(person)
#多孩人数	(人)	Over Two Child	(person)
计划内出生人数	(人)	Number of Birth In - planning	(person)
计划外出生人数	(人)	Number of Birth Out - planning	(person)
育龄妇女人数	(万人)	Number of Women at Child - Bearing Age	(10000 persons)
已婚育龄妇女人数	(万人)	Number of Marriged Women at Child - Bearing Age	(10000 persons)
#已有一孩	(万人)	1st Birth	(10000 persons)
*#已婚育龄妇女一孩率	(%)	Rate of 1st Birth of Marriged Women at Child - Bearing Age	(%)
初婚妇女人数	(万人)	Number of First Marrige for Women	(10000 persons)
已昏育龄妇女节育率	(%)	Rate of Controlling - Birth for Marriged Women at Child - Bearing Age	(%)
采取节育措施人数	(万人)	Number of Controlling - Birth Method	(10000 persons)
年内节育手术例数	(例)	Number of Controlling - Birth Surgery in This Year	(case)
年内取环例数	(例)	Number of Remove Contraceptive	(case)

Basic Statistics on Family Planning by Region

	全市 Total	市区 Urban District	# 鄞州 Yinzhou	余姚 Yuyao	慈溪 Cixi	奉化 Fenghua	象山 Xiangshan	宁海 Ninghai
	98.97	99.57	99.68	99.43	98.66	98.71	98.31	98.22
	40693	7846	5017	5783	8119	3720	4661	5547
	19595	3833	2467	2849	3901	1792	2207	2546
	34670	7390	4554	4925	6326	3212	3806	4457
	5958	453	459	851	1780	498	846	1071
	65	3	4	7	13	10	9	19
	40275	7812	5001	5750	8010	3572	4582	5448
	418	34	16	33	109	48	79	99
	158.14	35.50	19.59	23.95	29.57	14.96	16.25	18.32
	128.16	30.03	16.27	19.81	24.41	11.92	12.28	13.46
	87.13	23.55	11.45	13.62	16.29	8.06	6.93	7.24
	67.98	78.42	70.40	68.75	66.76	67.58	56.43	53.76
	30455	7439	4326	3374	4733	3094	2690	4799
	91.02	89.34	91.33	92.24	92.30	91.31	90.47	90.48
	116.65	26.83	14.85	18.27	22.53	10.88	11.11	12.18
	58590	7934	8699	7148	14114	6328	6368	7999
	17359	2424	2805	2820	3990	1901	1615	1804

13－11 各县(市)妇联工会组织及活动情况

(2003)

项目		Item	
机构		**Women Organizations**	
市、县(市)区妇联	(个)	Women Organizations in Municipal, County and Urban District	(unit)
镇、乡(街道)妇联	(个)	Women Organizations in Township, Town (Subdistrict)	(unit)
基层妇代会	(个)	Basic－Level Women Congress	(unit)
机关事业单位妇委会	(个)	Women Commission of Agencies and Institutions	(unit)
团体会员	(个)	Group Member	(unit)
人员状况		**Personnel of Women Organizations**	
市、县(市)、区级干部	(人)	Cadre at The Level of Municipal, County and Urban District	(person)
镇、乡(街道)级干部	(人)	Cadre in Township, Town (Subdistrict)	(person)
妇联工作情况		**Works of Women Organizations**	
双学双比及巾帼建功活动		Activity of Double Study And Double Compare, And Women Making Contribution	
参赛数	(万人)	Number of Participants	(10000 persons)
#女农民技术人员	(人)	Female Peasant Technician	(person)
先进女能手	(人)	Female Advanced Expert	(person)
巾帼建功先进个人	(人)	Advanced Women by Making Contribution	(person)
工会专职干部人数	**(人)**	**Number of Full Time Cadres of Labour Unions**	**(person)**
基层工会数	**(个)**	**Number of Labour Unions at Basic－Level**	**(person)**
建立工会单位全部职工	**(人)**	**Total Staff And Workers of Establishing Labour Unions**	**(person)**
#女职工	(人)	Female Staffs And Workers	(person)
工会会员	(人)	Member of Labour Unions	(person)
#女会员	(人)	Female Member	(person)
开展合理化建议的单位	**(个)**	**Number of Grassroots Unions Developing Rationalization Proposals**	**(unit)**
提出合理化建议数	(件)	Advanced Rationalization Proposals	(case)
合理化建议创造的经济效益	(万元)	Economic Benefit Created by Carrying out Rationalization Proposals	(10000 yuan)

Basic Statistics on Organizations of Women Federation and Labour Unions by Region

全市 Total	市区 Urban District	#鄞州 Yinzhou	余姚 Yuyao	慈溪 Cixi	奉化 Fenghua	象山 Xiangshan	宁海 Ninghai
12	7	1	1	1	1	1	1
148	37	20	22	20	11	18	20
3749	1056	603	269	307	580	705	832
241	132	23	7	33	19	29	21
6	4	1	1	1			
88	54	7	7	9	7	5	6
167	76	38	22	20	11	18	20
105.65	29.65	19.45	18.81	21.96	9.80	12.79	12.99
293	117	84		56	120		
190	48	15	44	45	5	22	26
243	94	10	34	64	22	15	14
604	**436**	**20**	**67**	**23**	**22**	**18**	**38**
8097	**3513**	**1038**	**1133**	**1302**	**786**	**737**	**626**
1200510	**547043**	**205871**	**147916**	**250264**	**70588**	**82277**	**102422**
582057	260128	104632	71377	120116	39545	34169	56722
999155	439420	144197	128750	202506	65017	71266	92196
472464	206462	76841	63301	85965	36108	29398	51230
1656	**499**	**23**	**297**	**759**	**22**	**41**	**38**
34152	23411	1229	2754	6617	327	491	552
22474	13505	611	2480	5542	187	59	700

13-12 部分年份律师、公证工作基本情况
Basic Statistics on Lawyers and Notarization in Partial Years

项目	Item	1997	2001	2002	2003
律师工作情况	**On Lawyers**				
律师事务所数(所)	Number of Lawyers Offices(unit)	40	42	55	60
#合作制律师事务所	Cooperative Law Offices	7	14	14	15
合伙制律师事务所	Law Offices in Partnership		38	41	45
律师数(人)	Number of Lawyers(person)	483	545	561	580
#专职律师	Full-time Lawyers	249	466	486	555
聘请担任常年法律顾问单位(家)	Number of Units with Permanent Legal Advisors(unit)	2688	1972	2200	2326
民事案件代理数(件)	Agent of Civil Cases (case)	2085	6006	6000	6326
经济案件代理数	Agent of Economic Cases	5784	3939	3699	3538
#索回赔数(万元)	Debt and Indemnity Claimed (10000 yuan)		17023	7666	12268
刑事辩护和代理数(件)	Agent of Criminal Defense (case)	3302	2851	2450	2270
非诉讼法律事务	Non-Litigious Legal Affairs	1364	964	1414	1430
行政案件代理数	Agent of Administrative Action	59	197	317	521
涉外及港澳台法律事务	Legal Affairs With Foreign, HongKong, Macao and Taiwan	302	106	52	100
解答法律文书	Legal Advisory Services	15065	11150	22552	12500
代写法律文书	Legal Document Written on Behalf of Clients	9512	4319	5919	4127
公证工作情况	**Notarization**				
公证处(个)	Notary Offices (unit)	12	12	12	12
#办理涉外公证(人)	Registered Foreign Affairs (person)	12	12	12	9926
公证人员人数(人)	Notarial Personnel (person)	85	59	91	68
#公证员	Notaries	52	59	40	39
办理公证事项(件)	Notarized Documents (case)	28248	74016	94918	97156
国内经济公证	Domestic Economic Affairs	12669	48983	59714	65588
国内民事公证	Domestic Civil Affairs	9463	12144	19644	21497
涉外及港澳台公证	Documents on Foreign, HongKong, Macao and Taiwan	6116	11859	15560	10051
接待来访(人次)	Reception(person-times)	37993	65966	61275	134
处理来信(件)	Treatment(case)	271	416	147	165

13－13　基层司法工作及人民调解情况

Basic Statistics on Basic－Level Judicial Work and People Mediation

项目	Item	1997	2001	2002	2003
司法助理员人数(人)	**Number of Judicial Assistants (person)**	**381**	**282**	**313**	**270**
专职司法助理员	Full－Time Judicial Assistants	121	240	247	237
兼职司法助理员	Part－Time Judicial Assistants	35	42	66	33
基层法律服务所(所)	**Basic－Level Service for Legal Advice (unit)**	**163**	**108**	**98**	**91**
配备工作人员(人)	Provide Staff (person)	443	512	994	486
代理讼诉事务(件)	Agent of Litigious Affairs (case)		8434	16413	7824
代理非讼诉事务	Agent of Non－Litigious Legal Affairs		2013	8883	1740
调解纠纷	Mediating Disputes	34516	1747	2771	1214
协办公证	Handling Document Jointly	582	152	158	238
见证	Witness		500	437	360
担任法律顾问	Taking Legal Advisors	1559	1262	1285	1328
代写法律文书	Legal Document Written on Behalf of Clients	7167	7629	7977	5656
解答法律咨询人次(人)	Legal Advisory Services (person)	25875	27172	35639	32619
挽回经济损失(万元)	Economic Loss Avoided and Reclaimed(10000 yuan)	13081	29628	28481	48551
办理法律援助事务(件)	Handling Succorab leLegal Affairs(case)		399	364	470
参与司法行政工作(人次)	Participating Judicial Administration(person－times)		688	670	445
人民调解委员会(个)	**Peoples Mediation Committees (unit)**	**7419**	**5716**	**5587**	**5537**
调解人员数(人)	Number of Mediators (person)	19232	15204	17851	18087
调解纠纷总件数(件)	Number of Mediating Disputes(case)	34516	28732	25494	26466
调解成功件数	Number of Success	32676	27419	27505	25650
婚烟	Marrige	7337	5114	4732	4780
继承权	Right of Inheritance	830	840	836	555
瞻养抚养	Supporting and Fostering	1910	1492	1363	1176
房屋宅基地	Ground of Building	4331	3378	3126	2436
债务	Debt	2271	1969	2233	1438
生产经营	Production & Management	2005	1308	1485	999
邻里关系	Relation of Neighborhood	5922	5532	5868	5104
赔偿	Compensation	5063	5012	4845	5111
其他调解	Other Mediating	2724	2132	3409	3613
调解纠纷成功率(%)	Rate of Mediating Success (%)	95.00	95.43	96.53	96.90
防止可能发生非正常死亡事件(件)	Avoiding Accident of Abnormal Deaths(case)	106	76	35	32
防止可能发生非正常死亡人次(人次)	Avoiding Accident Times of Abnormal Deaths (person－times)	151	76	37	36

13－14　二级人民法院收,结案情况

Cases Accepted & Closed by People's Court

单位:件　　(2003)　　(case)

项目	Item	上年留案 Retained in Last Year	全年新收案 New Accepted in This Year	办结案件数 Number of Cases Closed	年末未结案件 Retained Case at Year－end
总计		**1078**	**60997**	**61062**	**1013**
一审案件数	**Number of First Instance Cases**	**542**	**36261**	**36351**	**452**
刑事	Criminal Case	10	6052	6057	5
民商事	Civil & Economic Case	528	29630	29716	442
行政	Administrative Case	4	579	578	5
二审案件数	**Number of Second Instance Case**	**59**	**2359**	**2330**	**88**
刑事	Criminal Case	1	395	396	
民事	Civil Case	39	1147	1143	43
经济	Economic Case	19	553	559	13
行政	Administrative Case		264	232	32
审判监督	**Number of Cases Judged and Supervised**	**7**	**118**	**115**	**10**
刑事	Criminal Case	1	8	9	
民商事	Civil & Economic Case	6	109	106	9
行政	Administrative Case		1		1
执行	**Carry out Case**	**452**	**20141**	**20171**	**422**
刑事案件(有财产部分)	Criminal Case (With Property)	27	202	190	39
民事	Civil Case	394	13550	13614	330
行政	Administrative Case				
行政非审查与执行	Administration No－examine and Carry Out	18	5371	5361	28
其他案件	Others Case	13	1018	1006	25
申诉申请再审	**Appeal and Applying for Review**		**654**	**631**	**41**
司法赔偿	**Juridical Compensation**				
减刑	**Commutation**		**1437**	**1437**	
假释	**Parolee**		**27**	**27**	

13－15 人民法院及检察院补充信息

Added Information of People's Court and Procuratorial Organ

（2003）

项目		Item		总计 Total
人民法院		**People's Court**		
办结申诉申请再审案件	（件）	Appeal and Applying for Review Closed	（case）	631
处理群众来信	（件次）	Deal with Letter from People	（case－times）	17429
群众来访人数	（人次）	People Come to Appeal for Help	（person－times）	21458
判决被告	（人）	Adjudge defendant	（person）	8071
五年以上有期徒刑直到无期徒刑	（人）	Fixed－term Imprisonment of More than 5 years until Life Imprisonment	（person）	1208
不满五年有期徒刑	（人）	Fixed－term Imprisonment of Below 5 years	（person）	4243
缓刑	（人）	Probation	（person）	1336
宣告无罪	（人）	Declare Innocent	（person）	8
免于刑事处分	（人）	Avoid Criminal Sanction	（person）	23
其他处理	（人）	Others	（person）	1253
判处罪犯		Sentence Criminals		8063
#18－25周岁罪犯	（人）	Between 18 until 25 Years Old	（person）	2747
#少年犯	（人）	Juvenile Criminal	（person）	653
#女性犯罪	（人）	Female Criminal	（person）	327
一审民商案件中解决争议标的	（万元）	Solve Amount of Disputed Bid for Civil & Economic Case in First Instance	（10000 yuan）	627400
执行案件中执结标的	（万元）	Carry out Amount of Money in Carry out Case	（10000 yuan）	278800
办结经济犯罪	（件）	Closed Economic Criminal	（case）	416
为国家，集体挽回经济损失	（万元）	Retrieve Economic Losses for State & Collective	（10000 yuan）	3327.36
办结申请公示催告和支付令的案	（件）	Closed Apply to Show the Demand Commonly & Indemnity	（case）	612
标的	（万元）	Total Amount of Money	（10000 yuan）	10544.04
检察机关		**Procuratorial Organ**		
立案查处贪污贿赂	（件）	Cases Registered for Corruption and Bribery	（case）	169
立案查处贪污贿赂	（人）	Cases Registered for Corruption and Bribery	（person）	169
立案查处职务犯罪	（件）	Cases Registered for Duty Crime	（case）	11
立案查处职务犯罪	（人）	Cases Registered for Duty Crime	（person）	17
批捕各类犯罪嫌疑人	（人）	Approve to Arrest Crime Suspects	（person）	7541
起诉各类犯罪嫌疑人	（人）	Accuse Crime Suspects	（person）	8401
受理举报控告来访	（件）	Accept Public Report, Accuse Crime and Visit	（case）	2372
提出民事行政抗诉	（件）	Submit Civil and Administrative Counterappeal.	（case）	60

13－16　各县(市)火灾情况

(2003)

项目		Item	
火灾起因情况		**Cause of Fire**	
放火	(起)	Arson	(case)
电器	(起)	Electric Appliances	(case)
违章操作	(起)	Operation Against Rules	(case)
用火不慎	(起)	Careless	(case)
生活用火	(起)	Fire for Living Purpose	(case)
生产用火	(起)	Fire for Production Purpose	(case)
吸烟	(起)	Smoking	(case)
其他原因	(起)	Others	(case)
重大火灾		**Heavy Fire**	
起火	(起)	Fire	(case)
损失	(万元)	Losses	(10000 yuan)
死亡	(人)	Deaths	(person)
损失情况		**Situation of Losses**	
起数	(起)	Number	(case)
死亡	(人)	Injuries	(person)
伤人	(人)	Deaths	(person)
损失	(万元)	Losses	(10000 yuan)

Basic Statistics on Fires by Region

全市 Total	市区 Urban District	# 鄞州 Yinzhou	余姚 Yuyao	慈溪 Cixi	奉化 Fenghua	象山 Xiangshan	宁海 Ninghai
8	3	3		1	1	1	2
33	18	7	4	7	1		3
23	11	2	3	6	3		
8	6	1	2				
6	4		2				
1	1						
4	3			1			
57	22	15	5	20	3	2	5
8	1	1	1	5	1		
479.13	197.77	197.77	51.20	229.96	0.20		
7				4	3		
140	28	28	16	35	8	3	10
26	9	3	1	12	3		1
26	13	7	3	8		2	
1502.75	637.36	459.58	160.03	517.08	89.28	30.40	68.60

13－17　交通事故情况

(2003)

项目	Item	合计 (Total) 事故次数(次) Number of Accident (case)	死亡人数(人) Deaths (person)	受伤人数(人) Injuries (person)	直接损失(万元) Direct Pecunlary Losses (10000 yuan)
总计	**Total**	**4046**	**947**	**3288**	**2701**
特大事故	Extraordinarily Serious Accident	29	21	50	266
重大事故	Heavy Accident	984	926	314	16
汽车	Automobile	2650	497	2068	723
#运输部门	Transportation Department	160	41	111	147
公共汽车	Bus	39	5	38	19
机关团体	Organ and Organizations	78	11	66	78
个体户	Individual	1689	311	1321	40
农村单位	Rural Unit	117	29	89	86
其他	Others	554	99	430	507
摩托车	Motorcycles	636	185	665	149
拖拉机	Tractors	254	58	236	104
非机动车	Non－motor－driven Vehicles	234	92	167	44
其他及行人	Others and Pedestrians	125	70	69	28

Basic Statistics on Traffic Accident

城市 (Urban)				农村 (Rural)			
事故次数（次）Number of Accident (case)	死亡人数（人）Deaths (person)	受伤人数（人）Injuries (person)	直接损失（万元）Direct ecunlary Losses (10000 yuan)	事故次数（次）Number of Accident (case)	死亡人数（人）Deaths (person)	受伤人数（人）Injuries (person)	直接损失（万元）Direct Pecunlary Losses (10000 yuan)
1332	**208**	**1063**	**783**	**2714**	**739**	**2225**	**1918**
9		8	89	20	21	42	177
224	208	67	6	760	718	247	10
931	121	691	664	1719	376	1377	60
64	11	45	67	96	30	66	80
22	5	19	11	17		19	8
32	2	26	24	46	9	40	54
569	66	408	38	1120	245	913	2
33	5	34	15	84	24	55	71
203	31	151	150	351	68	279	351
201	36	201	58	435	149	464	91
52	11	53	20	202	47	183	84
82	25	67	18	152	67	100	26
	7	19	2	103	63	50	26

13－18　全市档案人员及馆藏和编研情况

Conditions of Files Stored and Used in the Archives

(2003)

项目		Item		全市 Total	市局馆 Municipal	市区合计 Urban District	县市合计 County
机构数	**(个)**	**Number of Institutions**	**(unit)**	**25**	**2**	**12**	**11**
档案行政管理机构(局、科)	(个)	Administrative Department of Archives	(unit)	12	1	6	5
档案馆	(个)	Archives	(unit)	13	1	6	6
现有工作人员数	**(人)**	**Number of Staff and Workers**	**(person)**	**166**	**37**	**54**	**75**
档案行政管理机构	(人)	Administrative Department of Archives	(person)	135	37	23	75
档案馆	(人)	Archives	(person)	31		31	
馆藏档案		**Archives Stored**					
全宗	(个)	Whole Volume	(unit)	2185	360	694	1131
案卷	(卷)	Files	(volume)	648052	92631	189310	366111
以件为保管单位档案	(件)	Archives Which Regard a Storage Unit by Files	(pieces)	7588	1468	1544	4576
录音、录象影片档案	(盘)	Records, Films on Videotape	(copy)	1288	134	153	1001
照片档案	(张)	Pictures	(pieces)	67269	10713	25151	31405
馆藏资料	**(册)**	**Number of Material Stored**	**(volume)**	**86982**	**21033**	**24589**	**41360**
档案馆总建筑面积	**(平方米)**	**Floor Space of Archives**	**(sq.m)**	**15775**	**1430**	**6581**	**7764**
档案库房建筑面积	(平方米)	Floor Space of Storerooms	(sq.m)	7690	750	2646	4294
本年档案资料利用		**Use of Material in This Year**					
利用人次	(人次)	Number of Persons Using Material	(times)	10267	840	4033	5394
利用档案	(卷件次)	Number of Archives Used	(times)	37178	5426	12982	18770
利用资料	(册次)	Number of Material Used	(times)	6302	2849	2778	675
复制	(页数)	Copies	(pages)	75197	37213	26678	11306
本年编研档案资料内部参考	**(万字)**	**Compiling and Researching Material Restricted**	**(10000 words)**	**339**	**133**	**112**	**95**

注:统计范围:市,县(市)区档案局,国家综合档案馆。
Note: Statistical Limits are Archives of Each District and County.

主要指标解释

【全年供水总量】 指公用自来水厂和自备水源的社会单位全年的供水总量,包括有效供水量及损失水量。

【城市人口用水普及率】 指城市用水的非农业人口数(不包括临时人口和流动人口)与城市非农业人口总数的比例。计算公式:

用水普及率=(城市用水的非农业人口数÷城市非农业人口数)×100%

【公共绿地】 指供游览休息的各种公园、动物园、植物园、陵园、以及花园、游园和供旅游休息用的林荫道绿地、广场绿地。不包括一般栽植的行道树及林荫道的面积。

【废水排放总量】 包括生产废水和生活污水。生产废水指企、事业单位在生产、科研过程中向外排放的所有排放口的废水量总和。生活污水指城镇居民区和企、事业单位职工集中居住区排放的污水量。

【工业废水排放量】 指经过企业厂区所有排放口排到企业外部的工业废水量 。包括生产废水、外排的直接冷却水、超标排放的矿井地下水和与工业废水混排的厂区生活污水,不包括外排的间接冷却水(清污不分流的间按冷却水应计算在内)。

【工业废水排放达标量】 指各项指标都达到国家或地方排放标准的外排工业废水量,包括未经处理外排达标的和经过处理后外排达标的和两部分。国家排放标准见 GB8978-88。

【工业废气排放量】 指企业厂区内燃料燃烧和生产工艺过程中产生的各种排入空气的含有污染物的气体的总量,以标准状态(273K,101325Pa)计。

【工业粉尘排放量】 指企业在生产工艺过程中排放的颗粒物重量。如钢铁企业的耐火材料粉尘、焦化企业的筛焦系统粉尘、烧结机的粉尘、石灰窑的粉尘、建材企业的水泥粉尘等。不包括电厂排入大气的烟尘。

【工业粉尘回收量】 指经生产工艺废气净化处理装置处理回收的粉尘和尘泥量(包括干法和湿法)。不包括电厂的烟尘。通常情况下:

工业粉尘产生量=工业粉尘排放量+工业粉尘回收量

【工业固体废物产生量】 指企业在生产过程中产生的固体状、半固体状和高浓度液体状废弃物的总量,包括危险废物、冶炼废渣、粉煤灰、炉渣、煤矸石、尾矿、放射性 废物和其他废物等;不包括矿山开采的剥离废石和掘进废石(煤矸石和呈酸性或碱性的废石 除外)。酸性或碱性废石是指采掘的废石其流经水、雨淋水的 pH 值小于 4 或 pH 值大于 10.5 者 。

【社会福利事业单位】 指集中收养社会孤老,残,幼的机构。包括由民政部门管理的社会福利院、儿童福利院、精神病人福利院和城镇集体办的福利院,以及农村集体举 办的敬老院。

Explanatory Notes on Main Statistical Indicators

【Annual Volume of Water Supply】 refers to the total volume of water supplied by the public water – works and those owned by individual enterprises and institutions during the whole year, including both the effective water supply and loss during the water supply.

【Percentage of Urban Population with Access to Tap Water】 refers to the ratio of urban non – agricultural population (excluding temporary and mobile population) with access to tap water to the total urban non – agricultural population. The formula is:

Percentage of Population with Access to Tap Water = (Urban Non – agricultural Population with Access to Tap Water ÷ Urban Non – agricultural Population) 100%

【Public Green Area】 refers to green areas of various parks, zoos, botanical gardens, cemeteries, amusement parks, tree – flanked boulevards, green – land squares for tourism and relaxation. Area with trees planted along – side the streets and boulevards are excluded.

【Total Discharge of Sewage】 includes production sewage and domestic sewage. Production sewage refers to the total discharge by the enterprises and institutions in their production and scientific research. Domestic sewage refers to the discharge by urban and rural residential communities and the residential neighborhoods of the enterprise/institutions staff.

【Volume of Industrial Waste Water Discharged】 refers to the volume of industrial waste water discharged, through all outlets, to the outside of industrial enterprises, including waste water produced, direct cooling water, underground water from mines that does not meet the standard of discharge, and the domestic sewage mixed up with industrial waste water when discharged, but excluding discharged indirect – cooling water.

【Volume of Waste Water up to the Standard for Discharge】 refers to the volume of discharged industrial waste water that, with or without treatment, has come up to the national or local standards for discharge.

【Volume of Waste Gas Emission】 refers to waste gas emitted from burning of fuels and from production process in the area of the factory, and is measured by 10000 standard cubic metres each year under normal condition.

【Industrial Dust Discharged】 refers to the total weight of solid dust discharged by industrial enterprises in the production process, such as dust of refractory materials from iron plants, dust from coke – screening system or from sintering machines of coking plants, dust from lime kilns, cement dust from building material enterprises, etc. but excluding smoke and dust discharged by power plants.

【Volume of Recovery of Industrial Dust】 refers to the volume of dust and dirt recovered by production process purification devices, including both dry process and wet process, not the fly ash emitted into the air by power station. Generally, the formula goes:

Industrial Dust Produced = Industrial Dust Emitted + Industrial Dust Recovered

【Volume of Industrial Solid Wastes Produced】 refers to the total volume of solid, semi-solid or high concentration liquid residue produced by industrial enterprises in their production process, including dangerous wastes, residues from melting, slag, powdered coal ash, gangue, chemical residues, tailings, radioactive residues and other residues, but excluding stripped or dug stones in mining (except gangue and acid or alkali stones which are stones washed or soaked by water with a pH value smaller than 4 or larger than 10.5.)

【Social Welfare Institutions】 refer to institutions taking care of old people without children, handicapped people and orphans. They include social welfare institutions run by civil affairs departments, children's welfare institutions social welfare institutions for mental patients, and collective-owned old people's homes in tualareas.

14

企业景气指数

CHAPTER 14 PROSPERITY INDEXON ENTERPRISES

企业景气指数
Prosperity index on Enterprises

主要统计指标
Major Statistics Indicators

		第一季度 1st. Quarter	第二季度 2st. Quarter	第三季度 3st. Quarter	第四季度 4st. Quarter
企业家对宏观经济的信心指数	Index of Confidence on Macro Economy by Enterprisers	145.40	133.68	149.83	148.85
综合经营景气指数	**Prosperity index on General Production and Operation of Enterprises**				
企业综合经营景气指数	Total	144.28	131.81	140.69	153.42
工业企业综合经营景气指数	Industrial Enterprises	144.50	133.66	133.85	150.79
建筑业企业综合经营景气指数	Construction Enterprises	180.31	192.11	194.23	190.85
交通运输、仓储和邮政业企业综合经营景气指数	Transport. Storage and Post Enterprises	135.88	129.53	140.90	148.87
批发和零售业企业综合经营景气指数	Wholesale and Retail Sale Enterprises	133.65	124.24	143.74	153.02
房地产企业综合经营景气指数	Real Estate Enterprises	155.56	142.11	150.00	144.44
社会服务业企业综合经营景气指数	Social Services Enterprises	110.00	60.00	140.00	150.00
信息传输、计算机服务和软件业企业综合经营景气指数	Transmission, Computer Service and Software EEnterprises	153.85	148.84	118.07	153.85
住宿和餐饮业企业综合经营景气指数	Hotels and Catering Trade Enterprises	147.55	21.18	167.24	157.94

14－1 企业家信心指数

Index of Confidence on Macro Economy of Enterprisers

（2003）

项目	Item	第一季度 1st. Quarter	第二季度 2st. Quarter	第三季度 3st. Quarter	第四季度 4st. Quarter
企业家对宏观经济的信心指数	**Index of Confidence on Macro Economy by Enterprisers**	**145.40**	**133.68**	**149.83**	**148.85**
按登记注册类型分	**By Registration Status**				
国有企业	State－Owned Enterprises	148.99	139.16	150.23	153.34
集体企业	Collective－Owned Enterprises	149.40	105.92	160.87	156.52
股份合作企业	Share Cooperative Enterprises	133.33	120.00	135.71	128.57
有限责任公司	Limited Liability Corporations	143.83	127.77	145.42	143.41
股份有限公司	Share－holding Corporations Ltd.	167.74	139.52	172.51	169.42
外商及港澳台企业	Foreign,Hong Kong.Macao and Taiwan Funded	150.33	137.76	152.85	162.11
按行业分	**By Sector**				
工业	Industry	151.57	132.30	146.34	147.43
建筑业	Construction	161.68	183.56	193.04	159.13
交通、仓储、邮政业	Transport.Storage.Post and Telecommunications Services	121.30	135.88	139.79	146.94
批发和零售业	Wholesale and Retail Sale Trade	119.61	126.13	143.74	139.92
房地产业	Real Estate	163.16	168.42	157.89	168.42
社会服务业	Social Services	120.00	80.00	150.00	160.00
信息传输计算机服务及软件	Information Transmission,Computer Service and Software	169.23	141.14	164.22	161.54
住宿和餐饮业	Hotels and Catering Trade	154.84	71.19	169.13	160.00
按特殊企业群体分	**By Special Group**				
国家重点企业	State－point Enterprises	183.95	103.78	187.74	187.74
国家试点企业集团成员	Member of State－test Enterprise－groups	100.00	100.00	100.00	100.00
乡镇企业	Town and Township Enterprises	155.73	143.43	149.13	146.63
上市公司	Listed Company	179.98	126.51	184.22	180.34
按企业规模分	**By Size of Enterprises**				
特大型及大型	Large－scale and Oversize Enterprises	171.67	148.26	181.68	181.21
中型	Medium	152.58	136.08	151.55	148.45
小型	Small	139.20	117.61	141.14	142.20

14－2　企业景气状况

Prosperity index of Enterprises

(2003)

项目	Item	第一季度 1st. Quarter	第二季度 2st. Quarter	第三季度 3st. Quarter	第四季度 4st. Quarter
企业综合经营景气指数	**Prosperity index on General Production and Operation of Enterprises**	**144.28**	**131.81**	**140.69**	**153.42**
按登记注册类型分	**By Registration Status**				
国有企业	State－Owned Enterprises	160.11	124.59	148.33	160.26
集体企业	Collective－Owned Enterprises	132.01	97.23	169.57	160.87
股份合作企业	Share Cooperative Enterprises	113.33	106.67	128.57	92.86
有限责任公司	Limited Liability Corporations	143.35	131.62	136.21	150.93
股份有限公司	Share－holding Corporations Ltd.	157.88	136.55	142.29	173.49
外商及港澳台企业	Foreign, HongKong, Macao and Taiwan Funded	137.79	118.28	140.31	150.34
按行业分	**By Sector**				
工业	Industry	144.50	133.66	133.85	150.79
建筑业	Construction	180.31	192.11	194.23	190.85
交通、仓储、邮政业	Transport. Storage. Post and Telecommunications Services	135.88	129.53	140.90	148.87
批发和零售业	Wholesale and Retail Sale Trade	133.65	124.24	143.74	153.02
房地产业	Real Estate	155.56	142.11	150.00	144.44
社会服务业	Social Services	110.00	60.00	140.00	150.00
信息传输计算机服务及软件	Information Transmission, Computer Service and Software	153.85	148.84	118.07	153.85
住宿和餐饮业	Hotels and Catering Trade	147.55	21.18	167.24	157.94
按企业规模分	**By Size of Enterprises**				
特大型及大型	Large－scale and Oversize Enterprises	169.65	142.43	149.17	188.90
中型	Medium	151.55	125.77	141.24	149.48
小型	Small	131.61	116.48	135.06	143.02
按特殊企业群体分	**By Special Group**				
国家重点企业	State－point Enterprises	187.74	103.78	103.78	200.00
国家试点企业集团成员	Member of State－test Enterprise－groups	100.00	100.00	100.00	100.00
乡镇企业	Town and Township Enterprises	154.42	153.65	154.43	157.61
上市公司	Listed Company	170.94	125.27	138.83	186.30
按观察指标分	**By Indicator Observed**				
生产(经营)情况	Production(Operation)	117.64	116.35	138.46	149.64
盈利(亏损)变化	Changes of Profit(Loss)	110.25	108.20	128.12	128.08
资金情况	Funds	116.91	106.60	114.34	116.79
货款拖欠情况	Payment for Goods in Arrears	107.49	97.83	99.29	106.50
劳动力需求	Demand on Labors	109.36	105.71	118.07	120.72
投资情况	Investment	117.46	118.42	128.48	124.46

14－3 工业企业景气指数

Prosperity index of Industrial Enterprises

(2003)

项目	Item	第一季度 1st. Quarter	第二季度 2st. Quarter	第三季度 3st. Quarter	第四季度 4st. Quarter
企业家对本行业信心指数	**Index of Confidence on This Industry by Enterprisers**	**151.57**	**132.30**	**146.34**	**147.43**
企业综合经营景气指数	**Prosperity index on General Production and Operation of Enterprises**	**144.50**	**133.66**	**133.85**	**150.79**
按登记注册类型分	**By Registration Status**				
国有企业	State－Owned Enterprises	175.57	141.22	141.22	174.55
集体企业	Collective－Owned Enterprises	144.44	144.44	155.56	166.67
有限责任公司	Limited Liability Corporations	146.42	139.93	136.73	151.50
股份有限公司	Share－holding Corporations Ltd.	146.57	130.62	136.19	159.97
外商及港澳台企业	Foreign,HongKong,Macao and Taiwan Funded	137.45	127.22	133.10	147.06
按企业规模分	**By Size of Enterprises**				
特大型及大型	Large－scale and Oversize Enterprises	173.73	145.49	140.10	188.51
中小型	Medium and Small Enterprises	139.29	131.55	132.74	143.98
中型	Medium	146.67	141.67	130.00	145.00
小型	Small	135.19	125.93	134.26	143.40
按特殊企业群体分	**By Special Group**				
国家重点企业	State－point Enterprises	187.25	100.00	100.00	200.00
国家试点企业集团成员	Member of State－test Enterprise－groups	100.00	100.00	100.00	100.00
上市公司	Listed Company	164.43	134.29	142.96	185.05
按观察指标分	**By Indicator Observed**				
生产成本	Cost of Production	68.58	84.29	81.44	33.06
生产总量	Total of Production	111.22	119.31	133.73	152.14
产品订货情况	Production Order	120.96	116.88	136.38	144.28
#国外订货	From Overseas	121.12	111.37	116.51	121.01
产品销售量	Total of Production Sales	104.50	113.07	134.61	155.83
产品销售价格	Price of Production Sales	100.90	79.84	91.91	111.67
产成品库存	Stock of Finished Production	131.61	122.45	130.44	136.39
盈利(亏损)变化	Changes of Profit(Loss)	114.16	122.13	127.78	133.08
资金情况	Funds	113.40	108.18	116.72	117.66
货款拖欠情况	Payment for Goods in Arrears	104.12	95.18	99.94	104.40
劳动力需求	Demand on Labors	116.54	108.40	115.90	126.99
投资情况	Investment	119.61	121.32	125.22	126.15
科技开发情况	Scientific and Technological Development	112.26	119.28	115.42	116.50
原材料及能源购进价格	Purchase Price of Raw Mater and Power	42.58	75.44	134.13	23.41

14－4　建筑业企业景气状况

Prosperity index of Construction Enterprises

(2003)

项目	Item	第一季度 1st. Quarter	第二季度 2st. Quarter	第三季度 3st. Quarter	第四季度 4st. Quarter
企业家对本行业信心指数	**Index of Confidence on This Industry by Enterprisers**	**161.68**	**183.56**	**193.04**	**159.13**
企业综合经营景气指数	**Prosperity index on General Production and Operation of Enterprises**	**180.31**	**192.11**	**194.23**	**190.85**
按登记注册类型分	**By Registration Status**				
国有企业	State－Owned Enterprises	200.00	100.00	200.00	200.00
有限责任公司	Limited Liability Corporations	183.33	200.00	183.33	196.55
股份有限公司	Share－holding Corporations Ltd.	172.89	200.00	200.00	184.50
按企业规模分	**By Size of Enterprises**				
特大型及大型	Large－scale and Oversize Enterprises	175.39	190.14	192.79	188.56
中小型	Medium and Small Enterprises	200.00	200.00	200.00	200.00
中型	Medium	200.00	200.00	200.00	200.00
小型	Small	200.00	200.00	200.00	200.00
按观察指标分	**By Indicator Observed**				
工程合同签定情况	Project Contract Signed	153.41	148.15	141.87	183.04
#来自国(境)外的工程合同数	From Overseas	100.52	121.65	121.65	121.65
建筑产品实物工程量	Project Quantity of Construction Productions	101.77	163.48	188.81	178.82
施工产值	Output Value of Buildings Under Construction	92.97	164.15	178.81	190.85
竣工产值	Output Vyalu of Buildings Completed	112.68	138.48	120.67	181.36
工程结算收入	Revenue of Settlement of Projects	110.61	139.68	153.55	165.59
建筑材料购进价格	Purchase Price of Building Materials	49.46	11.87	34.48	7.96
工程结算成本	Cost of Settlement of Projects	76.01	56.09	48.55	17.04
盈利(亏损)变化	Changes of Profit(Loss)	100.30	101.93	135.72	117.77
资金情况	Funds	76.42	56.43	70.23	88.19
货款拖欠情况	Payment for Goods in Arrears	143.39	68.13	80.35	82.28
劳动力需求	Demand on Labors	97.27	162.63	165.15	151.37
投资情况	Investment	105.15	116.02	173.04	135.86

14－5 交通运输、仓储和邮政业企业景气状况

Prosperity index of Transport. Storage and Post Enterprises

(2003)

项目	Item	第一季度 1st. Quarter	第二季度 2st. Quarter	第三季度 3st. Quarter	第四季度 4st. Quarter
企业家对本行业信心指数	**Index of Confidence on This Industry by Enterprisers**	**121.30**	**135.88**	**139.79**	**146.94**
企业综合经营景气指数	**Prosperity index on General Production and Operation of Enterprises**	**135.88**	**129.53**	**140.90**	**148.87**
按登记注册类型分	**By Registration Status**				
国有企业	State－Owned Enterprises	157.97	157.97	145.47	156.76
集体企业	Collective－Owned Enterprises	200.00	100.00	200.00	200.00
有限责任公司	Limited Liability Corporations	66.67	66.67	100.00	100.00
按企业规模分	**By Size of Enterprises**				
特大型及大型	Large－scale and Oversize Enterprises	140.45	142.68	154.52	176.83
中小型	Medium and Small Enterprises	133.33	122.22	133.33	133.33
中型	Medium	150.00	125.00	150.00	125.00
小型	Small	120.00	120.00	120.00	140.00
按特殊企业群体分	**By Special Group**				
国家重点企业	State－point Enterprises	200.00	200.00	200.00	200.00
国家试点企业集团成员	Member of State－test Enterprise－groups	100.00	100.00	100.00	100.00
上市公司	Listed Company	100.00	200.00	200.00	200.00
按观察指标分	**By Indicator Observed**				
业务量	Business Volume	124.68	96.45	119.47	134.42
业务收入	Business Income	147.10	114.95	124.36	131.5
业务收费价格	Price of Business	107.14	100.00	107.14	100.00
营业成本	Cost of Operating	21.43	50.00	103.39	72.72
盈利(亏损)变化	Changes of Profit(Loss)	87.72	75.02	134.76	108.43
资金情况	Funds	119.47	89.91	93.83	97.06
货款拖欠情况	Payment for Goods in Arrears	118.84	91.99	111.17	111.91
劳动力需求	Demand on Labors	92.99	93.68	107.97	96.91
投资情况	Investment	122.25	129.38	152.92	127.28

14－6　批发和零售业企业景气状况

Prosperity index of Wholesale and Retail Sale Enterprises

(2003)

项目	Item	第一季度 1st. Quarter	第二季度 2st. Quarter	第三季度 3st. Quarter	第四季度 4st. Quarter
企业家对本行业信心指数	**Index of Confidence on This Industry by Enterprisers**	**119.61**	**126.13**	**143.74**	**139.92**
企业综合经营景气指数	**Prosperity index on General Production and Operation of Enterprises**	**133.65**	**124.24**	**143.74**	**153.02**
按登记注册类型分	**By Registration Status**				
国有企业	State－Owned Enterprises	155.56	136.36	145.45	154.55
集体企业	Collective－Owned Enterprises	100.00	100.00	200.00	200.00
有限责任公司	Limited Liability Corporations	118.75	126.67	118.96	120.00
股份有限公司	Share－holding Corporations Ltd.	159.24	122.10	159.24	191.49
外商及港澳台企业	Foreign, HongKong, Macao and Taiwan Funded	100.00		200.00	200.00
按企业规模分	**By Size of Enterprises**				
特大型及大型	Large－scale and Oversize Enterprises	144.50	102.10	166.20	191.49
中小型	Medium and Small Enterprises	129.63	132.14	135.71	139.29
中型	Medium	150.00	133.33	158.33	166.67
小型	Small	113.33	131.25	118.75	118.75
按特殊企业群体分	**By Special Group**				
国家重点企业	State－point Enterprises	100.00	100.00	100.00	100.00
国家试点企业集团成员	Member of State－test Enterprise－groups	100.00	100.00	100.00	100.00
上市公司	Listed Company	157.39	100.00	177.50	185.62
按观察指标分	**By Indicator Observed**				
商品购进额	Total Purchases of Goods	168.42	112.42	151.87	143.94
商品购进价格	Purchases Price of Goods	83.29	90.93	92.53	71.72
商品销售额	Total Sales of Goods	146.52	120.40	135.23	148.76
# 出口	Exports	110.29	109.08	102.77	128.14
商品销售价格	Sales Price of Goods	97.85	97.77	85.93	105.40
商品库存情况	Inventory of Goods	111.14	115.17	84.16	136.74
经营费用(营业费用)	Operating Expense(Business Expense)	69.12	82.60	65.84	68.15
盈利(亏损)变化	Changes of Profit(Loss)	115.93	108.00	123.72	130.12
资金情况	Funds	143.09	134.34	127.67	133.78
货款拖欠情况	Payment for Goods in Arrears	93.54	119.00	100.60	112.61
劳动力需求	Demand on Labors	98.34	96.36	107.64	105.84
投资情况	Investment	114.50	111.66	116.81	119.77

14－7 房地产业企业景气状况

Prosperity index of Real Estate Enterprises

(2003)

项目	Item	第一季度 1st. Quarter	第二季度 2st. Quarter	第三季度 3st. Quarter	第四季度 4st. Quarter
企业家对本行业信心指数	**Index of Confidence on This Industry by Enterprisers**	**163.16**	**168.42**	**157.89**	**168.42**
企业综合经营景气指数	**Prosperity index on General Production and Operation of Enterprises**	**155.56**	**142.11**	**150.00**	**144.44**
按登记注册类型分	**By Registration Status**				
国有企业	State－Owned Enterprises	200.00	100.00	100.00	100.00
集体企业	Collective－Owned Enterprises	100.00	150.00	150.00	100.00
有限责任公司	Limited Liability Corporations	160.00	130.00	150.00	150.00
股份有限公司	Share－holding Corporations Ltd.	200.00	200.00	150.00	200.00
外商及港澳台企业	Foreign, HongKong, Macao and Taiwan Funded	200.00	200.00	200.00	200.00
按企业规模分	**By Size of Enterprises**				
特大型及大型	Large－scale and Oversize Enterprises	200.00	100.00	100.00	100.00
中小型	Medium and Small Enterprises	152.94	144.44	152.94	147.06
中型	Medium	175.00	150.00	137.50	150.00
小型	Small	133.33	140.00	166.67	144.44
按观察指标分	**By Indicator Observed**				
土地开发面积	Land Space by Development	122.22	94.22	100.00	100.00
完成投资情况	Investment Made	133.33	138.89	122.22	116.67
新开工面积	Floor Space of Buildings Newly Started	127.78	94.44	94.44	111.11
房屋竣工面积	Floor Space of Buildings Completed	100.00	111.11	105.56	105.56
商品房预售面积	Floor Space of Commercial House Advance Sold	111.11	88.89	100.00	88.89
商品房销售面积	Floor Space of Commercial House Sold	116.67	100.00	100.00	88.89
商品房销售价格	Sale Price of Commercial House	144.44	122.22	138.89	122.22
空置商品房面积	Floor Space of Vacant Commercial House	127.78	122.22	122.22	127.78
盈利(亏损)变化	Changes of Profit(Loss)	138.89	105.26	127.78	127.78
资金情况	Funds	127.78	121.05	126.32	115.79
货款拖欠情况	Payment for Goods in Arrears	127.78	110.53	105.26	131.58
劳动力需求	Demand on Labors	100.00	100.00	105.56	100.00
投资情况	Investment	100.00	94.44	105.56	111.11

14－8 社会服务业企业景气状况

Prosperity index of Social Services Enterprises

(2003)

项目	Item	第一季度 1st. Quarter	第二季度 2st. Quarter	第三季度 3st. Quarter	第四季度 4st. Quarter
企业家对本行业信心指数	**Index of Confidence on This Industry by Enterprisers**	**120.00**	**80.00**	**150.00**	**160.00**
企业综合经营景气指数	**Prosperity index on General Production and Operation of Enterprises**	**110.00**	**60.00**	**140.00**	**150.00**
按登记注册类型分	**By Registration Status**				
国有企业	State－Owned Enterprises	100.00		150.00	150.00
有限责任公司	Limited Liability Corporations	100.00	40.00	100.00	160.00
按企业规模分	**By Size of Enterprises**				
特大型及大型	Large－scale and Oversize Enterprises	100.00	100.00	100.00	100.00
中小型	Medium and Small Enterprises	110.00	60.00	140.00	150.00
中型	Medium	150.00		100.00	150.00
小型	Small	100.00	75.00	150.00	150.00
按观察指标分	**By Indicator Observed**				
业务量	Business Volume	100.00	20.00	190.00	130.00
住房出租情况	Room Occupancy	130.00	100.00	155.56	150.00
旅游客源情况	Visitor's Source of Travle	116.67		183.33	160.00
业务收费(服务)价格	Price of Business(Services)	80.00	60.00	120.00	100.00
营业收入	Business Income	80.00	20.00	170.00	130.00
营业成本	Business Cost	70.00	70.00	40.00	40.00
盈利(亏损)变化	Changes of Profit(Loss)	60.00	30.00	120.00	120.00
资金情况	Funds	130.00	110.00	150.00	150.00
货款拖欠情况	Payment for Goods in Arrears	150.00	130.00	100.00	130.00
劳动力需求	Demand on Labors	80.00	70.00	130.00	90.00
投资情况	Investment	110.00	100.00	130.00	100.00

14－9 信息传输、计算机服务和软件业企业景气状况

Prosperity index of Information Transmission, Computer Service and Software Enterprises

(2003)

项目	Item	第一季度 1st. Quarter	第二季度 2st. Quarter	第三季度 3st. Quarter	第四季度 4st. Quarter
企业家对本行业信心指数	**Index of Confidence on This Industry by Enterprisers**	**169.23**	**141.14**	**164.22**	**161.54**
企业综合经营景气指数	**Prosperity index on General Production and Operation of Enterprises**	**153.85**	**148.84**	**118.07**	**153.85**
按登记注册类型分	**By Registration Status**				
国有企业	State－Owned Enterprises	100.00	100.00	100.00	100.00
有限责任公司	Limited Liability Corporations	175.00	200.00	175.00	200.00
私营企业	Private Enterprises	140.00	120.00	60.00	120.00
按企业规模分	**By Size of Enterprises**				
特大型及大型	Large－scale and Oversize Enterprises	200.00	167.43	167.43	200.00
中小型	Medium and Small Enterprises	145.45	145.45	109.09	145.45
小型	Small	145.45	145.45	109.09	145.45
按观察指标分	**By Indicator Observed**				
产品销售	Sales of Production	128.44	148.84	156.53	169.23
产品订货	Products Order	125.76	125.76	130.77	146.15
竞争能力	Competitive Power	152.90	161.24	144.57	158.33
销售价格	Price of Sales	100.00	71.91	94.99	107.69
营业收入	Business Income	133.45	120.75	133.45	161.54
营业成本	Business Cost	61.54	97.32	69.23	46.15
盈利(亏损)变化	Changes of Profit(Loss)	91.67	77.90	94.57	102.52
资金情况	Funds	112.70	107.69	84.62	100.00
货款拖欠情况	Payment for Goods in Arrears	79.25	69.23	76.92	100.00
劳动力需求	Demand on Labors	107.69	112.70	115.38	128.09
投资情况	Investment	135.78	138.46	115.38	123.08

14-10 住宿和餐饮业企业景气状况

Prosperity index of Hotels and Catering Trade Enterprises

(2003)

项目	Item	第一季度 1st. Quarter	第二季度 2st. Quarter	第三季度 3st. Quarter	第四季度 4st. Quarter
企业家对本行业信心指数	**Index of Confidence on This Industry by Enterprisers**	**154.84**	**71.19**	**169.13**	**160.00**
企业综合经营景气指数	**Prosperity index on General Production and Operation of Enterprises**	**147.55**	**21.18**	**167.24**	**157.94**
按登记注册类型分	**By Registration Status**				
国有企业	State - Owned Enterprises	150.00	50.00	175.00	175.00
集体企业	Collective - Owned Enterprises	142.86	14.29	200.00	185.71
有限责任公司	Limited Liability Corporations	148.55	15.22	100.00	140.34
股份有限公司	Share - holding Corporations Ltd.	200.00		200.00	166.86
外商及港澳台企业	Foreign, HongKong, Macao and Taiwan Funded	125.00	25.00	200.00	150.00
按企业规模分	**By Size of Enterprises**				
特大型及大型	Large - scale and Oversize Enterprises	193.49	14.16	179.33	159.55
中小型	Medium and Small Enterprises	140.74	22.22	165.38	157.69
中型	Medium	160.00	20.00	190.00	160.00
小型	Small	129.41	23.53	150.00	156.25
按观察指标分	**By Indicator Observed**				
产品销售	Sales of Production	122.41	3.23	158.11	119.42
竞争能力	Competitive Power	132.82	103.62	150.58	135.80
客房出租	Room Occupancy	119.60	36.44	140.96	131.03
业务收费价格	Price of Business	120.59	48.00	122.76	119.42
营业收入	Business Income	132.09	9.68	171.45	119.02
营业成本	Business Cost	64.12	138.15	80.61	98.98
盈利(亏损)变化	Changes of Profit(Loss)	118.35	6.45	164.76	119.67
资金情况	Funds	129.03	69.96	136.26	121.45
货款拖欠情况	Payment for Goods in Arrears	82.04	116.13	95.80	110.40
劳动力需求	Demand on Labors	130.26	19.75	153.74	107.28
投资情况	Investment	112.34	87.26	120.69	118.52

主要指标解释

【企业家信心指数】 也称宏观经济景气指数。是根据企业家对企业外部市场经济环境与宏观政策的认可看法、判断与预期(通常为对“乐观”、“一般”、“不乐观”的选择)而编制的指数,用以综合反映企业家对宏观经济环境的感受和信心。

【企业景气指数】 也称企业综合生产经营景气指数。是根据企业对本企业综合生产品经营情况的判断和预期(通常为对“好”、“一般”、“不佳”的选择)而编制的指数,用以综合反映企业的生产经营状况。

【景气指数的表示范围】 在0—200之间。新的表示形式含义为:100为景气指数的临界值,表明景气状况变化不大;100—200为景气区间,表明经济状况趋于上升或改善,越接近200状况越景气;0—100为不景气区间,表明经济状况趋于下降或者恶化,越接近0,状况越不景气。

Explanatory Notes on Main Statistical Indicators

【Entrepreneur Confidence Index】 as well as Macroeconomic Business Cycle Index, which is indexed according to the entrepreneurs' opinions, estimations and expectations (choice of "optimistic", "general" and "miserable") on outer economic environment and macroeconomic policies, to reflect general confidence about the macroeconomic environment of entrepreneurs.

【Enterprise Business Prosperity Index】 as well as Enterprise General Production and Management Business Cycle Index, which is indexed according to estimations and expectations (choice of "good", "general" and "bad") of general management of products, to reflect production and management status comprehensively.

【The range of Business Prosperity Index is between 0 - 200】 The meaning of new denotation method is: 100 is the critical value of Business Cycle Index which shows unobvious change of business cycle. 100 - 200 is the prosperous space interval, which shows ascending and improving economic status, closer to 200 more prosperous. 0 - 100 is the unprosperous space interval, which shows descending and deteriorating economic status, closer to 0 more unprosperous.

[illegible]

[illegible]

[illegible] on Main [illegible] Indicators

[illegible]